D1595592

WILDERNESS CALLING

WILDERNESS

THE HARDEMAN FAMILY IN TH

CALLING ⊁

MERICAN WESTWARD MOVEMENT, 1750–1900

by Nicholas Perkins Hardeman

THE UNIVERSITY OF TENNESSEE PRESS

Library of Congress Cataloging in Publication Data

Hardeman, Nicholas P
  Wilderness calling.

  Bibliography: p.
  Includes Index.
    1. Hardeman family. 2. United States—Genealogy.
3. The West—History. 4. Frontier and pioneer life—
The West. I. Title.
C571.H25918 1976   929'.2'0973   76–980
ISBN 0–87049–194–6

To Ada Mae, Jim, and Keith

WHO HAVE DONE A LITTLE PIONEERING IN THEIR OWN RIGHT

Preface

EVENING WAS STORYTELLING TIME after the farm chores were done and supper was finished. It had been so for generations in the Hardeman family. During the lean years of the late 1920s and early 1930s my sister and brothers and I would beg our parents to "tell us a story." We listened engrossed, content only after promises that succeeding nights would bring more installments of the legends. Our family lived on an isolated, wooded Missouri farm. We had no electricity or radio during my early childhood years, and, as did many rural youngsters, we relied on the older generation for amusement and entertainment to a degree which today's youth would find hard to believe.

My father and mother had stories to tell. They were distant cousins, and they shared family lore passed down from generation to generation, supplementing it with their own personal experiences and repertoire of general narratives. All I remember seeing that could be considered as testimony to the exploits of my forebears, however, was a single piece of ancient paper—a drawing of John Hardeman's garden on the Missouri frontier. From time to time there were admonitions from our parents that the trunk of old papers stored in the attic of our two-story frame house (built a century before I was born) should not be touched.

In the summer of 1962, long after my father and mother had died, I spoke about the documents to my brother, who still lived in the old home. The intervening years had whetted my interest in the material; I had taken my graduate degrees in history with an emphasis on the American West and had been teaching in colleges and universities for a decade. Our parents had been right; there were old papers in the attic—nearly sixty pounds of them—dating from the eighteenth century to the twentieth. The documents were frayed, dusty, and yellowed with age. Mice had nibbled at the edges of some, but most of the handwriting was legible.

A few hours' browsing turned up connections between the Hardemans and some well-known figures of the past, particularly of the frontier— James Robertson, Thomas Jefferson, Andrew Jackson, Thomas Hart Benton, Henry Clay, John C. Frémont, John J. Pershing, and others. The records shed light on the roles enacted by Thomas Hardeman (1750– 1833) and his direct family line for a number of generations in the westward movement. There were territorial and state representatives and senators, a state governor and state supreme court judge, leaders on great western trails, mountainmen, gold seekers, a Civil War general in the West, architects of independence, framers of constitution documents, and workers in a broad spectrum of frontier professions and occupations. The findings in these old accounts led to an extended search of many historical depositories in my attempt to give proper historical perspective to the saga of wilderness wanderings set forth in this volume.

Original spelling and grammar have been preserved in the quotations. Readers with an interest which is primarily genealogical should note that this account of the Hardeman family in the westward movement is intended to be a history, not a genealogy, and the genealogical table itself deals only with those people who figure in the account.

I am both indebted and grateful to a number of institutions and individuals for their assistance with this volume. A sabbatical leave and research leave were provided by the California State University and Colleges. Publication assistance was awarded by the American Council of

Learned Societies, under a grant from the Andrew W. Mellon Foundation, and by the Tennessee Historical Commission. Among the dozens of depositories of historical information used, the staffs and materials of several were heavily relied upon. The librarians at California State University, Long Beach, and particularly Fay Blackburn and Linda Steele, were very supportive. Richard S. Brownlee and Carol Sue Warmbrodt of the State Historical Society of Missouri and Western Manuscripts Collection, Columbia, were very helpful, as were Frances H. Stadler (a Hardeman descendant), Missouri Historical Society, St. Louis; Harriet Owsley, Tennessee State Library and Archives, Nashville; Harriet C. Meloy, Montana Historical Society, Helena; Myra Ellen Jenkins, State of New Mexico, Records Center and Archives, Santa Fe; and Chester V. Kielman, University of Texas Library and Archives, Austin. Also important were the staffs and resources of the Henry E. Huntington Library, San Marino, California; Bancroft Library, University of California, Berkeley; Texas State Archives, Austin; California State Library, Sacramento; State Historical Society of Wisconsin, Madison; and the Library of the University of California at Los Angeles.

Among the professional colleagues who assisted me, none other was as important as my friend and office mate, Robert W. Frazer, California State University, Long Beach. He read the entire manuscript and gave much in the way of time, helpful suggestions, and encouragement. Ralph W. Haskins of the University of Tennessee and Stephen D. Beckham of Linfield College, Oregon, made valuable comments on parts of the manuscript. Colin M. Maclachlan and James F. Noguer of California State University, Long Beach, assisted me with several translations, and Russell E. Orpet of the same university gave me much help with illustrations. Martin H. Hall of the University of Texas, Arlington, was likewise very helpful. Berenice Kinsman, graduate student at California State University, Long Beach, helped to trace the Hardeman trails.

Important information was supplied by Gladys Hardeman of Nacogdoches, Texas, Viola Hardeman Kraemer of Tyler, Texas, Albert L. Cooper of Shelbyville, Tennessee, and F. W. Brigance, Murfreesboro, Tennessee. Of significance, too, were the contributions of Russella Hardeman Matthews, Seattle; Pauline Hardeman Willis, Orange, Virginia; the late Hoyt N. Hardeman of Houston; Ward Nash Hardeman of

Austin; Eva Hardeman, Austin; Dorsey B. Hardeman, San Angelo, Texas; and Christine Wood, Lubbock, Texas. My sister, Townsend Hardeman Fenn of Sunnyvale, California, and brothers, Walker E. Hardeman, Pacific, Missouri, and Howard D. Hardeman, Cape Girardeau, Missouri, were helpful at various stages, particularly in supplying documents and photographs.

Finally, and by no means as an afterthought, my wife Ada Mae contributed very extensively in typing, editing, and encouragement. Our sons Jim and Keith assisted too by their understanding and by providing needed humoring and distractions.

Contents

[xi

Maps and Illustrations

WILDERNESS CALLING

And tell me now, sweet friend, what happy gale blows you . . . here?

Such wind as scatters young men through the world to seek their fortunes further than at home where small experience grows.

—SHAKESPEARE, *Taming of the Shrew*

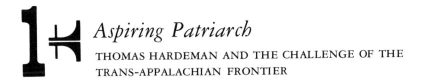

1 Aspiring Patriarch

THOMAS HARDEMAN AND THE CHALLENGE OF THE
TRANS-APPALACHIAN FRONTIER

AMONG THE TENETS which Thomas Hardeman passed on to his children
was one which seemed to characterize and foreshadow his activities and
those of many of his descendants. He would "rather hear about them doing
well a great distance away," he said, "than to see them daily doing
nothing."[1] This was more than a simple work ethic. It was an invitation to
travel; and the Hardemans worked and traveled. Their experiences constituted a microcosm of the American westward movement, a panoramic
view of the advancing frontier through the exploits of one pioneer couple,
Thomas and Mary Hardeman, and their direct descendants. Over a span of
150 years they pushed to and across the Appalachian Mountains and
spanned the continent along a number of routes, engaging in a wide range
of economic pursuits as they progressed. Canada, Mexico, Central
America, Brazil, and the Philippines as well as the United States frontier
felt the press of their migratory impulse.

The Hardemans were persistent yet reluctant in their westward ad-

[3

vance. Most were well educated and moderately well-to-do for the times. Frequently, almost flagrantly, they risked their stakes in the older, established centers of civilization, sometimes enhancing and at other times depleting their fortunes. If social and political pedigrees were abandoned when the wilderness called, new ones were acquired almost as soon as tents gave way to log cabins and stockades. Thomas Hardeman and his descendants flirted often with roles of political leadership, then just as often backed away from the limelight into obscurity. What kinds of ethnic, social, educational, occupational, and environmental backgrounds, what motivations drove the family, generation after generation, in this unique odyssey—this frontier *Forsyte Saga*? Undoubtedly the uniqueness was less in the makeup of the personalities than in the repetitive westering patterns—much as if the ancestral force had committed the family tree to branch toward the outlands.

The decade of the 1760s was a vintage season for frontiersmen of the Virginia-Carolina back country; John Sevier, James Robertson, William Bean, John Carter, and Daniel Boone were among the most prominent. Thomas Hardeman, less known but no less bold than these men, rivaled them in his crusade to master the wilderness; and indirectly, as the patriarch of a long line of westerners, he outdistanced all of his peers through his continued impact on the major phases of American expansion.

Tom Hardeman was a man of medium-heavy frame, about five feet ten inches tall. His eyes were blue and his round, ruddy face was topped with sandy hair; in late years he was balding noticeably.[2] He had considerable stamina, even at an advanced age. On one trip, at the age of eighty, he rode alone on horseback as much as forty and fifty miles a day over hundreds of miles of roads and trails. He was a strong-spirited type, with the pride of a Henry Clay in his humble background, the loyalty of an Andrew Jackson toward his friends and political allies, and the wilderness survival instincts of a Boone or a Simon Kenton. His pious Baptist father drummed the beliefs of the church and the virtues of Christianity into him, and when his own children were young, Thomas Hardeman exposed them to regular family worship. In later years he would rip the church dogma and the clerics with sharp literary slashes, but he seemed able to make practical distinctions between belief and behavior. According to acquaintances, Tom liked an argument and would go out of his way to challenge any act which he considered wrong. One unauthenticated bit of family folklore records that Hardeman was crossing Chesapeake Bay on a slave-trading trip when a heavy storm broke. The crew, paralyzed with fear, abandoned their posts and fell to praying. Apparently harboring his own notions about when to work and when to pray, he seized a rope and, with a few unchurchmanlike words, beat the crew back to their stations.[3]

Thomas taught his children and grandchildren several rules of life— rules that have been handed down in writing and by word of mouth to the present day: "First. Pay your honest debts. Second. Never disgrace the family. Third. Help the honest and industrious kin."[4] These guidelines, whatever their influences may have been, were less vital to the role of the family in American history than the persistent westward urge which Thomas passed on to them.

The stock from which Thomas Hardeman came may partly explain the wanderlust which later characterized him and many of his heirs. Five generations before him (some time prior to 1660), his ancestor Thomas Hardeman, the first recorded member of the family in America, moved from England to Virginia Colony. A grandson of this early arrival, John Hardeman I, sailed from Virginia to England, perhaps to secure an education abroad. He was jailed following his support of the Duke of Monmouth's unsuccessful rebellion. One of the more fortunate victims of the "bloody assizes," John Hardeman I was exiled to the New World from Bristol, England, in 1685. Returning to Virginia, he married Maria Eppes of Henrico County and became a cooper or barrel maker, a planter, and sometime justice of the peace of Charles City County and Prince George County. He held the rank of lieutenant colonel in the militia and was a member of the House of Burgesses from Prince George County in 1710. A number of his descendants would follow his example in both the military and politics. John died in 1711 after having been kicked in the chest by his racehorse.

One of his sons, John II, also a cooper and justice of the peace, married Henrietta Taylor of Charles City. A son of this marriage, John Hardeman III, was born about 1716. He too followed the cooperage trade. A man of stocky proportions, he was said to be "spunky as a wharf rat." The story was told that he and his brother-in-law were riding the same horse late one night on the way home from an election. The men became "boozy" and started to argue over one of the candidates. When words became inadequate to express their feelings, they seized each other and fell to the ground, grappling until they were pulled apart at daybreak. After sobriety set in, the two were again amiable companions.

At about the age of thirty John Hardeman III married an Irish immigrant, Dorothy Edwards. They moved out of the tidewater belt toward the frontier, settling first in Goochland County, Virginia, then in the verdant, rolling Piedmont region of Albemarle County, which had been split off from Goochland County. Two sons and seven daughters were born to John and Dorothy Hardeman. The first son and second child was Thomas Hardeman, born in Albemarle on January 8, 1750 (under the old, or Julian, calendar system).[5] On a nearby estate lived a red-haired youth of seven years, Thomas Jefferson, who would one day extend the flag of a new nation over vast lands which Thomas Hardeman and a number of his descendants were destined to cross and recross. Close at hand was a site later to become the birthplace of frontier explorer Meriwether Lewis, whose paths would be well known to several members of the Thomas Hardeman line.

As a young child, Tom Hardeman got a taste of the effects of frontier combat; his father fought against the French and their Indian allies during the French and Indian War. The backwoods military tradition would weigh heavily with Thomas and, in time, with a host of his descendants. One very significant event during his boyhood, life-shaping in its influence, was his parents' move southwestward along the Piedmont. They settled on the Dan River in Pittsylvania County, Virginia, east of Cumberland Gap, and built their cabin near some of the extensive lands once owned by William Byrd of Westover, an old friend of John's father and grandfather. The Hardemans' names appeared on the tax rolls of that county by 1767.[6] These frontierward moves were part of a trend rooted in the migration of John's ancestors from England nearly a century earlier, and destined to typify descendants of the family for four more generations. In time, three children of John and Dorothy—Deborah, Susannah, and John—moved south to the new Georgia Colony, and four others, led by Thomas Hardeman, took a course almost due west into the wilderness which would later become Tennessee. Meanwhile, in this Virginia-North Carolina border region Thomas became acquainted not only with the

Perkins family, who figured later in his matrimonial plans, but also with venturesome young fellows who, like himself, were beginning to direct their thoughts westward.

The trans-Appalachian West of the 1760s was a land which at once beckoned and intimidated prospective settlers. The French and Indian War had erased French control from the Ohio Valley, making it fair game for English colonial settlement. This struggle released latent expansionist impulses, as colonists felt that a prime purpose of the war was to give them entry to the land beyond the Mountains. But in 1763, Britain's Lord Shelburne mapped a Proclamation Line down the crest of the mountain chain, reserving the western watershed for the Indians. A series of treaties between Great Britain and several Indian tribes in 1765 and 1768 appeared to pull this restraining strand more taut than before. To the would-be westerners, this was precisely the wrong outcome of victory over France and her Indian cohorts.

In 1768, the year of the Creek, Hard Labor, and Fort Stanwix Indian treaties, eighteen-year-old Thomas Hardeman joined a group of "long hunters" and trappers in an expedition deep into the forbidden zone beyond the Proclamation Line. The cluster of woodsmen, which included Ben and Sam Crowley and Bill Faulin, crossed the mountains into the valleys of the Holston and Powell rivers. These prototypes of the legendary mountain men, called long hunters because they stayed in the back country for months and even years at a time, went as far west as the Cumberland Basin and the site of the present Nashville, shooting buffalo and quite possibly eyeing this fertile land with a view to future claims.

The hunting party of 1768 endured the usual hardships for such an expedition—danger from Indians, exposure, and hunger. Hardeman saved his last flour until Christmas Day, then rolled the dough in leaves, baked it in ashes, and declared that never in his life did bread taste better. His supplies of salt and other provisions were gone, and he was forced to live entirely off the country until he reached home.[7]

Nicholas Perkins and his wife, Bethenia Hardin Perkins, who had settled in the Dan River region about 1755, were neighbors of the Hardemans. In 1770 Thomas Hardeman married their sixteen-year-old daughter Mary, seventh of the nine Perkins children. John Hardeman III had apparently fared less well than some of his gentleman ancestors, for he was able to give his son Tom "little more than a father's blessing" to start his married life. The bride brought a dowry of only a small amount of property.

For several years Thomas and Mary rented acreage and worked as tenants in the Dan River lowlands. Signs of restlessness soon reappeared, and they shifted almost annually from one location to another, acquiring a few head of livestock but chafing under the "restraint and monotony" of tenancy. Doubtless Tom disliked his economic subordination to the tidewater planters, who held the hinterland in a form of vassalage, and he was under pressure to fill several new stomachs in the family circle. He had seen at first hand great spreads of opportunity lands across the divide. A few years after his neighbor, Captain William Bean, moved to Boone's Creek in the Watauga area of frontier North Carolina, Hardeman and a number of other land-starved settlers followed.

The Holston Valley had been settled previously but not permanently; Stephen Holston had built a cabin there in 1746. A handful of migrants followed, but all were sent scurrying eastward across the mountains by Indian attacks and threats. Bean cautiously reopened these lands when he built his well-secluded cabin in 1768. The promise of fertile land and freedom from oppression brought increasing numbers of ex-tenants, ex-Regulators, and other homeseekers to the Watauga, Nolichucky, and nearby regions. James Robertson and Jacob Brown arrived in the early 1770s. The Treaty of Lochaber (1770) underlined the fact that many of these trans-Appalachian pioneers were on ground recognized by Great Britain as Indian-owned. To make their tenuous position more secure, the settlers negotiated a treaty (with no foundation of legality) by which the Cherokees gave them title to the needed territory. A frontier government known as the Watauga Association was organized, and wagon roads were opened between the precarious settlements and the Great Valley of Virginia.

And so Thomas Hardeman, in late 1777 or early 1778, took his family to a region which seemed somewhat safer than it had been when he first looked down upon its green expanse a decade earlier. But experience soon proved that he had miscalculated. He established his wife and children in Watauga and returned to the Dan River Valley to look after unfinished business during the summer of 1778. Soon he headed west to rejoin the family, only to meet them on the road unexpectedly as they fled from a Cherokee threat. Thomas shepherded his wife and children back to the safety of Pittsylvania, where they remained until the following year. He then reestablished them in the same Watauga cabin which they had been obliged to abandon.[8]

Their first home in this area, newly organized as Washington County, was on Boone's Creek, a tributary of the Watauga River near its confluence with the Holston. Later Tom purchased from John Fuller Lane 100 acres of land at the falls of Sinking Creek. (This acreage had been previously acquired by William Bean and traded to Lane for one cow and calf.) By the end of the Revolutionary War, Hardeman had accumulated in the Watauga-Holston region at least 325 acres of land.[9]

The Revolution in the North Carolina back country was a combination of civil war, Indian campaigns, and battles against British regulars. A number of people in the hinterland, and particularly the defeated Regulators from the Battle of Alamance, despised the tidewater planters with such passion that they would have allied with the devil himself against the coastal "oppressors." It is not surprising that some of these settlers sympathized with England for this and other reasons. In 1778, Tom Hardeman joined a company of Whigs, Bean, Sevier, Robertson, and others, and drove a sizable party of Tories, including one Captain Grimes and Isam Yearley, eastward over the mountains.[10]

Indian problems along the border of settlement were aggravated by the Revolution, as the tribes were able to take occasional advantage of the war between the two groups of whites. The choice between the British and the ever-encroaching American settlers was not a difficult one for the aborigines. Thomas Hardeman was probably in William Bean's militia company which served with Colonel Evan Shelby in the campaign against the Chickamaugas in 1779. A few months later, Hardeman commanded an assemblage of Watauga woodsmen against a group of Cherokees in the Nickajack area. After this campaign, Thomas was known as "Captain," although his militia rank was apparently lieutenant at the time of the battle of King's Mountain.[11]

The record of the North Carolina militia in the Revolutionary War was uneven. Typical of the situation in most of the colonies, many of the militiamen would not be alarmed unless the enemy was slaughtering their

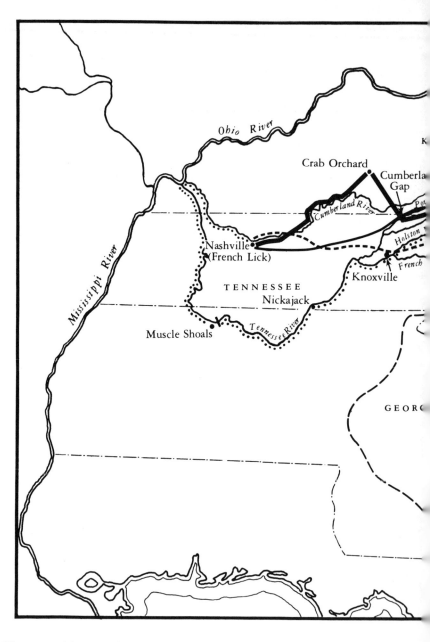

Map 1.   Travels of Thomas Hardeman to 1798.

10 }

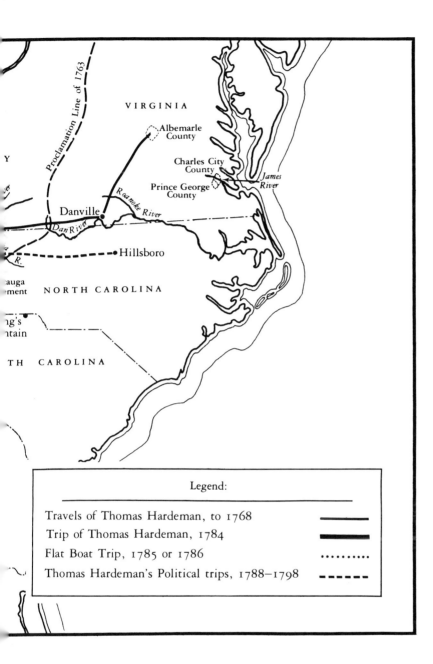

VIRGINIA

Proclamation Line of 1763

Albemarle
County

Charles City
County

James
River

Prince George
County

Roanoke River

Danville

Dan River

Hillsboro

NORTH CAROLINA

auga
ment

ng's
ntain

TH CAROLINA

Legend:

Travels of Thomas Hardeman, to 1768

Trip of Thomas Hardeman, 1784

Flat Boat Trip, 1785 or 1786

Thomas Hardeman's Political trips, 1788–1798

stock, trampling their gardens, and kicking in their doors. But King's Mountain was a notable exception. The severe setback administered by Lord Cornwallis and Colonel Tarleton to Horatio Gates's patriot army at Camden, South Carolina, on August 16, 1780, threatened the American cause throughout the South, and the subsequent British victory at Fishing Creek appeared to open the way for an invasion of North Carolina. Stirred by the threat to their homeland, North Carolina woodsmen rallied in unexpected strength, bringing into battle their years of experience as hunters and Indian fighters. Thomas Hardeman joined the Company of Watauga Riflemen, serving as an officer under his old acquaintance, Captain Bean.[12]

British Colonel Patrick Ferguson, contemptuous of the undisciplined militia, taunted them with threats of brute strength, then established his forces in what he believed to be an impregnable position atop King's Mountain, near the border between North and South Carolina. From this elevated redoubt on the left flank of the British position, he blustered that "all the Rebels from Hell" could not dislodge his force of 1,100 men. Colonels John Sevier, Isaac Shelby, and Benjamin Cleveland led 900 patriots in an unexpected thrust at Ferguson's position. The marksmanship of the frontiersmen quickly made a shambles of the British commander's boast; all of Ferguson's men were either killed or captured. King's Mountain was the turning point of the war in the South.

Every American war, from the French and Indian through the Spanish-American, has been followed by a lively period of westward expansion. These conflicts suspended expansion for a time; then the backlog of waiting settlers was released and they surged west to occupy the lands which had been opened by the successful conclusion of hostilities. Other forces contributing to postwar westward expansion were business booms, veterans' land grants as payment for military services, enticing messages from acquaintances, and a general restlessness laid bare by the enforced wartime wanderings and savagery. No doubt these factors were part of the driving urge which propelled Thomas Hardeman into the next phase of his confrontation with the West. In addition, he had seen for himself the promise of the Cumberland Basin and had reinforced his western hopes in 1782 by purchasing a tract of Cumberland acreage from Isham Cleaton for 20 pounds specie.[13]

Planning to return later for his family, Hardeman set off a second time for the French Lick region—the present vicinity of Nashville—in 1784. After arranging the sale of his 325 Watauga acres to William Elles, he went overland through Cumberland Gap, Crab Orchard, and Dripping Spring (in Kentucky Territory), taking a few cows and horses and a Negro slave to help clear a plot and start a corn crop. As part payment for his military service to North Carolina, Hardeman secured title to a 640–acre section on the Little Harpeth River. Lands near French Lick were so cheap that on the trip he was able to pick up, for a small consideration, another 640 acres, and on this tract near the Cumberland River he selected a cabin site.

Having laid claim to his new Canaan, Thomas Hardeman went back for his wife Mary and their eight children. Most settlers heading for the Cumberland Basin took the overland trail, but he selected a different course. Undoubtedly he had talked to some members of the John Donelson flatboat party. Donelson, later to become the father-in-law of Hardeman's close friend and political associate Andrew Jackson, had led a harrowing expedition down the Tennessee River.[14] Flatboats were the simplest of all designs to construct, and Hardeman built a large one out of heavy timbers which he no doubt expected to use again in erecting buildings at the end of his trip. Early in 1785 or 1786, he and his family, a few slaves, one or more canoes, some tools and household possessions, and his ever-present Bible, drifted out to midstream in the clear currents of the Holston River and began the 1,000-mile float to their new home.

The reputation of Thomas Hardeman as a frontiersman was becoming known. His companions on the trek of 1768, the Crowleys and Bill Faulin, had served and died in the struggle for the birth of the nation, and Tom had seen as much of the Tennessee country as most of his living contemporaries. Like Boone and Bean, Robertson and Sevier, he commanded some following whenever he doused the fire, called the dogs, and gathered his possessions for another wandering. Nicholas Tate Perkins, his wife's nephew, had followed him to Watauga, and, along with Thomas's sisters Lydia Crunk and Elizabeth Stone and their families, very soon joined him in the French Lick country.

Meanwhile, crowded on board the broadhorn flatboat with Tom and his immediate family were his sister and brother-in-law, Esther and John

Everett and their children. A Major Hay, with a smaller flatboat, accompanied them on the trip, as did a venturer named Williamson traveling in a canoe. Including slaves there were seven grown men in the party. This was scarcely a full count of able-bodied defenders, since frontier women such as Mary and Esther were adept with firearms. The story of the voyage, as Hardeman and his relatives told and retold it to their children and grandchildren, was written by a grandson, John Locke Hardeman.

That the voyage was begun in the dead of winter is less surprising than a first glance would indicate. Hostile Indians would have little concealment from foliage and would be unlikely to hazard an attack against boats shielded by the icy current. The prospect of high enough water to pass the shoals was better in late winter than in any other season. And the streams to be followed were sufficiently far south that, with luck, sojourners could avoid a freeze-over, arriving at the Ohio after the worst of the winter was past. Finally, the voyagers would be reaching their destination in time to take advantage of a spring planting and growing season.

Down the Holston, past the mouth of the French Broad River, and into the channel of the Tennessee Thomas Hardeman led the small fleet. The Tennessee River was known to be treacherous along parts of its meandering course. Piomingo, a prominent Chickasaw chief, for years known to the settlers as "Mountain Leader," agreed to serve the party as guide until the inhospitable 37-mile-long Muscle Shoals of the north Georgia backland (later to be included within the state of Alabama) had been negotiated. This chief was one of the "decided friends of the Americans,"[15] although he usually preferred traders over permanent settlers. Donelson's boats had threaded their way safely through the rapids at high water, but Hardeman and his crew were less fortunate. Although Piomingo pointed out the channel unerringly, the large, cumbersome boat was cast upon a rocky point. Agonizing hours and days dragged by as the party unloaded, pried with levers, repaired the box-like craft, and finally reloaded. A French settler and some friendly Indians helped the stranded travelers and informed them of the locations of hostile tribes. Not all of the Indians were so cordial to newcomers in the West. Many understandably fought with savage determination against the whites who encroached on their native grounds. The chance to get booty from the flatboats gave them added incentive to attack. Too, those parties such as Hardeman's, which fol-

Thousands of families, among them the Thomas Hardeman group, floated by
flatboat to their frontier homesites as pictured in this engraving "Emigrants
Descending the Tennessee." The Hardemans, guided by Chickasaw Chief
Piomingo, traveled down the Holston and Tennessee and up the Ohio and
Cumberland rivers to French Lick (Nashville) about 1786. *Courtesy Library of
Congress.*

lowed westward several years after the first wave of settlers, often met more Indian resistance than did the vanguards of the frontier. For the last crime committed by a white, the native attempted to punish the next white who came along. Likewise the emigrant contributed to the contagion of hostility by seeking vicarious retribution.

After ten days on the shoals, Thomas and his group got their arks afloat again, and none too soon. A party of about 300 Indians appeared on the bank. By various ruses they tried to take the boats.

> They sent an Indian on board to ascertain the force of the boats, and to see if there were any great guns aboard: they were told that the large boat had two. This was the famous John Taylor: he feigned himself drunk, with a view to detain the boats till evening, the hour of attack: and refusing to go ashore, was violently ejected.
>
> The Indians, foiled in their first plan of operations, hastened to a bend some distance below, where the river was narrow; they frequently showed themselves in parties of two or three and desired the boats to come ashore: they brought presents of meat, much needed by the whites: wanted to trade: said there were Frenchmen amongst them: wanted passports, or papers by which they might be known as friends among White men: finally said they: "We have a White-man bound, come and release him." They last showed themselves at the mouth of the Duck River, a place well calculated for their purpose. When after calling as usual, three of them came off in a canoe, pretending confidence and friendship: they stole the hat off Mr. Everett and making off, showed it at a distance, hoping . . . to provoke pursuit.

Despite the "great guns," whatever their nature and caliber, which transformed the boats into a miniature wilderness armada, Tom and Mary Hardeman, with their young children (none over fifteen years of age), must have spent some anxious days and sleepless nights. One can picture them scanning the deceptively beautiful branches that swayed and dipped along the river's margin, wondering if there were hostile eyes peering from beneath or behind, or catching a familiar sound from a canebrake. Was it the harmless call of a bird—or the signal of a deadly adversary? Often at night the group anchored in wide, deep stretches of water, posting guard and listening to the night noises, watching and waiting for the dawn. There were other nights spent drifting with the current, "trusting rather to an unknown and dangerous navigation than to the mercy of a daring and insidious foe." The parting of a cable cost the emigrants an anchor and much peace of mind. They fashioned another mud hook by heating and bending an iron bar which had been stowed on board the craft. This blacksmithing necessitated a perilous landing, but luckily the party was not detected while tied to the stream bank.

Other debarkations were required from time to time. Thomas Hardeman went ashore alone whenever the meat supply was low. Once while he was hunting, his family sighted a band of Indians, and when the hunter did not return, he was presumed dead or captured. The settlers, unable to go back upstream and deeming it folly to land, had no choice but to stay with the craft and the current. Several days later, upon rounding a bend in the stream, they saw Thomas at the water's edge, the carcass of a deer at his feet. He had outflanked his pursuers and had followed along at a distance, waiting until it was safe to return to the river and rejoin the flotilla. [16]

While on another hunt, he saw an Indian approaching. Concealing himself behind a tree until he was satisfied that the man was alone, he stepped into the open and slowly approached. The Indian, who appeared to be peaceful, was Panss Fallayah, or Chief Longhair of the Chickasaw, a relative of Hardeman's guide Piomingo. He was taken to the boat and given a meal and some provisions. Later, Longhair and his son were both to die fighting on the side of the settlers against Creek Indians in the battle at Duck River.

Shoals, Indians, and lost anchors were not the only hazards on the trip. A Major Kirkpatrick and other white pirates of the Cumberland country had raided flatboat traffic along the Tennessee River system during the 1780s. [17] But Thomas Hardeman's little group slipped through without such mishaps.

When the vessels reached the Ohio River and the mouth of the Cumberland, the physical hazards to navigation were magnified. Now it was necessary to go upstream, but flatboats were not designed for working against the current. Conditions worsened when the rains of late winter glutted the main channel of the Cumberland, swelling it out of its banks. At times the devout Baptist captain must have wondered if the Lord had broken his covenant with Noah. Mile after wearisome mile the square-nosed craft was poled, paddled, and cordelled upstream into the teeth of the flood. The boatmen pushed their vessels away from the main channel and through inundated woodlands where there was less current to fight against. Finally, at the mouth of Little River, the large flatboats had to be abandoned. The heavy items of freight were hidden in dense patches of timber; Tom would return for the supplies later.

His party proceeded in canoes, taking what items they could paddle and portage upstream against the flood.

> Those of the family who were able to walk and were not needed in conducting the canoes, walked on the margin of the river, that they might be more secure and by help of canoes be enabled to cross the creeks and deep rivulets in their way.

The long and laborious journey ended successfully on March 10, according to John Locke Hardeman; the year was either 1785 or 1786. In contrast to the pioneering Donelson float, which took four months and was made at a cost of several lives, Hardeman's group, having the advantage of smaller size, completed the trip in less than two and one half months and without losing a passenger. Thomas Hardeman pitched his tent and encamped the party three miles east of French Lick, or Nashville, as the "rude palisade fort and a few outhouses" had been renamed. The pioneer had learned his frontier lessons well; but he had scarcely time enough for a sigh of relief.

Most urgent of the tasks at the new home was the building of a small log cabin. This accomplished, it was necessary to "girdle" and cut trees for the clearing of corn land to add to the acreage which Tom and his slave had prepared earlier. The crops were planted in time for the spring growing season, a propitious circumstance, since the family would not have to weather a full cycle of the seasons without replenishing the bin and the stow room.

Equally important was good protection from the Indians, particularly since Hardeman had chosen for his cabin site an area that was some distance from the fort at Nashville. At that time and for a number of years it was unsafe for settlers to live in widely separated cabins. Each isolated neighborhood resided at one well-fortified "station" which typically consisted of several cabins in an enclosure of timbers. As soon as their fields were planted, Hardeman and his brother-in-law Everett, and their families, aided by several neighbors, built a stockade which appears on an early map of the region as "Hardeman's or Everett's Station."[18]

As for thirty-six-year-old Thomas Hardeman, he had found his promised land. Apart from journeys back to the Dan and on to Louisiana, he settled into his primitive niche, sank roots at last, watched—and helped—the country grow for the next thirty years before a resurgent restiveness drove him again westward.

The land was indeed primitive. Ringing axe and rasping saw had made little impression on the awesome countenance of the Cumberland wilderness in the several years since French Lick had been settled. The pioneer felt an ambivalence toward the deep stand of virgin timber. On the one hand, it meant wood in seemingly inexhaustible supply—wood for fences, fuel, and furniture, for buildings, barrels, boats, and a score of other uses. It also provided his meat supply little farther from his cabin door than the range of his rifle. Buffalo, deer, and bear abounded, as did small game such as the wild turkey, passenger pigeon, quail, squirrel, and rabbit. Numerous waterways teemed with fish, and the land was a trapper's dream, with the staple fur-bearers, beaver and muskrat, augmented by mink, weasel, wolf, fox, raccoon, and other small animals.

Yet, on the negative side, this bountiful forest concealed natives who were fighting back against the tide of invading settlers despite the Treaty of Hopewell, which stripped the Indians of their title to the Cumberland Basin in 1785. It was still a time and place "when a ploughman went to work with his gun swung to his back; and neighbors visited each other under arms."[19] Both Creek and Cherokee Indians were blamed for the bloodletting in the Nashville area. Early in 1788, James Robertson and Anthony Bledsoe wrote to Governor Samuel Johnston of North Carolina, requesting aid. Seven inhabitants of Davidson and Sumner counties had been killed recently, and forty over a twelve-month period, supposedly "by those barbarians the Creeks."[20]

Captain Thomas Hardeman mentioned taking part in many Indian campaigns. He served as a spy or ranger, scouting positions and movements of the enemy and carrying messages to and from the outposts. One reference to the Coldwater expedition implies that he was a participant, although there is no clear confirmation. This campaign occurred in 1787 after James Robertson's brother was killed by Creek warriors. A group of Cumberland Basin settlers hounded the Creeks as far as Muscle Shoals, killing several of their number. The aggressiveness of the Creeks from Georgia to the Cumberland was in part a result of armament and supply shipments which they received from Spanish Florida. Hardeman had been a close friend of the Robertsons since their comradeship in Revolutionary War scuffles, and it is unlikely that he would have missed Coldwater unless ill.

The Cumberland settlers had responded to recent Indian problems by contributing to a "hair buying" fund for those who brought in scalps of Indians. In May of 1787, Hardeman led a party of eighteen men from the Nashville locality in a "scout" against a group of Cherokees. Among his men were Ab Castleman, Isaac Roberts, Abraham Kennedy, and Thomas Hickman.[21] They passed Big Spring on the trail to Nickajack and set up an ambuscade. While most of the group lay in wait to dispatch and scalp passing Indians, Hardeman sent Roberts and another comrade for venison. They killed a deer and were carrying it back to the ambush when an Indian appeared in the trail ahead. Roberts fired, and the Indian fell. The two hunters, suspecting the presence of a party of Indians nearby, ran back to the main body of scouts. The entire group went quickly to the scene of the shooting, but the Indian, apparently only wounded, was gone, his trail blotted out by a brisk shower. The men had stopped in a canebrake for a "hurried repast" when suddenly a group of Indians came upon them. In numbers the two sides appeared evenly matched. Both instinctively leaped behind trees, but the Indians, flitting from trunk to trunk, escaped without a shot being fired by either party.

Two more weeks of trail watching yielded nothing, and Hardeman's group returned to Nashville. Scarcely had they arrived when Cherokee Chief Little Owl and two braves came from Nickajack bearing a white flag and asking to talk to James Robertson. Had they been an hour earlier the three would have been slain. The settlers despised Little Owl for his bloody reputation, and Hardeman's party returned to the trail to ambush him. But Robertson persuaded them to respect the truce flag in order to spare the Cumberland country "probable disastrous consequences." The only tangible results of the scout were several Cherokee horses seized by Hardeman's party.

Horse thievery worked both ways in the struggle between Indian and white. At first terrified by the settlers' mounts, the Indians soon learned to use them. Capturing or stampeding the enemy's beasts of burden was one of the most effective tactics in frontier warfare. At times Tom Hardeman would bell and hobble his horse and watch from a thicket, his rifle ready

Indian resistance to the ever-encroaching settlers often meant furious assaults on frontier communities such as Hardeman's Station in the Cumberland Basin. Shown here is such an attack pictured in Amos Kendall's *Life of Andrew Jackson, 1843–44. Courtesy Lehigh University Library.*

should an Indian be tricked by the decoy. But he related that he was never able to deceive an Indian with this ruse.

The feelings of Indian and settler toward each other were intense during these perilous seasons. Yet much later in his life Thomas seemed to soften his tone and minimize the brutality of his early struggles when recounting his experiences to his children and grandchildren. There was a twinkle in his eye, a smile, and a mellowness of voice which seemed to convey something other than hatred. Perhaps he toned down the harsh parts of his story to fit the sensitive feelings of his young listeners, or possibly as time went on he felt a sense of kinship with the bold and crafty sleuths of the forest. For his experience, too, was one of mixed boldness and craft and an apparent reverence for the wild, free, primeval land. And on occasion, like the Indians, he relied on primitive tools and weapons for survival.

Hardeman felt on more than one occasion that he owed his life to his dogs. The animals warned him of approaching Indians and were nearly indispensable in hunting the numerous black bears of the Tennessee cane-brakes. There were three objectives in hunting bears: their flesh made up a significant part of the frontiersman's diet; the skins were of some value; and the animals were a threat to livestock. Hardeman stated that he and two other men killed forty bears in one hunt. He sometimes made the kill with a knife thrust if shooting would endanger the dogs which held the quarry at bay. From these exploits Tom gained something of a reputation as a hunter.[22]

Inevitably, because of the influx of new settlers and the entrenchment of older ones, the Cumberland Valley evolved from the hunting, gathering, and defending stages of existence and entered a more civilized phase. The last major Indian resistance in Thomas Hardeman's locality was an attack on the night of September 30, 1792, by an estimated 300 to 900 Lower Cherokees and Creeks against the station of the John Buchanan family, less than a mile east of Hardeman's station. Runners sought help from neighboring stations and the assault was repulsed. By 1795, the Indian depredations had subsided—or the white depredations had succeeded. Thomas Hardeman's life reflected these changes as he acquired and developed economic assets, educated his children and himself (in that order), and plunged into politics. He had achieved some measure of security, success, and status. In the patriarchal mode of the day, he was established.

2 ⊞ *Established Patriarch*
THOMAS HARDEMAN AS PLANTER AND POLITICIAN

"THE DIFFERENCE IN VALUE between two saddle horses" was all that
Thomas Hardeman had paid for his 640–acre homesite near Nashville.[1]
With each move to an area of cheaper land he had bettered his holdings,
although at the cost of heightened dangers to his family and himself.
While it did not prompt his first trip to the Cumberland, inexpensive land
was undoubtedly an important reason for his moving there in the 1780s,
and the price of the hazard, since it was not demanded in specie, was one
that he was willing to pay. In that time and place the prime measure of
one's success and status was his land holdings—their extent, nature, and
utilization. As late as the census of 1840, about 90 percent of the nation's
people made their living from agriculture, and men who made fortunes in
nonagricultural pursuits usually directed much of their conspicuous consumption to landed estates. Tom lost no time in acquiring more spreads of
low-priced lands in the virgin valleys near Nashville. Far removed from

the doleful days of Pittsylvania tenancy, he was soon considered a planter of some means and prestige.

If the back-country land laws of North Carolina were liberal, they were nonetheless confusing, more so, in fact, than in most of the original thirteen states. Like several of her neighbors, North Carolina had a vague colonial sea-to-sea grant under the terms of her charters (1629, 1663, and 1665). The Peace of Paris ending the Revolutionary War established a closer and less nebulous western boundary, the Mississippi River.

The new nation was born gasping for fiscal oxygen to meet the costs of war; no longer could it expect to receive nourishment from the motherland. An appropriate experience, perhaps, since it acquainted the infant country with what was to remain one of its most persistent national problems. The military expenses in North Carolina were relatively high—much higher than the depleted state treasury could meet. Accordingly, that state's most bountiful resource, western land, was lavishly used to pay war veterans under land acts of 1782 and 1783. Land warrants for service, which would be a considerable boon to Thomas Hardeman, varied with the rank of the grantee—from 640 acres for a private to 12,000 acres for a brigadier general. In April 1784, North Carolina ceded her transmontane lands to the union, conforming to the ratification provisions of the Articles of Confederation as insisted upon by Maryland. But there were further motives for the bequest: to throw off the expensive burden of protecting the western settlements and to yield to the demands of some western residents and certain wealthy speculators. The Act of Cession specified that bounties to military personnel should be safeguarded by the national government. The Congress under the Articles of Confederation adjourned before action was taken on this cession, and after second thoughts, North Carolina's legislature repealed the act in October 1784. During the course of these actions, the movement for the state of Franklin in the Watauga region emerged and collapsed. Not until 1789, at least three years after Thomas Hardeman had moved to the Cumberland Basin, did North Carolina again cede its western lands to the United States. The Territory South of the River Ohio, embracing these lands, was created in 1790, and the state of Tennessee in 1796. Perplexing as these times were, and irrespective of the "critical period" theory as applied to the early national era under the Articles of Confederation, they were apparently good times to get western land, whether by deal or steal.

Although impossible to establish precise statistics on Hardeman's land holdings in all areas, it is clear from the original deed papers and from entries in deed books that he acquired at least 5,360 acres between 1784 and 1803. Apparently he did not own all this at one time. Several sections of this total were received as a result of his military service. One 640–acre spread of his holdings was situated near the Holston River in Hawkins County, North Carolina (later Tennessee), and was acquired while Hardeman was attending the Tennessee Constitutional Convention at Knoxville in 1796. The balance included 1,820 acres in Davidson County, near Nashville, and at least 2,900 acres on the Little Harpeth and Big Harpeth rivers in Williamson County, Tennessee.[2] Williamson had been formed from part of Davidson County in 1799. Hardeman had sizable plots in Louisiana by 1810 and an additional 640 acres in Smith County, Tennessee, by 1811.

What were his motives in acquiring some 7,000 acres of land? According to one modern-day observer, early Williamson County "deeds of twenty and twenty-five acre tracts appear more frequently than such large and obviously speculative ones as the 1,097 acres from William Blount to Thomas Hardeman."[3] This statement must be qualified on three counts. The seller was not William, but his half-brother Willie Blount, later a three-term governor of Tennessee. Secondly, Thomas acquired nearly three times this much land in the county. And finally, although speculation was quite possibly one motive, he appears to have been preoccupied far more with plans for the future of his brood of thirteen children. No child of his would be a tenant farmer; about that Thomas was determined! The financial considerations in land transactions are not always indicated in the deed books, but it is apparent that he gave each of five of his sons somewhere between 400 and 640 acres when they became of age. There were also later bequests of land to some and probably all of his daughters.[4]

Thomas Hardeman did not take part in the great land acquisitions engineered by William Blount, James Robertson, John Donelson, Armstrong, Martin, Caswell, and others, else he would have emerged as a very large holder. This "something-for-nothing" surfeit was well over by 1784 and 1785. As for Hardeman, he had too little land to qualify as a big speculator but more than ample for his primary purposes, a start for his children and a farm for himself, where he could raise corn, hogs, and other products.

If short-staple cotton was to become king in the South, corn—a contribution of the American Indian—was the staple of the Southern diet. Corn was one of man's most versatile crops. Thriving in a wide range of soil and moisture conditions, it fed humans and livestock equally well, and there was no waste to it. The grain could be eaten both in green and ripened stages, whole, or ground into flour. The dried grain would keep indefinitely—for decades if desired—and dried corn fodder carried cattle and horses through the winter. Cobs provided excellent kindling. Not least of the attributes of corn was that it could be converted into pork and whiskey. The corn-hog cycle has been important to American agriculture since colonial times, and whiskey, a high-value and low-bulk item, held a prominent place in western trade.

Understandably, planting corn had been one of Thomas Hardeman's first concerns after he arrived in the Cumberland Basin. In time, his was to become a rather typical corn, hog, and cattle enterprise, although both hogs and cattle were scarce during his early years at Nashville. He had brought cattle and horses on his homesteading trip to the area, and about four years later he purchased the cattle identification ear clip which had been registered to Obediance Gower. In two seasons Tom's potato crop had produced enough for him to sell several bushels to Hugh Gilleland for seed.[5] A small operation, yes, but it is symbolic of the margins of gain upon which frontier settlements were built. Years later, in Williamson County, Hardeman devoted heavy acreage to corn and hogs. Since he assigned some of his slaves the job of weaving, he apparently produced fibers such as cotton, flax, hemp, and wool. Other items included tobacco and a variety of fruits and vegetables.

Arduous though his duties were—clearing and building, planting crops, and protecting his family—they did not stay Thomas Hardeman's ambition to stand for election and represent his constituents in distant halls. No doubt his growing sons, Nicholas Perkins and John, along with the several slaves, were able to spell him at the stockade in the clearing, and the daughters Isabella and Nancy were able to assist with many chores. By 1788 he was a political "known" in Davidson County.

The road to political greatness in late eighteenth- and early nineteenth-century America was usually long and stony, and it nearly always began at the bottom. Unknown in those days, of course, were the elaborate party convention machinery, the mass media of publicity, and the scientific campaign management which could propel a "dark horse" candidate or a political nobody into high office overnight. A successful politician was characteristically a man who had established himself as a worthy leader in the eyes of his peers, as a planter perhaps, or a lawyer, a shipper, an Indian fighter, or a soldier. Given the keen consciousness of sovereignty in the local and state units of government, and small populations where candidates were likely to be well known by a high percentage of the electorate, the voters usually knew what kind of leadership they were getting. True, the voting franchise was restricted, and the leaders represented special, often selfish, constituencies then as in the post-Jacksonian era. The interests to be represented were less numerous and less complex than in later times. Western lands offered the best opportunity for corruption and personal gain from public office.

Thomas Hardeman traveled the path toward political prominence for some years. He ran for office a number of times in back-country North Carolina and Tennessee and won every election. There were no signs of greatness, only indications of strong individuality, suspicion of centralized power, and loyalty to his constituents. When he left the world of public affairs, it was because he had traveled that road as far as he wanted to go; he withdrew voluntarily, having had enough. This trait of disdaining a political career seemed to be a characteristic of those of his descendants who decided to have a fling at politics.

Thomas had started at the bottom. His first turn at public office came in Washington County, North Carolina, after he had emerged as a leader of settlers, an Indian fighter, and a participant in several Revolutionary War engagements. He served as tax assessor of his district and as a grand juror.[6] By the time of John Sevier's move to organize the state of Franklin from the Watauga settlements, Hardeman was either en route to the Cumberland Valley or was preparing to go, and he took no active part in the Franklin movement. But when he landed in the Nashville region, his political feet were in motion.

His first contest in Davidson County was for an office with implications for the Articles of Confederation and the new nation. Battle lines were already forming over the structure and ratification of a national document which had its wellsprings in Federalist discontent culminating in the Annapolis and Philadelphia conventions, and which heralded a "more perfect union." The North Carolina Convention to consider ratification of the United States Constitution met at Hillsboro, July 21, 1788. Conservatives usually took the Federalist or pro-Constitution side, and radicals became Anti-Federalists. North Carolina, however, was too unpredictable for such easy categorizations. Thomas Hardeman was chosen as a delegate from Davidson County, as were Thomas Evans, Robert Weakley, William Donaldson, and William Dobbins.[7] All were landholders of some status, yet all were Anti-Federalists.

The convention delegates sat uneasily through a long-winded pro-Federalist argument, then voted a resounding 184 to 83 rejection of the Constitution. They called for a second federal convention for the purpose of appending a bill of rights and a series of amendments. Hardeman voted with the majority, as did the other Davidson delegates. The prevailing opinion at Hillsboro was that the document as proposed was a threat to individual liberties, local governments, and states' rights. Possibly the western delegates feared that a stronger central government would overturn their somewhat clouded land claims, since North Carolina's land regulations had been loose. Charles A. Beard's economic interpretation of the ratification does not fit the Hillsboro experience. There is no demonstrable relationship between the economic assets of the delegates and their stands on the document.[8]

Thomas Hardeman, who had been elected, meanwhile, to the North Carolina state legislature in 1788, joined a group of active supporters of inaction from that body; they had met at Fayetteville after adjournment at Hillsboro. The House of Commons recommended against calling a second convention to reconsider the federal Constitution. The Senate voted to reconsider, and the House of Commons then reversed itself. Hardeman, however, held fast to his stand against reconsideration.

The Anti-Federalist triumph was short-lived; eleven of the thirteen states had ratified before the Hillsboro vote was taken, leaving North Carolina and Rhode Island in a nebulous category. A sharp reversal of public opinion brought an overwhelming vote in favor of ratification at the Fayetteville Convention of 1789.

The 1788 session of the House of Commons at Fayetteville, which Thomas Hardeman attended (along with Elijah Robertson), met under somewhat anachronistic circumstances; Davidson County was part of a region ceded to the national government, then taken back before the Articles of Confederation Congress could accept. In the meantime, the back counties, including Davidson, were represented in the state legislature, assuming, of course, that their delegates could keep track of the capital's location. This was no small feat, for Hillsboro, Halifax, Smithfield, Fayetteville, New Bern, Tarboro, Wake Court House, and Raleigh (which was laid out from a plantation as the capital city), were all capitals within the decade from 1782 to 1792!

The 700 or more miles of primitive country between Nashville and the seat of North Carolina government were to become familiar to Thomas Hardeman. He went to Fayetteville for the late autumn session of the 1788 legislature, attending every day of the thirty-four-day meeting and serving on the Committee of Propositions and Grievances, which was one of the busier committees. On the lively issue of separation of the back counties from the state, both Davidson County delegates, Hardeman and Robertson, favored the split-off, although their friend and fellow-westerner John Sevier was on the other side. Actually Thomas Hardeman favored territorial status instead of statehood, and he got his wish.[9] North Carolina ceded her western lands to the United States in 1789. The new Territory South of the River Ohio was formed in the following year, with congressional authorization for a governor, an appointed five-member legislative council, and an elected house of representatives based on population of free males.

Thomas Hardeman was elected as the one Davidson County delegate to the House of Representatives of this new territory, replacing Dr. James White, who moved from the territorial legislature to the position of delegate to Congress in November 1794. The legislative sessions were held at Knoxville, some 200 miles east of the Cumberland settlements. Hardeman's role at the new seat of government was a relatively active one. He was soon appointed to the upper house or Legislative Council and was a member of the committee of six appointed "to prepare such bills of a public nature as may be necessary to be passed into laws the present session" in June 1795. Tom opposed a measure to enumerate the inhabitants of the territory on grounds that it was not requested by the people and would lead to a change of government, with resultant increase in taxes. In addition, he was not satisfied that the tally would safeguard against counting the same travelers in each of several counties they passed through. These were poorly disguised subterfuges; his real objection was to statehood.[10]

The Cumberland Basin provides a good example of the often jagged, leapfrog pattern of settlement. The frontier was less like a tier or line than a loosely joined series of salients, tongues, and "bubbles." Davidson County was a bubble separated from the older Tennessee settlements by several hundred miles of wilderness. The county residents feared domination from eastern Tennessee; they had voted against statehood by a margin of 517 to 96, and although Hardeman was representing them as best he could, it was a lost cause. The census showed 70,000 free inhabitants in Tennessee by 1795, exceeding by 10,000 the Northwest Ordinance population requirement for becoming a state. A majority of Tennessee voters favored statehood, overriding the stockaded settlements in the West, and a committee of the council and the house was appointed to work out a statehood bill. Thomas Hardeman was a member of the committee, and his was the only vote against the measure. The territorial legislature voted in favor of statehood, with only one dissenting voice, again that of Hardeman, who fought for his Davidson constituents.[11] Territorial Governor William Blount issued a call for a constitutional convention.

The views of Thomas Hardeman may have been unpopular in Knoxville, but they still held up at the polls in Davidson County. When the convention to draft the organic law for a proposed state of Tennessee met at Knoxville on January 11, 1796, he was one of the five Davidson delegates.[12] Time would prove that he was in distinguished company. His home county colleagues were Andrew Jackson, James Robertson, John McNairy, and Joel Lewis. Jackson and Robertson were well-known western leaders; Judge McNairy and Lewis were prominent citizens and landholders.

The product of this convention was a constitution based on and similar

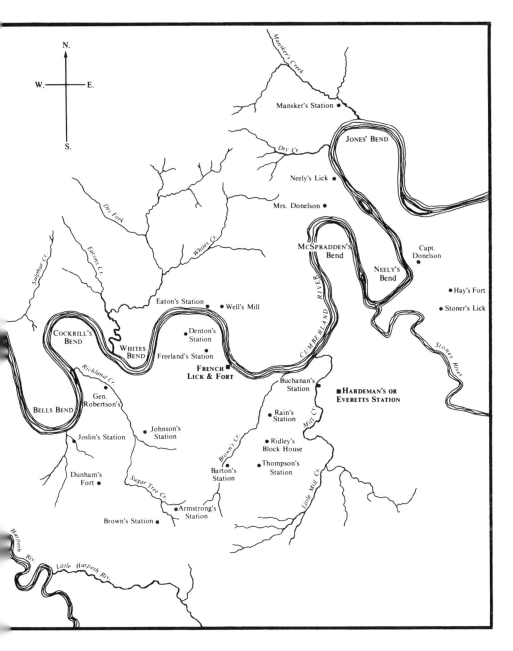

Map 2. Early Settlements in Davidson County.

to that of the mother state, North Carolina, but with some democratizing variations. These included proof of residence instead of property qualification for voting, popular election of the governor (rather than selection by the General Assembly), and representation based on taxable population instead of territorial units. Hardeman's deistic and anticlerical views, which in later years became almost fanatical, began to show up on several issues. He opposed the holding of civil or military office by clergymen and objected to exemption from military service on grounds of religious belief. His stand was upheld on the former and overridden on the latter. Moreover, he fought hard but unsuccessfully to strike out a clause providing that no person could hold a civil office in the state who did not believe in God, an afterlife of punishments and rewards, and the "divine authority of the Old and New Testaments."[13] One might safely guess that, a century and a quarter later, Thomas Hardeman would have opposed William Jennings Bryan in the notorious Scopes trial—part of the basis for which was contained in this constitutional provision.

Hardeman County is one of fifteen in Tennessee which bear the names of Constitutional Convention delegates. This was probably in joint recognition of Thomas and his sons Bailey and Thomas Jones Hardeman, the latter two having been among the county's founders.[14]

The new Tennessee constitution was implemented before it was accepted by Congress, and the first legislature met at Knoxville in March 1796. Later that year Tennessee followed Kentucky; trans-Appalachia had two states, and the nation's political scales started to tip slowly but perceptibly toward the West. In August 1797, Thomas Hardeman began another tour in state politics when he was elected as the state senator from Davidson County. Again he made the two-week trip to Knoxville; his was the farthest district from the seat of government, varying from 370 to 400 miles round trip.

A few changes had been made in travel conditions since he first probed the forest to Cumberland's shores in 1768. The Indian menace had ebbed after the Treaty of Holston, and enterprising ferrymen offered dry crossings at the larger streams. Tom, who would later operate a ferry much farther to the west, made six such crossings on this trip to Knoxville. By order of the North Carolina state legislature, a road had been cut from that town to Nashville in 1788, and seven years later the territory built another. But the 200 miles was still a wilderness, unorganized and sparsely inhabited, and Hardeman crossed it on horseback alone, sleeping along the trail and living off the land much as he had on earlier trips.

Upon his arrival at the capital, Thomas was appointed to two committees, Privileges and Elections and Propositions and Grievances, the latter handling petitions from citizens. He was active in supporting the payment of Andrew Jackson for services rendered as attorney general of the territory.[15]

Since 1788 Thomas Hardeman had put in many months of political duty far removed from his family; and he was a man seemingly devoted to family as he was committed to Tennessee. These conflicting loyalties had been a source of some distress. When in early November of 1798 he received word that his wife Mary had died, Thomas immediately went to his friend, Senate Speaker William Blount, and resigned his Senate seat to return home. Blount dispatched a letter to James Robertson via Hardeman, telling of the resignation "this moment" and stating that "it is Mr. Hardyman's most earnest wish you should succeed him." Blount added his own expression of hope that Robertson would be the replacement; the founder of Nashville acceded to the request, became a candidate and was elected.[16]

This was the end of Thomas Hardeman's career in Tennessee politics. Why he got out is known; why he stayed out is not. Although he was partisan, he had no part in the rough-and-tumble, dueling partisanship that was common in western politics of the times. In fact he maintained friendly relations with men who were bitter foes of each other, such as John Sevier and William Blount, Andrew Jackson and Thomas Hart Benton. Either he was not wanted inside such circles or had no desire to enter them. As the lone voice against statehood in both houses of the territorial legislature, he was in no position to be involved in deals on that issue. Unlike those of many western politicians, his land holdings do not seem to have escalated noticeably while he was in office. This is not to say that he had no personal interests. Reelection may have been in his interest, hence his loyalty to his constituents' wishes. Then too, political stewardship, or *noblesse oblige,* was a well-established southern concept, and political responsibilities were seen by planters as prestigious obligations, which, incidentally (and conveniently), offered the opportunity to look after the interests of one's own class, section, person, relatives, or friends.

One shortcoming which may have caused Thomas Hardeman some insecurity in the presence of political tycoons was his lack of formal education and literacy. He could read bear "sign" more readily than his Bible and could right a capsized canoe with greater ease than he could write a letter. Reportedly he was educated enough to be a handy amateur physician for frontier needs, yet the probable reason for the total absence of known letters by his hand during those ten political years was his inability to write well. Had he written much, his letters surely would have appeared in the papers of the Blounts, Jackson, Robertson, Sevier, and other Hardemans. When his children were in school, Hardeman began to write by learning with them and from them. Only after 1809 and 1810 do his letters appear frequently, and late in his life his long, articulate discourses on religion and philosophy appeared in local newspapers. The use of this tardily acquired medium of expression seemed to give him a sense of exuberant satisfaction. An acquaintance, Colonel John Reeves, later recorded that Thomas Hardeman studied law but never practiced.[17]

One of the many motivations for seeking public office, particularly in the West, was the opportunity to receive travel allowances, per diem, and other emoluments. Although the amounts seem small, they were important to planters and others who could leave their going concerns at home in the hands of their wives, other family members, and slaves. Throughout the correspondence of Thomas Hardeman, and indeed pervading much of the source material on the westward movement, was the cry of "cash shortage."[18] As English merchants held tidewater planters in a form of debt peonage, exacting payments in specie whenever possible, so business interests along the Atlantic seaboard passed part of the burden to the westerners. The trend carried over into postcolonial times. Even the assets of the wealthy consisted primarily of land, slaves, and equipment. Transactions were usually in the form of barter, credit, or both. Anyone with known liquid assets was frequently put upon by borrowers, and often the well-to-do planters would be hard pressed for $250 or $100, or even $50 in cash, which seemed ridiculously small in comparison with their assets.

At the state legislative assembly of 1788, Hardeman was paid the highest travel allowance, more than 80 pounds, for his 1,400-mile round trip. He was the second-highest paid member of the Territorial Assembly of 1795, receiving $64.07 mileage allowance and per diem for his travels, and ferry expenses were paid by the territory.[19] His costs were probably only a fraction of these amounts, since he lived off the country. From travel allowances alone on his many trips, Thomas received a significant amount of cash for the times, particularly so because more goods and services could be purchased for specie and bank notes than for credit or barter.

Hardeman's politics were Anti-Federalist; he was a strong and lifelong supporter of his "old friend" (from boyhood days at Albemarle) Thomas Jefferson. He was a states' rights and local control advocate, and in later years, a Jacksonian Democrat. During all of his public life, he resisted centralized authority and control—fighting Great Britain during the Revolution; opposing adoption of the United States Constitution; battling against statehood for Tennessee and against slighting of westerners by the states of North Carolina and Tennessee; and even challenging the power of clergymen and rejecting the concept of a personal and omnipotent God. Although this may be interpreted as an extension of resistance to parental authority, Thomas Hardeman's motives are not revealed in the documents.

At this juncture in his life he was content to relinquish his role in the political development of Tennessee, shifting to more vigorous economic activity and attending to his personal and family needs.

During the year following the death of Mary Perkins Hardeman, Thomas married her sister, Susan Perkins Marr, a widow who had seven children by her first marriage. In 1803, four years after the formation of Williamson County, Hardeman took his family to reside there. He had sold his section of land on the Little Harpeth River in 1800 and purchased the 2,160-acre tract astride the Big Harpeth. Here, five miles southeast of Franklin, the county seat, he established his new home, "Sugar Hill," an estate with a large three-story log house where he and Susan would reside for a dozen years. In 1805 he purchased from William Turnbull an additional 100 acres adjoining his new plantation.[20] Most of Thomas's children were grown, and his role as provider was diminishing; he could make a living from smaller acreage. Within several years' time he deeded most of these newly acquired lands to his offspring. In addition, he continued to assist them in other ways long after they were on their own. "Help the honest and industrious kin" was still an entry in his book of rules.

Soon after the addition of the Louisiana Territory to the United States, Thomas Hardeman purchased lands in Orleans Territory near Opelousas and Attakapas, in the southern part of what is now the state of Louisiana. He loaned and rented slaves, horses, some land, and tools to at least three sons and a daughter and son-in-law who sought their fortunes in that delta region. The repayment was to be delayed until they were well established in the new surroundings. Furthermore, Thomas helped to oversee their estates in Tennessee during their absence. He looked forward to settling his youngest son, Bailey, on 400 acres of this trans-Mississippi land.[21]

In regard to his own corn raising, salt pork business, and other agricultural enterprises, Thomas Hardeman was cutting back sharply. By 1809 and 1810, he was attempting to sell seven of his slaves—Mark, Jerry, Simon, Dann, Minty, Levi, and Ned—for $500 to $600 each, observing that several girls to do the weaving would serve his needs better. Two slave girls, Lattice and Harriet, were soon bought for this purpose.[22] Hardeman seems to have had none of the qualms about the slave trade which his son Eleazar would soon evince; he might have been surprised had he known that one of his grandsons would fight to free the slaves and that a great-grandson would by preference serve for years with the Negro Tenth Cavalry in the Far West of the late nineteenth century. Thomas's slaves had fulfilled their purpose for him, doubtless providing much of the economic well-being which he enjoyed, and now they were to be sold.

Problems of cash may have been reduced by his receipts as a holder of public office, but Thomas Hardeman's Tennessee politicking days were gone, and he was rapidly turning over his farm land to his children. It was not surprising that he cast about for better bargaining media than real estate, hogs, corn, and slaves; he sought something which most other people needed but did not have and which, at his age, would be less strenuous to manage than a large estate. He met that need by harnessing the swirling waters of the Big Harpeth River. On April 9, 1804, the Williamson County Court of Pleas and Quarter Sessions (later the County Court, housed in a building constructed under supervision of a commission of which Thomas Hardeman was a member) granted him permission "to build a water Grist and Saw Mill on his own lands on Big Harpeth." The decision, however, was delayed until the following October 8 because of appeals from the heirs of James Robertson and Matt Brooks, and from the Bookers, all of whom apparently had mills and thus resisted the increase of competition.[23]

Hardeman eventually won approval for his project and began construction, purchasing nails and a circular mill saw blade at the store of his sons, John and Nicholas Perkins Hardeman, in nearby Franklin. The cost of the steel blade was $17.90. By early 1805 the dual-purpose mill was slicing through the grain of timber and pulverizing the grain of the fields. And whether or not his mill was better than others in the vicinity the world was soon beating a path to his door, for, on April 5, 1805, the County Court authorized the building of a road from the town of Franklin to Thomas Hardeman's mill five miles away.[24] Mill and "still," or distillery, were frequently associated with each other in frontier areas, with grain the common denominator, and Hardeman produced both whiskey and ale at his power plant on the river. The value-bulk ratio made these commodities economical to transport. Soon Thomas was selling the products of his mill, including beverages and barrel staves, to the store of his sons.[25] The staves reveal his only known involvement in the cooperage trade followed by his ancestors. Now, because of the mill, the elder Hardeman could afford to reduce his acreage and slaveholdings sharply. Immediately after construction was completed, his recorded credit purchases from his sons' store dropped off to a small fraction of their former level, showing that he had increased his cash and barter buying power.

An accounting of Thomas's recorded purchases on credit at the store over the years would fill a number of pages, and there were probably many cash and barter sales not listed in the official ledgers. Household utensils and equipment, cloth, livestock-related items, farm and shop tools, nails, books, and imperishable groceries made up the bulk of the recorded purchases. As one window into his life, they provide a view of an established planter and business man of moderate scale, concerned with self-sufficiency, luxury, and intellectual activity in a situation not far removed from frontier conditions. This was the high tide of his success in material things.

Tranquil days these may have been at his Sugar Hill, but Thomas

Hardeman's mind was not entirely at peace. He noted that an unspecified member of the family was not living up to his expectations of industry and thrift. A son and son-in-law were captured by the British in the battle of New Orleans in 1815. Thomas himself suffered attacks of rheumatic fever, and his wife Susan was chronically ill before her death in 1815. His children all grown, Thomas felt a return of the old wanderlust which had recurringly pushed him on to new frontiers. Thus in June 1816, at the age of sixty-six, he took his rifle and headed westward across the Mississippi, where he found not only new land but a new life of vigorous activity, returning briefly to Tennessee to close out his business.

For nearly fifty years Thomas Hardeman's life had been bound up with trans-Appalachian North Carolina and with Tennessee. And for thousands of miles he had walked, ridden, and paddled, facing Tory, Indian, wild beast, and rampaging waters. He was a rough, "Leatherstocking" type of frontiersman by most standards, yet there was something of civility and romanticism that showed through the crude exterior. His efforts to tame the wilderness and to harness the waters of the Harpeth were matched by labors to educate himself, albeit past the noontide of his life, and to ready his family for a new era. The excursions into politics at times appeared to be pointed toward stopping the chronometer of civilization. Yet he applied his newly won literacy to reading classics and putting his ideas to paper. While not a full-fledged precursor of James Ohio Pattie or of Sinclair Lewis's Martin Arrowsmith, Hardeman administered smallpox vaccine and performed some surgery for his fellow frontiersmen. Added to this, his challenge of time-honored religious views suggested a tincture of the Age of Enlightenment which was visiting itself on more civilized areas. Having done with his share of taming the wilds, he now found them too tame—and so he moved on. His influence on the development of Tennessee had come to a close, except for the roles played by his descendants. Indeed, years before he left, several of his children had sculptured features of their own on the visage of the Cumberland Basin.

3 ⊣ᴴ *The Second Generation*
MERCHANDISING ON THE "SETTLED FRONTIER" OF TENNESSEE

IT MUST HAVE GIVEN patriarch Thomas Hardeman a sense of satisfaction to see his children established on ample acres and to know that he had been able to provide them with such a substantial start. Helping hands, it developed, could extend in both directions. A large family of small children was a worrisome responsibility on a wilderness-bound flatboat, but later, in the simple frontier economy, growing children meant additional workers. As he diversified his activities, Tom was aided by all of his children, and particularly by the two oldest sons, Nicholas Perkins and John. They were mature enough to assist in the more dangerous episodes in Tennessee, and they could handle farm chores and help their mother and the slaves run the plantation during their father's absences. The sales and marketing functions which they performed as part of the operation of their general store in Franklin, the Williamson County seat, coincided with the development of Thomas Hardeman's new enterprises in the same county and were important to his success.

[39

Typical of the small country store of the South in the early national period, the Hardeman business was a diverse, grass-roots operation. The many hundreds of yellowed pages in the half-dozen ponderous ledgers, journals, and day books show that the store was closely tied to an agrarian economy, part subsistence and part commercial. The entries further point out the existence of a "settled frontier," or a blend of the settled, stabilizing West with the more primitive frontier.

The proprietors of this house of merchandise were almost as unlike in temperament as brothers could be. Perkins, as Thomas and Mary Hardeman's oldest son was called, was born in the Dan River region in 1772. He was a blue-eyed youngster of thirteen or fourteen when he had to shoulder the emotional and physical burdens of an adult on the flatboat trip down the Tennessee River. Life in the West had a way of rushing at him. At only twenty-two years of age he assumed the duties of sheriff in Davidson County; the responsibility for law and order in the river town of Nashville and its not-so-placid environs, where a floating population turned up more than its share of ruffians, was no small task for any peace officer. Public service kept its hold on him all the rest of his life, however, as his plantation and store duties were frequently interrupted by the job as Williamson County Clerk, a position which he held for eighteen years.

Perkins seems to have been outgoing and a loyal business partner but somewhat volatile and intemperate. With whiskey selling for one to two dollars a gallon and brandy plentiful, drunkenness was a common frontier problem. Perkins's imbibing aggravated a liver ailment that eventually claimed his life. Oddly, he made a better living during the years when he drank heavily.[1] In this overindulgence Perkins, unlike his more temperate brothers and sisters, caused some anxiety to his father.

The records of the Williamson County Court reveal that the mercurial Perkins Hardeman may have been intemperate on another count, resorting to the direct and violent action which was not unknown in the West. This former peace officer was convicted on a charge of assault and battery.

Perkins Hardeman married Ann Neely, a friend of Martha Washington. Ann was to outlive him by nearly half a century. Their children, including Thomas (known as Clerk Tom) who took over the position of county clerk after his father's death, resided in Williamson County.

The younger partner of the Hardeman firm was John, second son of

Ann Neely Hardeman, a friend of Martha Washington, out-
lived her husband, Nicholas Perkins Hardeman, an early store
proprietor of Tennessee, by nearly half a century. *Courtesy the
Hardeman family.*

Thomas, and named for a long line of John Hardemans. It was fitting that he was born in the year 1776. He was of independent mind and had a breadth of interests and talents that were reminiscent of Jefferson. A confirmed Anglophobe like his father and brothers, John combined a strong devotion to his convictions with an appreciation of things cultural and philosophical. He was not the typical frontiersman, however, for he fought his battles with the pen rather than the sword. An obituary notice, possibly indulging somewhat in customary exaggeration, described him as "a gentleman of fine mind, liberal education, just principles, and most excellent temper. . . . His conversation was . . . particularly attractive and delightful, being thoroughly imbued with a chaste and delicate wit, and perpetually enlivened with good humor."[2] Possessed of an irrepressible fondness for literature, poetry, and philosophy, he nevertheless spent his life in the one environment where a man of such interests might be least expected to live—on the farther edge of civilization.

John Hardeman was five feet nine inches tall, of medium build, lean-faced, with brown hair, and his blue eyes contrasted with a somewhat dark complexion.[3] As did many members of the family, he had the prominent nose and chin which suggested that they had been hewn or chiseled. John was the balance wheel in the store's operation—sober, temperate, well schooled in mathematics, and willing to do the distant marketing and buying which the enterprise required. It may be speculated from his hospitality that he offered a garrulous welcome to his patrons. John and Perkins divided their time and investments between the soil and the store. Both proprietors were active in early Tennessee Freemasonry and were fellow lodge members with James Robertson, Andrew Jackson, John Overton, and other well-known westerners during the period of their store operation.[4]

The time span of the Hardeman store, 1802 to 1806, was a formative period for merchandising trends and institutions in the agrarian South and Southwest. Short-staple cotton was a dominant ingredient in the economy. Eli Whitney's cotton gin and growing textile markets had made that crop king of exports in the South; by 1800 it was firmly entrenched. The care required in tobacco processing tended to favor smaller agricultural producers, whereas cotton production was better adapted to the large planters. Before the advent of "King Cotton," many small farmers and planters alike had hauled their own products by flatboat to Atlantic coastal or Gulf cities and had marketed the crops directly. On these trips the men would often buy merchandise in New Orleans, Mobile, or Charleston for resale back home. With the era of the Hardeman enterprise, however, two local institutions emerged in the South to take the producer's crops and to supply his merchandising needs.

One of these, an institution in himself, was the cotton factor, who dealt primarily with the larger plantations. It was no longer practical for the planter to manage all the functions of his huge enterprise single-handed. The factor bought his cotton and made store goods available to him, thus freeing the planter to concentrate on the other business involved in running his plantation. The factor provided credit to the planter and generally took care of the transportation problems, in addition to marketing the cotton and purchasing merchandise in the large coastal and northern commercial centers. In those sections where large plantations were predominant, the factor was the principal merchant. With his orientation toward quantity buying and selling, the factor was not often attracted by the needs of small farmers.

What the factor was to the large cotton producer, the country store was to the small-scale farmer and planter. There were, of course, exceptions to the usual pattern, but the general store of a country town, such as the Hardeman establishment at Franklin, met most of the local economic needs above the subsistence level. This included supplying goods, providing a market for surplus products from the fields and forests, and offering much-needed credit. The general store was the most accessible and stable means of economic exchange.[5] Its significance was magnified by the fact that its clientele, the small farmers, comprised the largest class in the South, although literary classics have focused more upon big planters and poor whites.

Williamson County, Tennessee, was an area of small farms and small plantations, and much of it was served by the Hardeman house at Franklin. Despite the fact that it came into existence early, the store was remarkably like those which typified the next five decades in the Southern economy. Records are continuous from August 1802 to October 1806, although the operation appears to have been well developed by 1802. This indicates that it may have been a going concern which the brothers bought. Like William Byrd I of Virginia and many other men of the trade, its proprietors were planters as well as merchants. This provided a partial buffer against the seasonal troughs in the mercantile trade. As were numerous other stores, the Hardeman firm was owned and operated by several members of the same family, thus hopefully minimizing dishonesty and keeping the profits in the family. John and Perkins were the owners, but the handwriting in the daybooks shows that their younger brother Peter worked in the store much of the time.

Franklin was in one of the most agrarian regions of the most agrarian section in an overwhelmingly farm-oriented nation. It was far to the interior of the continent, thereby to a great extent geographically insulated from competition with cheaper goods in the coastal and northern cities. This advantage was somewhat offset by the alternative economic channels available to the individual producers because of the proximity of the Cumberland, Ohio, and Mississippi river systems and the overland route from the lower Mississippi to the Cumberland Basin (known after 1806 as the Natchez Trace). The circuit involving shipment to New Orleans by water and the return overland to Franklin from Natchez in Mississippi Territory was probably more useful to the store proprietors than it was to individual farmers. Thus Franklin, from the standpoint of production, market, and transportation, offered good prospects for merchants' profits.

Unfortunately, yet typically, there are no records showing profits of the Hardeman store. The four-year period of known operation suggests that the proprietors made a reasonable living—no fortune was amassed, but there was enough income to enable John Hardeman to "retire" as a well-known and moderately well-to-do experimental farmer and Perkins to be considered as prosperous. Wholesale costs and transportation expenses were rarely noted in the records of 1802 to 1806. Spoilage and losses caused by boating accidents, river gangs, Indians, and seasonal variations in business cannot be determined; nor can gains or losses from deflation, inflation, and cyclical fluctuations in the national economy. Complicating the historical post-audit further are the many unrecorded sales for cash or barter—it has been estimated that the average country store transacted from one-quarter to one-third of its business in cash—and the considerable losses from bad debts. In stable rural settings where everyone knew everyone else, social pressure dictated that most people would pay their debts, but in this area of transient population along the Natchez Trace and the Cumberland individuals listed in the accounts receivable occasionally skipped out and left the merchant holding the bag.[6] Both counterfeit character and counterfeit currency were prevalent in the region.

The merchant preferred cash or barter transactions, but money was scarce in the South and West of this time because the economy of these regions was "colonial" in nature and was tied to raw materials. Thus southern and western settlers usually paid more for manufactured goods than they received from the sale of raw materials. For example, the principal product recorded as sold by farmers to the Hardeman store was raw cotton, for which the sellers received 13 to 15 cents per pound. The biggest purchases from the store by these same farmers consisted of cotton cloth, and for this they paid a sum which included the original sale price, transportation costs to and from northern mills, value added by manufacture, and profits and incidental expenses. Only by producing a large surplus of crops could the farmer hope to "get ahead" in cash under such conditions, and even here he was not very successful. He had difficulty selling his surplus for cash, since specie was very scarce in the section. The people of Williamson County apparently did little buying with cash, in spite of the fact that prices were probably 20 to 30 percent lower for cash purchases than for credit. The store owner too was short on cash and was willing to pay a premium in goods for it.

Lacking cash, the agricultural producer hoped for direct barter or trade. The Hardemans accepted payment "in kind" for most of the store goods which they sold. Thereby they became marketing agents for the farmers, assuming the responsibility for shipping the country produce by wagon to Nashville and down the rivers to New Orleans markets.[7] This was not an unmixed evil; it gave them a chance to profit from both ends of the transaction—the sale across the store counter and the resale of farm products. The long-range marketing function was a vital service to farmers and small-scale planters who simply could not regularly sell their goods on an individual basis at great distances. Barter had its limitations. Not only were patrons addicted to buying more than they could barter for, but nature had dictated a seasonal economy. Crops matured in late summer and early fall and were marketed once a year, while settlers' needs and desires arose all year long.

The store met this imbalance by extending credit. On the average, two-thirds to three-fourths of all sales were made on this basis, with payment in kind, or occasionally in cash, once a year at harvest time and during the fur-trapping months (as will be described later). The need for credit was so pressing that without it the store could not have begun, much less survived. As a marketing agent, the country store was a banking institution of major significance. It helped to solve the chronic cash shortage by allowing farmers to buy at the time of need and pay later with produce. This was the universal pattern in the South. It was accentuated by the scarcity of banks and by the widespread tendency to plow farm profits back into land and slaves while debts continued to mount at the merchandising houses. Once credit was extended it could not be easily stopped. It made the merchants' operations more predictable and stable by legally tying the farmer to the store in a long-term contract, as clearly shown in the Hardeman store accounts.

A number of other features were built into the credit merchandising business of the Cumberland Basin. An early-day credit rating system evolved as people carried letters from previous business contacts attesting to their reliability as credit risks. Longer credit terms were usually allowed on imperishable goods than on groceries. To cover the losses from credit sales and to finance the loans, prices charged in such transactions were generally at least 20 percent higher than for cash sales. Moreover, because of the seasonal nature of debt collection and the necessity to "stock up" ahead of the demand, proprietors were in turn dependent upon credit at the wholesale houses in the large, distant cities.[8]

The seasonal business trends at the Hardeman trading establishment were in most ways similar to those prevailing at many stores of the time. The fortunes of merchant and farmer rose and fell as one; the Hardeman brothers' store was closed down for days at a time during the slack months, but during August, in keeping with the harvest and crop-marketing of late summer and fall, the records show a sharp upswing in sales of merchandise, purchases of crops, and payments on accounts. The pace leveled off and dipped noticeably but not markedly through January, then rose in February and March. Unlike the southern pattern as described in

At least seven members of the Hardeman family operated frontier stores—important trading and shipping centers in pioneer life, as well as sources of credit to farmers. Illustration is from *Harper's Monthly*, May 1870. *Courtesy State Historical Society of Missouri.*

the writings on the subject, this late winter and early spring quickening of the business tempo at the Hardeman store was very sharp, equaling and even surpassing the fall flurry, although it was not sustained as long. Part of this trend was normal and predictable, that is, the purchase of spring supplies to meet the heavy demands of seasonal tilling, planting, cultivating, and harvesting. The additional element at the Hardeman store, however, was the existence of a more primitive activity—trading in furs and skins. Winter was the season when the coats of fur-bearing animals became "prime," developing thick, warm undercoats which increased their market value. The farmers, freed from their fields by frosts and snows, had time on their hands to harvest this indigenous cash "crop."

Not only were late winter receipts of furs heavy, but in February and March there was a sharp increase in cash payments on accounts at the store; probably this indicated that cash-paying fur buyers visited the area from New Orleans and the East. Undoubtedly the relatively high level of business throughout the late fall months resulted from purchases made in anticipation of a good winter catch. Too, it is likely that the unrecorded winter and early spring barter transactions were high, with furs going directly over the counter for equivalent values in merchandise. By April, store business had dwindled to half the previous month, and May, June, and July of each year were the doldrums. It was apparently during this summer hiatus that the Hardeman brothers traveled to distant markets to replenish their stock for autumn. [9]

The frayed pages of ledger and daybook show that hundreds of products were sold at the store. Obviously the proprietors stocked or ordered whatever available merchandise was demanded. One can picture the back-country patron browsing through dark, crowded aisles, fingering the honed edge of a knife, shouldering a "rifle gun," eyeing a bundle of steel traps hanging from a wall peg, squinting at prices and the few labels, feebly resisting his own desires and the blandishments of his family, whose attentions had been caught by a colored bolt of cloth, a Barlow blade, some pearl buttons, a hatchet, or a necklace, and finally testing his future credit by purchasing more than he had come for.

Several business trends at the Hardeman brothers' store reveal much about the times and the locale. The groceries sold were the dry imperishables—coffee, tea, loaf sugar, chocolate, spices, wafers, and the like. There were no canned goods, preserves, or perishables such as those available in present-day stores. Probably all edibles not sold at the early country store were home-produced or taken from the natural environment. Despite the heavy use of salt, for preserving meat among other things, no salt was sold at the store. This critical need was met by the salt licks in the area, which had been a major reason for the "bubble" of frontier expansion near Nashville. As to matters of food, the farmers were nearly self-sufficient.

In clothing, self-sufficiency was less pronounced, however. Some wool and cotton cards were sold, indicating that spinning and weaving were not lost arts, but there were more sales of cloth and sewing accessories than any other class of merchandise. With the exception of hats, shoes, hose, and gloves, ready-made clothing was seldom sold, and particularly was it rare to market ready-mades for women. Rather, most garments were made at home from materials such as buckskin or store-bought cloth.

Local craftsmanship was by no means confined to tailoring, as evidenced by sale records on a variety and quantity of wood-working and cutting tools. Among these was one of the few brand names of the day, the Barlow knife. The general absence of brand names made the task of stocking goods easier since only one make or design of a particular type of merchandise need be carried. Nor were all the store's manufactured items stocked from wholesalers in distant commercial centers. John and Perkins Hardeman handled some locally manufactured or processed items, including coffins, buckskin, and considerable quantities of whiskey. Pleasant Glass, a local blacksmith, made various metal goods, particularly nails and horseshoes, which were resold at the store. The large quantities and numerous shipments of cast and bar iron brought in and sold by the trading house—1,200 pounds in one consignment—point to an active blacksmithing trade. The proprietors bought and resold some guns from a local gunsmith and manufacturer.[10]

High on the list of sales were powder, lead, flints, and knives necessary to kill and skin wild game, indicating that west central Tennessee was at most a step removed from the frontier. Guns and traps, on the other hand, were stocked but were less frequently sold; most residents in this newly settled area probably owned guns long before they came, and traps were often made and sold directly by local blacksmiths. But the other hunter-related items passed across the counter with almost monotonous regularity. The brothers Hardeman must have looked upon these sales with feelings other than monotony, however. Not only did they bring direct sales profits; they were fundamental to another part of the business, the acquisition of furs and skins for resale at a profit.

In their role as buyers and marketing agents for the producers of the Williamson County region, the Hardemans received two types of commodities—furs and skins and agricultural products. The peltry, providing off-season income and exchange for both farmer and merchant, was a dependable partial insurance against a bad growing season. The enterprise was also well adapted to the backland economy because of the favorable bulk-to-value ratio and the somewhat imperishable nature of the commodity. The variety and prices of these pelts are demonstrated by the 253 skins and pelts Thomas Hart Benton sold during only one month (early in 1806) for about $120. He received roughly $1.00 for each beaver and bear skin, $2.00 for otter, 50 cents each for fisher, wolf, and panther, and 25 cents each for wildcat, raccoon, fox, and muskrat pelt.[11] The merchants must have made a substantial profit upon resale since fur prices were much higher in major fur centers. This overlapping of the fur business with settled agricultural development was not confined to Williamson County or to Tennessee. It extended throughout much of rural America, where furs continued to be an important source of cash well into the twentieth century. Scholars have neglected the story of the fur trade in settled areas. The shift of an area's population from Indian, long hunter, and mountain man to settled farmer and planter did not signal the end of significant fur trade.

Cotton and tobacco were the leading crops received from the farms and plantations, with the fiber crop clearly first. The Hardemans provided cotton ginning services at the store, and from September through the winter months, there are many entries of "G. C."—ginned cotton received from growers.[12]

Corn acreage probably exceeded that of either cotton or tobacco in the Cumberland Basin, but this grain itself was rarely purchased directly by the store. By-products of corn, however—lard, salt pork, and whiskey —had a higher value per unit of weight, and were regularly sold to the Hardeman brothers. Whiskey was uniquely valuable to the trade since much, if not most of it, was sold locally. Transportation costs were thus minimized or eliminated. Brandy was both bought and sold locally also, as were beeswax, livestock, deerskins, horseshoes, and nails. Thus, the store was more than a marketing agent; it was a clearinghouse for the local exchange of goods produced in the neighborhood.[13] Nevertheless, the bulk of the merchandise bought by the store had to be sold at faraway markets, which presented transportation problems of staggering proportions.

The transportation dimension of the store involved three distinct phases: local, up river, and down river. Most of the local hauling appears to have been done by individual farmers who brought their produce to the store in wagons and carried their purchases home in the same creaking conveyances. Saddle horses were probably used for the lighter carries. The Hardeman brothers also peddled their wares to individual estates about the countryside, and from time to time they hired wagoners to transport goods to and from Nashville, which was the head of navigation for their long hauls.[14]

Some, and probably most, of the manufactured supplies sold at the store of John and Perkins Hardeman were shipped from Philadelphia to Pittsburgh, thence down the Ohio River and up the Cumberland to Nashville. By the mid-1790s, this flatboat and keelboat route had effectively displaced the commercial hauls by wagon through the Cumberland Gap. Water transportation going with the current was the cheapest. An abundance of timber in Tennessee, particularly along the streams, simplified the important task of boat building. In a transaction culminated on February 23, 1804, John Hardeman paid Andrew Jackson $45.00 for a flatboat forty-five feet long and twelve feet across the beam. This craft was one of twenty-eight which the federal government had contracted with Jackson to have built. The purpose was to carry military forces downstream to Natchez on the Mississippi River above New Orleans.[15] The boat which Hardeman purchased undoubtedly made that trip, but with produce from the store rather than troops.

As they bought primarily from the Northeast, so the Hardeman brothers shipped to the Southwest, taking advantage of cheap, downriver hauls in both types of transactions. In 1795, Pinckney's Treaty with Spain temporarily opened New Orleans to western trade down the Mississippi by giving the traders duty-free "right of deposit" on goods for transshipment. Spain abrogated the treaty in October 1802, but restored the right of deposit in May of 1803. Despite the threat of another close-down under Napoleonic control, this route to the sea lanes remained precariously open until purchase of the Louisiana Territory by the United States in 1803 settled the question permanently. The records of the store at Franklin begin just two months prior to Spain's temporary interruption of the right of deposit in 1802. The prompt resolving of the matter was a source of relief to the entire trans-Appalachian West, which hoped to profit from cheap flatboat transportation to New Orleans.

John and Perkins Hardeman were among the frequent users of the river system from Nashville to Natchez, Baton Rouge, and New Orleans. They hired boatmen to move the cotton, tobacco, peltry, pork, and whiskey, but they were not content to entrust all the distant negotiations to others. Perkins was apparently tied down by his court clerk duties, but John went periodically to the towns near the Gulf Coast in order to give the business first-hand direction.[16] The residences which he maintained at Baton Rouge and Natchez until late fall of 1805 were probably established as an outgrowth of the need to be on hand to market the produce, although he also acquired land, hogs, cattle, and slaves in the lower Mississippi country. Undoubtedly John bought some goods for shipment up the river by keelboat, since the rates were not much greater than buying out of Philadelphia. His return trips were usually overland by way of the Natchez Trace.

The distant business dealings caused the Hardeman brothers some anxiety over financial matters. Not only was theirs a credit-oriented society, but monetary values were chaotic. The issuing of bank notes was not strictly regulated; merchants had to contend with multiple specie standards, fractional currency, coin clipping, and—not the least of their difficulties—sluggish communications. Dollars, pesos, pounds, shillings, bits, pence, debt statements or promissory notes, and the ever-questionable bank notes and bills of exchange had to be cross-evaluated[17] routinely without benefit of slide rule, telephone, calculator, or computer. The widespread use of barter meant that every item had to be given a monetary value before trade in order to arrive at a common value denominator. A change of prices in New Orleans, New England,

Philadelphia, or Europe could cause unanticipated profits or losses many months later. Difficulties in physically transferring money, and a shortage of banks in the West, further compounded the Hardemans' problems. They often used bills of exchange or drafts to transfer credit from one geographical locality to another, thereby reducing the danger of losing money in transit. The mails were not safe in the early 1800s, and it was often just as well that money was shipped in the form of produce which was less difficult to steal. Numerous problems notwithstanding, considerable sums of money were successfully transferred. John and Peter Hardeman carried cash to settle store accounts, [18] and many of the letters refer to sending money in the care of relatives or trusted friends.

Kinfolk and close friends played another, even more important part in the success of those frontier merchants than carrying money for the store; they carried business *to* the store. The big clans of Hardemans and Perkinses, added to the Holts, Edwardses, and Neelys and supplemented by friends, provided a comfortable business cushion in the form of a built-in clientele. Here and there a luminary emerges from the pages; there were the Bentons, the McGavocks, and Dr. John Sappington; William Neely, who collaborated with Benton in an anti-Aaron Burr meeting; and a cousin of the Hardemans, Nicholas Perkins, who attracted attention by his role in capturing Burr and collecting the reward.

The records of the store unaccountably end in October 1806. Subsequent ledgers and daybooks may have been lost or destroyed; or the business may have been sold. The latter is probable, since both John and Perkins Hardeman seem to have gotten out in possession of their shirts and taken up more leisurely pursuits as planters in reasonably comfortable circumstances. Their business had covered years of relative prosperity in the West, years marked by fortuitous circumstances: the purchase of Louisiana, the clearing of the Mississippi trade and right of deposit question, and rapid population and market expansion in Tennessee. Before the year 1807 had passed, new trade problems were to arise: Jefferson's shipping embargo, the expiration of Jay's Treaty of 1794, and intensified British and French seizures of American ships. The brothers must have felt particularly relieved that they had done with the trade when President Madison's commercial restrictions and the War of 1812 further darkened business horizons in the West.

4 ⊨ *From Plantation to Frontier*
RESTLESSNESS IN THE SECOND GENERATION

MARY POLK HARDEMAN and her sister-in-law, Elizabeth Owen, waited at Franklin for word from their young husbands who had gone off with several other sons of Thomas Hardeman to join General Jackson in Louisiana. Then came the news, cruel as a saber thrust: Thomas Jones Hardeman and Glen Owen had been killed in action against the British near New Orleans on December 23, 1814. Christmas came and passed, and it was weeks later when the families of the men learned that they were not dead but were captives of the "savage foe." They would live and return home, and in time would push on westward into the very lands which the war had made more secure and accessible for American settlers.

The War of 1812 and its conclusion signaled a sharp change in the activities of Thomas Hardeman and most of his progeny, a turn away from Middle Tennessee. John and Perkins Hardeman had stimulated the local economy with their store at Franklin and had long since left it for other pastimes. But before they took leave of their home of several decades to join the volunteer army and the migration farther west, Thomas's children played other roles in the growth of the state.

Tennessee stretched due west like a huge board from its eastern end, imbedded in the Appalachians and the Watauga settlements, to the distant shores of the Mississippi. Entering its wooded expanses with the late eighteenth-century line of pioneer settlers, Thomas Hardeman and his family had balanced precariously at first, then ensconced themselves firmly. Eventually most of them would use this foothold in the wilderness as a base from which to set off anew to other frontiers.

The children of Thomas and Mary Perkins Hardeman took up a variety of occupations in Tennessee. There were the merchants, planters, and politicians, but there were also housewives, soldiers, lawyers, mill owners, and a physician among them; and their substantial degree of material success may have stimulated rather than satiated their appetites for further ventures.

Thomas and Mary had fifteen children, five daughters and ten sons. Isabella, oldest daughter and first child, was born in October 1770.[1] She married John Holt, who was a frequent patron of the Hardeman store. Nancy, born in 1774, married Judge Seth Lewis and lived in Louisiana until her death from cholera in 1833. Susanna, or Julia Ann, migrated to Texas with her family in 1835. Dorothy, who was born in 1786, married George Burnet, and they later moved from Tennessee to Missouri. One of their sons was to become well known in Oregon and California. The last daughter, Elizabeth, was born in 1791. She moved to Missouri by 1819 with her husband, Glen Owen; after his death she went back to Tennessee and later remarried.[2] Women were, of course, deprived of an equal chance to leave their marks in the recorded history of the American frontier. They were relegated to positions as childbearers, homemakers, farm hands, and child carers—and thus were less active in the actual physical conquest of the frontier than were the men. The pioneer women's role in stabilizing the home and farm base was integral and indispensable to the achievements of the wandering menfolk. Women were characteristically denied the education which would have enabled them to leave better written records of their activities and contributions.

Of the ten sons of Thomas Hardeman, two died in infancy, Pitt in 1793 and Franklin in 1796. Two others, Constantine or Constant and Eleazar, became plantation owners and spent their lives in Tennessee. Constant helped to found Rutherford County (formerly a part of Davidson and Williamson counties) and built a mill there, at Smyrna on Stuart's Creek. The remaining six sons, possessed of the wandering spirit which characterized their father, acquainted themselves with new frontiers.

After these Hardeman sons moved west, they apparently were stimulated to greater creativity and individualism than they had shown in Tennessee. Perhaps it was because they were in the shadow of their father as long as they remained in the Cumberland Basin; possibly there simply were too many other planters and farmers in that area for the Hardemans to become prominent. The second generation of Tennessee Hardemans may exemplify a reason for one of mankind's enduring and worsening emotional problems, namely that as population increases in a given area, one's personal sense of satisfaction through recognized achievement seems to diminish. It was easier to stand out in a small crowd than a large one, particularly if the small group was pioneering. Compared with the inhabitants of older, established centers an inordinately high percentage of the frontier population has been recognized and written about in historical accounts.

Youthful life for the first eight or ten of the Hardeman children was a thrilling and fear-fraught adventure: flight from Indians in the Holston area, apprehensive months while their father was away at Nickajack, Nolichucky, and King's Mountain, talk of Tory depredations, nights of terror on the flatboat trip, uneasy years at the stockade in the Cumberland country. These and lesser-known episodes must have left indelible marks on the young minds. But there were also pleasant times, and there was room to grow and burn excess energy. It may be significant that, against this background, most of the Hardeman sons and two of the daughters later staked their claims in dangerous environments.

Familiarity with forest, stream, and field was essential, and Tom Hardeman's boys were schooled early in the art of the practical; the use of guns and tools was second nature to them. Like most of their contemporaries, they were inclined toward earning at least a substantial part of their living from the soil. All eight of them owned and worked sizable acreages, and boyhood experiences equipped them well. Yet Thomas Hardeman knew first hand the value of being prepared for something more. As he resolved that his children would not experience his own discomfort of tenancy, so he was determined that they would have the educational benefits which he lacked. This involved freeing them from farm chores for periods long enough to provide for study. Thomas arranged, often at considerable time, expense, and inconvenience, to expose them to book learning, relating that he "had frequently to guard his children to school in the morning and return for them at evening; often bidding them go, as though there was no danger, and following unobserved at a distance."[3]

Testimony to the effectiveness of this schooling exists in the form of letters written by most of his children in literary styles which would have passed in any company. Beyond this backwoods learning there was some more advanced education. John, Bailey, Blackstone, and Thomas Jones Hardeman probably outdistanced the others in formal training. John's life became a veritable patchwork of interests. In 1796, at the age of twenty, he was a mathematics student at Nashville, perhaps at the Davidson Academy (which became the University of Nashville). Three years later he pursued courses in surveying, geometry, and plane, rectangular, and oblique angular trigonometry. He was admitted to the Tennessee Bar in 1810, although he practiced law very little during his lifetime. Perhaps he never intended to. A well-read man on a variety of subjects, he may have passed the examination as an exercise in achievement with little special effort. Legal training was not comprehensive at that time. The store ledgers indicate that John, Peter, and Perkins Hardeman were adequately versed in elementary accounting. Bailey and Thomas Jones Hardeman also were licensed to practice law, but Bailey apparently did not establish a legal practice at any time. His best-known contribution to education was his creation of an academy at Hardeman's Crossroads (now Triune), Tennessee. Blackstone Hardeman was a medical doctor.[4]

Education for these sons of the frontier was like enrichment of the soil in a garden; it broadened the foliage and enhanced the blooms, but it did not basically alter the species. Agrarian and western was the stock, and agrarian and western it would remain, no matter the periodic ventures into other places and endeavors. The base operation, the common denominator of the livelihood of Thomas Hardeman's children, was land, amplified by slaves and work and crops. Because in this milieu they were usually indistinguishable from the multitude of other farmers, inevitably they became least known to history for what they did most, and best known for what they did least. (John's unique contribution to western agriculture in later years was the exception to this rule.)

Unhappily, few records of these Tennessee farming operations are available, apart from the none-too-revealing acreage statistics. The soils of the river and creek valleys were doubtless as good as the typical overcropping techniques were bad. Soil erosion and exhaustion often accounted for a family's move to fresh lands in early American history, and this may explain some of the Hardemans' wanderings. Since Thomas provided sizable tracts for his sons, they were endowed with a guaranteed income. These lands were located chiefly in Davidson, Williamson, Smith, and later Hardeman counties, but Mississippi and Louisiana soils were soon broken by their plows.

Some of the family correspondence suggests the breadth of their farming operations. Peter Perkins, writing to his cousin and partner Peter Hardeman while the two were on business trips in 1809, advised: "If you cannot get fifteen cents per pound for our cotton we had as well sell as much as will pay Mr. Murray and barter the balance for goods." Thomas the elder and John Hardeman looked after Peter Hardeman's Big Harpeth plantation from late 1809 to early 1815. John wrote in 1810 that Mr. Andrew Craig offered to buy Peter's estate for "10 thousand weight of tobacco payable in two annual payments one half in March 1812 the other half in 1813." Regarding Peter's corn crop, his father wrote, "I will take 200 bushels of your corn at 50 cents a bushel." While doing his own butchering in the winter of 1814–15, John looked after his absent brother's hogs. "Your pork I have salted up . . . about 14 hundred weight." Meanwhile, former store clerk Peter Hardeman was the chief liaison between the Tennessee Hardemans and their Louisiana holdings.[5]

It was appropriate that a philosophical agrarian and physiocrat, Thomas Jefferson, added the Louisiana Territory to the United States. The purchase in 1803, which doubled the country's area in one swing of the nationalistic scythe, took in not only land in general but much excellent river bottom and delta soil. The Jeffersonian myth of an inexhaustible land supply for all time to come must have appeared healthier than ever. But the very appetite with which these rich expanses were engorged should

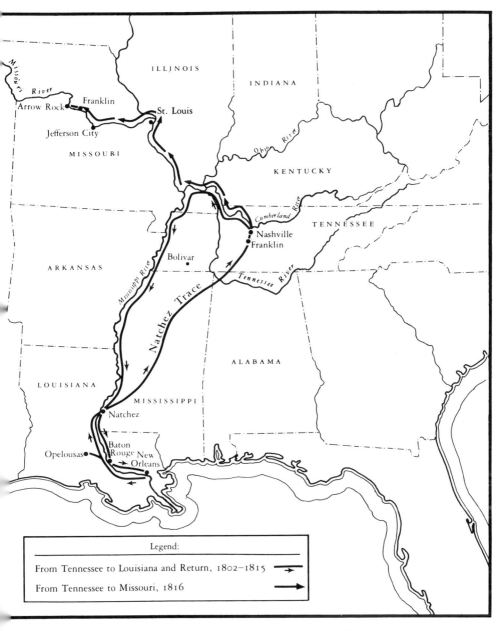

Map 3. Travels of the Hardeman Family, 1802–1816.

have been read as a sign with mixed meaning. It bespoke at once an optimistic, opportunistic temper and an ominous awareness that soils of the older sections had been mined to their depths and were getting "tired." Almost before the ink was dry on the final Louisiana Purchase agreement, John Hardeman acquired property below Pointe Coupee near Baton Rouge, and soon he was producing cotton, corn, cattle, hogs, and sheep there. His brothers Thomas, Peter, and Blackstone and his brother-in-law Seth Lewis, with much financial aid from old Thomas Hardeman, operated a kind of annex to their Tennessee enterprises in Attakapas and Opelousas, Louisiana.[6] The patriarch himself purchased but apparently did not work land in the delta region.

Most of these Louisiana holdings were given over to the production of rice, cotton, and sugar cane. Seth Lewis, Judge of the Fifth Judicial District of Louisiana from 1812 to 1839, wrote to Peter Hardeman in 1815, explaining some of his experiences and woes on the Opelousas plantation. His cotton "failed totally," and in the face of plummeting land values during the war, he turned to sugar production.

> But a heavy expense was still to be incurred before anything could be made of that plant. Works were to be erected and stills for a Distillery, or Boilers for a sugar works to be procured. I adopted the former as best adapted to my force and . . . have finally got my Distillery in operation on a scale that will easily yield fifty Gallons of double distilled spirits in 24 hours.[7]

This, along with an account of his grave illness, was offered as reason for his delinquency in repaying a loan from Thomas Hardeman.

The Hardeman sons, like their father, accomplished their labors with much more help than their use of the pronoun "I" indicated. All of them owned slaves. By 1820, Thomas Jones Hardeman had ten and his brother Eleazar eight. Judging from the frequent mention of slave transactions it must be assumed that there was heavy dependence on slave labor and much concern with the financial investment in the Negro work force. The average market price for men was $500 to $600, although Ned, one of Thomas Hardeman's slaves, was valued at $1,800, undoubtedly because he was a skilled craftsman such as a blacksmith or cooper. John's purchase of a slave for $500 in July 1806 illustrates a not-so-typical aspect of the trade—Richmond was bought from a Cherokee Indian named John

Chisholm.[8] There was slaveholding in all of the civilized tribes of the Southeast, but most of the slaves were held by mixed bloods.

At times there were difficulties with the purchase and sale of slaves. Peter Perkins, buying laborers near Baltimore for himself and Peter Hardeman in the summer of 1809, reported, "I have bought nine negroes (to wit) 5 fellows, one of which is an excellent blacksmith. Three negro women and a girl about 12 years old."[9] Although the letter was written on July 4, it was obviously not Independence Day for everyone. A few days later, having bought three more slaves, he wrote again, sounding a note of alarm about the security of his chattels:

> The Quakers and Abolitions have been so violent on men of our business that I'm afraid to leave the place for fear they turn my negroes out of Gaol [jail] and if they should and no person hear to take charge of them we would lose them of course.[10]

As slaves in the intercontinental trade had been caged on the ships until they could be brought to America and broken, domesticated, or intimidated to remain on plantations, so they were often jailed after purchase in the domestic slave trade until the new buyer was ready to transport them to his destination. Referring to conditions in Louisiana, where his son Peter was attempting to sell some slaves, Thomas Hardeman observed in 1811 that "the late rebellion amongst the blacks may have occasioned dull markets for such merchandise."[11]

There were instances where slaves and ex-slaves were placed in a category more respectful than "merchandise," and indications of opposition to slavery or to some aspects of it began to emerge in the South. Seth Lewis and Peter Hardeman appealed to the Humane Society for the Abolition of Slavery, Richmond, Virginia, to help

> to recover the freedom of a family of people of colour whose case in our opinion calls aloud for assistance. . . .
>
> You will be relieving the injured and oppressed and may essentially contribute to the restoring to freedom of no less than fourteen human beings whom we verily believe to be unjustly held in slavery by Cuthbert Coleman of Virginia and South Carolina. . . . We feel confident that you will readily give us your assistance in freeing them from the shackles of an unjust and cruel slavery.[12]

How much of this sentiment was humanitarian and how much was legal fee of course cannot be determined, although it is doubtful that the monetary consideration, if any, could have been very great. Eleazar Hardeman sought to negate the purchase of a slave by his son Seth from Judge John Overton of Nashville, stating that he was "determined never to . . . encourage any man in the slave trade."[13] Here too, the motive may be questioned, since Eleazar was a slaveholder and Elbert, the slave boy in question, was considered a poor investment owing to his chronic rheumatism. It was not unusual for slaveholders to be opposed to the slave trade, however.

Several of Thomas Hardeman's sons, while they maintained and worked their lands, branched out from farming to other activities. Typical of many planters—even small planters—they were from time to time active in public affairs, although with the exception of Bailey in Texas they were less prominent than their father had been. The designation of the oldest, Perkins, to the office of Davidson County Sheriff may have been a patronage appointment by Territorial Governor William Blount, well known to the appointee's father. The eighteen-year term as Williamson County Clerk has been noted. Peter Hardeman served as deputy sheriff and collector of public and county taxes in Williamson County; and at the age of twenty-one, Bailey served as deputy sheriff of the same county. John and Eleazar were appointed to the County Road Commission in 1806, to lay out and mark a road to Newton Cannon's horse mill, and John served with Cannon on the County Court Jury in 1810. Shortly thereafter, the two opposed each other for the state senate seat from the district composed of Williamson, Bedford, Maury, and Rutherford counties. Thomas Hart Benton, who had held that position just prior to the Cannon-Hardeman contest, supported John, but Cannon was elected[14] and later became governor of Tennessee. This was the only time that John Hardeman ran for office, although his acquaintance with political figures such as the Blounts, Jackson, Clay, and Benton could have been used to his advantage were he politically inclined. In connection with the last named, John and Perkins made a contribution to the success of a political figure who was to gain considerable prominence in the West.

The occasion was December 1804. Twenty-two-year-old Thomas Hart Benton, still smarting, no doubt, over his expulsion from the University of North Carolina on a charge of petty theft, left the Williamson County plantation of his pious, widowed mother and took a school-teaching job at Duck River in west-central Tennessee. Much impressed by the command- ing figure of Judge Andrew Jackson at Nashville several years before, and by what he had seen of Jackson's legal proceedings, Benton decided to take on a spare-time reading program to acquaint himself with the law. The library of his father Jesse Benton afforded him a start, but he wanted more books as well as personal supplies. Accordingly, he wrote to his friends the Hardeman brothers at their store in Franklin and took John up on his offer to help Benton and keep him from selling land to meet his needs.

> I am now at Duck, where I shall remain for the winter.
> Those books I spoke of when with you, I request you will now send me: They are: Millott's General History 5 volumes; Legar's Frederic William 3 volumes; Cook's Voyages 2 volumes; Goldsmiths Natural History 2 volumes; Gray's Fables, and Sheridan's dictionary.[15]

Benton made other and more extensive book purchases from the Harde- mans on a buy-now, pay-later basis. Among them were Tucker's *Black- stone,* Homer's *Iliad,* Chambana's *Grammar,* Mallet Dupan's *Switzerland,* Lavater's *Physiognomy,* Chestupulas' *Letters,* Silanas' *Demosthenes,* Blair's *Letters,* Prossaus' *Confessions,* Montesquieu's *Spirit of the Laws, Burlamaqui,* Robertson's *America, Locke on Understanding,* Milton, and Sevogne's *Let- ters.*[16] A comparison of this list with other book sales at the Franklin store shows that, if not representative of the volumes which people were reading, it was a good cross section of what they were adding to their shelves.

The nature of Benton's nonintellectual needs may be only partially determined from the letter of December 1804.

> Further, I want you to send me an almanac, not a last year's one; a penknife, best double bladed; a comb to straighten out my hair with; a pair of black cotton stockings; half a dozen quires of common writing paper, and one pair of strong coarse shoes.

With nontypical tact, revealing his impecunious straits, he continued:

> In an idle hour to prevent the evaporation of Peter's industry, I would be glad if you would set him to transcribe my account; and when he has finished it, I desire that Peter will remind you from time to time of sending it to me; as a

knowledge of its amount will assist me in the regulation of my financial concerns.

And if he was accurate in his closing Bentonesque line, "I am, dearest sir, more thine than mine own,"[17] he was to remain so for several years. Thomas Hardeman, too, gave the young teacher and lawyer assistance when the latter returned to Williamson County and hung his shingle in Franklin.

Twenty-five years later, now a highly influential United States senator from Missouri, Benton humbly acknowledged the aid he had received. Upon John Hardeman's death, he wrote to the eighty-year-old father:

> I will do all I can for you, and the family of my deceased friend, Mr. John Hardeman, without fee or reward, and through gratitude for past services and friendships from you both.
> I can never forget that when I mentioned to your son then a merchant at Franklin that I wanted law books and intended to sell land to buy them, he answered that I should not, that he would buy the books for me, and wait for reimbursement till I made the money, which was done: and out of these books I studied law, and it was several years before he was repaid. This is a favour not to be repaid in money: my friendship is still a debtor to you and to his children in his place, and I shall omit no opportunity to show it.[18]

This favor was by no means the extent of the Benton-Hardeman contacts. Thomas Hart Benton, his mother Nancy, and his brother Jesse were very frequent customers at the Hardeman store in Franklin. Benton was also closely associated with Thomas Jones Hardeman during the War of 1812.

The second American Revolution, as the War of 1812 has been called, was essentially a westerners' war. Acquisition of territory in Canada and Florida, a cessation of Indian hostilities, and freedom to ship their agricultural products on the seas were high on the list of objectives of western war hawks. Tennessee's own hawk, Felix Grundy, summed up his and his constituents' Anglophobia with the remark: "We shall drive the British from our continent. They will no longer have an opportunity of intriguing with our Indian neighbors." He asserted that Britain would "lose her Canadian trade, and, by having no resting place in this country, her means of annoying us will be diminished."[19] How ironic that the declaration of "Mr. Madison's War," jammed through Congress by western and southern votes, would bring the British lion nearly to the point of closing that sacred channel of western commerce, the mouth of the Mississippi.

Tennesseans had a big stake in an open trade route to New Orleans and the Gulf. The same water and land connections which had been essential to the Hardeman store were no less vital to all central and western Tennessee. Although the state was little affected by military action until the war was nearly over, judging from the number of Tennessee settlers in General Andrew Jackson's army by late 1814, the term "Volunteer State" might well have been adopted a third of a century before that nickname was applied (during the Mexican War).

Among these volunteers were at least three of Thomas Hardeman's sons—Thomas J., Peter, and Bailey—and his son-in-law and nephew, Glen Owen. All four ultimately elected to serve under Thomas's former neighbor and political confrere, General Jackson, who had known the three Hardeman boys since they were infants.

Thomas Jones Hardeman was born on the frontier, at the stockade near Nashville in 1788. As the lean-faced youngster grew to maturity, so did the Cumberland Basin; and as he worked his father's plantations and took to the legal profession, it began to appear that he would not again know the fright and excitement of his early years. In 1814 he married Mary Polk, daughter of Ezekiel Polk of Mecklenburg, South Carolina. Mary was an aunt of James Knox Polk, who would become the eleventh president of the United States.

But Thomas Jones Hardeman's blood was not that of the settled life, and, bristling at British insults, real or fancied, he joined the war hawks and the war. In September 1814, he was a lieutenant in Colonel Thomas Hart Benton's Thirty-Ninth Infantry.[20] Benton had been itching to join the fray during the better part of three years—against Indian or Tory. Owing to an almost comical succession of circumstances, he had been denied his moment of action. The nearest he could come to it was to join his brother in a knifing, pistol-shooting brawl against Andrew Jackson and Colonel John Coffee. Now, with Napoleon Bonaparte temporarily humbled and powerful contingents of Britain's army en route to punish the upstart republic of the stars and stripes, it appeared that Benton would have his chance. But he was ordered back to Tennessee, and his enemy,

Jackson, reaped the accolades in several battles against British Major General Edward Pakenham's forces in late 1814 and early 1815.

The assignment of Lieutenant Thomas Jones Hardeman was changed, and he and his brother-in-law, Captain Glen Owen, went into the crucial days of the conflict as members of the First Regiment of Volunteer Mounted Gunmen in the Brigade of the towering John Coffee (who had been recently promoted to brigadier general). Lieutenant Peter Hardeman was in the Forty-Fourth Regiment under Coffee. Peter, the fifth son of Thomas and Mary Hardeman, was born in the Watauga country in 1784, the year after the close of the American Revolution. Now he was on hand for the closing battle with the former mother country. He had received his lieutenant's commission in September 1814.[21] Eleven months earlier, eighteen-year-old Bailey Hardeman had been commissioned a first lieutenant in Captain Ota Cantrell's artillery company, which was attached to the Second Regiment of Mounted Gunmen. Bailey, Thomas Hardeman's youngest son, had enlisted in September 1813. Judging from his later activities, he must have found life on the campaign trail stimulating. His artillery experience would prove to be an asset in the future.

The campaign against Pakenham was viewed as a do-or-die encounter by the states of the Southwest. Should they lose control of their Mississippi lifeline, the westerners would be open to untold depredations by both the enemy from abroad and Indians who might take heart and attempt to avenge such defeats as Horseshoe Bend. After jabbing successfully at British forces in Spanish Pensacola and parrying a thrust at Mobile in late fall 1814, the ailing Jackson hurried his 12,000 Tennessee volunteers westward to New Orleans in order to meet an expected British onslaught in the delta country. His forces threw up breastworks to protect against a land approach to the city and felled timbers to clog bayous and lake entrances. But the one entrance which was neglected, Bayou Bienvenue, nearly proved Old Hickory's undoing.

As the first day of winter broke over the bayou country, an English exploring party located this waterway where Jackson's guard was down, and by December 23 they had placed just below New Orleans several thousand soldiers seasoned in European battles. But for exaggerated reports of Jackson's strength told by American prisoners and believed by their British captors, this force could probably have taken New Orleans

Three of Thomas Hardeman's sons fought with General Jackson at New Orleans. In this scene from Kendall's *Life of Jackson*, the General's troops drift stealthily down the Mississippi toward the target city. *Courtesy Lehigh University Library.*

virtually unopposed. An escapee warned Jackson, who, like a cornered animal, attacked immediately and almost instinctively.

Using the cover of the long winter night of December 23, he sent out a three-pronged force, one unit by sea and two by land. The schooner *Carolina* drifted stealthily down the Mississippi and suddenly began bombarding the encampment of the redcoats. General Coffee and his men, including the First Regiment of Thomas J. Hardeman and Glen Owen, accomplished the "swamp fox" maneuver and waded to a silent readiness on the enemy's flank. After half an hour of shelling by the *Carolina,* Coffee's men attacked from the flank as the main force of Tennesseans struck from the front. The spur-of-the-moment strategy threw the enemy into confusion and bought time to erect earthworks around the approaches to the city.

But the attacks gained only a reprieve, and at a cost of a considerable number of men. The First Regiment paid dearly in killed, wounded, and missing. Thomas Jones Hardeman and Glen Owen, reported killed at first, were taken prisoner. Hardeman was taken aboard a British warship and questioned at length about the size and disposition of Jackson's army. For his refusal to answer he was wounded on the head by a blow from a British officer's saber. Perhaps old Thomas Hardeman, with some battles against redcoats in his past, had some precognition of such treatment as this when he commented on the imprisonment. Writing to Peter at Jackson's camp, he observed, "They will suffer no doubt in the hands of such a savage foe, but there is still . . . hope."[22]

Peter and Bailey Hardeman may have fought in the Battle of New Orleans, January 8, 1815, as both were in the vicinity of the battleground about the time of the encounter. Peter's military service continued until May 13, but Bailey returned to Franklin soon after the engagement. The New Orleans battle was one of the most one-sided in the history of warfare, thanks to the time bought by the December 23 attack and to the timing which Pakenham employed when he attempted to send a column across the Mississippi to assault the American artillery emplacements. The British commander and 2,000 of his soldiers were killed. Only six of Jackson's men lost their lives in the battle.

Unknown to the participants, the battle of New Orleans had been fought fifteen days after the war was over and thus influenced neither the decision nor the peace treaty. Few Americans would have been willing to take away their most brilliant victory because of the mere technicality of slow communications, however, and there is no doubt that the triumph enhanced the diplomatic position of the United States. Nowhere was the victory celebration more jubilant than in Tennessee. From his plantation twenty miles south of Nashville, John Hardeman wrote, "I heard even at this place, the sound of cannon fired in rejoicing at Nashville."[23]

War's end was followed by one of the most vigorous releases of pent-up energy and pulsations of frontierward force in the entire national experience. Peace, like war, left the Tennessee Hardemans restless. Following their habit of answering the wilderness call when settlement began to wall them in, most of them left Williamson County—as they had departed Davidson a decade and a half before. In 1818, led by Thomas Jones Hardeman, whose father-in-law, Ezekiel Polk, had preceded him, one group moved to the sparsely settled Hardin County in southwest Tennessee. Five years later, Hardeman County was created in that part of the state from parts of Hardin and Madison counties. The same year, as his father and his brother Constant had done farther east, Thomas Jones Hardeman built a mill on Pleasant Run Creek, two miles west of the present county seat of Bolivar. His activities included the purchasing of lands in Hardeman, Fayette, and Henderson counties, serving as clerk of the county court at Bolivar from 1823 to 1833, and holding the posts of town commissioner and county road overseer. He found time to take active roles in the York Rite Masonic Lodge and the Episcopal Church.[24] Not the least part of his influence on the area was his attracting of other settlers.

Four of the children of Thomas Hardeman the elder developed a closeness which kept them and their families together through several westward moves. Thomas Jones Hardeman seems to have been the pivotal figure in this sequence, first to southwest Tennessee, and later to Texas. Blackstone and Bailey and their sister Julia Ann Hardeman Bacon joined in these changes of residence.

Blackstone Hardeman, seventh son and tenth child of Thomas Hardeman of Albemarle, was born near Nashville in 1790. It was the time of his grandfather's death, and Thomas was apparently back at Guilford, North Carolina, managing the affairs of the estate. Blackstone, named for the eminent English jurist, spent his early childhood in Davidson County.

His mother died when he was eight, and several years later the family moved to Williamson. He studied medicine, probably at least in part under the guidance of his uncle Dr. Hardin Perkins.

Blackstone and his wife, the former Anna Bunch, moved on a number of occasions—to eastern Tennessee, then to Orleans Territory, then back to Tennessee (Maury County) on lands acquired from his father at Globe Creek near Duck River. In 1826 he moved west to Hardeman County, taking with him two nephews, Peter and Glen Burnet, who were visiting from Missouri. He assisted Peter in finding a job at Bolivar.[25] As for his own livelihood, Blackstone divided his time between his two occupations of physician and farmer. He served on the county jury in 1827. Five years later he was in Rutherford County, near his brother Constant, but he kept in touch with Thomas Jones Hardeman and was ready to uproot himself from Tennessee soil, despite his forty-five years there, and follow his older brother when the time came.

Southwest Tennessee was the last frontier area east of the Mississippi which the Thomas Hardeman line helped to settle. A number of descendants remained (and some still reside) in Tennessee. Nicholas Perkins Hardeman died at his Williamson County home in 1818 at the age of forty-six. Two years later, thirty-six-year-old Peter Hardeman died at his plantation near Franklin.[26] Most of Thomas Hardeman's surviving children, like the patriarch himself, crossed the Mississippi and staked their claims in various parts of the big new West beyond. They had been part of the heartwood of Tennessee's adolescent years, working at its agriculture, its trade, its struggles for adulthood. But Tennessee was no longer a sapling in the expanded grove of western states, and a large part of the Hardeman clan seemed driven to surround itself with the environment of young and changing growth.

5 ⊨ *Eden by the Wild Missouri*

"ELK HEAVEN!" exclaimed sixty-six-year-old Tom Hardeman as he check-reined his horse in the Boon's Lick country along the Missouri River. There were herds and "sign" of big game animals about him, elk and deer and buffalo. And there were fine stands of oak, walnut, sugar maple, elm, hackberry, ash, and mulberry, their boles contrasting with the bleached trunks of sycamore and cottonwood. Hardeman felt at home in the virgin forests, but, furrow turner that he was, he could see future fields under the mantle of trees. In the bottomlands along the muddy, wide river, the earth was black and rich, and behind was gently rolling country. No doubt he thought of what his sons might say of this vast, sylvan expanse with cheap transportation just a step away—this land that looked like the Tennessee of old—the unspoiled Tennessee. "Elk heaven!" This would be his new home.[1]

A series of geographical circumstances stamped Missouri for a unique and prominent role in the American frontier advance, first as a salient, and later as the base of departure for most overland travel to the Far West. Its eastern boundary, the Mississippi, which Thomas Hardeman had followed to St. Louis, not only provided a main north-south artery through which pulsated much of the economic lifeblood of settlements near its banks, but also enabled frontiersmen to move along its course and enter the New West at points of their own choice from Minnesota to the Gulf of Mexico.

But north of the Gulf Plains it was the Missouri route which most of the overlanders followed. The "permanent" Indian frontier limited the Arkansas Valley gateway; the Ozark Highland deflected migrants north or south; and above the mouth of the Missouri there were no important streams leading to the Far West. If not the mythical Northwest Passage, the Missouri was the best substitute the continent could offer. It divided the northern plains almost to the Great Stony Mountains (later called the Rockies), and funneled overlanders to the Platte and points westward. Water transportation was by no means its only attraction. Soils , timber, and wild game were such as to enable settlers and travelers from the trans-Appalachian West to adapt with little adjustment. The valley west of St. Louis was ripening for American settlement, but foreign flags and Indians held up the rate of movement.

The purchase of Louisiana Territory, a major landmark in the westward movement, overcame the technical obstacle to large-scale settlement of Missouri; with the exception of the delta country, however, it was not until the end of the War of 1812 that trans-Mississippi migration became more than a trickle. Previously, save for the Gulf Plains, the agricultural frontier was some distance east of the Mississippi, and until 1808 the Osage Indians made good their extensive claims in Missouri. In that year they surrendered these lands and followed the receding herds of buffalo to the Great Plains west and southwest of Missouri. As the East convalesced, the frontier convulsed with migrants and prosperity after the Peace of Ghent. United States census reports show that a heavy percentage of early Missouri settlers came from Carolina, Virginia, and particularly Tennessee and Kentucky. The latter two states were settled several decades earlier than Indiana and Illinois and had a bigger population to export to lands farther west. This fact largely accounts for the southern, slaveholding views which prevailed in Missouri's formative years. The Tennessee,

Cumberland, Ohio, and Mississippi rivers provided easy travel to the New West. The Hardemans and many other settlers of Tennessee and Kentucky knew those waters from their trade contacts with New Orleans and had seen Missouri soil from the mouth of the Ohio southward.

In June 1816, shortly after the death of his second wife, Thomas Hardeman bade farewell to Sugar Hill and Williamson County.[2] Like Gulliver in the land of the Lilliputians, he had seemed bound by a thousand thin threads. Yet the tranquil life at his comfortable house, his plantation, his mill on the Harpeth, the satisfactions which came from the closeness of his friends and his prosperous sons and daughters and his grandchildren, the infirmity stemming from his advancing years—all these were not enough to stay his wanderlust. His youngest child, Bailey, became of age in 1816, leaving him with no further responsibility to minors in his immediate family, and old Tom set off alone to try new trails and stir new soils in the lately created Territory of Missouri. St. Louis, that half-century-old hangout for Spanish traders and French voyageurs, had little appeal for him. There were stories of fine country up the Big Muddy, and he pushed on to the farther edge of settlement more than 150 miles west at Boon's Lick in what was later to become Howard County.

This area had been visited by explorers Lewis and Clark and by surveyor Ira Nash in 1804. Nathaniel and Daniel M. Boone, sons of the Kentucky colonizer, arrived in 1807, began salt excavations, and sold their product in St. Louis. Hence the name Boon's Lick. The following year Benjamin Cooper took his family there, but Territorial Governor Meriwether Lewis told him to return eastward to the mouth of the Gasconade River because of Indian danger. In 1810, the Coopers, Wolfskills, and a few others became the first permanent settlers. Sharp encounters with the Quapaw, Sauk, and Fox Indians restricted settlement until about 1815, after which time wagons rolled west in swelling numbers from St. Louis, St. Charles, and other points down river.

Thomas Hardeman examined this newly opened area in mid-1816, and by late summer he was back in Tennessee closing his old homestead. He parceled out most of his land among his heirs and selected his lawyer son, John, to handle his legal and financial affairs. Taking two or three slaves, a one-horse cart, saddle horse, and long-barreled rifle gun, he retraced his course to Missouri.[3]

Unlike his real estate acquisitions in Tennessee, Thomas Hardeman's first land purchase in Missouri led to complications. Because of the multiple changing of hands—France to Spain to France again, and finally to the United States—Louisiana Territory was torn by confused land titles. While passing through St. Louis in October 1816, Thomas bought a Boon's Lick claim of 1,200 arpens, or arpents, from Pierre Barribeau. This Frenchman had received the title from Spain in 1800. Four years later United States Deputy Surveyor Ira Nash was sent to map out existing grants in the area before the American government commenced land sales there. Barribeau's claim was confirmed, but in the meantime the original survey certificate had been lost. Taylor Berry, a well-known central Missouri landholder (who was later killed in a duel with Abiel Leonard), challenged Hardeman's claim and sought a patent for the land through the nearby Franklin, Missouri, land office, which had been opened in 1819.[4]

With some aid from Thomas Hart Benton, now in St. Louis, Thomas Hardeman fought back. In the columns of the *Missouri Intelligencer,* the territory's first back-country newspaper, he accused Berry of "fraudulently" claiming his land and stated, "Whoever purchases from the said Berry may expect a lawsuit for the above land." Later he accused Berry of making a business of such claims.[5] Berry responded that the claim was a "pretended" one and that "If every settler in this country under the Spanish gov't who says he once had a grant and lost it is to hold land, we may bid adieu to all safety in land titles." But when the matter came before the Circuit Court of the territory, Hardeman had a battery of authoritative witnesses: surveyor Ira Nash, his chain carrier Stephen Jackson, and Spanish land surveyor Anthony Soulard. The court denied Berry's claim.[6]

Thomas Hardeman secured other lands near the Barribeau tract. In August 1820 he made good a preemption claim to an odd-shaped 275-acre area, sheared by the Missouri currents and known to surveyors as a fractional section. In a deal with his old antagonist Berry, he bought another 80 acres in the same vicinity. By 1819, a road had been laid out from the Missouri River town of Franklin to his farm.[7]

As for his livelihood, the stocky old settler of western lands repeated much of his Tennessee experience, raising grain, cattle, horses, and hogs, and garnering recognition from his neighbors as one of the more successful producers of the region. His farm was not as large as the Tennessee operation, reflecting his lessened family needs. In 1820 he paid taxes on 1,200 acres of land, four slaves (sixteen to forty-five years of age), and three horses.[8]

In politics too, Hardeman sought to reenact his earlier roles in constitution making at Hillsboro and Knoxville. Missouri was pressing to emerge from its territorial stage into infant statehood, and the mother nation was experiencing some of the most severe labor pains of its young life. Twenty-two states, eleven free and eleven slave, formed the Union in 1819, and Missouri, peopled chiefly by southerners, sought admission as a slave state. This threat to break the balance of power in the Senate was first met by the Tallmadge Amendment, which would have made Missouri a free state after a period of gradual emancipation. It passed in the House of Representatives but was blocked in the Senate. Not until 1821, after the nation was shaken by its awareness of the deep fracture in its makeup, was the issue resolved by the Missouri Compromise, balancing slave Missouri with free Maine, preserving the standoff in the Senate, and providing that no additional slave states north of 36° 30' north latitude would be fabricated out of Louisiana Purchase lands.

When Thomas entered the race as a "reluctant" candidate for delegate from Howard County to the state constitutional convention for the election of May 1820, he may have been thinking that his experiences qualified him well. But his campaign was a political soft-sell of humblest design. He spoke of some popular attempts to persuade him to run for territorial delegate to Congress in 1818. Referring to the importance and responsibility of the convention delegate, he stated that the office called for

> a man of talents much superior to mine, & the knowledge of my own inability to perform so arduous a task, makes me almost shrink from the attempt. Holding it, however, as a correct principle in republican gov'ts., that the citizens have a right to the services of any man, whom they think best qualified to serve them & in whom they can place the greatest confidence, I offer myself, not as such a man, but to gratify those who have solicited me to do so.

Hardeman's political principles were still Jeffersonian Republican; he supported a progressive tax "higher in proportion to numbers" on large property holders; and he pledged himself to help devise a constitution which would "guarantee the blessings of liberty." Liberty for whom? Regarding the thorniest problem, Thomas Hardeman argued in a public speech: "As for slavery, that political hobby horse of the general government, I will remark an exalted benevolence will, in my opinion, extend it as wide as the nature of the case will possibly admit."[9] The election of May 1, 1820, came and passed, and he lost his first election; lost it rather badly, in fact, as he placed fifteenth among the nineteen candidates who ran for the five seats from the county.

Thereafter, the only hint of political activity on the part of Thomas Hardeman was an unverified allegation that he had used his influence with President Jackson to get a friend appointed as Receiver of the Public Moneys at Lexington, Missouri. He was willing to share his political opinions, however, and apparently eager to bring into play his late-acquired but pungent literacy. When Kentuckian Henry Clay gave his support to John Quincy Adams over Jackson in the presidential selection waged by the House of Representatives in 1824 and 1825, Hardeman was fighting mad, despite some ties of friendship that his son John had with Clay. To Judge John Overton of Nashville he penned a 2,000-word diatribe which was a vigorous defense of Jackson and a condemnation of the practices used in blocking him from the presidency. His reaction was typical of the white caps of sentiment whipped up on back-country political waters by the episode. Accusing Clay of willfully mistaking the powers of office for personal powers, he advanced the "corrupt bargain" argument, charging that Clay had backed Adams to get a Secretary of State appointment as a stepping stone to the presidency.

"Bad construction should never be put on any proposition that will bear a good one," Thomas argued after quoting relevant passages of the Constitution. Clay and his henchmen, he charged, chose a president by their own "discretion" rather than "by ballot" as required. Ballot implied acceptance of the apparent will of the voters' ballots, which had given the highest number of votes to Jackson. Except in case of a tie, there should have been acceptance of the front runner or else "further investigation or canvass upon the subject." He noted that the legislature of Clay's home state had instructed its representatives to cast the state's vote for Jackson. There were strong words against the Kentuckian in Hardeman's message, such as "dereliction of public duty and a base desertion of the confidence reposed" in the "great demagogue" who had acted for the "pecuniary interest and aggrandizement of Mr. Clay."[10] These could have been fighting words under some circumstances. None of the Hardemans ever dueled, but Clay, in fact, did fight a duel (fortunately bloodless, with bad aim on both sides) against another individual over this same issue, and over similar words. For whatever reason, no known confrontation came from the arguments advanced by the seventy-five-year-old Missourian.

In a sense other than political, Thomas Hardeman more successfully reenacted the role of his earlier trans-Appalachian migrations. The Indian threat in postwar Missouri was minor by comparison with his experiences in North Carolina and Tennessee. But he was still the patriarch of the family and an influential leader in the eyes of his friends. His reports of the rich Missouri bottom soils and high crop yields probably were persuasive. Within a short time his sons John and Bailey joined him, as did his sons-in-law George Burnet and Glen Owen and their families. Peter Burnet later wrote that his family's move was directly attributable to Thomas Hardeman.[11] Close friends such as the Sappingtons also may have followed his lead.

John Hardeman, like his father, had recently experienced a shallowing of his Tennessee roots. He had quit the mercantile trade and was a planter and creator of a luxury garden and experimental farm at his estate in Williamson County. In June 1805 John had married eighteen-year-old Lucretia Nash at Baton Rouge. Seven years later, Lucretia's life was claimed by that scourge of womanly existence, childbearing, and John was left with the couple's two children, John Locke and Lucretia Nash Hardeman. If there were plans for moving west at that time, they were delayed by the war, but in late summer of 1817 he followed his father to Missouri.[12]

The St. Louis area, although it failed to attract as a permanent home, appealed to John's business instincts. He stopped off and bought four lots in Carondelet, adjacent to St. Louis. As Nashville and Franklin had become, St. Louis was already too populous for his tastes. Seeking a more primitive setting for his pursuit of culture, he proceeded up the Missouri and invested in the deep-timbered alluvial soils near his father's farm five miles beyond the last settlement on the frontier.

Land-rich and cash-poor, a chronic complaint of the times, apparently did not apply to John Hardeman when he moved to Missouri, although it may have soon after he arrived. Two of his four lots at Carondelet cost him a total of $500, and he promptly paid out several thousand dollars for some 2,000 acres in central Missouri. He bought 275 acres from his father, 1,600 arpens from surveyor Ira Nash, and additional amounts from Taylor Berry, lawyer George Tompkins, and the federal government. More than three-fourths of the total was in Howard County, comprising his experimental "Fruitage Farm" and garden; the remainder made up his auxiliary estate, called "Penultima," in Cole County near Jefferson city.[13]

Having secured essential agricultural bases on the Missouri—bases which would be worked largely by their slaves—Thomas and John quickly broadened their economic pursuits. Thomas had a closer relationship with John than with any of his other sons and daughters. Both had recently lost their wives; they owned adjoining farms and lived for years in the same house. There was teamwork in their plantation activities, and when they branched into other enterprises, they often invested jointly. Tom opened an inn or tavern, apparently to take advantage of the increasing traffic across the river. Dovetailing with the inn was a ferry boat service which father and son ran as a partnership, linking the Fruitage Farm dock with Pierre à Flèche, or Arrow Rock, on the south bank of the Missouri.[14]

Five miles downstream from their landing, both Thomas and John Hardeman made investments in Franklin, the westernmost town in Missouri at that time. Franklin was organized and platted in 1816, the year Thomas arrived. All sources report that it was named in honor of Benjamin Franklin, as it was, indirectly at least. But it was undoubtedly called Franklin because a number of its founders had come immediately from the Tennessee town of the same name. Thomas Hardeman purchased three of the twelve lots fronting on the public square.[15]

By 1819 the town had 120 log houses, several brick and two-story frame dwellings, thirteen general stores, two blacksmith shops, mills, taverns, billiard parlors; there were also a post office, printing press, court house, and two-story log jail. The population of about 1,000 included a number of people who, along with settlers in the nearby tributary area, would loom prominent in the New West and the state. There were future mountain men Ezekiel Williams (who lived next to John and Thomas

Hardeman), Antoine Robidoux, William Wolfskill, the Workmans, and a saddlemaker's apprentice, Kit Carson. Santa Fe traders William and Thomas Becknell, Augustus Storrs, Alphonso Wetmore, and the McNees were there. So was Dr. John Sappington, who went about the Missouri countryside scattering bluegrass seed, and who sold his pills throughout the land from St. Louis to Santa Fe. Artist George Caleb Bingham, judges Nathaniel Beverly Tucker and George Tompkins were on hand, as were future Missouri governors Claiborne Jackson and Meredith Miles Marmaduke, and War of 1812 generals Thomas A. Smith and Duff Green. In 1819, Smith, later a business partner of John Hardeman, opened and headed the United States land office at his store. Green also opened a general store at Franklin.

Like his father, and possibly with his father, John had some Franklin business interests. Along with the many record books of his Tennessee store, he saved for posterity a single daybook of a general store in Franklin, Missouri. John was connected with this operation, but to an undetermined extent—in all likelihood as an investor. The entries begin November 26, 1817, several weeks after he arrived at Franklin. He was an experienced merchant with capital to invest, and he wrote a number of the headings in the record book. Samuel Williams (perhaps the same who was a patron at the Hardeman store in Tennessee) and Byrd Lockhart appear to have tended the store, as they signed out goods for peddling to farms in the adjoining countryside, and Lockhart wrote many of the entries. The goods handled were typical of the general store of rural nineteenth-century America, and thus the same as in John's Tennessee merchandising. Franklin merchants rode horseback to Philadelphia, Pennsylvania, to order goods which would be shipped to them the following spring. The entries in the daybook end May 2, 1818, at the last page, suggesting that they were probably continued in another book.[16] Notwithstanding his connection with this house of trade, Hardeman's chief energies were to be devoted to agriculture.

He had extensive plans for his estate up the river. There he and his Negro bondsmen cleared towering cottonwoods, elms, and oaks, and grubbed dank willow thickets from the waiting soils. The issue from these labors was Fruitage Farm and Hardeman's Garden, his Eden on the north bank of the wild Missouri.

The scope and character of John's farming, gardening, and household operation can be roughly gauged by the personal property inventory that was compiled following his death in the fall of 1829. (The appraised value was probably one-third to one-half of the market value of the items.) Property at his other estate near Jefferson City, Missouri, was not included in the listing, and in all probability neither were numerous items belonging partly to his father but shared in their closely linked activities.

The most valuable listings on the inventory were the twenty-six slaves, more than half of whom were women and children. Since their station in life condemned them to having first names only, their identities cannot be accurately traced beyond the occasional recording of their names on an inventory or purchase slip. To them goes a large share of the credit for the achievements of their master. William, who was always left in charge of operations when John and Thomas were absent, was valued at $450. Most of the women were assessed at $300 to $350, and children $100. Their number was considerably larger than for the average slaveholder.

Livestock ranked second in value. The possession of a jack, or donkey, appraised at $200, a very high figure, confirms that John Hardeman was an early breeder of the legendary Missouri mules. The overall stock picture is one of diversity, including 40 hogs, 7 horses, 7 oxen, 9 milk cows and calves, 60 sheep, and 22 black cattle. There were numerous items related to the livestock business—wagon, ox cart, saddle bags, barrels and hogsheads, 50 pounds of tallow, leather, sheep shears, butcher knives, a meat axe, a butter churn, 200 pounds of corn, and numerous stacks of hay, wheat, and corn fodder.

A full range of general farming, woodworking, and light timber tools, a quantity of lumber and "curled" grain walnut planks, and many general household items added bulk to the list. The amount of high-grade lumber, particularly walnut, indicates that there was a double value to the clearing of the land, that is, farming and selling timber. Miscellaneous entries on the list included brandy, a shotgun, a pocket compass, a canoe, twenty-five pounds of cotton seed, and some beeswax.

Finally, several listings point to specialties; a cooper's adz and a set of blacksmith's tools indicate that barrel-making and metal work were handled at the plantation. Perhaps some of the slaves were skilled workmen, as John himself may have been. The five beehives show that he produced honey domestically, although bee trees were reportedly abundant. The trans-river ferry boat was the principal nonagricultural business equipment on, or related to Fruitage Farm, and apparently it served an important cash-producing function.[17]

But the bulk of John Hardeman's business was agriculture— commercial production, experimental cultivation, and the botanical show garden, three distinct but interrelated activities. Commercially, he stayed with, but did not limit himself to, the items that he had produced successfully in Tennessee—cotton, tobacco, corn, pork, and beef. From December 1825 to November 1826 he sold 14,000 pounds of beef, pork, tallow, and lard in addition to quantities of hides, corn, and butter through the firm of Ward and Parker of St. Louis. Hardeman was one of the early producers of hemp in central Missouri. This fibrous plant was used for making rope and coarse fabrics and was well suited to the river bottom soils. By early 1823 he advertised ten or twelve bushels of fresh hemp seed for sale, indicating that his production was sizable, assuming that he kept enough to seed his own acres.[18] Two years later he corresponded with a fellow experimental farmer, Henry Clay, on the subject of hemp breakers, which were in the early stages of development. Clay had tried one on his farm the previous summer and reported to Hardeman that:

> It broke out several tons of hemp, without any rotting. . . . I consider the matter as . . . premature for any farmer to have one erected. The hemp is broke out, without being either dew or water rotted, and may be applied to the Brake in a week . . . properly cured. I sent upwards of two tons of the hemp thus prepared to the Eastern cities, where it commanded the price of Russian hemp.[19]

Both John Hardeman and (later) his son designed and built hemp breakers. The breaking operation was essential to the removal of waste material so that costs of transporting to market would be kept down.

John's marketing arrangements involved locations both near and distant. Some of the sales he made personally in St. Louis; at other times Lemon Parker sold goods for him in St. Louis and New Orleans, and some of his transactions were handled by merchants Thomas A. Smith and George Knox of Franklin. Parker wrote of the worsening competitive position of Missouri products in the New Orleans market. "I must confess that the year has nearly satisfied me with the New Orleans trade particularly in anything Missouri furnishes for that markett."[20] New Orleans was an entrepôt for much of the South and West, and perhaps because St. Louis was not directly subject to competition from such a wide area, the latter city was looked upon with increasing favor as a market for Missouri produce.

American agriculture in John Hardeman's era was essentially conservative in its methods. Progress had been slight for centuries, indeed for several thousand years. Farmers were traditionally slow to accept changes, and it was too early to get help from those two institutions which were to become modernizers of farming—the land grant colleges and the government. Experimental farmers, in tune with the scientific spirit of the Enlightenment, were the leaders in the realm of agricultural innovation. Gentleman farmers such as Henry Clay, Elkanah Watson, and Edmund Ruffin had the capital, the spare time, and the spark of interest to break out of the hand-to-mouth cycle of existence and engage in innovative farming. Central Missouri had several such men in the years of the earliest settlements. One of these was General Thomas A. Smith, who operated "Experiment Farm" just south of the Missouri River in Saline County.

Preceding Smith's establishment by a number of years was the first such operation in this frontier area, John Hardeman's Fruitage Farm. Here large sums of money and much time were poured into experimental breeding, seeding, cultivation, and, in the Jeffersonian tradition, extensive record keeping. Thomas Hart Benton had doubtless known of the experimental farming interests of his friend and benefactor John Hardeman at "Crabstick," the latter's plantation in Tennessee. Benton was interested in propagandizing for the new western state of Missouri, which he now represented in the United States Senate. Having visited Fruitage Farm during 1822, he asked for agricultural specimens and a description of the farming conditions of Howard County. John's lengthy reply was printed in the Washington *National Intelligencer,* and later run in the *Missouri Intelligencer* at Franklin. Benton's cover letter to the Washington paper noted that "the facts stated . . . relative to the vegetable productions of Missouri will give correct data for forming opinions about the soil and climate of that country. The writer is a gentleman of science, character, and fortune, greatly attached to the pursuits of agriculture, and entitled to an implicit confidence in all his statements."[21]

John Hardeman treated every plant or farm animal, whether raised for profit or pleasure, as an experiment. "Agreeably to your request," he wrote Benton, "I have forwarded to you some of the largest specimens of plants which have been reared in my garden this year. . . . You will bear in mind, that I have not traveled for these samples out of my own garden." This, he said, was "laid out on the poorest part of my land, and on which there has not a particle of manure been spread: It is a rich sandy loam . . . and has too great a portion of sand in my own estimation." In his pragmatic style, he continued:

> It is known to most, that an individual of any species of plant may accidentally attain to great size, even on a poor soil; and that some soils abound with salts peculiarly adapted to the nurture of particular species of plants; and that, consequently, the whole species will be reared to great perfection on them. But, it is not known . . . that a great *variety* of plants can be raised, to great perfection, for a series of years in succession, unless the soil and climate be both rich and warm. Let me not theorise, but leave it to others to conjecture the causes of the great fertility of our country: facts are all I vouch for; and these not conjectural, but such as I have determined by the trial.[22]

There followed a long list of his recorded production statistics: cotton "in the seed," 1,200 pounds per acre, radishes as long as three feet, turnips up to 30 inches in circumference, 4,468 squashes on only two vines, 672 pounds of citron melons from one vine, two generations of corn raised in one season of four months and ten days. These and other data on the growth rates of trees, the size of hemp, and the fecundity of Jerusalem artichokes and asparagus undoubtedly had some influence on migration to Missouri.

On his frequent trips back to Tennessee, John had encountered a widespread ignorance about Missouri. His acquaintances found it difficult to believe that it was not a mountainous land too far north for good farming. Henry Lee of Westmoreland County, Virginia, was intrigued with the descriptions of the Missouri River lands.:

> I have seen your letter of the 24th of November last to Col. Benton describing the productiveness of the soil on which you reside, and being about to prepare for an emigration, . . . take the liberty of proposing the following questions to you. . . .
> I have a wife who has been politely bred and educated, and expect to carry with me about 40 slaves, little and big.

A long list of questions followed; Lee inquired about ague and fever, steamboat service, the price of 3,000 to 4,000 acres of land "such as yours," availability of wild game and fish, and so on.[23]

John Hardeman's attentions to western agriculture were not limited to the improving of plant species and attracting settlers. He operated a nursery and was a supplier of fruit trees, grapevine cuttings, ornamental shrubs and trees, and many types of seeds for central Missouri as well as more distant places such as St. Louis and Tennessee. Often these were provided without charge.[24]

Among his varied activities, the one for which John was best known was "Hardeman's Garden," the elaborate and somewhat expensive showplace on Fruitage Farm. This was the heart of his establishment. It has been given a place in practically all the volumes which treat the early history of Missouri or of Howard County in detail. The prominent location of the garden, directly on what soon became the principal artery of travel to the Farther West and Far West, with its own steamboat landing and ferry boat facilities connecting with Arrow Rock and the Santa Fe Trail, contributed to its recognition, as did the welcome extended by its creator. Of the numerous references to, and descriptions of Hardeman's Garden, several are eyewitness accounts, providing a moderately detailed picture of this splash of refinement on the frontier. Alphonso Wetmore was not only a neighbor who knew John Hardeman and Fruitage Farm well; the two men traveled together into the Far West in 1828. In his characteristic style, Wetmore wrote:

> When the town of Old Franklin was in the most prosperous condition . . . Mr. John Hardeman, a gentleman of peculiarly fine taste, was carrying forward improvements in his horticultural and botanic garden, about five miles above this place, on the bank of the Missouri. . . . Ten acres, laid off in an exact square, had been set apart, and no labour or expense was spared to render this garden, in the richness and variety of its productions, a perfect parallel to the most happy description of Eden. This spot of the earth was adorned with fruits, . . . and *sombroso* foliage, that lent enchantment to the labyrinth through which the serpentine paths led the admiring visitor. Fruit-trees and ornamental shrubbery were transported, with successful care, more than a thousand miles, to perfect this favoured spot. The native grape of Missouri and the Skauppernong of Carolina were introduced into the society of distinguished foreign vines from Madeira and Oporto; and these, in rich clusters, contributed to the ruby streams of pure and exhilarating juice that

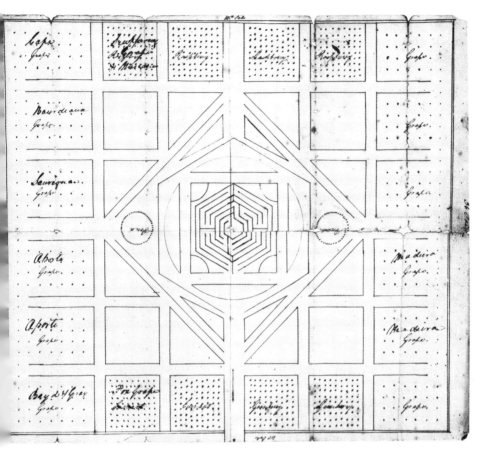

TOP: An unexpected cultural oasis on the frontier was this ten-acre Elizabethan garden laid out by frontier merchant and Santa Fe trader John Hardeman (1776–1829) near Franklin, the westernmost Missouri town at that time. Here he freely dispensed wine and hospitality to visitors. *Courtesy State Historical Society of Missouri.* LOWER: Silhouettes, usually fashioned by women, predated photography. This is the clipped likeness of Hardeman. *Courtesy the Hardeman family.*

[85

flowed from the wine press, here successfully trodden. It would be more than
passive ingratitude for all the survivors of the gay and cheerful groups who once
trod the avenues of this court of Flora, to refrain from making record of the
unostentatious hospitality of this tasteful devotee of that goddess. Here the
fruits of the varying season were dispensed with an open hand, moved by a
generous and joyous heart. It was the joy of reason, chastened with the
influence of philosophy.[25]

The *Missouri Intelligencer* contained a brief reference to the botanical
layout in its issue of October 29, 1822.

Mr. Hardeman's ingenuity in forming the plan of his garden, and his
industry in introducing into it exotics and valuable plants, shrubs and fruits,
are only equalled by his urbanity and hospitality to those who have the pleasure
of visiting it.[26]

John's own description is preserved in the form of a plat of the garden.
The design is reminiscent of English gardens dating back to the Elizabethan age. The overall size was slightly different from what Wetmore
reported, containing a total of nine acres. In its outside dimensions it was
36 poles (594 feet) by 40 poles (660 feet).

Europe, Central America, New Mexico, Sonora, Chihuahua, the upper
Missouri River country, North Carolina, Pennsylvania, Tennessee, Virginia, St. Louis, Louisiana—these were among the areas from which
Hardeman got the thousands of plants, cuttings, seeds, sprouts, and bulbs
for his garden. He visited most and perhaps all of these places, including
northern Mexico and Central America. There were numerous trips to
Tennessee, some for the purpose of transplanting from his earlier botanical
showplace there, and his visit to Washington City sometime before July
1819 may have been for a similar purpose. Apparently the garden was
taking shape in his thinking when he arrived at the Boon's Lick country in
1817; it was a well-known arboretum by 1820, although he added new
specimens for a number of years.[27]

This extensive plant collection was not entirely a product of John's own
travels. On occasion, the steam-spewing and bell-clanging boats which
docked at Hardeman's landing brought sprouts and cuttings which the
naturalist had ordered. And visitors from time to time brought or sent
gifts of plant specimens. George Champlin Sibley, who surveyed and
marked the Santa Fe Trail for the United States government in 1825 and

1826, must have been such a visitor to Hardeman's Garden, for he wrote to John Hardeman from Mexico: "I sent you in 3 small parcels some cuttings from the very fine Grape Vines that are cultivated in this country." The grapes were of both black and white varieties, and were procured from various parts of New Mexico.[28] Army Captain Charles Pentland wrote from Council Bluffs in May 1824 that he was leaving for the upper Missouri River, and, knowing of John Hardeman's interest in gardening, he stated his intent to collect curious plants and fruits for him.[29]

A prominent businessman, John O'Fallon of St. Louis, leaned on the resources of John Hardeman in creating his own ornamental garden. Correspondence extending from 1821 to 1828 indicates that these two men furthered each other's botanical and horticultural interests. O'Fallon asked Hardeman for the North Carolina mountain raspberry, an edible gooseberry, the Arkansas grape, Oporto grape, and many other fruits, vegetables, and ornamental plants, writing in appreciation: "The liberal disposition you have uniformly manifested towards persons who take pleasure in propagating whatever is rare and curious of the botanical kingdom is my apology for thus troubling you."[30] That O'Fallon of the St. Louis crossroads would rely upon an area on the frontier some 150 miles westward for his supply of exotic flora was perhaps a commentary on the success of central Missouri agriculture. Although he blamed his lack of know-how for the loss of some grape cuttings, O'Fallon's cultivating skill must have improved; his garden and farm later became a part of the well-known O'Fallon Park in St. Louis.

Another prominent St. Louis botanist, Henry Shaw, had come to that city by 1820 and entered the merchandising and fur trading business. Long before establishing his garden in St. Louis, he visited John Hardeman's botanical showpiece. Shaw got many of his gardening ideas from his longtime acquaintance, John O'Fallon. According to the *Centennial History of Missouri,* "Hardeman's Garden became the showplace of the Missouri river country. It was in its generation what Shaw's Garden became fifty years later."[31] The personal and business association between Hardeman and Thomas A. Smith suggests that the latter may have acquired much of the inspiration and collections for his "Experiment Farm" from John Hardeman. John also gave plants from his collection to

General Henry Dodge, Missouri Senator David Barton, and many others.

There were troubled times ahead for Hardeman and for his botanical creation. It had taken a great deal of his time and a sizable share of his fortune, and added to this burden were entertainment costs. The welcome mat was a status symbol of these times. Hosts took pride in being able to afford lavish hospitality (or to convince people that they could afford it) and were eager to command the cordial attentions of eminent visitors. According to the *St. Louis Beacon*, Hardeman was prone "to reciprocate visits with his friends, and to dispense from his own board a liberal hospitality which knew no distinction between honorable men in all stations and conditions of life."[32]

The sinister serpent in John's Eden was the rapacious current of the Missouri, which undercut the banks and snaked its way ever closer to the garden until, in 1826, a major part of this development was swept away by the rampaging waters. Although embellished, Alphonso Wetmore's description is the only detailed one.

> The destructive vagaries of the river were not then well understood; and it was believed that a bottom, protected with a fine growth of forest trees, as Mr. Hardeman's plantation was, would be secure against the surges of the annual freshets. . . . Like an infinite amount of anticipated enjoyment, the fascinations of this spot, too, were evanescent. When the mountain snows melted and poured their waters in redundant volumes upon this alluvial bank, the earth itself dissolved in the excessive floods, and this garden, with its poetic symmetry, was carried away by the resistless action of Mad river. Its evergreens and richly-laden fruit-trees were uprooted, and dead apples floated upon the waters: and now a neglected corner, with a section of unpruned orchard, alone remains to mark the spot once devoted to mental and material luxury. It is a just conclusion to arrive at, that the learned and tasteful proprietor of the Elysium, thus ravished from his possession, felt the pain of kindred bereavement when receding, step by step, from the encroachment of the fluid destroyer. The exodus of trees he had planted and pruned, the departure of foliage beneath which he had pored over his classic volumes, in relaxation from the manly toil to which he was then accustomed, inflicted pain, like night-watchings of a parent over his expiring progeny![33]

In all, the river claimed considerably more than half of Fruitage Farm, leaving only 645 acres.

Nor was the Missouri satiated. Stephen Long observed in 1819 that the town of Franklin was not wisely located and predicted that it would fall victim to the currents. The same flood which took away much of John Hardeman's acreage also destroyed a major portion of the town.[34] Old Franklin, as it was thereafter called, was abandoned, and New Franklin was laid out and built nearby on higher ground.

The losses in productive property sustained by both John and Thomas Hardeman in Franklin and on their farms were serious if not disastrous. The stream which had given the alluvium and had contributed so much to the "bumper" crops described in the letter to Benton had now taken away. The lesson was not new. Man has long gambled where the stakes are high, in rich river bottom soils beside treacherous currents: the Nile, the Tigris and Euphrates, the Ganges, the Yangtze, the Colorado of the Yuma Indians, and now the Mississippi and the Missouri. John Hardeman had gambled and lost his floral creation and a major part of his livelihood. But he would turn the wheel of fortune again, with the expectation of replacing what the flood had taken. Such was his interest in culture and agriculture that he hoped to put in another garden near the site of the first one (but on higher ground); and he planned and began to develop a botanical showplace at his other estate, Penultima.[35]

Culturally, John was a man of varied interests. He seemed to have been at home with books and farm tools, with plants and poetry. From penetrations of distant frontiers to excursions into philosophical discourse he moved with apparent ease. What is known of his library is at best a crude index of his reading tastes. John Gay's *Fables,* Samuel Johnson's *Dictionary,* William Cowper's *Poems,* and Thomas Gray's *Practical Works* were on his shelves, as were Dobson's twenty-one-volume encyclopedia, Alibey's *Travels,* Gibbon's *Decline and Fall of the Roman Empire,* Plutarch's *Lives,* Marshall's *Washington,* Hamilton's *Works, Gil Blas, Don Quixote,* the *Bible,* and various works on botany and natural history.[36] Not all westerners had the finances, the time, or the literacy for such reading. That these and his many other books were probably more than ornaments and dust catchers is attested by Alphonso Wetmore.

Such fascination as John Hardeman had with the science of soil, climate, and crops would be logically complemented by an interest in other aspects of the natural environment and Indian artifacts. Tennessee political figure Willie Blount wrote to E. Earle (probably Ralph E. W. Earl), Nashville collector of museum materials, that John Hardeman of

Missouri, who was "intelligent and well informed in natural history," would be able to assist him in the collection of "relics of antiquity."[37]

The same Governor Blount and Judge John McNairy, also of Tennessee, engaged in spirited philosophical debates with John Hardeman. Their beliefs were Christian, as opposed to Hardeman's scientific agnostic views. McNairy expressed concern over Hardeman's afterlife if he remained preoccupied with "metiphisical incomprehensibilities. . . . A man of your mind and talents must not fall into nonentity or rather infinite punishment and misery."[38] John Hardeman responded:

> To give even the "shadow of a shadow" . . . of foundation for your hope of immortality, you must first *imagine* the existence of something not *known* to be—You must thus imagine a *mode* of perception of pleasure not now known—and finally you must imagine pleasure now inconceivable. Strange aggregation of imaginary existences!

Taking off from this suggestion of pre-Comtian positivism, he wrote that:

> We cannot infer from the facts which we see, that there is any one only mode of salvation pointed out for man, even supposing there should be a God, and supposing that we are immortal.

Such agnosticism was less than popular in America at that time. Applying Lockian conclusions that perception comes not from revelations, but from one's own senses, Hardeman assailed the Christian views of Blount.

> There are five of these witnesses [senses] who have been forever with me—they have reported 100,000 truths to me, for every single lie. . . . These witnesses have told me a thousand times, that Jesus Christ was no more a God than you are . . . , that St. John never had anything revealed to him . . . more . . . than has been revealed to you in your dreams. . . . They have told me, and I believe them, that the whole tissue of supposed facts, the foundation of your faith, is nothing more than a damnable Hoax.

(Small wonder that the writer had named his son John Locke.) John Hardeman then questioned whether a God who supposedly created man as a fallible creature could in fairness subject him to eternal damnation for unintentionally violating a law of God. "Intention then constitutes the crime."

There were other dimensions to his philosophical outlook. As a relativist, he observed:

TOP: John Locke Hardeman built this plantation house in 1844 near Arrow Rock, Missouri. It was ransacked repeatedly by bushwhackers during the Civil War. *Courtesy the Rev. Howard D. Hardeman.* LOWER: Hardeman sat for this portrait by famed Missouri artist George Caleb Bingham, a long-time friend of the family. *Courtesy State Historical Society of Missouri.*

Were we so constituted, that pleasure could be perceived without its contrast, we might wish to perpetuate that perception: But . . . they must alternate before we can have a consciousness of either.

Semantics, too, came in for some attention as he labeled terms such as "infinity, eternity . . . , soul, spirit . . . counterfeits, and rank ones too." Lastly, in the temper of the Enlightenment, John expounded on the scientific method as he understood it.

The science of mathematics is the only one which has arrived at any tolerable degree of *certainty*. And it seems to me, that each other science, might be rendered equally certain, so far as we could go in them, by the use of the same means, to wit, definite and distinct ideas, expressed invariably by the same terms.[39]

Beyond these two letters, one can only speculate as to whether John Hardeman's philosophical views were expanded in the numerous letters to the Blounts, McNairy, Benton, Clay, and others—letters which have not been found. Would his suggestions of epicureanism and hedonism have been developed, or would Locke have been more clearly tempered with the transcendental ideas of Kant and the logic of Hegel? Certainly when matters of his personal feelings were involved, John was capable of surrendering his objectivism to sentiment in the manner of Rousseau, as his lines of poetry demonstrate.

After the death of his young wife Lucretia, John remained single for eleven years. Among his papers are several love poems written during this period. In their timeless flavor and depth of feeling they suggest further dimensions to his thought and personality. Typical of his rhymed sentiments are the following stanzas from "Moorland Mary."

> . . . Swift flew the moments through the sky;
> I knew not time by measure
> And held as naught if she were nigh
> The world's all other treasure.
> Not India's stores of costly gems
> Or Diamond's richest quarry
> No! these my soul in pride contemns;
> My all is Moorland Mary. . . .
>
> Still glows my heart with fervent pray'r
> That guardian angels tend her

And make my Mary all their care
Nor suffer aught to offend her
E'en shield from death's severe behest
Till time with age grows weary,
Then gently soothe to sweetest rest
My lovely Moorland Mary.[40]

On March 25, 1823, John Hardeman crossed the river (literally and figuratively) and married Nancy Knox of Boonville. She too was a descendant of a Virginia family and was a sister of George Knox, Jr., who was later one of Hardeman's business partners. Three children were born to John and Nancy—Leona, Glen, and George. The boys were twins, but George died in infancy.[41] In terms of his continuing role in American expansion, John's remarriage was significant, for his surviving son Glen, and Glen's sons as well, were active members of the family in the West.

Thomas and John Hardeman continued their close business and personal associations after the latter's marriage. Although now in his advanced years and eclipsed by his son's activities as gardener, experimental farmer, and trader, Thomas was by no means out of the public eye. Despite chronic diabetes and "the stone" (gall- or kidney-stones), he was active and alert. Having long since taken leave of his Baptist faith, in the 1820s he plunged into a vitriolic denunciation of Christianity and the clergy.

Like his son, Thomas Hardeman hitched his philosophical wagon largely to the ideas of Locke, although he evinced some familiarity with other theorizers. The *Missouri Intelligencer* published several of his caustic pieces in 1824. Man was born "without an inclination for either vice or virtue," he argued. "The mind of an infant is like a blank sheet of paper." Expanding on this, he observed that ideas were acquired not by supernatural means, but through "education . . . in the large sense of the word," through all the five senses, and by natural means only. Thus Thomas, whose literacy (and much of his education) came late in life, placed great store in education as the hope of mankind. He disavowed divine revelation and the divinity of Christ in a manner which his son agreed with, then departed from John's agnosticism and, like his friend Jefferson, embraced a deistic view of the Cosmos. "The Deity must be as completely circumscribed within the pale of his own perfection, as we are within the pale of our nature." Infinite wisdom, he averred, would set up natural laws "in the best possible manner at first," with no error, no need for adjustment, and "leaving no cause for miracles." No doubt his Deism and Romanticism complemented each other in shaping his benevolent view of nature and the wilderness which he so persistently sought out.

Quoting Biblical passages and adding his refutations of Christianity, Thomas fired a denunciatory barrage at the clergy. Soul, spirit, divinity, he argued, were "engendered in the brain of priests . . . demagogues, for the purpose of cheating ignorant men out of their natural rights, in order to live upon their labor. . . ." And with an air of finality, he wrote:

> As there is nothing in me but what is finite and perishable, I believe that my last gasp will be my utmost limit, except the matter of which I am composed, and time will soon dissolve the mass into its original elements, leaving nothing but the name of THOMAS HARDEMAN[42]

Ironically, even his gravesite is unknown.

But while Thomas and John Hardeman were on the scene, they leavened and livened the western edge of settlement by propounding their beliefs. In his eighty-third year, Thomas wrote at length to an old Missouri friend, elaborating on the same Lockian, Deistic, and anticlerical views.[43] As a new wave of westward expansion turned the spotlight away from Missouri, it caused both John and his father to take leave of that state—permanently, as it developed—and one cannot but conclude that both their material and philosophical contributions were missed.

6 ⊬ *The Santa Fe Trail and Trade*

JOHN HARDEMAN WEPT as he quilled his last lines before embarking on a new venture into the Far West. "If I be in any way fortunate," he wrote, "I have strong hopes that it will enable me to spend the remainder of my days with my family."[1] He had banked the fires of his westward wandering impulse for a decade; but the embers snapped and flared anew, and like his brother and brother-in-law he took to the Santa Fe trade.

Santa Fe! That was a name which stirred feelings—and spurred dealings—out on the peopled rim of the American West. The reasons were no doubt many: turquoise skies and tawny velvet landscapes, the piercing brilliance of the stars, an exotic culture with quaint tastes, a foreign tongue, dark-eyed señoritas. Certainly one of the major appeals was the chance for profit, an option to blunt the economic vassalage which westerners suffered at the hands of eastern merchants and bankers; a solution to the specie shortage was offered through the tapping of the Mexican silver mint at this veritable Baghdad of the backlands. Like ants,

[95

many followed where a few first dared inch their way over the shimmering trail. In the broad picture, this commerce was a romantic linking of two empires, two contrasting cultures, and widely separated economies which reached half fearfully, half invitingly toward each other from their advanced stations. But in the microcosmic view, the saga was a story of people—of individuals whose day-to-day successes and setbacks on the dusty, mirage-veiled passage often seemed less than romantic. Bailey and John Hardeman and their relative, Glen Owen, were among those who challenged the rigors of the road to Santa Fe in the 1820s.

All three men lived near Franklin, on the Missouri. Although the focus of written accounts has been primarily on the town of Independence, Franklin was the starting point for the most famous caravans to Santa Fe during the 1820s. Some early venturers had launched expeditions from other points and traveled over parts of what was to become the Santa Fe Trail—Francisco de Coronado, Juan de Oñate, the Mallet brothers, Pedro Vial, Zebulon M. Pike, McCallan, McLanahan, Patterson. Between the expeditions of Vial in 1792–93 and the early 1820s, several key events lent their weight to the conditioning of the southwest for trade: the United States' purchase of Louisiana Territory, Mexico's independence from Spain in 1821, and statehood for Missouri in the same year. The several communities of New Mexico were willing, even eager, to find goods which were cheaper and better than those moving over the Chihuahua trail, or El Camino Real, from Old Mexico. Missouri merchants, pressed for coin and salable commodities such as mules and furs, were willing to accommodate. The attitude of Mexican officials toward the trade was more inviting than had been that of Spain with her closed, mercantilistic system.

The commerce that developed was not merely an exchange between the two outposts. New Mexico was an entrepôt for goods and specie which were freighted north from the homeland, and Missouri became the funnel for goods from St. Louis, Philadelphia, New York, and other eastern centers. Both Missouri and New Mexico appear to have welcomed the opportunity to worm their way from under the control of economic overlords in the respective motherlands.

It was William Becknell of Franklin who first took wagons westward to settlements in New Mexico. Like his frequent traveling companion Bailey

Hardeman, he was a veteran of the War of 1812 and a seasoned frontiersman. Becknell's initial trading trip to Santa Fe was made in the fall of 1821 with goods carried by pack animals. The expedition was warmly received, and the trade profits were good. Hence Becknell set out again from Franklin in May 1822, this time with twenty-one men and three wagons laden with merchandise. These undertakings won for him the title "Father of the Santa Fe Trail."

Old Tom Hardeman, with thousands of miles of frontier travel in his past, was interested in Santa Fe, and he is believed to have accompanied one of the early expeditions. Confirmation of this legend is lacking, but there is no doubt that he had contact with and influence upon many, if not most, of the Santa Fe expeditions which left Franklin during the 1820s. By the fall of 1821, and perhaps earlier, he had established a ferry across the Missouri River. Later his son John held the license for the same ferry, which crossed that stream five or six miles above Franklin and connected Fruitage Farm on the north bank with Arrow Rock on the south. This was variously referred to as Hardeman's Ferry and Arrow Rock Ferry (although there may have been two ferries known by the Arrow Rock name). Hardeman's Ferry was the means of crossing for at least one, and perhaps three Becknell expeditions, the M. M. Marmaduke party of 1824, the Wetmore-Hardeman group of 1828, and probably others. The Arrow Rock ferry described by Edwin James of the Stephen Long expedition was a catamaran structure with two large parallel canoes. These hulls were joined by a deck with a livestock guard rail. The craft was "peculiarly adapted to the navigation of a rapid stream."[2]

While the ferry boat of Thomas and his oldest living son, John Hardeman, was shuttling westbound men and animals and wagons across Missouri currents, Tom's youngest son, Bailey Hardeman, plunged into the trade. At the age of twenty-six he was on hand at Franklin by the time the first Santa Fe expedition departed. This lawyer and former artillery officer was involved in various phases of the Santa Fe trade. Yet, like his close associate Ewing Young, but to a greater degree, Bailey suffered the fate of obscurity; records of his Santa Fe exploits have been heretofore undiscovered or unnoticed. He is well known for his later role in the Texas independence movement, but no mention of his part in the trade has been published.

Bailey was a man of medium heavy build with a boyish face, a prominent nose and chin, large blue eyes, and dark, almost black hair. As though moved by the counsel of Polonius, he gave few men his voice. His pen, too, was as silent as his tongue. Typical of his brevity was a line from his later correspondence written from a seething Texas in the trauma of its birth as a nation. "Relative to the political situation of our country I have not time to say one word."[3] Such terseness may explain Bailey Hardeman's obscurity despite his role of leadership in the West.

He was born on February 26, 1795, at the Hardeman stockade near Nashville. His mother died when he was three years of age. Bailey grew up in the farm environment of Davidson and Williamson counties, became a War of 1812 artillery officer at eighteen, and at twenty-one was a deputy sheriff back in Williamson County. His father provided him with a landed legacy and a good education. Like several of his brothers, Bailey took training in the law and was admitted to the bar in Tennessee. In 1820 he married Rebecca Wilson of Williamson County. Six months later, Bailey was with his father and his brother John on the Missouri frontier.[4] It was here that he met William Becknell.

Family legend holds that Bailey Hardeman was a member of the Becknell expeditions which opened the trade with New Mexico in 1821 and 1822. No documentary evidence has been found to bear this out, although it is known that he was closely associated with several members of those expeditions. The land purchases which he made in Tennessee in 1822, 1823, and 1824[5] offer no positive clue, since some, perhaps all of these, were made in his absence by his wife Rebecca or by one or more of his brothers. Possibly he was able to buy the land with proceeds from the Santa Fe trade.

If Bailey was not a veteran of the Turquoise Trail by 1824, he was soon to become one. In that year, he and his brother-in-law and cousin, Glen Owen (who was in Missouri by early 1819), assembled their trade goods and joined the swelling traffic on that parched ribbon of commerce.[6] Perhaps they went together, or possibly Glen Owen went with the Braxton Cooper caravan. Bailey's outfit was captained by the enigmatic mountain man and trader, Alexander Le Grand. But the expedition is most closely identified with Meredith Miles Marmaduke, whose diary of the trip has been preserved. Marmaduke was a Virginian by birth, a

From Tennessee to the Great Plains, ferry boats such as this one were used or operated by a number of the Hardemans. Their ferry near Arrow Rock carried the caravans bound for Santa Fe during the 1820s. *Courtesy Library of Congress*.

veteran of the War of 1812, and, in later years, lieutenant-governor of Missouri, then chief executive (after Governor Thomas Reynolds took his own life with a rifle bullet). His diary is a valuable source of information on the early commerce with New Mexico, although his heretofore unpublished letters to his friend John Hardeman are much more explicit as to the actual techniques of the business.

John Hardeman, too, had a finger on the pulse of the Santa Fe trade of 1824. Before the expedition left Missouri, Marmaduke appointed John as his agent to care for his slaves and business.[7] In view of the usual family connections it is probable that John and his father had invested in the enterprise of Bailey Hardeman and Glen Owen. Where the trail crossed the Missouri, John was instrumental in facilitating the movement of the big wagon train of 1824.

The Marmaduke caravan was the largest and best organized to tackle the New Mexico road up to that time. It consisted of "81 persons and 2 servants, . . . 2 road waggons, 20 dearborns [light wagons], 2 carts, and one small piece of cannon," and 150 to 200 horses and mules. The value of the trade goods was estimated at $30,000, although it is not clear whether at Missouri or Eastern prices. On Sunday, May 16, 1824, this aggregation was hauled across the Missouri River to Arrow Rock on the ferry of John and Thomas Hardeman. No small piece of work to perform on the Sabbath!

Once across the Missouri, the travelers passed through Blue Spring and over the flower-blanketed prairie of western Missouri, then, after leaving Fort Osage near the border of the state, pursued a west-southwest course to the Arkansas River. They followed this stream for some 240 miles before breaking south to the Cimarron River and moving in a westerly direction to Taos, New Mexico. "We saw but very few Indians on our way out," Marmaduke noted, "yet I believe we were seen by many who were afraid to visit us."[8] They would be less fortunate on the homeward haul.

Despite good planning and leadership and the absence of Indian troubles, the cavalcade met with many obstacles. The land was inhospitable, an expanse with a split personality: hauntingly beautiful yet hell to the traveler, swollen streams or sweltering jornadas. And if, as the nineteenth-century adage allowed, God took care to stay on His own side of the Mississippi, the trail to Santa Fe must have strongly influenced His decision. It seemed never to rain enough, except when it rained too much. There was little timber to conceal the Indian, but as little wood for fires to cook food and to break the chill of the night. Bailey Hardeman and his companions made numerous camps with neither wood nor water. Buffalo chips proved to be adequate for fuel, but the water problem was more serious. They dug wells in the dry sand beds of "upside-down" streams at the bottoms of ravines and filled buckets with the water which seeped out. At times they were able to cross streams only after digging cuts through the banks and lowering the wagons by ropes, then covering the stream beds with bushes and felled trees.[9] Broken wheel spokes and other wagon parts were quickly repaired, but keeping the draft animals from getting lost was a bigger problem.

The innumerable buffalo, while providing fuel and food, constituted a mixed blessing. In a letter to John Hardeman, Marmaduke included a description which supplements the information in his diary.

> About 2 o'clock at night on the morning of the 12th day of June, [1824] a great [herd] of buffalo crossed the A. River [Arkansas] exactly opposite our encampment and part of them passed thro the [area] assigned the horses to graze. It appears that the guard could not check them—and they . . . frightened our horses so that they broke by the guard—and could not be checked—and to the no. of 25 or 6 were entirely lost.[10]

Antelope, elk, and deer were numerous, but they were dwarfed by the tens of thousands of buffalo, the staple of the trail. The diarist noted of one of the large herds that it consisted chiefly of bulls. This imbalance was increasingly evident. Long before white marksmen with Sharps rifles slaughtered the shaggy beasts to the edge of extinction, the fate of the buffalo had been nearly sealed by Indian hunters. Spanish ponies supplied the mobility with which the Indians could overtake and slaughter the animals. The cows were killed off more rapidly because their meat and hides were superior for the Indian's needs and their strength inferior to the bulls. This practice had largely destroyed the balance of the sexes, leaving a preponderance of bulls. Before acquiring the horse, the Indian, by using the buffalo jump and by hunting on foot, apparently killed animals of both sexes in approximately equal numbers. In fact, bulls had been at times readily killed by hunters on foot because of their tendency to turn and fight.

Bailey Hardeman and his companions reached Santa Fe at dusk on July 28, 1824, after safely traversing an estimated 931 difficult miles in 73 days. "The Dearbourn held out well," Marmaduke reported to John Hardeman. "Not a wheel or axle tree gave way, and I yesterday refused 4 mules for it, notwithstanding it has been capsized twice." The members of the party promptly began to size up the market, pay the 25 percent *ad valorem* tariff, and bargain with buyers of their wares. The group quickly dispersed, peddling to the various New Mexico towns.[11]

They had brought cotton, woolen, and silk textiles, cutlery, looking glasses, and "many other articles necessary for the purposes of an assortment." In exchange, they received "Spanish milled dollars, a small amount of gold and silver, in bullion, beaver fur, and some mules."[12] The bulk of the coin and bullion had been brought north from Chihuahua and was used for trade with the foreigner more than as a local medium of exchange. It became quickly apparent that coin was less plentiful than had been hoped. Disposing of the goods in Santa Fe was going to be difficult. According to Augustus Storrs, about half the party went to northern Mexico in an attempt to "effect better sales" in "New Biscay" (the province of Nueva Vizcaya).[13] Concerning the first American merchants to follow the Royal Road south from the New Mexico settlements, little is known. Perhaps, as Josiah Gregg states, this leg of the trade attracted Americans as early as 1822. On the other hand, the unprecedentedly large Marmaduke party may have been the first to glut the New Mexico market and spill over to the lower country.

Quite possibly Bailey Hardeman was among these merchants on the Chihuahua Trail; his brother-in-law, Captain Glen Owen, definitely was. Glen had bought out the goods of a Mr. Reamy. In mid-October, Marmaduke wrote John Hardeman that:

> Capt. Owens left this, I think about 6 weeks since, for the lower country. He had not then vended many goods, and I have understood that the prices below of goods is much lower than in this section of the country—and that the lower country is full of goods. I hope however he will do well. He was in fine health and spirits.

Although Marmaduke said little in his journal as to the marketing techniques employed, he wrote his business associate, John Hardeman, in succinct detail about the operation.

Bailey and John Hardeman and their brother-in-law Glen Owen were among the
weary but jubilant travelers who celebrated the first sight of Santa Fe in the
1820s. *From Josiah Gregg,* Commerce of the Prairies, *1844*.

We are now engaged in vending our goods by retail, which we find to be a very tedious business, as the country is actually overrun with goods. One remains in Sta. Fee, and the other with a pack endeavors to vend wherever he can in the neighboring villages. . . . Money is exceedingly scarce in this country. [The mode] of operations is this—To remain in St. Fe and the neighborhood around and vend for cash all the goods we can, perhaps the whole winter, and so soon as we shall have succeeding in effecting a sale of the most salable goods—and reduced our stock considerably say $2000—then with the balance of the goods to go to the lower country and exchange them for mules and take them around by San Antonio to the US and vend them to the best advantage we can in the states. Thus you find we cannot return very soon to Missouri if no accident befals us—I fear none of us will succeed as well as we at one time expected.[14]

The practice of keeping one person in Santa Fe while another, or several others, packed and sold goods to the nearby settlements was later extensively employed, particularly by Jewish traders; but this may have been the first use of the technique in New Mexico. The Marmaduke expedition carried on some of the last of the extensive retailing by American traders who brought goods over the Santa Fe trail. Soon the common method of operation was to rent a room, perhaps a private home, and to wholesale the goods from that base.

As these sales operations were progressing, Andrew Jackson was seeking to become the first President from a western state. Another friend of the Hardemans, William H. Ashley, was working out the first rendezvous of mountain men ever to be held in the Rockies. And Bailey Hardeman himself had turned mountain man, heading north from Taos in search of beaver. The decade of the 1820s was a boom time for the fur trade in the trans-Mississippi West. Spain and Mexico, which had expended immense energies in the pursuit of precious metals but had little tradition of fur trapping, were largely uninterested, even when chance placed them in the heart of the fur-bearing kingdoms—the sea otter haven of the Pacific coast and the numerous beaver streams of the southwest.

The Spanish-speaking communities of New Mexico—Santa Fe, Taos, Santa Cruz, Albuquerque, and other settlements—inadvertently provided strategically situated all-year rendezvous grounds for American mountain men of the Southwest. Fur gathering by Americans in Mexican territory was illegal; only Mexican citizens could get licenses to trap, and some Americans became citizens of Mexico for that purpose. Since there were no organized fur companies in the Southwest at that time, in contrast with several well-known operations to the north, the records of the southwestern fur trade are, by comparison, much less complete. Many of the famous members of the "reckless breed of men" at one time or another trapped out of the New Mexico towns; Walker, Waldo, and Wolfskill, Young and Yount, de Mun and Dye, Jackson and Fitzpatrick, Smith and Carson and Williams, the Patties, the Robidoux, the Subblettes, were among them.

Certainly there were more, and probably many more of these mountain men than history has thus far recorded. Bailey Hardeman was not the first member of the family to evince an interest in the fur business. His father had trapped trans-Appalachia fifty-six years before, and when Bailey was but a small boy his brothers John and Perkins Hardeman had bought peltry at their store in Franklin, Tennessee. The family legend that Bailey subsisted on horseflesh while on a trapping expedition in the Rockies is corroborated through William Becknell's account of that harrowing experience. [15]

Becknell, along with twenty-nine-year-old Bailey Hardeman and seven other men, left the crude adobes of Santa Cruz, New Mexico, on November 5, 1824, to trap what they called the "Green River" country. By modern maps, this was the Colorado River of southern Utah. Becknell stated of these men that they "had seen better days, and had never before been supperless to bed, nor missed a wholesome and substantial meal at the regular family hour, except one who was with me when I opened the road to Santa Fe." There was no such regular bill of fare on this journey! Some forty days from the nearest settlements they were marooned by three to four feet of snow. They made winter camp and conserved their strength, confining themselves to hunting and resting. Prisoners of the numbing cold and driven to the verge of starvation, the men killed a lean horse "to break our fast" and considered the meat "excellent." When they fell to eating the animal's bones, however, they were unable to digest them properly, and all members of the party became so ill that they feared for their lives. They "subsisted two days on a soup made of a raw hide," and on the following day ate rawhide hash. Starvation was fended off when they killed a bear. Its meat was described as good, although it reminded the chronicler of coyote flesh, a tribute to other hard days on the trail.

The trappers saw numerous remains of Indian habitation, furnaces, stone houses, kivas, and painted pottery, apparently of ancient Pueblo tribes near the present Four Corners. When they came upon a camp, the men were shocked at witnessing an Indian method of solving the problem of the aged. A sick, uncomplaining elderly squaw was placed on a funeral pyre of pine wood and burned to death.

The catch of this Colorado River foray must have been less than a fortune. Trapping was impractical during part of the time because of the cold weather and deep snows. Fall and spring were the best times to trap beaver, since water sets were the rule and ice interfered with trapping. One account states that $10,000 worth of peltry was brought back by the Marmaduke expedition,[16] and it may be presumed that part of this take came from the William Becknell–Bailey Hardeman party. The little band of weakened, emaciated men concluded their hunt when they reached a New Mexico settlement on April 5, 1825, having weathered five months in the winterswept wilderness.

Becknell returned to Franklin directly from Taos, and Hardeman first rejoined Marmaduke at Santa Fe. Becknell stated that Bailey Hardeman was to lead another expedition to Santa Fe upon his return,[17] but no evidence has been found to indicate whether or not he made this projected trip.

Part of the Marmaduke group had returned to Franklin in the fall of 1824, but the Colonel himself remained for ten months, leaving Santa Fe on May 31 of the next year. In addition to Marmaduke and Hardeman, there were at least fourteen traders, and probably more, in this eastbound party. There were mountain man Ewing Young and Frenchmen Henry Gratiot and Joseph Bezet; Mexican merchants of the trail Garcia, Escudero, and Pasquez, and a Negro trader whose only name given was William. Other blacks had gone to the West, such as mountain men Jim Beckwourth and Edward Rose and a number of residents in California, but William was quite probably the first free Negro to engage in the New Mexico trade from the United States. Along the trail west of Missouri, the Osage and Kansa Indians attacked the homeward-bound caravan, stampeding and capturing many horses and mules and inflicting losses totaled at more than $1,600. All the above-named men suffered financially;

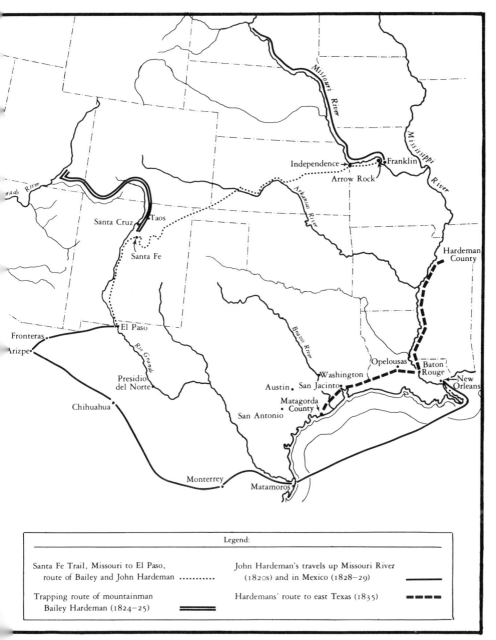

Legend:	
Santa Fe Trail, Missouri to El Paso, route of Bailey and John Hardeman ··········	John Hardeman's travels up Missouri River (1820s) and in Mexico (1828–29) ————
Trapping route of mountainman Bailey Hardeman (1824–25) ═══	Hardemans' route to east Texas (1835) ▬ ▬ ▬

Map 4. Western Travels of the Hardeman Family, 1820–1836.

Bailey Hardeman lost to the Osages two horses and one mule, valued at $100 to $108 total, and William, the Negro, was robbed of one horse worth $35.00.[18] Nevertheless, as serious as these setbacks were to the individuals concerned, they did not negate the overall value of the trip.

The Marmaduke expedition reportedly brought back $180,000 in gold and silver, in addition to furs, mules, and other goods. Becknell reports that a 3 percent export duty was levied on all specie brought east out of the province. Despite his early feelings of gloom about the trade, Marmaduke and his companions appear to have come off well for their endeavors. Probably their profits were enhanced by selling techniques which "stretched out the market": peddling the goods over almost a year's time and covering a wide geographical range that included both New and Old Mexico.

Bailey Hardeman himself apparently reaped a respectable profit from his several New Mexico investments, despite the $108 loss to the Osages. In the summer of 1825, after his return from the ordeal of snow and famine, he financed the Santa Fe trading expedition of William Scott. The contract stipulated that the two men were joint owners of $100 worth of silversmith tools, which were probably held as partial security by Hardeman until Scott's return after two years. The profits of Scott's trip were to be divided between himself and Hardeman. (William Scott was listed by the customs officials in Santa Fe as one of the traders of 1825.)[19] Several years later, Bailey's gifts, loans, and business activities in Tennessee show that he was a man of considerable means.

Not all members of the expedition were able to enjoy the fruits of their strenuous labors on the trail. As noted, Captain Glen Owen, husband of Thomas Hardeman's daughter Elizabeth, had led a group of traders, including William Wolfskill, to northwestern Chihuahua. They traded their goods for horses and mules which they planned to sell in the southern part of the United States. In 1825, near Presidio del Norte on the Rio Grande, they were attacked by a Comanche war party; the herd was stampeded, and Glen Owen was killed. Enough horses and mules were recovered and sold in Louisiana and Alabama to prevent the venture from being a total loss. Owen's share was taken to his widow at Boon's Lick by Wolfskill.[20] Glen Owen, like a handful of others—McNees, Munroe, Means, Wixon—had paid the supreme price for his pioneering spirit.

Perhaps Josiah Gregg was right when he wrote years later that married men were "peculiarly unfitted for the chequered life of a Santa Fe trader. The domestic hearth, with all its sacred and most endearing recollections, is sure to haunt them in the hour of trial, and almost every step of their journey is apt to be attended by melancholy reflections of home and domestic dependencies."[21] Elizabeth Hardeman Owen published notice of a sale of her deceased husband's personal property to be held July 7, 1825; the property was to include "Well blooded Mares, Horses, Mules, A stock of cattle, Sheep, Farming Tools, Ploughs, Hoes, Axes, Saws, Bench tools . . . &c."[22] Some time after the sale she returned to Franklin, Tennessee.

The losses in livestock and men spurred Santa Fe traders to press their political representatives for protection from the United States Government. Senator Thomas Hart "Old Bullion" Benton, whose hard-money views were doubtless influenced by the specie rolling into his home state on Santa Fe wagons, led the move for government help. His interest was as old as the trade, but his ammunition came largely from the expedition of 1824, and specifically from Augustus Storrs of the Marmaduke caravan. Federal aid had been limited to allowing traders to cross Indian Territory and accepting pesos from Mexico in place of United States currency at the Missouri-based federal land office. Benton's bill, which passed Congress and was signed by President Monroe on his last day in office, provided for safe passage of the traders through the Indian lands and for a survey and marking of the route. Later that year the desired treaty with the Osage and Kansa Indians was negotiated, and in 1825 and 1826 the survey and markings were carried out. The treaties were successful, but Indians farther west continued their resistance for two decades, caravans often pushed on heedless of the path pointed out by the trail markers, and trade termini changed from time to time, rendering the survey partially obsolete. The captain of a later company of traders opined that the survey was not necessary, as the traders themselves had left satisfactory trail markings.[23]

The surveying and trail-marking expedition came in contact with Missouri ferry owner and gardener John Hardeman. On July 5, 1825, the party was transported across the river to Arrow Rock, apparently on Hardeman's Ferry. One of the survey commissioners, George C. Sibley, and Hardeman had conversations about the flora at the former's Fruitage Farm. As mentioned previously, early the following year Sibley addressed John from San Fernando, New Mexico, stating that several parcels of grape cuttings were being sent to him from the New Mexico settlements. Presumably there was some time for cultural as well as military matters.

Efforts to secure federal payments for losses at the hands of Indians and to get military escorts along the trail met with little success. Marmaduke sought the counsel of Benton in an effort to recover the losses sustained by himself, Bailey Hardeman, and others in 1825. He was presented to the Senator by Benton's old friend, John Hardeman, who wrote, in August 1825:

> . . . To introduce my friend Col. Marmaduke who has lately returned with my brother [Bailey Hardeman] from New Mexico—and of whom I cannot say less than that he is a gentleman at all points. Conversation with him will be of interest to you touching the Santa Fe road. . . .[24]

The efforts of Marmaduke and others probably had a cumulative effect. But it was the plea stemming from losses on the return from Santa Fe in 1828 which brought about the one noteworthy example of government escort, the military forces under Major Bennet Riley in 1829.[25] Ultimately the traders found protection in their own ranks and armament, and by increasing the percentage of oxen. These animals pulled the wagons, supplied emergency food for the traveling company, and, most important, were of little use to the Indians, who preferred buffalo to ox flesh. They were much more interested in raiding caravans for the sorely needed horses and mules, and the switch to oxen sharply curtailed Indian attacks.

John Hardeman, through his trans-Missouri ferry boat service, investments, and correspondence, had shown more than a passing interest in the New Mexico trade since its opening. In 1828, he immersed himself in it directly. Complex person that he was, he no doubt succumbed to the tugging and pushing of more than a few forces. Merchandising was by no means foreign to him, although foreign merchandising was. His previous experiences as a store proprietor provided valuable background for the Southwest trade. He was currently marketing crops as far away as New Orleans. Furthermore, he had been literally standing astride the profitable artery of commerce at his ferry landing; and there were examples of success close at hand in the persons of his brother and friends. The fate of Glen Owen may have been as much a challenge as a dissuader. John was by some standards a well-to-do gentleman farmer. His twenty-six slaves, his acres, garden, busy ferry boat, and popular winepress—all were touchstones of success. However, the general cash shortage of the area had not been entirely relieved by the Santa Fe trade. John's expenditures for his show garden and for the hospitality which he had proffered numerous visitors had been a drain upon his assets, and above all, the piracy of the Missouri River flood had been nearly disastrous. In his statement, "Were it not for the strong necessity that is now pressing me, I should not leave . . . the family as I am about to do,"[26] he hints at an overriding economic motive for the gamble. But his broad background of trading and farming gave him other—and safer—options than Santa Fe.

One can picture John Hardeman—planter, businessman, lawyer, philosopher—applying his chilly logic to the various facets of the undertaking, then perhaps allowing his sentiments or his unaccountable restiveness to cast the dice. The combined logic of all his philosophers would not be enough to hold him back. If he had apostasized from the religious faith of his childhood, he was never able to abandon his frontiering cult. At fifty-two his hair was still a youthful brown, and his health was equal to the rigors of the trail. For eleven years his urge to push farther west had lain dormant, but now it was stirred up and revitalized by all the talk and the activity surrounding Santa Fe.

From the business standpoint, John Hardeman's trading operations in the Southwest were backed by a three-way partnership which included his brother-in-law George Knox and General Thomas A. Smith. On occasion the firm of Smith and Knox in Franklin, Missouri, had purchased large supplies of goods from Philadelphia and resold to traders who were headed for New Mexico. George Knox may have been in the Marmaduke caravan to Santa Fe in 1824; he definitely made the trip in later years.[27]

The functions of the three partners were clearly differentiated in their trading enterprise of 1828. Smith supplied much of the capital, and the proceeds were to be "joint stock." George Knox probably had less than a full share of interest in the enterprise. He went to Philadelphia in the spring of 1828 and purchased $8,000 worth of assorted goods, which were shipped to Hardeman's landing by steamboat. Alphonso Wetmore was in

New York at the time, buying his supply of goods for the same trip, but Knox concluded that Philadelphia prices were better.[28] John Hardeman's part of the bargain was to take the goods to New Mexico, sell them, and return with the proceeds.

The diplomacy of the Santa Fe trade was becoming somewhat more complex than it had been in the first years. Joel R. Poinsett, United States minister to Mexico, announced in 1827 that every trader was required to obtain a regular passport signed by a Mexican agent before arriving in New Mexico. John Hardeman sent a request to Senator Benton for passports for himself, M. M. Marmaduke, Damen Sappington, and ten others. Benton responded by sending the necessary blanks, along with his opinion that Mexico would probably oblige. Hardeman's passport was signed on January 25, 1828, by Secretary of State Henry Clay and endorsed on the following day by Obregón, an official at the Mexican Legation in Washington.[29]

The job of preparing for the Santa Fe run was no small one. Smith's lead mining interests in southern Missouri needed his attention. (True to its preeminent role in opening the Far West, Missouri supplied large amounts of lead for bullets.) Two weeks after the arrival of the steamer with the trade goods, John wrote to his father that "the General went to the mines & left the whole of the business relative to the Santa Fe expedition to my charge & I have not slept any night since, earlier than 2 o'clock."[30] Hardeman left his own business affairs in the hands of his son, John Locke, with instructions to turn over any surplus funds beyond the family's needs to General Smith. John also consigned to Smith two of his slaves, Ephraim and Dick, to work in Smith's lead mines until his return from Mexico. William, another slave, was given the large task of operating Fruitage Farm.

May was the time for wheels to roll on the deep-rutted road to Santa Fe, and late in that month, in 1828, John Hardeman ferried his wagons, loaded with assorted merchandise, to the south bank of the Missouri River. On May 28, the customary rendezvous for traders was held at Blue Spring. Alphonso Wetmore was elected captain. A reference to the Wetmore-Hardeman party indicates that John Hardeman may have been chosen second in command.[31]

The westbound leg of Hardeman's Santa Fe journey was in all likelihood the easiest on record to that date, but the return experiences for these very traders would be the worst in the entire history of the trade route. There was no borderline starvation on the outbound leg, although on July 26 Wetmore, with his usual touch of subtle humor, noted: "This evening when threatened with a famine, or a mule feast, two black specks appeared far off. . . . These were buffalo, and they cost us only two ball cartridges." No hostility from the Indians was encountered; no drinking of hot mule blood to fend off death from thirst while crossing the jornadas. Quite the contrary, it was feast instead of famine, as the season was unusually wet, and the men were able to kill game and find water at the temporary ponds dotting the landscape. Mud, downpours, and swollen streams were problems, to be sure, but a caravan could survive these well enough.

Mules, which figured so prominently in the New Mexico trade, as usual provided no little entertainment and anxiety on this expedition. Wagon races were frequently noted by Wetmore, who provided an explanation almost as classical as it was comical: "It is one of the foibles of mule teams, that after they have travelled four or five hundred miles, and when it is supposed that they are about to tire, to take fright from a profile view of their shadows, and run like the antelope of these plains." Nevertheless, the eccentric hybrid animals were heavily depended upon in this era of the trade, and it was apparently considered something other than poetic justice when a member of this company—none other than the centurion Wetmore—shot his own mule through the head while chasing a buffalo!

The caravan traced closely the path of the federal survey of 1825 and 1826, arriving at Santa Fe about August 3, 1828. Reports of trade prospects and profits in the New Mexico villages for that year are mixed. Some members of this expedition, and a number of men from the Marmaduke group which also reached Santa Fe and vicinity that summer, disposed of their goods in New Mexico, and returned home in the fall. However, one observer reported, "Those that sold out at St. fee got but 20 per cent on cost—a bad prospect," and some of the Hardeman-Wetmore party "intended to go lower down."[32] John Hardeman disliked the marketing picture in the northern province and sought clearance to take at least part of his goods into Chihuahua and Sonora. By August 20, his wagons were creaking south on the Royal Road. He entertained the possibility of "selling off at wholesale" at El Paso, but stated that "should the reports of prices of goods in Sonora be found to be true, I shall have a fair chance of making something for the trouble I have already encountered."[33]

The latter course appealed to him, and he drove southwest to distant Fronteras, Sonora Province, where he checked in with the customs house on October 2, 1828. Peddling what he could dispose of there, he headed his teams eastward to the Sonoran city of Arizpe, the former Spanish headquarters of the Commanding General of Internal Provinces. Here too, after a customshouse clearance dated January 13, 1829, he sold goods from his wheeled warehouses. In all, Hardeman took to the lower country nineteen bales, fourteen boxes, and eight barrels of assorted goods, in addition to nine bundles of clothing. The trade items were chiefly textiles. The finished goods included cotton and silk shawls, coats, hats, blankets, and saddle covers. And there were many kinds of cloth, buttons of several materials, thimbles, and dress patterns. Pocket knives, files, dinnerware, pen nibs, cow bells, and tin trays were among his stores, as were some special items to strike the fancies of *señoras* and *señoritas*—German mirrors, ivory and bone combs, powder and rouge boxes, pendants and chains, umbrellas and parasols, and a few sprays of artificial flowers.[34] This was a fair cross section of the goods brought by the Missouri traders.

John estimated that the Sonoran markets were as far from Santa Fe as that town was from his home. This calculation, which was roughly accurate, placed his farthest trading point nearly 2,000 miles by road from Fruitage Farm. Adding the miles of hostile terrain which he then covered from northwestern Sonora to the Gulf of Mexico, he had driven his wagons some 3,000 miles since leaving Franklin. By any standards, this was an expedition of large dimensions, comparable to a wagon trip from New England to California.

The members of the 1828 trading parties which returned home in the fall of that year suffered heavy losses from Indian attacks. Hundreds of head of livestock were lost, and three men, Robert McNees, Daniel Munroe, and John Means, were killed.[35] The returns from the trade were sharply cut by these assaults. In contrast, John Hardeman had been lucky. But time would soon prove him to be less a favorite of fortune than his brother Bailey. He embarked for New Orleans from the port of Matamoros near the mouth of the Rio Grande on August 10, 1829. Two days earlier, a letter from New Orleans to the *National Intelligencer* sounded an ominous note. "The yellow fever is raging here with great violence. Yesterday, it is said, thirty persons fell victim to it." On Wednesday, September 2, at the age of fifty-three, John died from the disease at New Orleans,[36] the fourth victim of the ill-starred caravan of 1828. The Santa Fe Trail had become for him a Daedalian labyrinth, an alchemist's conjuring which turned his sterling silver hopes to tinsel. Fifteen arduous months he had toiled on mockingly beautiful desert trails. He had only a month to travel, and that in the relative comfort of a river boat berth, when his dream broke up like ice that shatters with the spring thaw.

As Hardeman had been susceptible to the dreaded yellow fever, so his fortune from the trade was apparently vulnerable to the avarice of an opportunistic physician. For a few days' lodging at Knight's Inn, for visits on four successive days by Dr. Jonas E. Kerr, and for his interment, all of which should not have cost more than $100, according to Thomas Hardeman, John's estate was charged $1,643.63½. Most of this went to the man whom Thomas called a "robber of widows and orphans," Dr. Kerr.[37]

How much profit John Hardeman had extracted from his labors is not known. A Missouri River traveler and friend of Hardeman, fur magnate William H. Ashley, noted that "the death of Mr. John Hardeman is regretted here by all who knew him. . . . Am glad to learn that the money which he had collected was safely deposited in bank."[38] A legal opinion offered to General Smith from New Orleans indicated that a saving of about $1,000 would accrue to Hardeman's family if some friend would administer the estate in that city.[39] However large, the total amount which this reflected was small in comparison with John's biggest investment in the trade—his life. Like Jedediah Smith, Glen Owen, and a score of others, he had paid the ultimate price for his vision, his daring, his folly. Perhaps he had a premonition that his southwestern oasis would become a mirage. He had penned a farewell message to his son just before leaving home, expressing his devotion and concluding with a hint of finality, "May you prosper as I think you deserve."[40] It was little short of prophecy that, in the wake of the floods at Fruitage Farm, he had just begun his new botanical show garden and named it Penultima.

Senator Benton assisted the survivors with some of the legal problems in the aftermath of John Hardeman's death. Marmaduke, who was appointed guardian of the minor children of his fallen fellow trader, got a negative opinion about Hardeman from his devoutly religious Virginia cousin, Samson Porter, to whom he had written of the death of his "great friend." Porter replied, "He might be as respects this world. . . . I recollect some two or three years ago Reading in some paper or other . . . the sentiments of a Mr. Hardyman a Retched Infidl, it is to be hopt he is not the man you call your friend, which I fear he was."[41] Undoubtedly this was a reference to the Lockian or deistic views of John or Thomas Hardeman.

The Santa Fe trading—though not the western travels—of the Hardemans was ended with the death of John. In spite of, or perhaps because of the tragedy brought to the family by the trail, his son Glen would choose the same route twenty years later, but in search of California gold rather than Mexican silver.

The value of the Santa Fe trade was not large in the 1820s compared with the flourishing thirties and forties, but it was foundation and framework for the larger structure soon to be erected. The increase in Missouri's wealth and prominence was already notable. Alphonso Wetmore informed Secretary of War Lewis Cass in 1831, "With all the disadvantages which have been encountered, this trade has continued to increase for a period of nine years, and the circulating medium of Missouri now consists principally of Mexican dollars."[42] That state, as a result, enjoyed a more favorable balance of payments position relative to the older, established economies of the eastern seaboard.

Certainly Missouri was influencing the Southwest as much as, or more than, she was affected by it. Had "Mother of the West" titles been awarded, Missouri would have been in the forefront along with Tennessee. Despite increasing penetrations of Chihuahua and Sonora by Missouri traders, New Mexico too improved its balance of payments situation from the trade. The 5,000 inhabitants of Santa Fe and the 40,000 to 45,000 population of New Mexico, much of which was living in poverty, could not absorb the total quantity of incoming goods. New Mexico traders overbought in order to resell American products in the lower country, and they insisted more and more upon hard money in their commercial interchange with the merchants to the south. The large receipts in customs duties further stimulated the economies of the northern Mexican provinces.

The Hardemans had been members of at least three and perhaps more expeditions during the first seven years of the commerce. They invested in other caravans and ferried the wagons, goods, and livestock of hundreds of traders across the Missouri River. As some of the early developers of the first great American trail in the trans-Mississippi West, their wagon ruts were an indeterminate but not inconsiderable part of the braided, cable-like tracks which seemed destined to bind the United States and the Southwest inexorably—and inextricably—into one shared future.

7 ⊬ From Tennessee to Texas
THE INDEPENDENCE MOVEMENT BEYOND
THE SABINE

JOHN HARDEMAN'S DEATH seemed to take the momentum from the family's westward impulse. For over half a century since taking leave of his Dan River neighbors, Thomas Hardeman and his children had pushed at the outer edge of American settlement. John himself, the widest ranging, had spanned the continent from the Atlantic colony of Virginia to the Pacific province of Sonora and from the north central plains to Central America. Now his death signaled a moratorium, or more properly a retrenchment. Suddenly the central pivot had slipped. Had not John been the spark, the intellectual leader, had he not taken in and teamed with his aging father, hired his younger brother Peter, and provided a hearth for young Bailey and hospitality and financial help for his kin, he might have been missed less keenly and fallen from view—as did his brother Perkins—without slowing the family effort. The Hardemans' frontier enthusiasm, however, was stilled for six years after the passing of the Missouri gardener.

By 1830, once-wild Missouri had quieted like a newly bridled colt which would not again kick over the traces until western border turmoil took hold in the 1860s. Few representatives of the Thomas Hardeman line were in the state. John's immediate family remained, that is, his wife Nancy and their children John Locke, Lucretia, Leona, and Glen, as did the Burnets. Some of these would later resume the frontierward effort. Meanwhile the others had returned to Tennessee. Elizabeth, some time after her husband Glen Owen was killed by Indians, went back to Williamson County. Later she married Dr. Reese Corzine. And the patriarch Thomas, who had lived with John and his family most of the time since 1817, concluded that he would be a burden, unable "to do any essential service" for Nancy and for his Missouri grandchildren. Past the midpoint of his eighty-first year, he returned alone to Tennessee in September 1830, displaying considerable energy as he rode horseback as much as fifty miles in a day. [1] Sixty-two years had gone by since he had first visited the Cumberland country. Over that span he had opened a half dozen plantations and put up enough log buildings to make a small town if they had been gathered at one place; he had seen and helped three states rise out of the forests that embraced his lands. He had harbored no illusions about the frontier, having met it again and again on its own terms. Now time had dulled his vision and robbed his step of its spring. The unexpected loss of his closest son had left him stunned, resigned.

Thomas Hardeman knew that he was going back to Tennessee to die. "Destiny having determined," he wrote to Nancy, "we shall never meet again . . . I can only wish you, and yours, all the health, prosperity, and happiness, you and each of you can possibly enjoy." His ailments continued to plague him, and despite his stoicism, he wrote, "My greatest desires are to be off." [2] He lived for some months with his son Thomas J. at Bolivar, then moved to Franklin with his daughter Elizabeth. Thomas's eyesight failed completely, and it was a source of frustration to him that he could no longer write letters to his relatives and friends. His mind was alert till that June 4th, 1833, when, in his eighty-fourth year, he crossed with characteristic calm into his last frontier.

Around this time two other westward migrating members of the family, sons of Eleazar Hardeman, died, James in Arkansas of unknown causes, and Seth from drowning in the Mississippi River.

Meanwhile the silent Bailey Hardeman, like his father, had back-tracked to Tennessee, not out of resignation, but presumably to take up another life and invest earnings from the Mexican trade. Not only was he able to finance the expedition of another trader to Santa Fe, but he made a large loan to his nephew Locke, and was recognized as one of the most prosperous members of the family. By early 1828 he had secured a license to keep an "ordinary," or tavern, in Williamson County.[3] For the next several years he lived near Wilson Creek, where his in-laws resided. As a small boy Bailey had been familiar with his brothers' house of merchandise, and he had tasted the business more personally following the War of 1812, when he owned and operated a store. Shortly after his return from Santa Fe and Missouri he opened another general store, this one at Hardeman's Cross Roads, a Williamson County village named for him. His tavern at the same location[4] was an asset since patrons of such stores sometimes traveled long distances and remained overnight.

Like his older brother John, Bailey blended his urge for the action of the frontier with a commitment to culture. He donated a parcel of land to Wilson Creek Baptist Church. But his best known contribution to things cultural was his establishment of the Hardeman Academy near Hardeman's Cross Roads, now called Triune. Colonel John L. Jordan described the institution in his history of Triune.

> Hardeman Academy was a famous school prior to the Civil War. It stood on an eminence about a half mile west of Triune in a grove of beautiful beech trees. In ante-bellum days many young men from other counties and states boarded in the neighborhood and attended this school.[5]

(Nearly eighty years later, Dr. Nicholas B. Hardeman, another descendant of Thomas, would become a co-founder of Freed-Hardeman College, also in Tennessee.) In a very real sense these bequests of Bailey Hardeman were monuments to the Santa Fe trade. He was one of the trustees for his school and also for a female academy in the same town.[6]

It was autumn of 1835, the time of year when stars glittered with unmatched brilliance over southwestern trails, when crystal streams were shallow and fordable and, along their banks, the broad, trembling cottonwood leaves were turning gold from crisp fall nights. A season's clandestine traders—poachers on the north domain of Santa Anna's Mexico—were herding droves of mules and lugging silver east in Santa Fe

Trail ruts fifteen years deep. A small army of gruff mountain men was preparing to bivouac in the defiant Rocky Mountain cordillera for another fall beaver hunt. High up on the Green River in South Pass, Dr. Marcus Whitman had pulled an arrow from Jim Bridger's back. Tough Tennessean and distillery operator Isaac Graham was entrenching himself in California, where he would soon plot revolution against the improvident Mexican government. And Bailey Hardeman, whose tracks were already large across the Southwest, was off again for Mexico's northern provincial fringe.

What turned the taciturn Bailey's head from Tennessee can only be guessed. Was it the decline of his business fortunes? Or some velvet-tongued *empresario* such as Sterling Robertson, who persuaded many Tennesseans to go to Texas for new lands and opportunities? An urge to join his countrymen against the imperious Santa Anna? Perhaps it was simply that the lure of the frontier had lain dormant in his veins and flowed again like sap in the springtime, impelling him to branch out anew. Two headstones lying side by side in the Polk cemetery of Hardeman County give mute testimony about the mood if not the motive of the Texas venture. One marks the grave of Emeline Hardeman, eight-year-old daughter of Bailey and Rebecca, who died September 3, 1835, and the other commemorates Mary Polk Hardeman, whose death occurred twenty-one days later.[7] Mary's husband, Thomas J. Hardeman, and Bailey probably had plans for the move southwest before these events. One does not read far in the personal correspondence of that era without an awareness that death lurked a mere step away in every household. It was no doubt a crucible which helped to temper the pioneer spirit of the times.

Texas was no reprise of Bailey's previous southwestern experience. Santa Fe was a foray; Texas was a migration. Santa Fe was half a journey away; Texas was journey's end. The lure of New Mexico was quick profit; the appeal of Texas was more akin to a desire for permanence. Bailey was by no means alone in this move; it was the largest single pilgrimage of Hardeman clan members since the flatboat trip to the Cumberland Basin in the 1780s. Three sons and a daughter of the late Thomas Hardeman were in this company of sojourners—Bailey, Blackstone, and Thomas J. Hardeman and Julia Ann Hardeman Bacon. Also present was John Marr Hardeman, a son of Constantine and grandson of Thomas, who (like

Blackstone) had taken an M.D. degree. D. Hardeman, a son of the late merchant Perkins, also opted for the move. The entire group numbered some twenty-five people.

Bailey, Blackstone and Thomas J. Hardeman settled first in the "cradle of Texas history," Matagorda County, on the Gulf Coast. The Caney Creek bottom lands, which were ten miles wide in places, with rich soils and abundant wild game, promised them a good start in the new country. Within several years the land holdings of various members of the family extended inland to what would become Bastrop, Henderson, Washington, Travis, Gonzales, Nueces, and Caldwell counties. The grant policies of the Mexican government had been suspended during the 1830s but were restored by the time the Hardeman brigade arrived. After 1836, additional lands were made available through county land commissioners, acting on behalf of the government of the newborn Republic of Texas. Not only did these emigrants receive headright grants, but soon most of the adult males among them were given bounty grants for service in the Texas revolution.[8]

The Texas of Bailey Hardeman and his fellow expatriates had been the first area outside the United States settled by large numbers of Americans, and the patterns of Manifest Destiny and conquest which unfolded there were to be substantially reenacted farther west. The fixing of the Sabine River as the southwestern boundary of the United States in the agreement of 1819 appeared to fence settlers from the United States outside of what many wishfully believed to be a legitimate part of the Louisiana Purchase. Doddering Spain's grip on her empire relaxed, and Texas became an outpost of youthful Mexico. Although this new nation twice rejected United States offers to buy Texas, she did accept American settlers. Through the efforts of Moses and Stephen Austin, then of numerous empresarios or colony promoters, thousands of farmers from the southern states and Missouri peopled eastern Texas. Grants of land to empresarios and common settlers were liberal, slavery was tacitly permitted, and in the early years little was asked in return save lip service to Mexico and the Catholic faith. But genuine harmony never existed between Mexican authorities and the Anglo settlers. The Texans chafed under the "alien" culture, control, and hazy land titles, and Mexico distrusted the haughtiness of the newcomers. In 1830 the inevitable crackdown began. American immigration was sharply curbed, importation of slaves was stopped, goods from the United States were taxed heavily, and to further salt the wounds, Mexican troops were sent in, giving spine to the new regulations. Then came President and General Antonio Lopez de Santa Anna with his centralized regime, replacing federalism and negating his own liberal promises of statehood. These brickbats were more than the spirited Texans could or would endure, and the seedlings of revolt quickly sprouted.

The cultural and institutional chasm, wide at the outset, grew steadily broader as each side interpreted the other's acts in the least favorable light. The assumption by many historians that Mexico magnified its problems by failing to recognize the clear loyalty which most Texans felt toward their newly adopted country is no doubt partly correct. However, in the long run it mattered little, for Texas was certain to break free eventually whether the reins of government were slack or tight.

On the eve of the armed uprising, the Hardeman platoon arrived in Texas. Judging from one opinion, Bailey must have been squarely in his element. A Santa Fe trading companion, Samuel McClure, sized him up in a letter to M. M. Marmaduke. "I have no doubt but our old Friend and fellow traveler Don Bayle Hardeman is a pretty good Moddle of the Citizens of that country [Texas]. I know he could breed a mutiny in any camp or Regiment."[9] But the mutiny was already bred when "Don Bayle" and his crew arrived. Had they come a few months earlier, they would have helped foment the revolution; a few months delay, and they might have been accused of playing the carpetbagger. Bailey and his nephews Monroe, William, and Dr. John Marr Hardeman promptly assessed the situation and joined the fight.

Mexico had a number of military posts in the eastern half of Texas— San Antonio, Goliad, Nacogdoches, and Anahuac (on Galveston Bay). San Antonio, although commercially outclassed by new, American-dominated centers such as Brazoria, Nacogdoches, San Felipe, and Matagorda, was still the Mexican military stronghold of Texas. And it was natural that the bastion of Bejar located there, decaying though it was, would be the hub of military planning and action in the impending struggle. The Fredonian Rebellion of 1826 and 1827 was a harbinger of the times ahead, but seizure of the military and customs post at Anahuac by William B. Travis in June 1835 turned up the heat to boiling temperature. Fearful of reprisals for this act, some of the settlers called a convention which moved toward the establishment of a provisional government, while professing loyalty to the federalist Mexican Constitution of 1824.

At about this time the first genuine battle of the revolution occurred. Colonel Domingo de Ugartechea, who commanded the Mexican soldiers at San Antonio, sent a force of about 150 men to Gonzales on the Guadalupe River to seize a small brass cannon. The six-pounder had been issued four years earlier for repelling Indian attacks on the colony of empresario Green DeWitt (who would soon become the father-in-law of Thomas J. Hardeman). As at Lexington and Concord, the colonists resisted this attempt to confiscate weapons. Messengers rode hard and minutemen rallied. "Yesterday we were but eighteen strong, today we are one hundred and fifty, and forces continually arriving."[10] Thomas Monroe Hardeman, twenty-one-year-old son of Thomas J., heard the call several days after arriving from Tennessee and joined the Texans in this brief encounter, fought on October 2, 1835. The leader of the Anglo-Texan force, Captain John Moore, ordered his men to fire, and after a brief exchange Captain Castañeda pulled the Mexican troops back to San Antonio; the very cannon he had come to seize had been used against him. The Texans had fired the first shot, and now the cry "To arms" went out. Settlers tucked their hunting rifles in the crooks of their arms and descended on the little hamlet of Gonzales by the hundreds.

Except for the Gonzales action, the first battle probably would have been fought beside the Colorado River rather than the Guadalupe. It was along the banks of the former that the Texans had planned a hostile reception for President Santa Anna's brother-in-law, General Martín Perfecto de Cós, who was pushing toward San Antonio from his landing at Matagorda. Inadvertently, the Gonzales gun served as a diversion, and the general was able to slip through to Bejar without a fight.

But Cós was not long neglected; the Texans at Gonzales, having repulsed the enemy and killed one of his troops with no loss to themselves, were seized with a feeling of euphoria. They hitched several longhorn steers to the cannon and marched on San Antonio, starting with 300 troops and gathering many more along the way. General Cós, instead of fighting in the open where his regulars might have acquitted themselves more ably, allowed his force to fall victim to siege and to a sniping, house-to-house attack. This type of encounter was ideally suited to the settlers and the large numbers of trouble seekers who had recently arrived from the southwestern American states. These latter reinforcements had heard about the war and scurried to join in.

Unhappily for the Texans, the Gonzales cannon carriage suffered a broken wheel, and the gun had to be abandoned. The artillery was now all on the side of General Cós. Bailey Hardeman had joined the Texas force as soon as he arrived, and now he and his nineteen-year-old nephew William P. Hardeman (brother of Monroe) accompanied by a few other men, set forth on what must have been familiar duty to the former War of 1812 artillery officer. He and his company hurried to Dimmitt's Landing near the mouth of Lavaca River to secure an eighteen-pound cannon, which had been delivered from Matagorda Pass by schooner, and proceeded to wheel the weapon to San Antonio. News of the approach of this artillery piece and the accompanying force of men (which had swelled to seventy-five, including twenty "Mobile Grays") reportedly reached General Cós and prompted his surrender on December 10, 1835.[11] He was permitted to take his 1105 soldiers back to Mexico, and thus, for the moment, Texas was cleared of Santa Anna's troops. As an additional byproduct of this action, young William Hardeman learned a few lessons in artillery handling which he would carry into another war a quarter-century later.

Meanwhile, political machinery was devised to keep pace with military developments, and Bailey Hardeman's name figured in numerous deliberations. On November 28, 1835, the General Council of the infant Provisional Government elected Bailey, along with Jefferson George and Hamilton Cook, as a commission to organize the militia of Matagorda Municipality.[12]

Texans were still divided over their ultimate goal—greater autonomy but with allegiance to the Constitution of 1824, or outright independence. The Provisional Governor, Henry Smith, and the General Council were all but helpless in offering direction, although as their last gasp the temporary officials called for a convention, the delegates to which were given plenary authority. This group would draw up both a declaration of independence and a constitution, and the election date was set for February 1, 1836. Sixty-two delegates were chosen, fifty-nine of whom were actual participants in the proceedings of the convention. Newcomer Bailey Hardeman and Samuel Rhoads Fisher were the delegates from Matagorda. Bailey was elected *in absentia* while on duty with the military. Upon learning of his selection, he hurried to Washington on the Brazos River and joined the delegation on March 1.[13]

Once organized, the convention considered a motion by former Nashville editor and lawyer George C. Childress of Milam to create the Declaration of Independence Drafting Committee. Even loyalist Stephen Austin had stated, in November 1835, that Texas would be jusified in asserting its independence, and there was no doubt about the sentiments of the delegates: the motion passed. Convention chairman Richard Ellis appointed Childress, Bailey Hardeman, Edward Conrad of Refugio, James Gaines of Sabina, and Collin McKinney of Red River to the committee.

The details of the proceedings of this committee apparently were not recorded. Childress, the chairman, presented the Declaration of Independence to the convention on March 2. Most historians have assumed that Childress wrote the document unassisted, as the Childress family legend attests. Statements made long after the convention by contemporaries support this. Assumptions at one stage of historical writing may be judged as facts at a later time, however. One author goes to interesting lengths to speculate on why each of the other four committee members would not have been capable of contributing materially to such an intellectual feat as paraphrasing the more famous Declaration of July 4, 1776. McKinney, Gaines, and Conrad were disposed of for lack of education. Bailey Hardeman perhaps offered more of a challenge because of his legal training. The writer states that Bailey "had been out of touch with affairs of state while with the military," but this was mild speculation compared to the conclusion that he "may be considered as not having been endowed with the initiative required to prosecute such an effort."[14]

As to whether or not the forty-one-year-old frontiersman lacked initiative as alleged, his record in Tennessee, Louisiana, Missouri, New Mexico, and Texas must be left to speak for itself. His nephew Peter Burnett recorded that Bailey was a well-educated man of fine mental capacity. A fellow delegate at Washington, James Power, stated that he had a good intellect, though not brilliant, and that "although he made no effort to push himself to the front during the deliberations of the Convention, nevertheless, his talents and worth were soon recognized."[15] The small number of his writings that have been preserved leave no doubt that he was literate. Unfortunately for his chances to prove his ability in Texas matters, however, Bailey died soon after the convention. Edward Conrad was so vocal and tenacious in later debate on the constitution that it would be unwise to assign to him a rubber-stamp role in any proceeding. The fact that the declaration had to be referred back to committee to correct the many errors indicates that it was hastily framed, rather than drawn up in advance by such an experienced editor as George Childress,[16] and was, in short, not a great credit to the committee.

In view of the lack of evidence, all that can be said with certainty is that the document was prepared by the committee and was the property of the entire committee when chairman Childress presented it to the convention. Soon it would be the property of the Republic of Texas. Whatever the truth may be as to credits, these two Tennessee cousins, Childress and Hardeman (related through the Perkins family), made trenchant pleas for its adoption. After the presentation by the chairman, Bailey Hardeman—his hair worn in the French republican fashion, his boyish face belying the miles and years of exposure to wind and sun—delivered a typically brief supporting statement which reportedly "caused great enthusiasm among the delegates."[17]

The declaration was signed with the zeal of a John Hancock, and the delegates turned to the next order of business, the framing of a constitution. Bailey Hardeman moved that "all subjects not directly connected with the constitution of this republic lay on the table until that instrument be adopted by this convention." The motion was passed after a brief delay, having been amended to permit setting aside constitutional consideration only by a two-thirds vote of the delegates.[18] On March 2, three members of the Declaration of Independence committee were appointed to the twenty-one-member committee charged with drawing up a constitution for the republic. They were Gaines, McKinney, and Bailey Hardeman. Like his father, Bailey not only played a military role in the birth of a new nation; he had a hand also in the deliberations involving its new constitution. Washington on the Brazos was no copy of Hillsboro or of Knoxville, but there was a recurrent theme of interest and participation in affairs of state.

The constitution committee reported out a working draft on March 9, 1836. After considerable debate and revision, particularly regarding land grant policy, the document was approved on March 16 or 17. Not all the delegates were on hand for the vote, some having left fearing the approach of Santa Anna's army. Bailey Hardeman asked to be allowed to return at once to the army, but he was persuaded to stay until the convention had completed its work.

The chief business remaining before the convention was the creating of a provisional government and the choice of a military commander. Delegate James Power observed that Hardeman's reputation for loyalty to the colonists' cause was well known.[19] His record of service on the Declaration of Independence, Constitution, tariff payment, and militia committees had earmarked Bailey for something other than return to the battlefields, and the convention designated him as secretary of the treasury of the provisional government. Because of the absence of Samuel P. Carson, secretary of state, Hardeman also served for a time in that capacity. On April 1 he signed one document twice, as secretary of state and as secretary of the treasury of the Republic. The other governing officials were Bailey's cousin, David Burnet, President; Lorenzo de Zavala, Vice President; Thomas J. Rusk, Secretary of War; Robert Potter, Secretary of the Navy; and David Thomas, Attorney General. Sam Houston was named commander in chief of the Texas armed forces, and the newly organized republic braced for its most severe test.

The convention business was concluded none too soon, as the Texans were in immediate peril on the military front. General Santa Anna had arrived with a large force bent on avenging the seizure of San Antonio and bringing the rebels to heel. Even as the convention deliberated weighty matters at Washington on the Brazos, the Mexican chieftain was sending wave upon wave of his troops against the beleaguered men under William Travis and James Bowie at the Alamo. Travis dispatched several "victory or death" messages, pledging that they would never surrender and appealing for reinforcements. One group of thirty-two Texans, led by Albert Martin and George Kimball, reached the Alamo on March 1. The fortress was overwhelmed on the morning of March 6, 1836, and its defenders were massacred.

Several relief parties were on the way when the end came at the Alamo. Commander Sam Houston was assembling one of these, and he ordered James W. Fannin to close in also. Their plans were abandoned on March 11 when news of the capture of the Alamo was confirmed. Earlier, the nineteen-year-old volunteer William P. Hardeman joined a group of about twenty men and rode hard to reach the Alamo in answer to Travis's call. They were not so fortunate as Houston had been. According to Hardeman's long-time friend, General Alexander W. Terrell, this little group, in an attempt to enter the Alamo the night before the fall of its defenders, rode their exhausted horses among the Mexican pickets but were unable to break through the ring of soldiers around the building. The volunteers wheeled their mounts about and escaped, but the horses were so weakened by the forced pace to San Antonio that they had to be abandoned. The men retreated on foot along the Guadalupe River, suffering severely from lack of food.[20]

Upon his return from this abortive campaign, William Hardeman was sent on another errand by his uncle Bailey to raise more militiamen. Illness from exhaustion and exposure on these combined missions (on one occasion he swam the San Bernard River and slept wet and uncovered that night on the prairie) prevented him from joining his brother Monroe in the Battle of San Jacinto.[21]

Santa Anna held the Alamo, but March 6 was a Pyrrhic victory of classic dimensions. More than 1,500 of his own men lay dead, the price of storming the old mission building and killing 187 defenders of Texas soil. Two precious weeks were lost, and the frightened but infuriated Texans were united as never before. The slaughter of about 370 prisoners by Mexican armed forces at Goliad on March 27 further firmed up the Texans' resolves, if such was possible. Like the Israelites in Pharaoh's land, they seemed to gain strength and numbers from every act of mistreatment. Santa Anna selected one thousand of his best troops and picked up others en route as he pursued the settlers eastward.

The officials of the provisional government were prepared to leave Texas if Santa Anna should succeed in overrunning it and overwhelming Houston's army. According to legend, Bailey Hardeman and President David

Burnet took the diminutive archives of the Republic and fled on horseback only a jump ahead of the pursuing Mexican troops; the "Ark of the Covenant" was salvaged in their saddlebags. At Harrisburg, they narrowly escaped capture by fleeing to Morgan's Point on Galveston Bay. They found a small boat and shoved off just in time as enemy bullets skipped across the water toward them. A number of the government party, including Bailey and Rebecca Hardeman and their two sons, Sam and John, boarded the privateer *Flash* on April 22 or 23, 1836, and were taken by Captain Luke A. Flavel to Galveston Island, preparatory to a voyage to New Orleans if necessary. (This was one of several instances when control of the coast by the small Texas naval forces was significant to the outcome of the conflict.) Then came word of a military encounter on the plains at San Jacinto, and Bailey left the island on the steamer *Laura* to provide supplies and aid for the victorious Texas soldiers.[22]

While the tiny Texas government had been fleeing for its life, Houston and his motley aggregation faded before Santa Anna's pursuit. The "Raven" Sam fell back, recruited, drilled, and fell back again until not much of Texas lay to his rear. At San Jacinto River, the retreat was over. On April 21, he sent his 700 men in a surprise charge against a force now nearly twice as large and gained a triumph as decisive as Jackson's at New Orleans; more than 600 Mexican soldiers were killed, 208 wounded, and 730 captured, against 9 dead and 33 wounded among the Texans. Santa Anna himself was taken prisoner, and the war was effectively over. Lean-faced Monroe Hardeman fought in this fifteen- to twenty-minute battle.[23] His participation was a seemingly fitting sequel to the family's role in several of the most one-sided battles in the history of the continent—his grandfather at King's Mountain, his father at New Orleans, and now Monroe at San Jacinto. It must have been a source of frustration to his brother William Hardeman that sickness kept him out of the San Jacinto encounter; he would be an inveterate warrior in scores of battles over a thirty-year span.

The curtain having fallen on Santa Anna's acts of war in Texas, sword yielded to pen as negotiations began, and Bailey Hardeman now found himself in the position of a diplomat. Santa Anna's bargaining position was weak; he knew that most Texans itched to dismember him personally. Yet a lynching or a firing-squad execution would have discredited the

Texas Republic, and the Mexican general might be diplomatically useful. So he was threatened but kept alive, and on May 14, 1836, at Velasco, he signed two treaties with Texas, one open and one secret. The first would end the war honorably for Texas and remove Mexican soldiers across the Rio Grande. By the second agreement, Santa Anna promised to support Texan independence, diplomatic recognition of the Republic, a satisfactory commercial treaty between the two nations, and recognition of the Rio Grande as the international boundary. Bailey Hardeman, acting secretary of state, was one of the negotiators and signatories of these two treaties with the general.

The diplomatic maneuvers were only beginning for the Texas leaders. Apprehensive lest Mexico disavow the Velasco agreements, they decided to send negotiators to Mexico City with Santa Anna so that, with his assistance, they might secure ratification at the other end of the line. It had been agreed at Velasco that the Mexican general would be sent promptly to Vera Cruz and that he would then work for recognition of Texas' independence. Two officials from the Republic, Bailey Hardeman and Lorenzo de Zavala, were commissioned and readied for this assignment in Mexico.[24] The three men were scheduled to sail for Vera Cruz about June 1, 1836, aboard the schooner *Invincible* (which had been purchased in the United States), but a sharp dispute raged as to whether or not Santa Anna should be allowed to get away. Burnet had the ship held in port several extra days to provide time for full instructions to Hardeman and Zavala. Meanwhile, a force led by Thomas Jefferson Green arrived, removed the Mexican leader from the ship, and placed him under guard. Santa Anna was held for several months before being taken to Washington, D.C.

Bailey was thus deprived of, or perhaps spared, another important assignment. Since Mexico promptly repudiated the Velasco agreements, and Santa Anna had no intentions of keeping the promises he made under duress, the Hardeman-Zavala mission would have been doomed to failure before it started.

Of Bailey Hardeman's place in the affairs of Texas after this abortive assignment in diplomacy, little has been found. He must have had a minimum of work as treasurer, since Texas had a debt of $1,250,000 before the end of summer 1836, and the treasury notes were inflated to a nearly valueless level. He could have as well left his post and gone to

Mexico City to negotiate a treaty. President Burnet called for a regular election (to be held in early September), which would designate officers to replace the provisional government. Sam Houston, presidential candidate, scored almost as lopsided a victory at the polls as he had won at San Jacinto. The constitution and the proposal for annexation by the United States were overwhelmingly endorsed by the voters, and Houston assumed the duties of president some weeks before the October date when the provisional government was to yield the reins. At most, Bailey could have served only a few days in the new Houston administration. The veteran of the Santa Fe trade died of congestive fever at his home on Caney Creek, September 25, 1836, one year after he arrived in Texas.[25]

The year had been a busy one for Bailey Hardeman. Nearly half of it was spent in the militia; then came the rise to political prominence. It was as if he had battled the currents to help spawn the Republic and died of exhaustion from the task. It had been a life of crowded years, packed with thousands of miles of frontier adventure. His career was cut short at a time when he showed some promise as a leader in the Lone Star Republic.

8   On the Frontiers of the Texas Republic

WINNING INDEPENDENCE had been a matter of only a few months' struggle; but keeping it intact would be a drawn-out and costly process. The United States vacillated for nine years over the annexation matter, unable to harmonize its domestic and foreign problems with the acquisition of Texas. Northern spokesmen opposed to slavery expansion and Easterners suspicious of increasing western political power added their weight to the views of those who shied away from the probable complicating of relations with Mexico and England. The Texans, meanwhile, anxious to join the United States but unwilling to yield to Mexican or Indian forces on their borders, fought for the young life of the Republic.

There were other descendants of Thomas Hardeman to take up where the fallen Bailey had left off his work for Texas. To a less prominent degree, Bailey's brother Thomas Jones Hardeman of Matagorda picked up the political torch, extending the civic role which he had developed in Hardeman County, Tennessee. He was elected to serve in the Second and

Third congresses of Texas from 1837 to 1839, and it was his suggestion and motion which resulted in the choice of the name Austin for the capital.[1] (Bailey too had been an Austin booster, urging the colonizer to run for president of the Republic.) In the mid-1840s Thomas was elected associate justice and chief justice of Bastrop County, and between 1847 and 1851 he served in the House of Representatives for the new State of Texas, representing first Bastrop and later Travis County. During the early 1850s he was president of the Colorado Navigation Company, an organization commissioned by the state legislature to open navigation from Galveston inland along the Colorado River (of Texas). The principal obstacle was the "raft," which consisted of miles of floating debris extending upstream from the mouth of the river.[2]

Two years after he reached Texas, Thomas Jones Hardeman married Eliza DeWitt Hamilton, daughter of empresario Green DeWitt. Hardeman died on January 15, 1854, at the age of seventy-four. His four sons by his first marriage, Monroe, William, Owen, and Leonidas, would one day carry the military banner to other frontier battlefields in the tradition of their father at New Orleans.

Monroe and William, the oldest sons, were particularly restless types who bore the stamp of both father and grandfather. They had arrived just in time to lend their youthful hands to the task of manufacturing the Texas republic on the battlefield—these two hard-tempered models from the Tennessee forge. Monroe had graduated from the University of Nashville before shipping off to Texas[3] and had fought at Gonzales and San Jacinto; William had missed the Alamo carnage by the whisker of a Mexican picket. Thomas Monroe was named for his grandfather and for the fifth president of the United States (who held office at the time of his birth). William Polk's middle name came from his mother's family, which produced the man who would soon become the eleventh president.

William, also a former University of Nashville student, drew the nickname "Gotch," reportedly from his habit of canting his head to one side when he talked. The tag clung for life. Whatever the label, in the course of his more than fifty military battles and numerous wounds he emerged as a military leader who was either able or lucky, or both. He usually won, and when he lost, it was in the face of overwhelming odds—odds from which he was always able to extricate himself and his men, often in daring escape. William Hardeman did not exactly fit the pattern set by his progenitors. He had caught the communicable family fascination with the frontier—caught it well, for life—and he wore it with a difference. Many of the Hardemans *traveled,* but William *wandered.* If their aim was to *use* the frontier, his aim *was* the frontier. He was Leacock's knight, donning his armor and riding off in all directions. A veritable Daniel, he was invariably spared in the lairs of Comanche, Mexican, and Unionist lions. Perhaps his drift toward adventure was a natural byproduct of revolution, border clash, and war—both internecine and international—nurtured by later sectional strife and civil war and blended with the family trait of restlessness.

Yet with all his preference for thorny situations and less than comfortable surroundings, William Hardeman was pictured by his military associates as loyal, kindly, cultured, even gentle, conciliatory in disposition, and deliberate in forming opinions. He wept for his fallen soldiers; he defied official military orders, risking loss of his commission by sending home on furlough men who had fought their hearts out and were too battle-weary to continue. On occasion he was seen to pause in battle and hold his canteen to the lips of a wounded enemy soldier who begged for water. "I never knew a more steadfast friend," wrote a fellow officer.[4]

If he counted his own most dependable friends at any given time, William surely must have ranked his horse high among them. As a ranger and cavalryman, he knew the value of a fine and fast mount. His steed was to save him on more than a few occasions. And he was well tailored for life in the saddle—six feet tall, ramrod straight, and 140 pounds, no great burden for a good horse. Wiry? Yes, if the analogy is to barbed wire! He had a long, lean face and auburn hair, and during his middle and later years he wore a moustache and beard.

In the 1830s, however, William Hardeman was a slender mast like his brother Monroe, almost frail in appearance, but eager to test his fiber against the blasting of Texas gales. And younger brother Owen Bailey Hardeman, born in Tennessee about 1818 and named for two uncles who had been in the Santa Fe trade, was nearly as venturesome. None of the three was of a mind to settle into the furrow to enjoy the bounty grants earned for service in the revolution or the landed legacies from their parents. Their work was stretched out for them on the vast Indian-inhabited plains of the frontier—beyond the Balcones Escarpment, over the treeless Grand Prairie and Edwards Plateau and the Staked Plains, south and west to the Rio Grande, among clusters of mesquite and prickly pear and herds of wild longhorned cattle, and up the crooked stream beds where occasional timber sentinels stood. How little this new homeland resembled the sylvan expanses of their birth and youth back in Tennessee!

For years a dual problem played havoc with this border region and often threatened the very existence of the settlements in eastern Texas. The battle with the Comanche was only warming up, while the raid-and-run encounter with angry Mexico was far from finished. Sometimes these two war fronts seemed to merge. Indeed, part of the reason that Mexico had accepted colonists from the United States was the hope of building a raid-proof human buffer between its northern provincial centers and the mounted scourge that was the Comanche and Kiowa. Like British officers in Canada several decades earlier, Mexican leaders were suspected of buying settlers' scalps.

Nowhere in Anglo-America were the wars between Indian and white more bloody, more rapacious, more fraught with hatred and cruelty than in Texas. Both Texan and Comanche were culture-conditioned to strong feeling and brutal action. If circumstances did not, in some form of Gresham's Law, drive out all but the bad, they banished all but the bold. The Texans had learned to hate the Indians in Tennessee and Kentucky; the Comanches detested the Euro-American foes from contact which dated back several centuries. Both transferred their hatreds readily when they met west of the Sabine. It was obvious from the first contact that no quarter would be given by either side, and equally certain that, despite the protestations and peace efforts by Indiophile and Cherokee tribe member Sam Houston, there was scant possibility that the two groups could coexist peacefully along a common border. By the mid-1830s, settlers were moving up the Colorado and the Brazos into Comanche country. White encroachment on Indian lands, the time-honored genesis of conflict between the two races, was part, but only part of the problem. The Comanches were marauders by tradition, and they had long raided, kidnaped, tortured, and raped their neighbors, dark or white; Texans were no exception.

Mirabeau Buonaparte Lamar, who succeeded his arch rival Houston in the president's chair, launched an aggressive policy against both the Indians and Mexico, a policy which, despite his early popularity, was to be his undoing after the failure of raids into Mexico. The expensive anti-Comanche program was the more successful of the two, although frontier defense problems persisted for decades. Eastern woodland methods of warding off Indian attacks or retaliating were useless against the Comanches, who were reputed to have been among the world's finest light cavalry. Like Genghis Khan, they struck with incredible swiftness and surprise on fast ponies. At first Texans lacked the horses, the horsemanship, and the weapons to fight these Indians effectively. The long-barreled rifle, which had been meal ticket and life insurance to the Hardemans, was too cumbersome to use with dispatch while riding at full speed, and it was too slow to reload. Not until the late 1830s and after were the Texans able to match and surpass the weaponry of the Comanches. The Colt six-shooter and the later Walker-Colt could be fired accurately enough at close range while riding at top speed, and the tide began to turn. Even so, after a typical Comanche raid it was too late to assemble an Indian-hunting party and go in pursuit. The Anglo-Texans could not sustain a permanent guard in all areas to fend off the thrusts.

They fell back on an old institution, used in New York and Tennessee, and organized the famous Texas Rangers. Young, tough, devil-may-care volunteers—like Jack Hayes, Ben McCulloch, or the brothers Monroe and Owen and William Hardeman, who knew the ways of the Indians and could ride and shoot—were paid (when money was available) to roam the frontier, warn of approaching raiders and, when the opportunity presented itself, carry the war home to Comanche camps. In these years they were light cavalry, not like the later peace officers.

The three Hardeman brothers were among this border breed of rangers in the embryonic stage of that legendary institution. Perhaps they were bent on revenge against the Comanches for the death of their uncle Glen Owen a decade earlier. They took part in numerous actions. For four months during 1837, William and Owen Hardeman accompanied Erastus "Deaf" Smith of Natchez on frontier ranger duty.[5]

About a year and a half later, Colonel John H. Moore, Texas leader in the opening battle of the revolution, assembled a force of more than sixty rangers and a small cadre of Lipan Apache Indians (who had some old scores of their own to settle with the Comanches), and moved northwestward up the Colorado River to the domain of the Penateka Comanches. William Hardeman, now twenty-three years old, joined this force.[6] The Apache scouts, covering the plains like bird dogs ahead of the hunter, reported a Comanche camp on Wallace's Creek, a tributary of the San Saba River. On February 22, 1839, Moore and his men concealed their horses, stealthily approached the encampment on foot, caught the Comanches by surprise, and inflicted heavy casualties. However, more than forty of the Texans' horses were used by Indians to escape, and some rangers had to return on foot to the settlements.

William probably remained on the frontier between this battle and the Córdova clash. Underlying the frequent hostilities along the Comanche front from San Antonio through the new capital at Austin to Belton was the fact that Mexico had been trying to create an Indian confederation to help them drive the settlers from Texas. For several years Vicente Córdova had attempted to persuade Chief Bowles and the recently transplanted Cherokees in the eastern part of the republic to adopt this plan. The bait consisted of secure land titles for the Cherokees and a relatively Texan-free Texas. It was attractive, to be sure, but the Indians were in a tight spot. They were civilized, settled farmers; the response to Córdova was spotty and unenthusiastic. In April 1839, two months after the frolic at Wallace's Creek, William and Owen Hardeman participated in an attack led by Edward Burleson against the Córdova forces, many members of which were captured.[7] Córdova himself escaped to Mexico. Subsequently, after the seizure of Mexican-Indian "conspiracy" documents and supplies, President Lamar and Secretary of War Albert Sidney Johnston had their excuse to move against the Cherokees, who, along with most other tribes in east Texas, were ruthlessly cleared from the young republic.

The scene of conflict shifted quickly back to the Comanches. Mutual harassment picked up tempo after the Council House battle at San Antonio on March 19, 1840. A dozen chiefs headed a party of more than sixty Comanches (including women and children) who came to negotiate the sale of a number of white prisoners then in Comanche hands. When fighting broke out after talk bogged down, more than half the Indians were killed and the remainder captured. Led by Chief Buffalo Hump the infuriated Comanche nation struck back, first by harrying the settled

William P. Hardeman served with the Texas Rangers from 1837 through the
Mexican War defending the frontier against Comanche and Mexican adversaries.
Reproduction of "Texas Rangers" by Frederic Remington, Harper's Monthly, *1896.*

fringe, then with a massive summer thrust by hundreds of warriors. Smashing the frontier line between Austin and San Antonio, they killed or drove out settlers, seized several thousand horses, and scorched the earth in a path which carried to the Gulf of Mexico. In this prototype of Sherman's march, they took Victoria and completely sacked Linville, gathering in a haul of booty from the store and warehouse of the latter town on Lavaca Bay. The Council House losses thus avenged, Buffalo Hump turned his force from smoldering Linville back toward the high plains and home, having scored what ranks among the great victories in the annals of American frontier warfare.

But the latter-day Paul Reveres were riding hard day and night to every hamlet and hacienda. Before the war party could herd its valuable horses and loot-laden pack mules to safety, Texas forces converged at Plum Creek, near the present site of Lockhart, and awaited the arrival of the Indians, who were being closely watched by Tonkawa Indian scouts. General Felix Huston arrived on August 11 and took charge of the entire Texas force. Some well-known frontiersmen commanded various units —Colonel Moore; Captains Wallace, Jones, and Caldwell; and Major Monroe Hardeman. The latter's brother William was also on hand for this battle, and soon they were joined by Owen Hardeman, who had ridden to tell the early arrivals at Plum Creek that strong reinforcements under Burleson would soon join them.[8] Few battles of the frontier could have been more colorful than this one. The Indians and their horses were bedecked with brightly colored ribbons and cloth, umbrellas, a stovepipe hat, and various other items of booty from Linville, in addition to the usual Comanche regalia. Chief Placido and his twelve Tonkawa scouts wore white armbands to avoid being mistaken and shot for Comanches. Unwilling to abandon their plunder and fight in traditional fashion, the Comanches were without maneuverability or an effective battle plan. While the main Texas force attacked from the front and sides, Monroe Hardeman, assisted by Jones and Wallace, led 100 men against the enemy's rear. The horses and mules were scattered and the Comanches put to flight. More than eighty Indians died in the initial melee and twelve- to fifteen-mile running fight, and a number of the women and children were captured. Two thousand horses and mules and much of the booty were retaken. Monroe Hardeman chased one of the warriors who fled on foot.

The Comanche turned and shot arrows as he ran, and Monroe was narrowly missed by a bolt which drove eight inches into his horse. Burleson was hit by an arrow from the same warrior, who was finally killed by John Jenkins. Only one Texan died at Plum Creek.[9]

The rout at Plum Creek was a turning point in the frontier warfare against the Indians. No more big Comanche war parties attacked the settlers, although small raiding bands continued their guerilla tactics for years. Two months after Plum Creek, Moore and his rangers (probably including one or more of the Hardeman brothers) conducted a highly successful raid deep into Comanche territory. Lamar's Indian policy, although costly, had been worthwhile from the Texas viewpoint, opening vast areas of land to safer settlement.

Scarcely had the big battles with the southern Comanches died down when border scuffles with Mexico flared. As in the struggle with the Indians, both Texas and its enemies played the aggressor's role. There had been a prelude in early 1837 when "Deaf" Smith, assisted by Owen Bailey Hardeman and twenty other Texans, had made an abortive attempt to expand the territory of the republic by attacking Laredo.[10] President Houston publicly condemned this escapade, and as it turned out Texas was fortunate that Mexico was too busy with both domestic and foreign problems to respond. Now President Lamar, flush with his successes against the Indians, launched an ill-fated campaign against the former mother country. After failing to secure Mexican recognition of Texas' independence, he ordered a force to Santa Fe in June of 1841 on the mistaken belief that New Mexico was ripe for trade with and annexation by Texas. It was a disaster on all counts, and Mexico retaliated with a threat to reconquer Texas.

The first of the *reconquista* expeditions was led by General Rafael Vásquez. This force of 700 Mexicans crossed the Rio Grande in February 1842 and captured San Antonio the following month. A group of militiamen, including William, Monroe, and Owen Hardeman,[11] harassed this army, but the Mexicans were too much for Texas to cope with, particularly in the face of the economy-minded administration of the recently reelected Sam Houston. Vásquez returned to Mexico laden with goods captured at San Antonio. In quick succession, Mexico followed with two more rapier thrusts: Corpus Christi was attacked in July, and General

Adrian Woll took San Antonio with his force of 1,200 men in September. The young republic was panic-swept all the way to the Sabine. Many settlers fled eastward from their homes, and others planned to follow. There were strong public feelings that Mexico should be attacked. Houston at last felt that he must choose between reduced taxes and a reduced Texas.

Three expeditionary forces were quickly assembled and hurled at various targets in Mexico's north border region, retaliating against retaliation. If there was a chance of success for any of the three, it was hamstrung from the outset by the freebooting nature of many of the men who signed on. Two of these expeditions, raids against Santa Fe trade, were dismal failures. The other force was led by Alexander Somervell, a veteran of San Jacinto and a former secretary of war for the republic. In November 1842 his 700 men left San Antonio for the Rio Grande. William and Monroe Hardeman, who seem to have been striving for the distinction of "most battles joined for the republic," moved south with Somervell.[12] The motley aggregation easily captured the towns of Laredo and Guerrero on the Rio Grande. Many of Somervell's men turned to looting and rape, and some 200 deserted when he tried to recover and return the pilfered property. Somervell, disgusted with this vandalism and fearing a strong Mexican force nearby, then declared the expedition ended and returned to Texas. But nearly half of the men defied him and assaulted the town of Mier, a short distance south of the Rio Grande. Apparently William and Monroe returned to Texas with their commander. The Mier attackers were captured, subjected to a death march, and finally whittled down by 10 percent in the famous Black Bean Massacre. More died of privations than execution, although some lived to seek savage revenge during the Mexican War. And to them, Mier was an Alamo, a Goliad crying for another round of retaliation.

Mexican soldiery could now invade southwest Texas almost at will; two-front warfare was taking its toll. The hour was a dark one when, in 1845, annexation by the United States made of the Mexican-Texas border fury a Mexican-United States problem. "Required to bring no dowry of land and chattels, Texas gave Uncle Sam two large and fierce frontiers, one occupied by a miscellaneous collection of Indians, and the other by several million irate Mexicans."[13] Mexico promptly broke diplomatic relations with the United States.

Notwithstanding a diplomatic overcast, 1846 dawned calm. True, the *National Gazette, Niles Register,* and other pulp observation posts in the United States pondered the prospects of war with Mexico and Britain; a large cluster of immigrants gathered for the now annual pilgrimage to disputed Oregon; and certain politicians were hoping to give John L. O'Sullivan's newly launched "Manifest Destiny" a daring trial run. Matthew Fontaine Maury, the hemisphere's most renowned living scientist, was pioneering in oceanography and discovering the "mitosis" of Biela's comet. He would one day join "Gotch" Hardeman in exile.

William Hardeman, meanwhile, was unknowingly on the verge of joining new battles against old enemies. Annexation had not resolved the Texas-Mexican conflict. It was the same explosive cargo carried in a new vehicle as Mexico and the United States glowered at each other across the disputed zone. Chauvinism on both sides and the implacable President Polk's brand of manifest destiny—which demanded the acquisition of California by purchase if possible, by force if necessary—soon brought the two nations into formal combat, albeit with much indecision in both camps. The Texans had their long-sought support.

When General Zachary Taylor moved south across the Rio Grande, he led an army composed of cumbersome dragoons, mounted infantrymen who, though not greenhorns in the saddle, were poorly trained and equipped for the kind of war or the type of terrain which faced them. If the *prospect* of expansion made a president of Polk, the *practice* of expansion molded another chief executive out of Taylor. Because of a comic-opera prelude to his invasion of Mexico—a condition only partly of his own making—Taylor might not have been thus honored but for the spying and light cavalry services of the battle-thirsty Texas Rangers. The rotund Taylor asked for four Texas regiments and got three. One of these was a spirited cavalry outfit under the command of Jack Hayes, with Sam Walker, Big Foot Wallace, John Ford, and Ben McCulloch in subordinate commissioned roles. Rarely in history has a group been so exactly suited to its task by temperament, experience, and motivation as was this ranger contingent.

Ben McCulloch's Guadalupe Valley group has been acclaimed the best ranger aggregation ever brought together under one command. It was destined to play what may well have been a decisive role in Taylor's successful campaigns. William Hardeman, cousin of the Polk in the White House, joined up as a private under his fellow Tennessean McCulloch of the steel blue eyes.[14] Perhaps it was fitting that the two were associates in many engagements; their fathers had served in the same unit during the War of 1812. Owen, Leonidas, and John Marr Hardeman also volunteered and fought in the Mexican War.[15] Gotch Hardeman crossed the Rio Grande as an invader, little suspecting that his next southbound crossing would be in search of protection in Mexico. McCulloch's outfit was assigned by Taylor to scout and select a route for the drive from Matamoros to the inland city of Monterrey. The ranger leader and his picked men searched out the way under considerable hardships and led the march after returning to Taylor's camp. They served both as feelers and lightning lead punch. Some of them, McCulloch and Hardeman included, had been on the Somervell expedition and perhaps knew something about the terrain immediately to the south of the border, but the country beyond was hard and unknown, and every inch was enemy soil.

The men of McCulloch first ferreted the Linares route to Monterrey. Ten days and 250 dusty miles they spent in the saddle—from Matamoros southwestward and back to Reynosa on the Rio Grande—with scanty equipment and slim rations which made Taylor's troops wince in admiration. Boots and spurs were never removed during this daring probe. With the speed and whoop of Comanches they descended on ranchos, towns, and haciendas, on one occasion putting an outlaw band to flight, and often circling and swooping in from the south to veil their direction of movement. A detour failed to turn up outlaw General Canales, the "Chaparral Fox" who had left a bloody trail on the Texas border. "Unacceptable" was the rangers' verdict on the Linares approach. A better corridor must be found for the General's cumbersome columns.[16]

The China route to Monterrey was now explored by McCulloch's rangers. This time they paused to sniff the cold trail of a turncoat, Colonel Juan N. Seguin, formerly a Texas patriot, who had defected to Mexico in 1842. After capturing the town of China and holding it for a brief reign of

Dr. John Marr Hardeman (1804–1891) forsook his medical bag for the saddle bags of the Texas Ranger and Mexican War soldier. *Courtesy Viola Hardeman Kraemer.*

terror, the rangers back-trailed to tell Taylor that this was not a satisfactory road to Monterrey.

Success crowned the third scouting foray of William Hardeman's ranger outfit. McCulloch remained behind because of illness, but his group sleuthed southward from Mier along the San Juan River toward Monterrey in mid-August 1846. "The eyes and ears" of Zach Taylor's army came back to report not only that the route was feasible, but that the rangers had captured and were holding Cerralvo. With this anchor point ahead, the General snaked his army out in a seventy-mile column from Camargo toward Monterrey. McCulloch's crew scouted and spied ahead of the column, serving as the cutting edge when the enemy was within reach. On September 14, 1846, the company of thirty-five rangers, back under the command of the now-recovered McCulloch, came upon an estimated 200 Mexican soldiers at the town of Ramos and put them to flight with battle cry and charge. On the following day, Taylor's 6,000-man army arrived at Monterrey. As the opposing forces eyed each other, the taunting Texans performed feats of riding under the guns of the emplaced opponents. "Their proximity occasionally provoked the enemy's fire but the Mexicans might as well have attempted to bring down skimming swallows as those racing daredevils."[17] Taylor soon ordered a stop to this sport. There was more serious business at hand.

Mexican General Pedro de Ampudia's defenders were well positioned on the northeastern approach to Monterrey, and Taylor sent General William Worth and Jack Hayes's Texans, with McCulloch's rangers in the lead, on a wide sweep around the city of 15,000 inhabitants. The plan was to amputate the supply and retreat line to Saltillo and attack from the rear (the west-southwest side). Near the Saltillo road beside Independence Hill, the party stopped for the night on September 20. A Texan was sent through the darkness with a message asking Taylor to launch a diversionary attack the next day.

Early on the following morning the ranger force rounded a hill by San Jeronimo hacienda and came face to face with a well-equipped and uniformed group of mounted Mexican lancers under the command of black-moustached Lieutenant-Colonel Juan Najera. Worth gave the order to dismount, but McCulloch's men, leading the force, failed to get the message and charged, throwing Najera's lancers into some confusion. The dismounted Texans, easily able to distinguish bright uniforms from the tattered garb of McCulloch, Hardeman, and the other mounted rangers, poured a heavy fire from the fringe. Najera and about one hundred of his men died in that very brief encounter and others fled to the Saltillo road. The path to the underbelly of the city's defenses was open.

Monterrey, lying peacefully in the bend of the Santa Catarina River, was about to flame into battle. On its west, two limestone heights, Independence Hill and Federation Hill, guarded the town with their heavy fortifications. The fatal flaw in this defense was the minimum armament on the very steep west faces of these abrupt uplifts—faces which rose hundreds of feet above the river bottom. Ampudia, thinking like Montcalm at Quebec eighty-seven years earlier, concluded that no enemy would scale such inclines. The Robert Wolfe of this encounter was William Worth. He had not a day to lose. With four days' rations, eight miles between his army and Taylor's main force, reinforcements moving out to meet him, an enemy well entrenched above, and unknown forces to the south, the situation was to say the least hazardous. Worth sent a detachment to choke off possible enemy columns from Saltillo. Booming guns to the east told that Taylor's diversion had begun. If William Hardeman had volunteered in hopes of going where the action was, he could scarcely have been disappointed. Worth's men stormed Federation, the rangers being the first to reach the top. A Mexican cannon was taken and turned on its former possessors, who were soon driven from the fortification. The regulars held the position while the rangers were withdrawn to lead next morning's assault on Independence Hill across the river to the north.

That evening, as opposing forces exchanged fire between the hilltops, an eerie symphony sounded. A heavy storm broke shortly after dark; there were flickers of gunfire and flashes of lightning. Booming cannon and crashing thunder echoed each other and reverberated from ridge to ridge. Smoke and clouds blended; rain and shot pelted down. Darkness quieted the guns, but the night was wet and short for the rangers, who were to start the ascent of Independence Hill at three o'clock the next morning.

In the summer of 1866, Generals William Hardeman and Hamilton Bee reminisced over their hard-fought victory at Independence Hill and took their fellow expatriates over the battlegrounds. General Alexander

Terrell marveled at the feat of scaling the bold escarpment into the very muzzles of enemy sniper's guns twenty years before.[18] The steep ascent had begun as planned at the appointed pre-dawn hour, but the footing was slippery from the night's rain. Daybreak caught the two columns of rangers only halfway up the 1,000-foot incline. Rifles above them spoke the message that they had been seen. The prospect was worse than gloomy; fresh soldiers on the heights above them were ready to gun down the weary toilers of the scarp.

Some Texan leader must have panted forth a command like "hold fire" and "whites of their eyes," for all the shooting was from above. The rangers were spared by a seeming miracle. Volley after volley was fired with no visible effect. The Mexicans consistently overshot. Heavy powder charges were later given as the explanation for this poor marksmanship. Gravity was probably more to blame. Bullets fired downward at a steep angle have a flat trajectory, and the defenders were, in their surprised excitement, allowing for drop as they would in level shooting. Since they had not considered an attack up the incline possible, no cannon were positioned to cover this approach.

The rangers, seemingly impervious to a hail of bullets, fired not a shot until they were only about twenty yards from the rim. Suddenly they opened fire, gave their famous battle cry, and charged. The encounter was very brief; Ampudia's men retired to the Bishop's Palace, a monastery turned fortress located on the northeastern end of Independence. Too exhausted to give chase, the rangers captured a cannon and awaited reinforcements from below. Later that day, Worth's men weakened the palace garrison by staging a fake retreat, then enfilading the pursuing Mexican troops from both sides. The palace gate was blown open by howitzer fire, and Worth's men, William Hardeman and Hamilton Bee among them, swarmed in.[19]

Within minutes the American flag floated over this last of the fortified heights, and cheers pealed from Taylor's hard-pressed men far below and to the east. Taylor's guns told of resumed attack, and Worth's western jaw of the pincer moved down the shallower incline of Independence Hill to close on the enemy. The fighting was block by block, house to house, and often hand to hand, with the scrappy rangers caught up in an unaccustomed type of warfare for the moment. Again, the Guadalupe Valley group was in the thick of it.

On the morning of September 24, 1846, General Pedro de Ampudia offered to negotiate. The American forces had suffered more than 500 casualties (only 77 of which were among Worth's men), many more would surely fall before the heavily fortified citadel could be taken, and Mexican reinforcements were feared. Furthermore, Taylor believed that General Antonio Lopez de Santa Anna, who had hobbled back into power on his remaining leg (he had lost the other in the Pastry War against France in 1837), wanted to end hostilities. The American general accepted a conditional surrender from Ampudia, who was permitted to retire southward with his army and much equipment. The Americans were in control of Monterrey, and an eight-week truce would prevail. Taylor's decision to grant virtual amnesty was not popular in Washington; and to the Texans, "Old Rough and Ready" was not rough enough in battle and too ready to let the enemy off. The rangers, their period of enlistment expired, went home. Taylor was glad to see them go. They had served their purpose—having probably won his battle for him—and they were for the moment an unruly, hell-raising liability.

But it was soon evident that without these daredevils he was a hound without a nose. When Santa Anna marshaled a major force to throw the Yankees off Mexican soil, Taylor reluctantly received Ben McCulloch and his ranger band back into the fold in January 1847. McCulloch had promised to return if the war flared up again. The gaunt William Hardeman was thus afforded more opportunities to vent his urge for adventure—opportunities, too, for a vastly increased knowledge of warfare on a larger scale than he had experienced before.

Zachary Taylor violated military rules twice within a few days after McCulloch's men joined him in north Mexico, and both infractions paid him large dividends. He refused to obey General Winfield Scott's orders to fall back northward to Monterrey from his recently occupied advance post at Saltillo. Then, since McCulloch's troop would not agree to enlist for the duration of the war or for any definite period of time, Taylor signed them up irregularly rather than deny himself their invaluable services. Santa Anna had a force of indeterminate strength at Encarnacion, thirty-five desert miles south of Taylor's army, and scouts from the main force of Americans had met with disaster in their attempts to probe across this stretch.

But McCulloch's men crossed with impunity, routing the outpost guard of a Mexican cavalry force at Encarnacion late at night on February 16, 1847. They returned by daybreak. Four days later, Taylor sent them back to determine the size of Santa Anna's force. This time the rangers slipped through the guard and inside the lines after dark, counting campfires and estimating the numbers from a rough formula. Their guess of 20,000 men was a safe one, if not completely accurate; the true count was about 16,000.

Taylor pulled back his much smaller army to a pass called La Angostura, near Buena Vista hacienda, and waited. Santa Anna, the stormy petrel, having received an intercepted message that the Americans were planning to withdraw, force-marched his men to catch them before they moved, but Taylor had already dropped back. Santa Anna interpreted this move as a retreat and advanced rapidly to the attack on Taylor's chosen ground. The battle of Buena Vista, fought on February 22 and 23, 1847, was a lucky event for the general from Louisiana. He squeaked out a victory, largely by dint of hunger among the Mexican troops, and he was happy to let the enemy retreat unmolested. This success, crowning the exploits at Monterrey, propelled him into the presidency. Santa Anna's heavy losses from starvation on the desert retreat further discredited that erratic general and did much to ensure Winfield Scott's later conquest of the Mexican heartland.

Very possibly the spying of McCulloch and his little band of daring men spelled the difference between defeat and victory at Buena Vista. Not only was the scouting report useful, but the initial thrust at Encarnacion may have given the American commander additional time which he sorely needed. The rangers fought with their usual savagery in the main battle and helped with the subsequent scouting operations. McCulloch's unit went home after six months of duty. Buena Vista was thus William Hardeman's last major engagement of the Mexican War, as he shifted for a time to a more settled life.

For the first time in 12 years, the inhabitants of Texas were able to devote themselves almost entirely to domestic pursuits. Acreage under cultivation increased, cotton and sugar cane production statistics multiplied, mills whirled, stores prospered, and slavery became more deeply entrenched. The next dozen years were the most vigorous the economy had experienced. The critical postnatal period was over, despite some Indian tilts ahead.

The sudden peaceful experience of the state was enacted on a small scale by most members of the Hardeman family there, as the four who fought in the Mexican War returned to their estates in Guadalupe County. William raised cotton and sugar cane on his plantation of more than 1,000 acres on the San Marcos River.[20] Influenced perhaps by the examples of his father, grandfather, and uncle, he built a mill on the river about 1850. He was married twice, first to Rebecca, the widow of his deceased uncle Bailey, and after her death to Ann Hamilton. He had two children by the first marriage and five by the second. Time would prove that all these earmarks of a settled life were misleading; Gotch had not said his final farewell to the frontier.

Monroe and Owen Bailey Hardeman were to make further, if indirect, contributions to the frontier through their sons. In 1843 Monroe had married Susan Burleson, great-niece of Edward Burleson, and they established the town of Prairie Lea on a tributary of the Guadalupe River in Caldwell County. They had two sons and two daughters. Owen and his wife, the former Sarah Berry, also settled to plantation life at Prairie Lea, where they reared five children. Leonidas Hardeman married Tullins Lenora Hamilton in 1852 and became a Caldwell County planter. Dr. John Marr Hardeman, who had married his cousin Mary Hardeman in 1828, returned to a civilian role and lived until 1891.

The plantation held no monopoly over the lives of the Texas Hardemans during these fat twelve years between wars. Dr. Blackstone Hardeman probably practiced medicine, although the most definite traces of his whereabouts and activities are his land holdings. He had gone first to Matagorda, but by 1837 he was in Washington County. Later that year he moved to Nacogdoches County and settled at Hardemans, which was subsequently renamed Chireno. Upon the death of his wife, Anna Bunch Hardeman, in 1842, the doctor moved to Gonzales County near his brother Thomas. Four years later he married a widow, Elizabeth Foster, and after Thomas's death he moved his family to an estate near his nephew

William in Guadalupe County. In 1867, shortly after his sons Blackstone, Jr., and Peter returned from the Civil War, Dr. Blackstone Hardeman died.[21]

Blackstone, Jr., or "Black," as he was called, had remained in Nacogdoches County. He was born in Maury County, Tennessee, in 1822 and had come to Texas in the mid-1830s. In 1842 he married Rebecca Jane Bruce Hunter. Shortly afterward he opened a country store at Melrose in Nacogdoches County, where he followed the merchandising business most of the remainder of his life. He received his goods by wagon and water from New Orleans, and his accounts show that the business was similar to the stores run by his relatives in Tennessee and Missouri. In the early years, his was the only store for miles, serving the cotton-producing region, ginning and marketing the raw product, and providing the clothing, hardware, and other commodities for the nearby planters. When his sons were old enough (he had sixteen children), they were given the job of hauling his store goods from New Orleans. On one occasion the home and store were smashed by a tornado which scattered goods as far as eight miles away and spread ginned cotton over the land like snow. Blackstone rebuilt his business.[22]

Disruptive though such "acts of God" may have been, they were less serious to the growth and security of Texas than the years of threatening storm from Santa Anna and Adrian Woll and Chief Buffalo Hump. And from these, the settled half of Texas was now safe.

The Hardeman tribe had expended no little energy to make itself and Texas secure. That state gave recognition to the contributions of Bailey and Thomas Jones by creating Hardeman County in 1858. The remains of Bailey Hardeman were exhumed in 1936 and placed in the State Cemetery at Austin beneath a monument which paid tribute to his service. The following year his brother Thomas's remains were also removed to the state cemetery.

The lull on the Texas front by early 1847 was by no means typical of conditions in all parts of the west. While the contest along the Mexican border had been building to a showdown, as raid and counter-raid were eclipsed by annexation and outright war, grandsons of patriarch Thomas Hardeman in Missouri were looking to western lands not yet tried by their frontiering kinsmen.

9 ⊞ *Peter Hardeman Burnett*
THE GREAT MIGRATION TO OREGON

ONE SATURDAY MORNING IN 1842, David Lenox took his fifteen-year-old son Henry to Platte City in the newly added bulge of Missouri's west side, where it was said a man would be talking about Oregon. The ride was not long—five miles west from the Lenox farm—and father and son were shortly rubbing shoulders with a gathering of listeners in front of a town store. A "rather striking looking man" of average height, fair complexion, dark brown hair, and sloping forehead, brought an old dry-goods box from his store. Stepping up on this platform, he looked over the crowd and began to talk about "the land flowing with milk and honey on the shores of the Pacific."

The speaker had a gifted tongue and a fund of information about Oregon. He lauded its fine climate, its rich soil, its bumper wheat crops. Then, with "a little twinkle of humor" in his "keen eye," this spellbinder with the folksy touch told his attentive following, "and they do say, gentlemen, they do say, that out in Oregon the pigs are running about under the great acorn trees, round and fat, and already cooked with knives and forks sticking in them so that you can cut off a slice whenever you are hungry."[1] This was Peter Hardeman Burnett, lawyer, judge, editor, merchant, and grandson of that incurable western traveler Thomas Hardeman. Lenox went into Burnett's store and signed up for the overland trip on the Oregon Trail.

> As the coming of the Winthrops' party of Puritans to Massachusetts Bay in 1630 largely determined the history of New England, so the arrival on the Columbia of Burnett's wagon train and Applegate's "Cow Column" are events of fundamental significance in the history of the Pacific Northwest.

So wrote western and agricultural historian Joseph Schafer.[2] Peter Burnett was the principal organizer and first elected captain of the first and perhaps the largest single immigrant wagon train ever to cross the North American continent all the way to the Pacific settlements, and he formed and led the first wagon train to go from Oregon to California. In both Oregon Territory and California he held prominent judicial posts. He was elected to the highest political office in the Golden State and was one of the foremost advertisers for settlers to come to the Pacific Slope. The frontier-ward impulse of Thomas Hardeman and his descendants reached its zenith in Peter Burnett.

Burnett's roots were in the Tennessee of 1807, when the chill and fading color of late autumn lay on the Cumberland Basin. George Burnet, a carpenter and farmer recently from Virginia, and his young wife Dorothy, a daughter of Thomas and Mary Hardeman, lived in a frame house which George had built.[3] On November 15 of that year, their first son was born. He was christened Peter Hardeman after a brother of Dorothy. When Peter was about four, his family moved a few miles south to Williamson County near Thomas Hardeman's Sugar Hill plantation. Six years later they followed old Thomas to Howard County, Missouri Territory. Here Peter met the frontier as the Burnets

> spent the first winter in a large camp with a dirt floor, boarded up on the sides with clapboards, and covered with the same, leaving a hole in the center of the roof for the escape of the smoke. All the family lived together in the same room, the whites on one side and the blacks on the other.[4]

After nearly five years in the "sickly" Missouri bottom lands, the Burnets shifted their abode westward to higher ground in Clay County, near the present site of Kansas City.

This too was rather primitive country. The rough conditions and the poverty made a deep impression on young Peter, who was faced with "too much hard work to admit of attending school, except at intervals during the summer."[5] He learned the elements of reading, writing, grammar, and arithmetic. From that point he was self-motivated and became an avid reader.

A visit from his uncle Constant Hardeman in 1826 prompted nineteen-year-old Peter to return to Tennessee. The diffident western youngster was taken aback by the knowledge, refinement, and wealth of his Tennessee kin. In their own time they had been as bumpkinish as he, but times had changed for them. "Conscious of my own poverty, ignorance, and homely dress," he later recounted, "I fancied that I was sometimes slighted by my relatives. I, however, said nothing, made no complaints, but laid it up in my heart that I would some day equal if not surpass them."[6] After a short stay in Rutherford and Maury counties, he went with his uncle Blackstone to Hardeman County in western Tennessee, where another uncle, Thomas Jones Hardeman, had settled. Blackstone found a position for the backwoods boy as a hotel clerk in Bolivar at wages of $100 per year.

About that time, in order to make his last name "more complete and emphatic," Peter added an extra "t." Hence the occasional variation from Burnet to Burnett in early documents. His brothers followed his example, as they were to follow his lead in later years to new territories.

Burnett soon shifted his employment to store clerk, and after several years' experience in that capacity, he bought out the store from his employer, Parson Peck. The problems of a credit economy in a newly settled region proved as troublesome for Peter as they had for his predecessor. Unable to collect his accounts receivable, he sent his young wife, Harriet Rogers Burnett, ahead to Clay County, Missouri, while he read law and attempted to close out the mercantile business without losing the raiment from his back. Fourteen lonely months later, when he rejoined his family in April 1832, he "had only sixty-two and a half cents left, was some seven hundred dollars in debt, had a wife and one child to support, and was out of employment."[7]

At his new home in Missouri, Peter combined his Tennessee talents and clerked in a store, gained admittance to the Missouri Bar, then entered two mercantile partnerships in 1834. Profits were encouraging for several years, but a long delay in completing a store building, the failure of his steam sawmill and distillery, and the Panic of 1837 and 1838 threw him deep into debt. By 1839 he was more than ready "to bid a final adieu to the mercantile business" and practice law.[8]

Burnett once observed that whatever he undertook, he was determined to do with all his might. His approach to the legal profession bore this out, at least for the time being. He updated his legal knowledge by means of a rigorous reading program, joined a debating club to polish his speech delivery, and in order to develop his writing style edited *The Far West,* a weekly newspaper in the town of Liberty. Specializing in civil and mercantile cases, he was moderately successful in his practice.

One of Burnett's cases brought him close to national notoriety if not popularity. In 1839 he became a member of the team of defense counsels for Mormon leaders Joseph Smith, Jr., Lyman Wight, Sidney Rigdon, and others who had been tossed into the Liberty jail. It was a seeming paradox that Peter Burnett had participated in armed militia activity against these Latter Day Saints, yet he defended their leaders in court. But whatever their offenses, he was convinced that they were not guilty of treason, robbery, and arson, the crimes of which they were charged. Given the anti-Mormon feeling in the area, he probably did not defend them for the sake of his reputation, and the financial considerations were in all likelihood small. Such was the emotional climate that after Burnett presented the first speech before the county judge of Clay County, he sat with a hand on his pistol, ready to administer "frontier justice" if any of the assembled mob attempted to lynch his clients. Meanwhile his associate A. W. Doniphan delivered an impassioned speech in defense of the Mormon leaders. The grand jury returned an indictment against them, and Burnett and his associates asked for a change of venue. While the prisoners were being transferred, they broke free and escaped to Illinois. Thus the case did not come to trial.

Soon afterward, Burnett accepted an appointment as district attorney in the area which had been appended to northwestern Missouri in 1837. He moved to Weston in Platte County near the Missouri River. Life as an attorney on the westernmost edge of the westernmost state provided a reasonable subsistence income, despite the depression which hit this section hard after the Panic of 1837. But Peter was $15,000 in debt, and the interest rates were so high that the $1,000 a year which he paid to his creditors scarcely dented the principal. He looked with despair upon the prospect of a lifetime of indebtedness. His wife Harriet was ill with consumption, and the climate was believed partly to blame. And it was becoming evident that ledgers and legal briefs and printer's ink had only temporarily covered his inner restlessness. Again he looked westward, and it was of necessity a far look, since the Near West was largely preempted by the so-called Permanent Indian Frontier and the lively myth of the "Great American Desert." At that moment in history Peter Hardeman Burnett spied Oregon, an event which had important consequences for both himself and that distant province.

During the second quarter of the nineteenth century, American frontiersmen were heavily occupied, but by no means entirely preoccupied, with the arid Far West. Now it was the *verdant* Far West that attracted greater attention. As in New Mexico and Texas, the penetration of Oregon Territory involved some international complications, but the United States had a much firmer foot planted inside the gateway to the Northwest. English claims were anchored deep in the past, from the voyages of Francis Drake, James Cook, and George Vancouver to the overland probe of Alexander Mackenzie and the 1825 treaty with Russia. The United States, however, had some bids of its own. There were claimants Robert Gray and John Kendrick, 1788; Lewis and Clark, 1804 to 1806; and John Jacob Astor's advance men in 1811. And there were French and Spanish claims, respectively picked up by the United States in the Louisiana Purchase of 1803 and the Adams-Onís Treaty of 1819. Thus, among the five strong contenders for Oregon, only two, Great Britain and the United States, remained in the running by 1825. They eyed each other and sparred cautiously, reluctant to close in combat over such a distant issue.

The fortunes of these two powers shifted from time to time. An early advantage accrued to the United States from its sea otter traders and the founding of Astoria by the Pacific Fur Company. But Britain wrested this outpost from the American grasp in 1813, and soon the Northwest Company, the Hudson's Bay Company, Fort Vancouver, and Dr. John

McLoughlin were the big names in that disputed area of the Pacific Northwest. Under terms of the joint occupation agreement of 1818, the United States kept a precarious grip and right of settlement against mounting odds.

While Burnett's uncles teamed and toiled on the Santa Fe Trail, propagandists John Floyd and Hall J. Kelley tried to awaken American interest in Oregon. During the 1830s, mountain men of the Rocky Mountain and American fur companies began to crack the Hudson's Bay Company's monopoly of the trade in that land of snow-capped Cascades, virgin-forested valleys, and warm chinook winds. Nathaniel J. Wyeth took a party of immigrants there, and American missionaries such as Jason Lee, Marcus Whitman, and Pierre de Smet stirred a lively interest in the territory. Despite the fact that the fur crop declined, missions failed to prosper, and immigration, although picking up by 1841, more accurately resembled a trickle than a gush, there was something building by the time Burnett keyed his interest to Oregon. It was a movement that drew its sustenance from many points, like a great stream gorging from the combined flow of its countless rivulets, and it was strong enough to force a quick showdown on the international dispute.

Perhaps it was a matter of accidental timing—the flood of Oregon propaganda, depressed farm prices in the Midwest, the lure of California, and the same pioneering spirit that had moved long hunters, mountain men, and Santa Fe traders. If the immigrant waters had welled up to flood stage from a myriad of coalescing headstreams, it was Peter Burnett who sent them over the spillway and along the Oregon Trail in unprecedented volume.[9]

At Weston in the winter of 1842–1843, Burnett pored "with great care" over a congressional report on Oregon and pondered a bill which Missouri Senator Lewis Linn had introduced in Congress. This proposal would provide free Oregon land for American settlers there, and Peter calculated that, if it passed, the size of his family would entitle him to 1,600 acres and a fair prospect of paying his debts. He first secured permission from all his creditors before deciding to go.

Another of Burnett's motives for moving to Oregon was noted by his fellow immigrant James Nesmith and was summed up by Peter himself in a later account:

Peter H. Burnett.
1849 Governor 1850.
Died May 17th. 1895.

Peter Hardeman Burnett, trail boss, gold miner, first elected governor of
California, and Oregon supreme court judge, possessed the characteristics
needed to "give solidity and respectability to the foundation of colonies."
*Painting in the California State Capitol, Sacramento, courtesy California State
Library.*

. . . The country was claimed by both Great Britain and the United States; so that the most ready and peaceable way to settle the conflicting and doubtful claims of the two governments was to fill the country with American citizens. If we could only show, by a *practical* test, that American emigrants could safely make their way across the continent to Oregon with their wagons, teams, cattle, and families, then the solution of the question of title to the country was discovered.[10]

Burnett set about with fervor to organize a wagon train, bringing to bear all the persuasiveness that his debating and legal experience would admit. He was to prove a successful salesman. In practically any company he was considered a sincere and trustworthy leader. David and Henry Lenox were but two of hundreds who threw in their lot with Burnett and his plan.

Peter had acquainted himself with what each person should take on the trip and with the conditions that could be expected en route as well as at the destination. For several months during late 1842 and early 1843, he stumped the counties of western Missouri, drumming up interest in an Oregon caravan for the coming spring and making speeches, as he put it, "wherever I could find a sufficient audience, and succeeded even beyond my own expectations."[11] His trenchant message was picked up by news-papers in Missouri and more distant areas. On March 14, 1843, the *Ohio Statesman* reprinted a column from the *Platte Eagle* of Missouri's west side.

> The people are again in motion here in relation to the emigration to Oregon this spring. Peter H. Burnett, Esq., one of our most estimable citizens is among the foremost here in exciting a laudable spirit in relation to the settlement of that desirable country. . . . Mr. Burnett delivered a very able lecture upon this subject, in which was embodied a vast fund of informa-tion. . . .[12]

A party of nearly 1,000 people, with about 120 wagons and several thousand head of livestock, turned out for the trip. The size of this migration brands it as a landmark in the history of American expansion. Nothing comparable to it had been undertaken in previous emigrations across the continent to the Pacific Slope. There had been only a few missionaries at a time on horseback, or a few dozen settlers who abandoned their wagons at Fort Hall or on the east side of the Sierra Nevada.

Did Burnett stir up this great wave, or did he merely catch it as it surged and ride it to notoriety? Obviously he was much closer to the crest

Peter Hardeman Burnett was the "Great Migration's" first "Wagon Boss"—a pioneer type captured here on canvas by Charles M. Russell. Burnett organized the earliest wagon train to cross the continent to the Pacific settlements. *Courtesy The Thomas Gilcrease Institute of American History and Art, Tulsa, Oklahoma.*

than the trough. John Minto, who came to Oregon in 1844 and who talked with various members of the previous year's Great Migration, stated that "no other single individual exerted as large an influence in swelling the number of home-building emigrants to Oregon in the years 1843 and 1844 as Peter H. Burnett."[13]

Several good sources on this mass migration have been preserved. James W. Nesmith kept a log of the journey, and Jesse Applegate's brief treatise "A Day with the Cow Column" is a well-known account, although he deliberately refrained from "burdening" the reader with the names of any members of the party except his own and that of Marcus Whitman. David Lenox, William T. Newby, and several others also produced useful accounts. The most complete and detailed of the known sources are those which were taken directly from the original Burnett journal. Among these, *The Recollections of an Old Pioneer* and the letters to the New York *Herald, Niles Weekly Register,* and many other newspapers are directly attributable to Burnett. Another account, published under the name of George Wilkes, a Pacific railroad propagandist, was a slightly fictionalized version of Burnett's journal, without credit to the original writer.[14] Like many such daily accounts, Peter's was less detailed in the later parts than at the fresh beginning.

The thrill of starting this new venture must have been tempered with both sorrow and apprehension as Peter, Harriet, and their six children departed their Platte County home on May 8, 1843, and headed for the rendezvous point twelve miles west of Independence: sorrow over the death of Peter's mother, and apprehension over the job that lay ahead. They took two ox wagons, four yoke of oxen, a small two-horse wagon, two mules, provisions, and a quantity of utensils and other household items. Many treasured possessions had to be sacrificed, but it was better to make those hard decisions before leaving than at some dumping ground along the trail.

The value of ox teams for hauling wagons across far western terrain was still debated despite considerable experience on the Santa Fe Trail, but the experiences of Peter Burnett were convincing.

> We fully tested the ox and mule teams, and we found the ox teams greatly superior. One ox will pull as much as two mules, and, in mud, as much as four. They are more easily managed, are not so subject to be lost or broken down on

the way, cost less at the start, and are worth about four times as much here. The ox is a most noble animal, patient, thrifty, durable, gentle, and easily driven, and does not run off. Those who come to this country will be in love with their oxen by the time they reach here. The ox will plunge through mud, swim over streams, dive into thickets, and climb mountains to get at the grass, and he will eat almost anything. Willows they eat with great greediness on the way; and it is next to impossible to drown an ox.[15]

Peter had anticipated success with these beasts when he advised recruits as to how they should equip themselves for the 1843 trip.

On May 17, Burnett reached the rendezvous. The following day a preliminary organizational meeting was held, and committees were picked to inspect wagons, contact Dr. Whitman (who knew the trail), and formulate rules for the journey. Although no captain was elected for a number of days, Burnett was the *de facto* leader. He had been the chief recruiting voice and had chosen the time and place of the rendezvous. Now he spoke to the emigrants thus far assembled, in a "glowing, florid address," lauding the resources of Oregon and assuring the group that they would "drive out the British usurpers who claimed the soil."[16] A follow-up meeting was held at Big Spring on May 20, and further details were arranged, including the very important one of engaging Captain John Gantt to serve as guide until the caravan reached Fort Hall.

Captain Gantt of the Sixth Infantry, United States Army, had been dismissed from service for falsifying pay certificates. It was his second offense, and, perhaps in search of relief from his disgrace, he took to the life of a mountain man. He was a trapper, Indian fighter, and sometime trading partner in Gantt and Blackwell Company of St. Louis. Gantt was tall, thin, wiry, and bald; his trade partner referred to him as "the crane," and the Cheyennes called him "Bald Head."[17] Like dozens of other mountain men, when trapping declined and canvas-covered wagons pointed their tongues toward the Pacific provinces, he became a guide. Burnett, Nesmith, and others persuaded Gantt to direct their party to Fort Hall for a fee of one dollar per person. The journey officially began on May 22, although wagonloads of latecomers rolled in for several days.

The white sheeted wagons and the fine teams, moving in the wilderness of green prairie, made the most lovely appearance. The place where we camped [Elm Grove, named for its two elm trees] was very beautiful; and no scene appeared to our enthusiastic visions more exquisite than the sight of so many wagons, tents, fires, cattle, and people, as were here collected. At night the sound of joyous music was heard in the tents. Our long journey thus began in sunshine and song, in anecdote and laughter; but these all vanished before we reached its termination.[18]

River crossings offered early challenges. As Burnett's uncles John and Bailey had done on the trail to Santa Fe, the Oregon-bound pioneers lowered their wagons with ropes down the steep banks of streams such as the Walkalusia, and twin canoes with joining platform, much like Hardeman's ferry, were devised to cross the Kansas. Repeated heavy thunderstorms scrubbed the landscape, and at the Big Blue (near the present Kansas-Nebraska border) a strong blow flattened all the tents.[19] Deep mires plagued the migrants, and the sunny dispositions of the Elm Grove camp began to cloud.

Beyond the Kansas River the party sensed that they were reaching wild country. Indian problems might arise at any time, and the wagons were drawn into a protective circle at night. It seemed wise to elect a captain and council and tighten up the organization. On June 1, near the muddy banks of Black Warrior Creek, they held an election—a unique one from the viewpoint of those unschooled in frontier ways. Actor and journalist Matt Field, who—like Harriet Burnett, Francis Parkman, and uncounted others—took to the bracing air of the Far West in an attempt to improve his health, was intrigued by a strange deployment of men which turned out to be a technique of choosing leaders.

> The candidates stood up in a row before the constituents, and at a given signal they wheeled about and marched off, while the general mass *broke* after them "lickety-split," each man forming in behind his favorite, so that every candidate flourished a sort of tail of his own, and the man with the longest tail was elected! . . . If the scene can be conceived, it must appear as a curious mingling of the whimsical with the wild. . . . These men were running about the Prairie in long strings, the leader, in sport and for the purpose of puzzling the judges, doubling and winding in the drollest fashion—so that the all-important business of forming a Government, seemed very much like the merry school-boy game of "Snapping the whip!"[20]

Literally "running for office," Field called it. He concluded his description with the remark, "They elected a young lawyer of some eminence, as we were told, named Burnett, as their Captain." Having emerged in a walk-away over his nearest competitor Jesse Applegate, "Pete," as he was called, took command. Nesmith was elected orderly sergeant, and nine or ten councilmen were designated in the same snake-dance manner.

The duties of the office now held by Burnett were spelled out in the company's regulations. He was to have "supreme military command of the company" and was empowered to "maintain good order and strict discipline" with the backing of the council. That body could hold a trial and expel a member from the company at its discretion.[21]

The new commander became disillusioned with his position after a few days. What he hoped would be remediable—the inexperience, recalcitrance, and blunt opposition on the part of large numbers of the travelers—grew worse instead of better. The column, Burnett concluded, was too large, too diverse in its needs, to move as a single body. Matt Field commented on the one thorn which, on June 1, had been festering and would break the company in two in a short time. On that peripatetic election day a rule was passed "that no family should drive along more than three head of loose livestock for each member composing it." This was soon rescinded because of the hardship it worked on many families. Burnett promptly divided the assemblage into four parts in a try at easier management.[22] Unfortunately, those with large numbers of livestock sometimes could not round them up before mid-morning, and there was chafing over the additional guard duty necessitated by the cattle. Burnett had brought enthusiasm and a knack for organization to the crucial first stages of peopling Oregon and had found his role as unofficial leader bearable during the initial "honeymoon" period. But these had been the stages of voluntary associations before nerves were frayed. The hard days were now upon the column—days which called for stern commands and rigid enforcement. Perhaps Burnett found this assignment distasteful. He stated in a letter that he was unable to continue as captain because of illness. Whatever the reason or reasons, on June 8 he stepped down. It was not the last time he would resign from an important office when the going was heavy. John Minto, who later worked for Peter in Oregon, stated that he was "generous in the extreme in preferring other men to positions they could fill more successfully than he could himself." He stated that Burnett resigned the captaincy as the best way to bring about a more manageable organization, that being division of the migrants into two distinct groups.[23]

Peter's abdication was quickly followed by action on what all observers agreed was the most serious problem, the dispute over the cattle. Those with considerable numbers of loose livestock simply had requirements which were different from the others. Now a division was made, Jesse Applegate commanding the "cow column" with its sixty wagons and large herd of loose stock, and mountain man William Martin heading the "light column" with the lesser numbers of cattle and horses. Families with as many as four or five head of loose stock went with the cow column. Both groups made about the same speed overall, but they were gaited differently at different times of the day. Dividing the company thus reduced the problems but by no means ended them. Before journey's end, Zachary would stab Wheeler with a knife, six-year-old Joel Hembree would be crushed to death under a wagon wheel, and six people in all would lose their lives.

Meanwhile the two columns coped with their respective chores separately although they remained within "supporting" distance of each other from the crossing of the Big Blue to Independence Rock on the Sweetwater. The Burnett family traveled in the Martin group, and Peter was still a frequently consulted leader despite his recent resignation.

Other than these problems, the party of 1843 had surprisingly few difficulties for its size in crossing the plains and reaching Fort Hall. Looking back from this trappers' and traders' entrepôt, Burnett called the Oregon Trail to that point "perhaps the finest natural road, of the same length, to be found in the world."[24] The "Great American Desert" concept of the Great Plains, so prevalent in the scientific and other literature of the period, is very little evidenced in his accounts of the trip. On the contrary, he seemed at times determined to dispel the notion, referring to the ample water supply and the great natural fertility of the soil and describing the Platte country as "a level plain of rich prairie land, equal to any in the world for farming purposes." Although he and John C. Frémont may have indulged their expansionist views by exaggerating the point, they would prove to be better prophets than their contemporaries. In one instance, however, Burnett compared the Platte with the Nile crossing sandy desert lands.[25] Unlike many settlers from the Midwest, when he reached Oregon he chose the plains for farming, undeterred by the "Great American Desert" notion that only timbered lands would have the fertility to grow crops.

Through the waving miles of bluestem and needlegrass, across the bunch and buffalo grass, and beside the elongated oasis of the Platte River, the party plodded and toiled; fifteen or twenty miles were covered in a day, and on one occasion twenty-five to thirty miles. The frequent deep ruts, chiseled for eons by the hoofs of thousands of buffalo headed for water, cut at right angles across the path of the wagons and jarred them sharply, resulting in several broken axles. The "glorious Fourth" of July was celebrated in a manner much more laborious than glorious—crossing the South Fork of the Platte. There was fording and swimming and converting of wagon boxes or beds into boats by covering them with buffalo skins. Some of the laborers spoke of their "hard fare" in comparison to the ice cream, mint juleps, and wine that were doubtless part of the celebrations elsewhere in the Republic.[26]

The same shaggy animals, the skins of which supplied boat waterproofing, also provided a major part of the food for the caravan. The first buffalo, a tough old bull, was killed by John Gantt, the guide, on June 12. Thereafter, these animals became increasingly numerous, and since they frequented the same streams which the travelers followed, they were easily killed. Burnett rated their meat superior to any other he had ever tasted, although he conceded that the rigors of the trail served to whet one's appetite. The diet was occasionally varied by flesh of the more fleet and wary antelope and deer. Some families, owing to their accustomed frontier generosity in the early days of travel, ran short of flour and other staples. However, such items were available—to those who could pay the price—at the Fort Laramie trading post.

Perhaps as serious to the sojourner as the problem of food supplies was the scarcity of fuel. With the exception of the serpentine wooded stretches in stream valleys, there was no timber short of the Rocky Mountains. Willow, cottonwood, abandoned wigwam poles, driftwood, and, further to the west, "sedge" or sage were the principal fire materials. According to Burnett, driftwood from the stream valleys was the most important, although it would be used up during the first several years of heavy travel. Small fire pits were dug to concentrate the heat and protect the fire from wind, conserving precious fuel. Later parties would have to cook over fires of buffalo chips, but as of 1843 not enough firewood scavengers had passed to reduce trailside chefs to that level.

The settlers' relentless search for firewood caused Peter Burnett to wince in feeling for the natural environment. He repeatedly deplored the stripping of branches and cutting of trees. His description of an incident at Lone Pine on the Powder River typified his feelings.

> This noble tree stood in the center of a most lovely valley, about ten miles from any other timber. It could be seen, at the distance of many miles, rearing its majestic form above the surrounding plain, and constituted a beautiful landmark for the guidance of the traveler. Many teams had passed on before me; and at intervals, as I drove along, I would raise my head and look at that beautiful green pine. At last, on looking up as usual, the tree was gone. I was perplexed for the moment to know whether I was going in the right direction. There was the plain beaten wagon-road before me, and I drove on until I reached the camp just at dark. That brave old pine, which had withstood the storms and snows of centuries, had fallen at last by the vandal hands of men. Some of our inconsiderate people had cut it down for fuel, but it was too green to burn. It was a useless and most unfortunate act. Had I been there in time, I should have begged those woodsmen to "spare that tree."[27]

The generations of nineteenth-century Americans were not kind to the environment. They plundered and despoiled selfishly and heedlessly. It seemed the resources were inexhaustible. Even the wise Jefferson thought, almost casually, that there was enough land in the country to meet its needs for all time to come. Perhaps it is noteworthy that amidst the plentitude there were already a few conservationists who were millions of acres and billions of board feet ahead of the rank and file of their time. There was John James Audubon, who cringed at the sight of timber "fast disappearing under the axe."[28] There were Henry David Thoreau in the East and George Catlin in the West, and poet William Cullen Bryant, editor Horace Greeley, and wanderers such as Francis Parkman and Washington Irving. Peter Burnett, their contemporary, shared their views on the environment. His letters and recollections show an often-stated feeling and concern for the stately timber, the clumped willow, and other vegetation, for the headstrong salmon, the antelope, and that "most noble animal," as he called the buffalo. And there were his frequent and detailed descriptions of mountains, plains, streams, and other landforms,

Indian and white, trader and traveler—all met at Fort Laramie. Peter H.
Burnett's Oregon-bound wagon train stopped here briefly in July 1843. *Painting
by Alfred Jacob Miller, 1837, courtesy The Beinecke Rare Book and Manuscript
Library, Yale University.*

which suggest that he was not a typical member of the plundering herd of migrants.

Likewise, Burnett's view of the Indians whom he encountered seems to have been at variance with that of most pioneers. True, his attitude toward the Osages and Kansas was at times one of annoyance at their "continual begging." But for most of the native Americans, he had only such words as "noble" and "fine looking" and "skillful." At Fort Laramie a troublesome member of the caravan insulted a Cheyenne chief. Peter, seeing difficulty ahead,

> followed the chief, and by kind and earnest gestures made him understand at last that this young man was considered by us all as a half-witted fool, unworthy of the notice of any sensible man; and that we never paid attention to what he said, as we hardly considered him responsible for his language. The moment the chief comprehended my meaning I saw a change come over his countenance, and he went away perfectly satisfied. He was a clear-headed man; and though unlettered, he understood human nature.[29]

No hostile Indians were encountered during the entire journey, although Nathan Sutton, while standing guard, claimed that he had shot an Indian. Daybreak revealed a dead mule in the grass, and, needless to say, Sutton was reminded often of his "four legged Indian." The reactions of the Indians to this great migration of the whites across their land can only be guessed, but Matthew Field gave some hint. He reported that the Sioux near Laramie, seeing this throng with large numbers of women and children for the first time, concluded that "the whole white village" had moved west.

Heeding the advice of Marcus Whitman—"travel, *travel,* TRAVEL. . . . Nothing is good for you that causes a moment's delay,"[30] the emigrants left Fort Laramie on July 15, one day after their arrival. Twelve days later they were on the Sweetwater, and as Indian danger was presumed over, the cow column slackened its pace and fell behind the Martin-Burnett group. On August 3, a "grand and magnificent sight," the snow-mantled Rocky Mountains loomed before them.[31] They went through South Pass by August 7, and there drank from water which, like themselves, was destined for the Pacific Coast. A short cut to Fort Bridger, and on, relentlessly on, to Fort Hall, which was reached in late August.

Between Fort Laramie and Fort Hall, Burnett and his companions had been overtaken by several groups under the leadership of men who were prominent among the trail-breakers of the Far West: Joseph Reddeford Walker, mountain man and discoverer of Walker Pass across the Sierra Nevada; Joseph Chiles, who had previously made the trip to California in the Bidwell-Bartleson party of 1841; Lieutenant John Charles Frémont of the army Topographical Corps; and the seemingly ubiquitous mountain man Kit Carson. Frémont took prudent measures to avoid close fraternization with the members of the wagon train as he passed them in the Smith Fork area and left them in his own trail of dust.

Beyond Fort Hall, as Burnett noted, was the "most critical period" of the journey, with "the untried and most difficult portion" ahead.[32] There was reason for gloom in the wearying company. They were tired from the strain of three and a half plodding months on the trail; more than a third of the distance still lay ahead of them. Thus far they had had relatively even terrain and a well-broken road to follow. Now they would have to break their own way between Fort Hall and the coast. James Grant, the factor at this Hudson's Bay post, told them he did not see how they could make it through with their wagons. Mountain man Joe Meek was supposed to have taken three wagons to Fort Walla Walla, but if so his trail was not found.

To further dim the weeks ahead, John Gantt, having well fulfilled the terms of his agreement, took the left fork in the trail and accompanied Walker and Chiles to California. Fortunately Dr. Whitman stayed with the Martin-Burnett column as far as Grand Ronde. He was paid $80 for his services on this leg of the trip. Stikas, an Indian guide sent by Whitman, gave them competent leadership for the remainder of the journey. Many of the young men, whose hands were desperately needed with the cumbersome vehicles, broke away and hastened west with pack animals. Several members of the party had recently died of "fever"— Clayborne Payne on August 4, and Stephenson five days later. And, as a harbinger of possible disaster, frost had been nipping the mountain air since mid-August, and in early morning the travelers broke thin ice on their cooking water.

No time to turn back; not a moment to waste; down the rock-strewn valley of the Snake, across intermittent stretches of wormwood or sage, where the first half dozen wagons had to be sturdy to break down this "melancholy shrub"; through groves of timber, weaving this way and that for lack of time to chop a roadway. On September 7, they reached Salmon Falls of the Snake River, where they bought dried and fresh salmon from the Indians in exchange for powder and lead. A boiling spring, its waters "hot enough to cook an egg," was passed a week later, and on September 20 Fort Boise came into view. By month's end they were in the beautiful Grand Ronde Valley. Here the diet of the pioneers was varied by the "quite palatable" camas root which they purchased from Indians.

Just beyond Grand Ronde were some of the most "terrible" conditions experienced thus far—rough, steep ridges which forced them to lock the rear wagon wheels on the descent, an ominous snowfall, and difficulty in keeping the cattle from straying. Added to these problems, "the exhausting tedium . . . and the attendant vexations" caused many members of the group to "become childish, petulant, and obstinate."[33] Beyond the blue mountains there was some reprieve, as the travelers were able to purchase fresh vegetables from the Indians, and on October 10 they pitched camp near Whitman's Mission, where they bought supplies.

Fort Walla Walla on the Columbia River was a high rung on the ladder to the Northwest, and the body of plodders must have breathed more easily when they reached it on October 16. Peter Burnett, indulging in the luxury of a backward look over the weary march, estimated accurately that they had traveled 1,692 miles from the rendezvous point to this fort in 147 days, for a daily average of eleven and one-half miles.

There were thrilling, often frightening days ahead, however. A majority of the members continued by wagon along the valley of the broad, blue Columbia to the Dalles, thence down the river on rafts to the Cascades, and from there to Fort Vancouver in canoes and boats. Burnett, his close friend William Beagle, and the remainder left their wagons and cattle at Walla Walla for the time being and went by boat from that point. Burnett's account is less precise after the arrival at Fort Walla Walla; he no longer kept a daily journal of happenings.

For their float down the Columbia, Burnett and Beagle bought an old Hudson's Bay Company boat from Archibald McKinlay, the factor at Walla Walla. This open craft, about forty feet in length, was strong enough to carry heavy loads and "shoot" rapids, yet sufficiently light to be carried by forty to fifty Indians around impassable stretches, or portages.

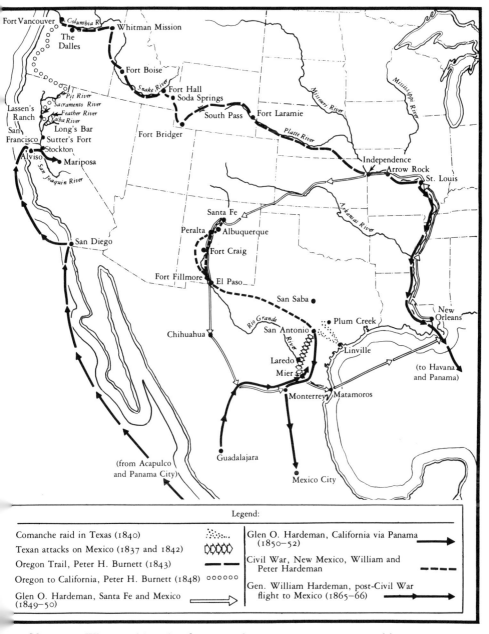

Fort Vancouver
Columbia R.
The
Dalles
Whitman Mission
Fort Boise
Snake River
Fort Hall
Soda Springs
Lassen's
Ranch
Pit River
Sacramento River
Feather River
Yuba River
South Pass
Fort Laramie
San
Francisco
Long's Bar
Sutter's Fort
Stockton
Fort Bridger
Mariposa
Alviso
San Joaquin River
Independence
Arrow Rock
St. Louis
Missouri River
Mississippi River
Platte River
San Diego
Santa Fe
Peralta
Albuquerque
Fort Craig
Fort Fillmore
El Paso
Arkansas River
San Saba
Plum Creek
San Antonio
Linville
Chihuahua
Rio Grande River
Laredo
Mier
Monterrey
Matamoros
New
Orleans
(to Havana
and Panama)
(from Acapulco
and Panama City)
Guadalajara
Mexico City

Legend:

Comanche raid in Texas (1840)	⋰⋱⋰	Glen O. Hardeman, California via Panama (1850–52) ⟶
Texan attacks on Mexico (1837 and 1842)	◊◊◊◊◊	
Oregon Trail, Peter H. Burnett (1843)	— —	Civil War, New Mexico, William and Peter Hardeman – – –
Oregon to California, Peter H. Burnett (1848)	oooooo	
Glen O. Hardeman, Santa Fe and Mexico (1849–50)	⟹	Gen. William Hardeman, post-Civil War flight to Mexico (1865–66) ⟶

Map 5. Western Travels of the Hardeman Family, 1837–1866.

A skillful Indian pilot took the boat and its party safely through, although three immigrants from the cow column of 1843 died in the surging waters of the Columbia just above the Dalles. These included a son and a nephew of Jesse Applegate, the leader of that caravan. Four decades after his wild ride down the river, Peter wrote with feeling—as if it had been yesterday—about the frightening rapids, the jutting rocks, and the "cool, determined, and intrepid" Indian pilot.[34] If he had time to reflect while he and his family knifed through the water at "racehorse" speed, perhaps he had fleeting thoughts of Thomas Hardeman and Piomingo and Muscle Shoals, a story that he no doubt heard many times at the knee of his grandfather.

A short distance upstream from the Dalles, the families were put ashore, while the men took the boat on through this funnel of foaming water. Here at the head of Columbia River navigation, where "there must some day grow up a town," Burnett "determined at once to settle."[35] He left his family at the Methodist Mission just below the Dalles and headed for Fort Vancouver to complete an arrangement made at Walla Walla regarding a possible exchange of cattle with the Hudson's Bay Company. The river was broad and smooth except for a portage at the Cascades, where boats were let through the rapids with the aid of ropes. Early in November, Burnett reached the fort.

At Fort Vancouver, the benevolent Hudson's Bay factor, Dr. John McLoughlin, and his co-worker James Douglas advised Peter to return for his family and settle nearer the ocean. His tribute to McLoughlin and Douglas was similar to many others written in admiration of the factors at this British post: "They were both gentlemen in the truest sense of the term." To Burnett, who came with an urge to strengthen the American foothold in Oregon, their behavior must have been puzzling, and perhaps soothing, to his paranoid feelings about British intentions toward the United States. "If these men were really opposed to American immigrants, they took the most extraordinary method of showing it."[36] They offered him round trip transportation to pick up his family, and it was that circumstance which brought Burnett again into the same path with one of the best-known frontiersmen of the decade.

John C. Frémont, leading the second of his five exploring expeditions to the Far West, had left his party at the Dalles while he went to Fort

Vancouver to purchase the supplies which would enable him to continue his exploration into California. The needed goods had been furnished by McLoughlin on the credit of the United States government, and Frémont was provided with a boat, three Chinook canoes, and a platoon of Indian and French Canadian laborers.

Burnett accepted McLoughlin's offer to go upriver with Frémont, and they set out on November 10. The two men shared the same boat and tent for ten days as they paddled and portaged up the Columbia.[37] At the Cascades portage they experienced wet weather, but clear skies smoothed the last part of the trip.

The Missouri lawyer and the explorer, in this close association, developed a high regard for each other. Burnett described Frémont as "modest in appearance, and calm and gentle in manner. His men all loved him intensely. He gave his orders with great mildness and simplicity, but they had to be obeyed. . . . I never traveled with a more pleasant companion."[38] Frémont's brief comment about his fellow voyager was that "Mr. Peter Burnett . . . possessed intelligence and character, with the moral and intellectual stamina, as well as the enterprise, which give solidity and respectability to the foundation of colonies."[39]

The Burnetts and their property were loaded in the Mackinaw boat and the three canoes at the Dalles. As traveling guests of the Hudson's Bay Company, they completed their six-month journey in luxurious style— passengers who had only to watch the scenery slip past them. In truth, a far cry from the summer's toil over jolting buffalo paths, alternate dust and mud, thick-matted sagebrush, and enervating incline. Yet the very luxury brought its anxious moments. Burnett had "shot" this same stretch of water less than a month before, but as an oarsman, seated with his back to the bow, having no time but to obey the commands of his Indian guide. Now, as an idle passenger with nothing to do but watch the rush of foaming water as the pointed craft jumped the rapids, he acquired an "adequate conception of the dangers."[40]

The second phase of Burnett's influence on the Pacific Northwest had drawn to a close. He had recruited settlers and done much to launch the great migration of 1843. And as traveler and sometime captain, he had made the long trek safely. The American population of Oregon country had tripled in one autumn, with the addition of nearly 1,000 new settlers.

10 ⊣ *Burnett of Oregon*
THE ROOTS AND THE UPROOTING

Whenever, since my arrival in California, I have seen a party of immigrants, with their ox-teams and white-sheeted wagons, I have been excited, have felt younger, and . . . anxious to make another trip.

—PETER H. BURNETT, 1879

THE THIRD AND FOURTH PHASES of the romance between Peter Burnett and Oregon, his function as propagandist and his role as citizen, unfolded simultaneously. If a prime reason for his activities was to promote American acquisition of the territory by filling it with a preponderance of settlers from the states, he recognized that there were two distinct ways of going about it. One, the great migration, was behind him. The second involved the pen, and occasionally the purse, as the means of attracting future settlers.

There had been Oregon boosters before him—Ledyard, Kendrick and Gray, Lewis and Clark, Floyd, Kelley and Wyeth, Walker and Disosway, Lee, Linn, and others. Oregon fever, as witness Burnett's own recruiting success, had reached near epidemic proportions by the time he wrote his propaganda pieces from Linnton on the Willamette. But in his messages there was fresh information, wide circulation, and an authentic, optimistic ring. It was Burnett's voice which first told to the nation the details of the largest immigrant body to cross the plains and Rockies, the first to take wagons all the way to Oregon; moreover, he said, it had been done with relative ease. He told what to take, what to expect on the trail, and what to anticipate upon completion of the journey. The effect on the heavy migrations which followed must have been appreciable, probably more significant than the letters of his uncle John Hardeman had been in promoting settlement of Missouri.

Of key importance to Peter's influence was the element of immediacy. Most journals and guides such as his did not come to light until years after the fact, but the expansionist-minded Missouri lawyer, upon arriving at his destination, turned and fired an urgent literary broadside, an entreaty to his countrymen to get on with the business of peopling Oregon.

Many newspapers spread Burnett's message before the American public. *Niles National Register,* in the fall of 1844, carried his account in two issues. In December of that year, and during the following month, five long letters from Burnett were serialized in James Gordon Bennett's flamboyant *New York Evening Herald.* They were written at Linnton in 1844, the trail descriptions having been taken almost verbatim from Peter's journal.[1] The *Herald* story was widely reprinted in many states, particularly in the West. Burnett also sent numerous letters directly to other newspapers; his account was printed widely enough that it is probable most of the reading public in the states had access to it. The *Washington Globe, Ohio Statesman, St. Louis Reporter, Jefferson Inquirer and Missouri Democrat,* St. Louis *Republican, Independence Journal, Platte Argus,* St. Joseph *Gazette,* Liberty *Tribune,* and Independence *Expositor* were among the papers which carried his message.

In a volume published in New York in 1845, George Wilkes presented a rationale for the construction of a railroad to Oregon, including a 50-page section which was plagiarized from the Burnett journal. Some fictitious names and incidents were added, and Peter was given no credit for the material, but the advice to prospective settlers was Burnett's. The impact may have been the greater because of this seeming corroboration of another observer telling the same enticing story. Beyond these published accounts, Burnett wrote numerous letters to acquaintances, describing the trail and the country.

What was the story, and how did he put it across? There was the journal itself, which was encouraging to prospective settlers yet carried enough flavor of day-to-day adversity to convince readers that blemishes in the trail were not being whitewashed. And there were specific words of advice for outfitting. The wagons, he said, should be "two horse wagons, plain yankee beds, the running gear made of good materials, and fine workmanship, with falling tongues." There were many other details on wagon design and construction. To draw the wagons, "the best teams for this trip are ox teams. . . . Horses need shoeing, but oxen do not. I had oxshoes made . . . but it was money thrown away."[2] Light tools also should be taken, he advised, as wagon repairs would be necessary.

For provisions he suggested taking 40 pounds of bacon and 150 pounds of flour per person in addition to "dried fruit, rice, corn meal, parched corn meal, and raw corn, pease, sugar, tea, coffee, and such like articles," but "let the quantity of sugar and coffee be small, as milk is preferable and does not have to be hauled."

Burnett enumerated other necessities. Cattle and horses would be both useful and profitable, and the expected loss of stock en route was only 10 percent, he wrote. Firearms and accessories, light farm implements, utensils, and a water bag would be needed, but all heavy articles, including furniture and beds, should be left.

What to do was as important as what to take. Leave Missouri by May , and earlier if possible, said Burnett. For the best performance from the teams, "drive a reasonable distance every day," normally not more than eight hours with a one-hour noon rest, and stop an hour before sundown. The travelers should not overindulge in the pursuit of the tempting buffalo. "Never stop your wagons to hunt, as you will eat up more provisions than you will save." The kills will usually be far from camp and the weather too warm to save much meat. "Those who have good horses can keep the company in fresh meat. If an individual wishes to have great amusement hunting the buffalo, he had better have an extra horse, and not use him until he reaches the buffalo region. Buffalo hunting is very hard upon horses." Instructions were included on the techniques of hunting buffalo and antelope and procuring fish.

These and numerous other bits of counsel flowed from Peter's pen, liberally salted with optimistic phrases. "The trip can be made, in ordinary seasons, in four months. It took us longer; but we . . . had the way to break." Concerning the role of his company as pathmakers, he observed, "The sedge, . . . we broke down completely, and left behind us a good wagon road, smooth and easy," so that property which the immigrant started with could be carried "clear through." In Oregon the property would be worth two to four times its value at the start of the journey. "I would even be most willing to travel the same road twice over again, had I the means to purchase cattle in the States," said the promoter. "Mrs. B. (who performed as much labor on the road as any other woman) would most gladly undertake the trip again." Such statements testify that women were by no means idle passengers on the trails. On the matter of the basic necessities of life, Peter reassured his reading public that "there is not the slightest danger of starvation, and not the least danger of suffering, if even ordinary care is taken. . . . There is no danger of suffering for water." All this at bargain rates! "The trip to Oregon is not a costly or expensive one"; no more so, he stated, than a move "from Tennessee or Kentucky to Missouri."

It remained for Peter to describe the bait at the end of the long line of march to Oregon. The resources of the Northwest were depicted with hues which leave little doubt that the writer was a crusading advocate of what was soon to be labeled "Manifest Destiny." "The fisheries of this country are immense," and "the water power . . . is unequaled, and is found distributed throughout this section," with "more fine mill sites than you ever saw,"[3] were typical of Burnett's descriptions. "The timber of this section of Oregon constitutes one main source of its wealth. It is found in inexhaustible quantities on the Columbia and on the Willamette, just where the water power is at hand to cut it up, and where ships can take it on board."

Regarding navigation and commerce, Burnett was again equal to the occasion, pointing out the primacy of Oregon as a present and potential supplier of timber to California, South America, the Sandwich Islands, China, and the Pacific settlements of Russia. In foodstuffs, too, he predicted that his newly adopted home would be a preeminent producer for that quarter of the globe. "I consider Oregon as superior to California," he recorded. "The climate of that country is too warm for men to have any commercial enterprise." This opinion he would later renounce.

Burnett attempted to sell the prospective migrants on Oregon's "most mild" climate, its "most beautiful scenery in North America," its thriving towns, its flour mills, and "the best business in this country," farming.[4] Since almost 90 percent of America's people were farmers, this last entreaty was a compelling one. Land hunger was a strong force in the westward moves of the 1840s.

Despite the general accuracy of his facts, he had indulged in some glowing phrases which were to bring verbal abuse upon him. The next wave of immigrants now had someone to curse for their troubles. Comments such as "This is more of Burnett's fine road" were common where the going was rough. And where he had quoted prices that changed over the succeeding months, he was charged with misrepresentation. Peter informed his accusers that he had tried to be a historian, not a prophet. The most recent arrivals also grumbled about the country and about the damp winter which greeted them so promptly after the fall arrival, but:

> In the spring, when the thick clouds cleared away, and the grass and flowers sprang up beneath the kindling rays of a bright Oregon sun, their spirits revived with reviving nature; and by the succeeding fall they had themselves become old settlers.

There was therapeutic value in having someone to criticize. To one lady's comments that her party had abused him much along the trail, Burnett replied, "Madam, that makes no difference. On a trip like that someone must be abused, and it is well to be someone who is not present."[5]

Overoptimism there may have been, but Burnett was read and believed, and his call to Oregon was affirmatively answered, as attested by the complaints, the praise, and the size of the trail parties. That some of Peter's messages influenced the next wave of migrants is shown in several journals and reminiscences turned out by western travelers of the 1844 season. John Minto, English-born resident of Pennsylvania, joined a party of some 800 immigrants in the spring of that year. General Cornelius Gilliam, a Southern soldier, was the captain. Both Minto and the Reverend E. E. Parrish made references in their writings to "Burnett's Trail" and the "Burnett Trace."[6] The use of these terms to identify a route much of which was well known and well marked for a decade before the migration of 1843 indicates that no little weight was given to Peter's accounts and to the success of that company. William Ashley's former mountain man, James Clyman, and a pioneer who had a date with destiny in the California lode, James W. Marshall, were among others who singled out Burnett for comment as they made their way over the Oregon Trail.[7]

Reaction on the part of older settlers to new immigrants varied with individuals. Especially during gold rushes there were occasional vicious attempts to thwart the newcomers, such as salting springs and deliberately despoiling pasture. More frequently, helping hands were extended. At about the same time that Johann Sutter of New Helvetia, on the Sacramento, was sending relief to parties crossing the Sierra Nevada, Peter Burnett was offering similar aid to Oregon-bound travelers. At Fort Hall, in 1844, James Marshall reported that Burnett had written a letter telling immigrants to send word ahead to him if they needed more food. The letter was in the possession of James Grant, the factor. John Minto and two other men hurried on to the Willamette and got assistance from Burnett for their party. James Clyman scribbled a message from a point west of Grand Ronde to tell Burnett that Cornelius Gilliam's caravan was "on the road and scarce of provision."[8]

Although by no means prosperous, Peter had endured the crop doldrums of winter and was harvesting his first Oregon wheat. The incoming caravans had exhausted their provisions and had winter's fasting before them. Like migrants of the previous year, their only currency was their good intentions to repay loans of wheat and other produce, and their few garments (with which they were usually unwilling to part). The "old settlers" and Dr. McLoughlin carried them through the winter, often providing them meals and a place to sleep on puncheon floors. Burnett tells of one man who promised to repay him three bushels for one in wheat, but the lender would accept only bushel for bushel. "Pete" observed a human tendency which was probably reenacted on most frontiers. Many of the old settlers remained impoverished because they could not resist the entreaties of the needy migrants who had just arrived. It was the generosity of Baucis and Philemon toward Jupiter and Mercury, but without the rewards.

Burnett himself was interested in the acres which he was advertising, and at the very time that his missives were spread across the pages of eastern newspapers, he was trying his hand at land speculation and farming. It is apparent that another motive for his campaign to popularize

Oregon was his desire to sell his lots at Linnton, which he had named after Lewis Linn of Missouri. Burnett and a trail companion, General M. M. McCarver, had founded the town for speculative purposes at what they believed to be the head of navigation on the Willamette River, a five-mile paddle above its mouth.

They built a wagon road through the timber from Linnton to the Tualatin Plains, hoping to sell lots in the town and profit from milling, lumbering, farming, and shipping. In his propaganda barrage of 1844, Burnett said of his town, "This place . . . is the nearest point on the river to the Fallatry [Tualatin] Plains, and the nearest eligible point to the head of ship navigation for large vessels on the Wallamette." However, in justice to his motives, he gave equal and in some instances greater play to other Oregon towns, such as Astoria, Oregon City, and Champoeg.[9]

Within a short time it became evident that Burnett and McCarver had not chosen the great entrepôt of Oregon's future. The head of navigation proved to be miles upstream at Oregon City. Lots sold slowly, and receipts were below expenditures. Seeing that "expenses were certain and income nothing," and that he was unable to make a living at his profession since there was not yet a demand for lawyers, Peter diversified his activities. In April 1844 he bought agricultural land on the Tualatin Plain and ten acres of fir timber nearby to meet the lumber needs of his farm claim.

Burnett had not farmed since his boyhood days, and the experience, he records, was a strenuous one both physically and mentally. For several years after he arrived, goods for sale in the territory fell far short of meeting the needs of the growing population. Clothing and shoes were very scarce. Newly arrived immigrants were often better dressed than earlier settlers, and one could tell an "old timer" from the patches. When Burnett's boots wore out, he worked barefoot in the fields to save his first wheat crop. He was embarrassed in church on one occasion when the parson asked him to start a fire and he had to pull his bare feet from under the table. After this experience, he made shoes for himself and several members of the family, but the leather was so stiff that the shoes had to be soaked in water every night to soften them up for the next day's wearing. Farming took up a large part of Burnett's five years in Oregon. It was successful enough for him to chip away slowly at his debts.

There was much besides self-seeking business and labor to entice the public-spirited in this young colony. Oregon residents had met at Champoeg and voted approval of organic laws in July 1843. But there were important unresolved constitutional and legal questions, and with the arrival of the party of 1843, revision of the regulations was indicated. A special problem grew from the joint occupation agreement with Great Britain. Both American and British subjects lived in the territory. Neither of these mother countries provided a formal political structure for its Oregon colonists, but despite some antagonism the two groups on the local scene cooperated rather well in implementing a provisional government.

Long before he reached the Willamette wilderness, Peter Burnett had been seared with the brand of leadership. He wished most to be left alone so he could mend his financial fences; the debts weighed heavily on his conscience. But as surely as his grandfather was pulled into Tennessee public affairs, and his uncles into matters of state in Texas, so the thirty-eight-year-old newcomer was drawn into the Oregon political vortex. The meeting at Champoeg had demonstrated the need for legal know-how, and as a lawyer, Peter's opinions were quickly sought. At first he doubted the right of the residents to establish a provisional government. He soon changed his mind, concluding that it was not only a right, but a necessity. Like several of his kin, he espoused Lockian views on this matter.

A legislative committee had been set up at Champoeg, and in 1844 a second such committee, consisting of nine members, was chosen to reorganize the organic laws of the previous year, using the Iowa Territory statutes as a guide. Burnett, one of the nine, contributed his legal experience to the process. The Oregon committee provided for a chief executive to be elected every two years, a house of representatives to be elected annually, and a supreme court judgeship.

Several laws with potential for emotional overtones were passed by the legislative committee at Oregon City in 1844. Burnett introduced a bill prohibiting slavery and allowing three years for slaves to be removed or set free. Despite the fact that his father had owned slaves, or perhaps *because* of it, Peter was firm in his opposition to slavery. He stated further that if the two races lived in the same area, the white would dominate the Negro with results that would be degrading to both. His answer to this dilemma was to propose a ban on free Negroes after a two-year period. Was this logic a mask for prejudice? Various Burnett statements indicate that it probably was. The bill passed, but the antislavery section was the only part to be enforced. Paradoxically, Burnett himself had sent provisions to mulatto immigrant G. W. Bush and his family of seven as they traveled from Fort Hall to Oregon in 1844.[10]

If Peter had entertained ideas of keeping Oregon white, he also hoped to keep it sober. About strong drink he harbored some stout convictions. He had briefly operated a distillery in Missouri but had concluded, perhaps in part through the influence of his wife Harriet, that alcohol was a social evil, and he became an advocate of prohibition. Accordingly he pressed for legislation to prevent the importing, distilling, sale, or barter of "arden spirits," and such a law was passed by the committee on June 24, 1844. Burnett directed efforts both toward getting drinking out and keeping it out. In one of his advertising messages to the States, he wrote, "No country in the world affords so fair an opportunity to acquire a living as this. I can see no objection to it, except it be by a man who loves liquor, for he can get none here."[11]

In all, forty-three laws were passed by this legislative committee. The original voluntary tax provision, or government by charity, was replaced by a law which made taxes optional, but failure to pay deprived an individual of voting rights and protection under the laws of the territory. Another measure entitled each married male, each male over eighteen years, or each widow to one claim of 640 acres of land. This was less lenient than the Champoeg measure which had provided that each person was entitled to 640 acres regardless of age or sex. On the overall legislative record, Peter remarked, "We improved upon their [the 1843 government's] labors and our successors improved upon ours."[12]

Although there were few demands for legal services in private life, there were public needs for men with legal experience. In August 1845 the Oregon Legislature elected Burnett Judge of the Supreme Court, the highest judicial office in the territory. He held this post for nearly a year and a half.

Burnett's concerns were wider than the judicial bench, however. He had pressed for a larger American population and a viable provisional government. These were necessary steps, yet they were short of his goal.

Oregon was still jointly occupied by two nations. The news of the great migration of 1843 hit the American press in time to inspire and help to sell James K. Polk's expansionist platform for the presidency. Without the burst of Oregon publicity it is quite possible that there would have been less emphasis on platform planks such as "Fifty-four forty" and less chance for a Polk victory, which was by a slim margin. But an expansionist had captured the White House, for whatever reasons, and either he must stage a backdown or a showdown with Britain. Burnett, pessimistic about Polk's intentions now that he was a president instead of a candidate, feared a backdown.[13] Matters were beyond the control of the settlers, as the United States and Great Britain, who were among each other's best trade customers, were in a compromising mood. Polk did not wish to complicate his plans to take a large parcel of Mexican territory. In a treaty of June 1846 he settled for the forty-ninth parallel, and without a fight, but it was enough to fulfill Burnett's imperialistic dreams if not Polk's.

Unilateral American control did not solve all of Oregon's difficulties. Numerous problems remained, and none was more pressing than the Indian question, as punctuated by the Marcus Whitman Massacre of November 29, 1847. There were tremblings, militia reactions, and calls for aid. Burnett, George L. Curry, and L. A. Rice were designated by the Territorial Legislature to petition Congress for the extension of laws of the United States to Oregon. Theirs was more than a petition for help; it was a call for territorial government, salved with a justification for the extralegal provisional government. "Our forefathers complained that they were oppressed by the mother country, and they had a just right to complain. We do not complain of oppression, but of neglect."[14]

The mother country responded. A bill creating Oregon Territory was signed into law August 14, 1848—and there was an extra item in the package, a judicial appointment from the President for his cousin Peter Burnett. By this time, however, Peter had other plans.

Two of Burnett's three stated goals in moving to Oregon had been achieved. A big growth in the American population had been followed by his country's outright acquisition. Moreover, Harriet had regained her health. She had been practically an invalid for the better part of two years, but after a month on the Oregon trail she was doing the cooking. By 1844 her condition, according to her own appraisal, was "wonderful."[15] But

Peter had made only small headway in paying off the $15,000 debt which he had incurred in Missouri. He had done his part for the public good, he reasoned, and now must look to his personal interests. On January 1, 1847, he resigned the supreme court judgeship, since it would be incompatible with his plans to practice law, and entered a partnership with another attorney, A. L. Lovejoy.

A return to the role of private attorney did not portend permanent retirement from public affairs in Oregon. Unlike the judgeship, the office of legislator was not incompatible with private legal practice, and Peter was elected to a second term in the territorial legislature in 1848. Later that year came President Polk's designation of Burnett as Justice of the Supreme Court of Oregon. Whether or not the appointment would have been accepted under normal circumstances must always remain a moot question. But circumstances were far from normal in the West of 1848. Burnett had already resigned the legislative seat, and he declined the federal judicial appointment when Polk's message caught up with him.

Peter Hardeman Burnett had left a mark on Oregon Territory—he had influenced its population, its constitutional structure and laws, and perhaps to some degree its nationality, at least in terms of timing. While paying tribute to other Oregon leaders, John Minto sized up Burnett's role in the following terms:

> No other single individual exerted as large an influence in swelling the number of home-building emigrants to Oregon in the years 1843 and 1844 as Peter H. Burnett. Without any disparagement of many able men who became Mr. Burnett's fellow emigrants . . . , it is, I believe, true that he was all round the best equipped man for the work to be done in organizing American dominion over the Columbia River Valley.[16]

Burnett had kept a rendezvous with the frontiering tradition of his grandfather, Thomas Hardeman. To a lesser degree, so had his brothers William, Glen, Thomas, and White Burnett, who followed Peter to Oregon about 1846. William became a judge in Oregon, Glen and Thomas were ministers, and White a farmer.

As Peter had helped shape Oregon's future, so the territory had returned the deed by stamping him in the mold of a public official. Despite short-term complaints voiced against him by some disgruntled immigrants on the trail and criticisms of his handling of constitutional and racial legislation, he was apparently considered by most Oregonians to be a worthy leader. He would soon command the political backing of those who joined him in another far western odyssey.

The summer of 1848 saw the beginning of a new epoch. The United States Senate had recently approved a treaty which stripped Mexico of more than half her territory. Democrat and Whig were squaring off for the quadrennial battle for the presidency when a vessel out of San Francisco Bay made a routine stop on the Willamette River to take on board a load of flour from the great grain plains of Oregon. Routine it seemed at first, but the ship's master knew a secret that he was keeping to himself for fear that he would have to pay more dearly for his cargo. His guarded news could not long be suppressed, however. From San Francisco to Honolulu and from Honolulu to Nusqualy to Fort Vancouver it had been relayed until, while the vessel yet took flour sacks aboard, Hudson's Bay officials spilled the story of the California gold strike.[17] The James Marshall who four years previously had taken note of Peter Burnett's helping hand extended to weary plodders on the Oregon Trail had dislodged the stone that caused the avalanche. It sent this same Burnett, along with several thousand other men from the Pacific Northwest and tens of thousands from other quarters of the globe, hastening to the Sierra Nevada foothills.

California, unlike Texas and Oregon, was a fruit nurtured to ripeness by settlers from lands other than the United States, and Americans were able to pluck it with a minimum of cultivation of the orchard. On the eve of the Mexican War, less than 1 percent of the people in that province were from the United States, while roughly 90 percent were Indian and 10 percent Spanish and Mexican. Yet alienation from the mother land had long since taken place.

Despite its agricultural, mineral, and commercial possibilities—the finest on the Pacific rim from Chile to China—Alta (upper) California was late on the timetables of colony builders. To the expansionist peoples of the last 450 years, it was one of the most isolated spots on the globe; it was vast oceans, wrong-way winds and currents, forbidding deserts, and bold mountain chains away from Portuguese, Spaniard, English, Dutch, French, Russian, and Oriental. Spain occupied it at the eleventh hour of her colonial cycle, and then only in a negative response to a vague Russian threat and because of personal ambitions of Visitor-General José de Gálvez in New Spain. Youthful Thomas Hardeman could not have known as he trudged home from his first trip to trans-Appalachia that the "sacred expeditions" were just schooling and tooling for the opening of the California which six of his grandchildren would help to Americanize.

California's resource potential remained largely undeveloped by the mother lands, Spain and Mexico, for several reasons. They were low-energy nations at the time they held California, and the most obvious products of that province were competitive with Spanish and Mexican economies and complementary to the economies of several seafaring nations. Ignored by its parents, the land was a naughty offspring from its early youth, flirting and commercially cohabiting with other than its mother countries despite mercantilist regulations to the contrary. In a sense it was held in deep freeze for some seventy-five years. Given Europe's delicate balance of power structure, the grasp was just heavy enough to keep that continent's rivals from seizing it, yet light enough to allow the United States to capture the prize.

Maritime pursuits, rather than settlers, gave the United States its early contacts with California as expeditions came in search of sea otters, seals, whales, and hides and tallow. The need for a traders' haven and a Pacific Squadron base caused American expansionists to place San Francisco Bay on the calendar for purchase or conquest. Mexican leaders, precariously perched on their thrones, rejected various monetary offers from the mid-1830s to 1846. Meanwhile, continuing maritime interests, a scattering of settlers, and several United States government–sponsored expeditions led by men such as Lieutenant Charles Wilkes and Burnett's boating compan-ion Frémont kept the sights on California. President Polk, bearing an expansionist platform labeled "Rush!" could stand the itch of delay no longer, and after his attempts to purchase California failed, he plunged his country into war against Mexico over the Nueces–Rio Grande pretext which had developed following the annexation of Texas.

The rope of connections between the United States and California had been growing steadily stronger, with new strands splicing in and overlap-ping at ever shorter intervals. There were the maritime interests, overland beaver trappers, attempts to buy the province, the arrival of American naval vessels to protect shipping, the government explorers, settlers by sea and land, and finally the showdown phase of Mexican War and Bear Flag

Revolt. It was typical of the accelerating tempo and overlapping of these developments that Marshall's gold discovery preceded by nine days the signing of the Treaty of Guadalupe Hidalgo, which finally knotted California to the United States. Hernan Cortés's dream had come true, but more than three centuries late. The legend of riches was verified, although the Spanish novelist who composed it was long gone. It was a cruel blow of fate for Spain and Mexico that the United States, the foster parent, cashed in on the inheritance of its newly acquired offspring with such quickness.

Oregonians were quick to clutch at the big chance in nearby California. Their roles in that land have been badly slighted in the historical writings on California and the West. Most of the single-volume treatments either have no mention of the Oregonians or cover the subject in no more than a single clause or sentence. Yet the discovery was made by a former Oregon resident, and miners from that new territory comprised perhaps one-fourth of the men in the mother lode country by the end of the so-called "local" rush of 1848. Peter Burnett guessed that "at least two-thirds of the male population of Oregon, capable of bearing arms, started for California in the summer and fall of 1848." Out of a mining population in the 6,000 to 10,000 range, probably 2,000 were from Oregon.[18] They were numerous and influential enough to help swing the gubernatorial election of 1849 to an Oregonian, even after the large population increase of that year. They helped write the constitution and made new discoveries of gold in the Siskiyou area near the California-Oregon border.

The reasons that so many gold seekers came from the Northwest early in the rush are similar to those which account for the preponderance of Californians in the first wave of miners. Compared with Easterners, people in Oregon got the news early and had to make only small sacrifices in order to join the rush. They had recently subdued the Indians and gambled (correctly, as it turned out) that they could leave their farms and families in safety. Many harvested their 1848 crops, went to the mines for the fall and winter, and returned to Oregon in time for the spring plowing and planting. Too, they were recent transplants, with relatively shallow roots. They had more to gain and less to lose than eastern and midwestern argonauts.

It was perhaps a fitting tribute (though not a finale) to the Hardeman family's almost century-old westward thrust that a number of Thomas's descendants participated in the early development of California. Five of his grandchildren in that area were Burnetts—Peter, Glen, George, White, Thomas, and Elizabeth—and a sixth was Dr. Glen O. Hardeman. In their moves to the land of gold, they tried several of the pathways: the Oregon Trail, the overland way from the Northwest, the Santa Fe Trail, and the sea route via Panama.

Peter H. Burnett, by a clear margin, was the best known. He was forty-one, much older than the average fortune seeker, but he observed that he substituted experience for youth. He had misgivings about break-ing his attachments to Oregon. The move called for another separation from his family, which in 1832 he had vowed would never happen again. "I had not the slightest idea," he said, "of leaving [Oregon] . . . until the summer of 1848."[19] He was apologetic lest he be judged as a drifter. He had become religious, changing from Deist to Campbellite in 1840, and switching again in 1846, this time becoming a devout Catholic, which he remained until his death. Except for a few French Canadian adherents, Catholicism was unpopular in Oregon, and Burnett was subjected to some abuse for his latest conversion. He said nothing about whether or not the Roman faith in California attracted him. His Oregon enterprises had not paid off his obligations, but debts or not, he probably would have been unable to resist the lure of the mining frontier. His writings hint strongly that he regretted the discovery of gold because the challenge it posed was irresistible.

And so, after hesitating to be sure that the alleged strike was neither a hoax nor a flash in the pan, Peter Burnett determined to leave Oregon. By September 1, 1848, he began preparations to go south. Many people had left earlier, and all had taken their belongings on pack animals, since there was no wagon road through to the California settlements. But while others were content with a mere trail, Burnett's thoughts were on double track. Had he not helped bring the first wagon train all the way to Oregon even when the Hudson's Bay man at Fort Hall said it was impossible? Again it was a Bay man whom he consulted, this time the good Dr. McLoughlin, who stated that he believed wagons could be taken through to California. That was enough for Peter; he would put it to a test.

Next on the docket of Judge Burnett was to organize a wagon train, and here he had both experience and a frontiersman's reputation in his favor.

Like Tom or Bailey Hardeman, he could attract some following any time he pointed his horse's nose or his wagon tongue toward the wilderness. At McLoughlin's suggestion, he persuaded Thomas McKay to serve as guide. McKay had known the Willamette Valley for twenty years and had several times taken pack trains to California, but he was skeptical about wagons. After an eight-day recruiting campaign in and around Oregon City, Burnett was ready to start with a party of "one hundred and fifty stout, robust, energetic, sober men," and more than forty ox-drawn wagons,[20] an improvement on the months he spent drumming up interest in Oregon in 1843.

The close call with snows on his trip to Oregon was still fresh in Peter's mind, and as if he needed the reminder, there was the well-known experience of the Donner party two seasons before. It was risky leaving Oregon in September with the encumbrance of wagons and with mountains to cross. Burnett's group carried six months' provisions, and their wagons and oxen were in good condition. They were prepared for both delays in opening a road and shortages of goods in California. Peter's equipage cost him little. He already had the two wagons, one ox team, two saddle horses, the wheat, beef, pork, sugar, clothing, and most of the tools, and purchased only one ox team, some tea, and two picks.

About September 10, the caravan moved south. For the second time in his life, Burnett was elected captain of a major pioneering wagon train. Anson Cone observed, however, that old Thomas McKay was not only the guide but the virtual leader.[21] There were obstacles ahead nearly as forbidding as those on the Oregon Trail. More of the terrain was timbered and mountainous, bearing no resemblance to the Great Plains and the open intermountain reaches on the road to the Northwest from Missouri. And there was greater likelihood of Indian hostility south from the Columbia. On the other hand, several factors promised to make this trip less trying. The party was much smaller and consisted almost entirely of experienced frontiersmen. There was no problem of loose cattle; and distance was materially shorter; and a wagon road had been opened as far as the California border.

A nationalist like his close friend Burnett, Jesse Applegate had been hopeful that a new southern wagon road, avoiding the treacherous Columbia River waters, would bring more settlers to Oregon and help to ensure American acquisition of that territory. Undoubtedly, too, both Jesse and his brother Lindsay had deep personal feelings about such a project—each had lost a son to the deadly Columbia rapids at the Dalles in 1843.

The Applegate brothers set out to open a southern road in time for use by the Oregon-bound settlers of summer, 1846. Their track from the Willamette to Goose Lake in northeastern California had adequate water and pasture, but from the lake eastward to the head of the Humboldt River the road was fit for neither man nor beast of burden. If Burnett was abused for his rosy portrayal of the path to Oregon, the Applegates were verbally crucified for luring settlers to this "Death Trail" across northwestern Nevada. They guessed badly in several particulars. The very Hudson's Bay posts which they wanted to outflank, Fort Boise and Fort Walla Walla, had been, under benevolent management, helpful to American settlers. Both grass and water in Black Rock Desert proved too sparse, and the road builders failed to allow for the fact that they were fresh from the lush Willamette while the immigrants were already exhausted when they reached this parched stretch.

Applegate's Road, nightmare for travelers from Missouri, was a boon to the Burnett wagoners. Up the narrowing Willamette Valley they creaked, the green Coast Range looming close on their right, and snow-capped Cascades to the left. From Mary's River (near modern Corvallis) they veered southeastward along the foothills of the Calapooya Range. The road wriggled up the Umpqua Valley and canyon, and thence to the top of the Umpqua Mountains. Here on the incline leading through Kanyan Pass, the oxen puffed harder than at any other climb on the trip. South along the crest of the mountains the party snaked to Grave Creek, across oak- and pine-dotted openings to the Rogue Valley and on to Immigrant Creek and the foot of the Siskiyous. Pushing eastward to the Klamath River, they swung an arc into California south of Lower Klamath Lake, on to Tule Lake and across the unique stone bridge (near the present Merrill).[22] Patches of rough lava bed terrain jarred their wagons as they drove around the north margin of Tule Lake. But the prairie and marsh lands provided easier going, and the group was soon at the southwest shore of Goose Lake. From this point the Applegate road bent toward the east to intercept the

California Trail, which branched southwestward from Fort Hall.

Burnett and company must have applauded Applegate's axemen every mile of the way. But now, having veered far enough eastward to avoid a head-on tilt with the worst of the Cascade and lava bed country of northern California, they left the beaten ruts and cut their own trail. Burnett, McKay, and five other men rode horseback ahead of the wagon train to find and blaze the best route for the vehicles. These trailbreakers traveled light and shot deer to keep the caravan in fresh meat. The teamsters followed blaze marks unless instructed by signs to stop and await directions. Sixty to eighty axe-swinging pioneers cut trees and removed fallen timber to provide passage for the wagons. This practice minimized backtracking, enabled the small advance force to get close to game before it was alarmed, and made for greater safety from Indian attacks.

The country through which they passed had known bloody encounters between Indian and white. All but three members in the party of Jedediah Smith had been killed by Umpquas in 1828. It was Burnett's guide, McKay, who with Alexander McLeod had been sent by McLoughlin to retrieve the furs which Smith's group had lost in the massacre. The 1848 train encountered Indians several times, and Cone stated that one Indian was killed in the Umpqua Valley.[23] Burnett reported, to the contrary, "We proved that we intended no harm to them, but were mere passers through their country. They evidently appreciated our motives, and the result was, that we had not the slightest difficulty with the Indians." However, in a letter of November 8, 1848, he stated that a member of the party was "shot through the wrist with an Indian arrow in a little skirmish at New Year Lake."[24] This relatively bloodless experience of Burnett's party would later degenerate into savage massacre and counter-massacre, beginning within several months and culminating in the sanguinary feud between the Army and Captain Jack's Modocs in 1872 and 1873.

The homeland of the Modocs brought privations upon the party from Oregon for the first time. The muddy, "almost putrid" puddles of Goose Lake offered no refreshment from a hot October sun, and the night spent on its marshy shores was little better than a dry camp. They struck south across the Modoc Plateau toward the upper Pit River, and after crossing twenty miles of open land south of Goose Lake entered a rocky, timbered

stretch which bruised the horses' feet. An Indian trail through a pine forest
gave some relief from sun and stones, but it was followed by a dry stopover
and somber moods.

Wild game was as scarce as water, but on the following morning a
member of the group, while staking a deer, came upon a clear stream. The
animal escaped, but the water was ample reward for the chase. The
trailmakers spent the remainder of the day enjoying the "luxury" of water.
For their fresh meat supply, however, they were forced to be content with
badger, which "to our keen and famished appetites . . . was splendid
food."[25] Breaking their own road slowed the party considerably. A group
of packers from Oregon easily overtook them and joked at their slow
progress. The prospect was sobering, with wide and uncertain expanses of
mountains between the caravan and the Sacramento Valley. But they had
moved scarcely ten miles that day when this dismal assessment was
brightened.

High up on the Pit River, where it was a mere creek troughing through
a half-mile-wide valley, the vanguard of the party ran into fresh wagon
ruts cutting abruptly across their course. A former Californian and member of the overtaking pack train guessed rightly that this fresh westbound
track was the "cutoff" of Peter Lassen (pronounced Lawson), a Sacramento
Valley rancher. Applegate's, Burnett's, and Lassen's roads had been
joined. The linkup was to be more of a boon to Oregonians than to the
Easterners and Midwesterners whom Lassen was trying to serve. A year
later his cutoff would be strewn with dead oxen and mules, broken
wagons, and grave markers of misled forty-niners.[26] But Burnett's party
had found another windfall.

Peter Lassen, a Danish-born emigrant, had gone to the Willamette four
years ahead of Burnett. In the spring of 1840 he sailed to California, where
he worked as a blacksmith, built a sawmill on the Cosumnes River a few
miles from Sutter's Fort, and raised livestock. While Burnett was inching
over the Oregon Trail in the heat of 1843, Lassen was chasing horse thieves
north into the Sacramento Valley. The Danish immigrant liked the land
he saw there, and in December 1844 he secured from the Mexican
government a grant of five square leagues in what is now Tehama County
near Deer Creek. He built a small mud house and presided over his estate
as lord over a feudal manor. He hosted Frémont's party for three weeks in

the spring of 1846, and the following year he returned eastward, perhaps as far as Missouri, to recruit settlers for his section of the valley, promising to bring them over an improved "cutoff."

The forty-eight-year-old Lassen led an immigrant train including ten or twelve wagons over the Oregon Trail to Fort Hall, down the California Trail to the upper Humboldt, then along the Applegate Road to Goose Lake. From this point his party turned south, reaching the Pit twenty-five days ahead of Burnett's wagons. Had the Oregon group followed Applegate's route several miles farther east at Goose Lake, they would have hit the Lassen Trail instead of paralleling it for more than twenty miles with a duplicate road. However, it now appeared that they might be spared all substantial road breaking, which would make of Peter Burnett something more than a prophet. It seemed that his Oregon guardian angel had scarcely given up control when another took charge from California.

But if he could have looked ahead, he would have seen that not all was a pre-cut pathway; he still faced 150 miles of lava plateaus, deep canyons, rushing streams, rocky ridges, and timbered mountains. Along the north banks of the Pit his party rolled west-southwest over the beaten road, occasionally improving on it; past the present site of Canby (named after an officer who, in a few years, would be battling with Peter's cousins William and Peter Hardeman in New Mexico); through Stone Coal Valley and Round Valley; across the river above Lookout and south to Bieber; then into the very shadow of 10,000-foot Mount Lassen's east side.

It was soon apparent to Burnett and McKay that they were following an uncertain homing pigeon; Peter Lassen was lost. Bewilderment, backtracking, forfeited mileage showed in the reading of the trail. Tracks and abandoned campfires daily became fresher. Profiting from some but not all of Lassen's mistakes, the Oregon train followed his road to the summit of the northern Sierra Nevada range in the area where it joins unobtrusively with the Cascades.[27] The summit was fairly level and studded with small pines. Just beyond was the western slope's "magnificent pine-timber."

A large, fresh blaze gleamed white on a roadside pine, and a penciled message on the sapwood addressed Burnett, directing him to a letter hidden beneath a rock. It was from his former law partner, Lovejoy of the pack train. The letter stated that Lassen's party had been overtaken, "lost in the mountains and half starved." That evening in late October, Burnett's company caught up with the Lassen group, "in the condition described by Lovejoy."

Lassen, according to Burnett, had not previously explored the route.

> The moment they came to heavy timber, they had not force enough to open the road. After reaching the wide strip of timber . . . [on the west slope of the Sierra Nevada], they converted their ten wagons into ten carts, so that they could make short turns, and thus drive around the fallen timber. This they found a slow mode of travel. One half of the party became so incensed against Lassen that his life was in great danger. The whole party had been without any bread for more than a month, and had during that time lived alone on poor beef. They were, indeed, objects of pity. I never saw people so worn down and so emaciated as these poor immigrants.[28]

Five of the carts had been abandoned by their owners, who packed what belongings they could on their oxen.

Burnett's group had ample provisions to carry the distressed immigrants the remainder of the journey. The army of Oregon axemen chopped a passageway "about as fast as the teams could well follow." For some miles they traced and widened the trail broken by Lovejoy and the other packers, but at length, where the pack train descended into a ravine too precipitous for the wagons, they kept to high ground and mapped out their own trail.

The roughest part of the entire trip still lay ahead of them as they went down from pine to scrub oak level a few miles east of the Great Central Valley. At one point they appeared to be hemmed in by two impassable chasms, one on either side. But like Jason steering between Scylla and Charybdis, these latter-day argonauts found a narrow "natural bridge" which took them safely between the hazards. A short distance beyond, it was necessary to lower the wagons by ropes and raise them by double-teaming to get around a massive outcropping of rock on the crest of a ridge. Before the travelers reached the valley, they suffered through several more dry camps. In these instances it was necessary to chain the oxen, or the beasts would wander for miles to get water. Two wagons broke down while crossing the rock-strewn base of the foothills near Deer Creek.

At last, on October 29, 1848, the caravan leveled out upon the broad, flat Sacramento Valley floor. "That was our Canaan," said Burnett; the land where "our serious difficulties, our doubts and fears, would be among the things of the past."[29]

11 ⊨ *At the Foot of the Rainbow*
BURNETT OF CALIFORNIA

THAT LAST LETDOWN of rope-suspended wagons onto the floor of the Sacramento Valley was symbolic. There would be work ahead, but Peter Burnett's road had begun to level out; the last half of his life would be an easier pull. At his Deer Creek ranch, Lassen repaid some of the favors to the Samaritans from Oregon. He killed a beef and provided several days of Elysian food and rest. Unhappily for the many who would suffer and die along its delusive miles in the next several years, Lassen's Cutoff was opened. It was by no means the path to everyman's Canaan.

"Cutoff" was a misnomer, since it added nearly 300 miles to the trek from the upper Humboldt to the mines. For the wayfarers of the California Trail, it was as much a snare as Applegate's Road and the Hastings Cutoff. Those who elected it at the Humboldt trail fork did so for several reasons—because of the deceptive word "cutoff," because of the Donner tragedy of 1846 on the Truckee–Donner Lake crossing, and because it was there. J. Goldsborough Bruff, Alonzo Delano, Israel Hale, James

Hudspeth, George Jewitt, Samuel McCoy, and hundreds of others who were lured down this primrose path uniformly cursed Lassen for his attempt to exploit them by selling supplies to those who were able to stumble exhausted to his Deer Creek estate. Perhaps Lassen's motives were not this diabolical; like Applegate and Hastings, he was myopically enthusiastic about his road.

In a very material way, it was more than Lassen's Trail. Properly it should have been called the Lassen-Burnett-McKay Road, although historians have given all the credit—or blame—to the Danish ranchero. The Oregon roadbreakers both fed and led the Lassen party over the last and worst section, and without this help it is probable that some of the Lassen group would have starved.

From the time of its opening in 1848 this trail had a distinctly dual character, its reputation depending on the origin of the traveler; it was a "Trail of Death" to the west bound, who hit this worst section when they were most exhausted, and a boon to the fully provisioned fortune seekers from Oregon. Avoiding the hellish link between the Humboldt and Goose Lake, the northwesterners had the best of both roads and were in the best condition to cope with them. Burnett and McKay swung open the gate for many hundreds of prospectors from Oregon, and in so doing they pierced another hole in the armor of the montane dragon which guarded the Golden Fleece of California's mother lode.

It was every man for himself from Lassen's place to the mining centers. There was no further need for the community-help projects like clearing timber, rolling heavy stones aside, and letting wagons over precipitous grades like spiders dangling on webs. Peter Burnett, accompanied by his wife's brother, John P. Rogers, and his nephew, Horace Burnett, spurred the teams. A day or two out of Lassen's, they heard hoofbeats and trail talk coming on behind them. It was the packers who had eagerly rushed ahead at Pit River. They had been hemmed in by mountain fastnesses, and after much backtracking had reached the valley some days after the wagons. Burnett, "surprised and very much amused," wryly observed that "they had plenty of provisions, and had suffered but little. We therefore rallied them heartily, all of which they bore with the best of humor. Our ox-teams had beaten their pack-animals, thus proving that the race is not always to the swift."[1]

The Sacramento Valley ranch of another European immigrant was Burnett's next stop. Johann Sutter, a native of Switzerland, had migrated to the American midwest, then on to Santa Fe, Oregon, and California. In 1841 he bought out the Russian colony at Fort Ross and moved its valuables to his fort, New Helvetia, at the present site of Sacramento. On that location he fulfilled a long-time ambition by establishing a semifeudal colony. For the moment Burnett's contact with Sutter was indirect and brief: a passing visit to his Hock Farm on the Feather River nearly fifty miles above Sutter's Fort. Named after a small Indian group in the area, Hock Farm was an adjunct to the barony at New Helvetia. Burnett talked with the farm agent about the most likely mining areas. "No material difference," was the answer, except that the agent knew the Yuba River was good. That stream, a tributary of the Feather River, was close, and after fording the latter the two Burnetts and Rogers turned northeast toward where the Yuba sliced through Sierra foothills. Following an overnight stop at the ranch of Michael Nye, an old Missouri friend of Burnett and Rogers, the trio pressed on toward the river. On November 5, 1848, after driving eight or ten miles, they topped a rise and looked down upon the North Fork of the Yuba at Long's Bar.

"The scene was most beautiful," as the swift current twisted its blue-green course through a narrow valley, sweeping around a half-moon bar of sand and gravel. A midday sun accented the "cloth shanties" and canvas tents and one log cabin which formed the mining hive on the far side of the stream below. Peter concluded that he would look no further; this was what he had come for. There was no impetuous scramble typical of the neophyte. Burnett's self-diagnosis of his gold fever was that he "had lived and suffered long enough" to renounce the haste and frenzy which seized many of the miners.[2] The balance of the day he spent looking about the camp and vicinity.

Before he lifted his first shovel of dirt, Peter came to feel at home on Long's Bar. He learned that the place was named for two of its miners, Dr. John P. Long and Willis Long, who were brothers of Burnett's brother-in-law, Dr. Benjamin Long. It was indeed a small world; smaller, at any rate, than it had seemed to Peter on the Oregon Trail. The camp had eighty men, three women, and five children. When the miners returned to their dwellings that first evening, Burnett found numerous familiar faces from both Missouri and Oregon, and undoubtedly he learned something about gold-mining processes and prospects.

Long's Bar, like most early mining sites, was a placer deposit. Streams over geologic time had cut into gold veins, washing loose the metal and matrix and tumbling the chunks downstream, breaking them until billions of gold particles had been scattered along past and present stream beds in the sand and gravel. The channels were like gigantic natural stamping mills and sluice boxes, cracking and eroding the gold loose from the rocks, then shifting and stirring the bits of glitter until they were deposited in potholes, pools, cracks, and other recesses of the bottom, and on bars where the inside of the current's bend ran less swiftly and dropped the heavy material more readily.

On the day after their arrival, the three newcomers from Oregon bought a twenty- by fifty-foot claim fronting on the river, agreeing to pay from future earnings $300 in gold at the going rate of $16.00 an ounce. Although Peter had never mined before—nor seen a mining camp, for that matter—he had had the foresight to carry some planks from lumber-rich Oregon on the beds of his wagons. Some of his father's carpentry skills had apparently rubbed off on him, and he set to work making a miner's rocker, or cradle.

The rocker was introduced to California miners at Coloma in the spring of 1848. Isaac Humphries, an experienced gold miner from Georgia, brought the idea west. It had been copied quickly, and its use soon spread to most mining areas. The design was much like a baby's rocker—a wooden hopper, open at the top, with a metal sieve beneath to prevent large gravel and rocks from going through. The hopper was fastened or hinged atop a sloping wooden trough which had cross cleats or riffle bars nailed or wedged on the inside bottom. Two rockers were fastened underneath.

Like the simple gold pan and the more stationary long tom, the rocker depended for its operation on the sloshing of water and the heaviness of gold. Sand and gravel were dumped into the hopper and washed down with buckets of water as the device was rocked with a jerking motion. The smaller "dirt" went through the half-inch-diameter holes in the sieve and was washed down the trough. Here the gold particles, because of their weight, settled and lodged behind the riffles as the lighter sand and gravel

The cradle, or rocker, was used for gold mining by both Peter H. Burnett and Dr. Glen O. Hardeman in the mother lode country of California. *From* Harper's Monthly, *1890*.

were swept over these cleats by the water. From time to time, the gold was removed from behind the riffles and panned or combined with mercury to separate it from the remaining grains of waste material. The rocker produced less gold than the long tom and more than the pan, although it lost a higher percentage of the gold dust than the panning process.

Burnett's rocker was finished after a day. The only material he had to buy was a small sheet of zinc for the sieve. There was no shortage of labor, as the device was suited to a three-man crew. Peter, laboring in his corduroy trousers, vest of homespun sleeves, and cap with green-glazed visor,[3] shoveled the dirt into the hopper, Rogers poured in buckets of water, and Horace Burnett agitated the contraption back and forth. "Within about three or four days we were making twenty dollars each daily, and we soon paid for our claim," Peter related. "We rose by daybreak, ate our breakfast by sunrise, worked until noon; then took dinner, went to work again about half-past twelve, quit work at sundown," thankful that the searing heat of summer had passed. Their base of operations was the Nye Ranch, where Peter kept his stock and wagons, but they slept at the mining camp, "under a canvas tent on the hard ground."[4]

The prices of goods and services on the Yuba, typical of all northern California, were steeply inflated as a result of the demands of a burgeoning population. Despite the sharing of large quantities of food with Lassen's party, Burnett was well provisioned. He had hauled enough goods from Oregon that, except for the claim, the zinc for the rocker, and some molasses, he bought nothing during his month and a half as a miner. On the contrary, he took advantage of the favorable market to sell his oxen and wagons. It was a fortunate case of all income and little expense. On December 19 he left Long's Bar and bade a permanent goodbye to mining, having saved enough to support himself for six months. As did uncounted others, he concluded that plying his specialty and "mining the miners" would pay best.

Gold mining was thus a small but important stepping stone in Burnett's transition from law and politics in Oregon to law and politics California-style. He had come to know the "silent tongue and downcast look" of the hard-luck miner and the "glowing countenance, and quick, high, vigorous step" of the more fortunate one. He had found old friends and acquired new ones. Campfire evenings had been pleasant—among the most enjoyable times of his life, in fact.[5] The rush was in its young stages and was less hectic and lawless than it was to become during the general migration and mining boom of 1849. And pickings were much better than during the frenzy of the following year. Official messengers, Lieutenants Edward F. Beale and Lucien Loeser, had arrived at Washington, D.C. in late 1848, confirming the gold discovery, and President Polk's announcement to the nation had come in December of that year, while Burnett was at Long's Bar. Months before that information had spilled its deluge of tens of thousands of argonauts into the diggings, the Oregon wagonmaster was rising, albeit unknowingly, toward long-sought fortune.

His arrival at Sacramento on December 21, 1848 seemed inauspicious enough; he had ridden straight through for forty miles in snow and rain, and was wet and cold, as he had often been during his frontier life. He sized up the location, speculated that it was destined for growth, and opened an office with his lawyer's shingle over the door. John Sutter, Jr., upon the advice of James King of William, Pierson B. Reading, and Samuel J. Hensley, hired Burnett as legal counsel and business agent for the multifarious interests of his father. Young Sutter had been placed in charge of the Swiss-born emigrant colonizer's estate just a few weeks earlier as a legal maneuver to prevent creditors from attaching the Sutter property. John Sutter, Sr., was deeply, almost ruinously in debt. Some of his livestock had been moved to Hock Farm as an added precaution.

Peter Burnett's services to the Sutters were performed primarily in two closely related activities.[6] Initially, by contract with the son, Burnett subdivided, advertised, and launched the sale of a large part of the estate in the Sacramento area between Sutter's Fort and the embarcadero on the Sacramento River. In so doing, he became one of the first in a long line of successful California real estate promoters. The contract stated that Burnett was to receive one-fourth of the proceeds from the lots in Sacramento. The second phase of his activities related to the Sutter debts. In six months Burnett had raised the money from land sales and systematically paid them off, including the balance owed to the Russian American Fur Company for the purchase of Fort Ross eight years earlier. Burnett personally carried $19,788 in notes and gold and delivered it to that company's representative in San Francisco on April 13, 1849. The discharging of all these obligations possibly averted disastrous foreclosures.

If opportunity hovered close over Burnett's new enterprise, so did some thorny problems—difficulties which were to tax his ingenuity and patience and even slightly tarnish his reputation. Most of these headaches stemmed from the foibles and weaknesses of the elder Sutter, who, himself a poor businessman, was becoming suspicious of his son's managerial acumen. Sutter was angry with his son and Burnett for creating a new city, Sacramento, which threatened to compete with his nearby Sutterville. As early as 1849 the rift became serious. It was aggravated when some of the so-called friends of John, Sr., got him drunk and persuaded him to sign over to them $20,000 worth of his properties in Sutterville. They promptly used these lands as bait in attempts to lure business from Sacramento to Sutterville, thereby threatening the promotional interests of Burnett and young Sutter, who responded by offering similar inducements to business to remain in, or move to, Sacramento. Then the older Sutter, without notifying Burnett, took back control of his lands from his son (who was ill at the time) and ousted Burnett. Peter was able to hang on long enough to pay off the last of Sutter's obligations—or rather, all his debts but one.

The sole remaining obligation was to Burnett himself, who attempted to hold Sutter to the terms of the original contract. Peter won his point in the summer of 1849, securing 82 square blocks and 109 additional lots in Sacramento as his one-fourth share. In August of that year he sold half of this property for $50,000 cash. The half which he kept was valued on the tax rolls at $343,722. Did Burnett fleece Sutter, as the feudal baron of New Helvetia believed? Historian William Franklin answers this question in the negative, observing that from a small fraction of Sutter's total holdings Burnett retired from business in 1854 at about the same time Sutter went bankrupt. Sutter undoubtedly would have become very wealthy if he had not fired Burnett.[7] Meanwhile, the last of the three goals which Peter had sought in the Far West was within reach (although for some reason he delayed paying off the principal on his Missouri debts for a number of months). He would now be able to settle to a peaceful life.

But somewhere along the pathways that linked Tennessee, Missouri, Oregon, and California, Peter Burnett had fastened his gaze on other goals. His days as a wagonmaster, the Oregon legislative duties, the judgeship had not satiated his desire to play the role of leader. The moderate fortune, which had seemed an end in itself, was now a means to an end in his quest for self-realization. Perhaps he had not yet shaken off the stinging insecurity nurtured years before by his association with those cultured Tennessee relatives.

Helping to institute new governments was a familiar task to members of the Hardeman clan. Burnett's early role in California was somewhat akin to his grandfather's in Tennessee, and his own part in Oregon, but it contrasted with the efforts of Bailey Hardeman in Lone Star country. Peter denied any intention of pushing for an independent California, holding that his only concern was an adequate provisional government to serve until Congress provided for statehood.

Americans in California quickly tired of the two chief controlling institutions there, military governors and Mexican-style *alcaldes,* and pressure arose for a civil government of a type to which they had been accustomed. California, the irresistible force, with its big population increase and its natural mint of gold, demanded action from the immovable object, Congress, which faced disruption of the house divided, half slave and half free. With fifteen free and fifteen slave states, the balance in the United States Senate would be upset no matter which way California entered the Union. Congress delayed, while California activists talked of self-government.

Peter Burnett, fresh from the proving grounds of Oregon's provisional government, was soon consulted by leading residents in and near Sacramento, and on January 6, 1849, he chaired a political meeting at that town. It was one of three seemingly spontaneous gatherings of its type held within a span of a few weeks. The others were at San Jose on December 11 and at San Francisco on December 21. Burnett took the position, as he had in Oregon, that the settlers had the "right to establish a *de facto* government" which could legitimately function until replaced by a government authorized by Congress.[8] Such a provisional government was urged at all three of these town meetings. Burnett appointed a committee to draw up resolutions embodying the views of those at the Sacramento meeting. Two days later the committee's resolves were amended and adopted. They called for an election of delegates to a constitutional convention at San Jose the following March, in order to set up an interim government. And they strongly opposed slavery, a fact in which Burnett later took considerable pride.

San Francisco, in order to cope with its chaotic problems of city control, moved for a local provisional government as well as one for California. In March, Burnett arrived at that city and assumed a role of leadership. On April 21 he expounded at length in the columns of the San Francisco *Alta California,* elaborating on the principle from the Declaration of Independence that governments "derived their just powers from the consent of the governed." Even President Polk, he argued, only "advised" the people of California to accept *de facto* military rule until Congress filled the void. And that gave the settlers latitude to set up a provisional government, particularly since Congress had failed to act. Peter's rationale, drawing upon the birthright of American citizens, supported the well-known pro-settler views of Missouri's Senator Thomas Hart Benton, which were widely read and cited. While Burnett was temporarily back in Sacramento, he was elected to the San Francisco legislative assembly. Upon returning to the Bay city, he moved for the appointment of a committee to urge that the people of California get on with a convention for the purpose of governing the entire territory. (The original March convention date had been postponed until May to provide time for including the southern country.) Burnett wrote the statement of principles for that committee—a call to action for a new California government.

At this juncture, after Congress had adjourned without acting, and before the San Francisco statement was published, Military Governor Bennett Riley took the initiative away from both Burnett and the Bay city by issuing his proclamation of June 3, 1849, calling for a constitutional convention. It is probable that neither Burnett nor Riley knew of the statement which the other was writing, but Riley was no doubt influenced by the San Francisco events, as indicated by his June 4 memorandum that the city had usurped powers vested in Congress. Like a major political party which destroys a third party by adopting its program, General Riley's proclamation swallowed up the San Francisco movement. The provisional government momentum may not have been indispensable, but it was useful despite the fact that the San Franciscans were more than a little nettled by Riley's action.

The stage was now set for the Monterey convention. Which direction would it take—independence, territorial status, statehood? Burnett and the rump government of San Francisco disavowed any intentions of setting up a Pacific republic, nor would they be content with a territorial government. The momentum of their booming population and needs had carried them beyond the latter stage. Burnett called a meeting at Portsmouth Square on June 12, in an attempt to prevent the anti-Riley mood from damaging the very cause for which the provisionalists had labored. Among those present were Myron Norton, William M. Stewart, Thomas Butler King, and William Gwin. Stewart, the presiding officer, called upon Burnett for the first speech, which was an appeal for state government. Others echoed this proposal, and a committee composed of Burnett, Norton, W. D. M. Howard, Edward Gilbert, and E. Gould Buffum was appointed (apparently with Burnett as chairman) to implement the wishes of the gathering. The *Alta California* of June 21 published this committee's report, which sparred with Riley but proposed election of delegates to his projected convention and indicated that such representatives should support statehood for California.

On the statehood matter, Riley attacked the San Francisco group, accusing it of plotting for California's independence. Burnett countered this in the columns of the *Alta* on July 12, scoring the military governor for charging them "with an intent to commit the highest crime known to the laws of the United States, without the shadow of a shade of proof." There were other barbs from Burnett, and the feud with Riley, though abating, continued until the election of delegates to the convention on August 1.

Peter Burnett might well have been a delegate at Monterey, but while he was back in Sacramento settling the Sutter affair, he was nominated Superior Judge from the San Jose–San Francisco district. Riley then appointed him to that position. Burnett polled three times as many votes as Kimball Dimmick, his opponent, and was selected Chief Justice.[9] He accepted the assignment and moved with his family (who had come by boat from Oregon to San Francisco in May 1849) to San Jose in August. As he settled into his judgeship, speculated in lands of the South Bay area, and watched the political developments unfold, he must have indulged in another kind of speculation: if he could win a judge's seat so handily, why not another office?

The delegates at Monterey decided promptly to bypass territorial status and draw up a state constitution. "The Supreme Executive power of this State," wrote the members at the convention, "shall be vested in a chief magistrate, who shall be styled the Governor of the State of California." Burnett set his sights on this office. In mid-September, before the document was completed, he announced his candidacy in Monterey. Late in October he returned to the familiar political ground of San Francisco and made it known in that city's newspapers that he would run as an Independent for the position. This was ideal campaigning; it was Burnett country, as the election for judge had indicated. Its voter population was high, and they were interested voters. Furthermore, it had well-established organs of publicity. Knowing better than to give much time to a constituency that was already in his pocket, the judge caught a steamboat for Sacramento. Despite heavy rains, he took a swing through the mining country to the east. This, too, appeared to be Burnett country; there were large blocs of ready supporters from Oregon and Missouri. And if Peter was no longer a miner, he was from the mines. His head might have reached greater heights, but his feet still trod the miners' earth; they were fresh from Yuba River sands. He spoke the miners' language without an accent and was practically a co-author of the settlers' political viewpoint. The campaign came to a close as Burnett doubled back for a speech at San Jose and a final address at San Francisco. In the course of this last stumping speech, all of the platform collapsed except the section occupied by Burnett. As he glanced at those dignitaries who had been unceremoniously dumped on the ground, he quipped that while others might fall, he would "be sure to stand."[10]

A gray, stormy election day, November 13, 1849, produced a light vote but a heavy majority for Peter Burnett. He defeated his nearest rival, W. Scott Sherwood of San Francisco, 6,716 to 3,188. John Sutter, John W. Geary, and William Stewart received among them a total of 4,295 votes. Burnett would be the presiding officer, and it appeared that he would have something over which to preside. The Constitution was approved fifteen to one. He took the oath of office at San Jose, December 20, amid rain and flood, and became the pioneer elected governor—the first nonmilitary chief executive of California. Peter had come "alone and unattended—no pomp, no ceremony—no venal guards, no useless parade of armed men,"[11] and his inaugural address before the legislature was brief.

> . . . To be chosen Chief Magistrate of California at this period of her history, when the eyes of the whole world are turned toward her, is a high and distinguished honor, and I shall do all in my power to merit this distinction by an ardent, sincere, and energetic discharge of the weighty and responsible duties incident to the position I occupy.
>
> Nature, in her kindness and beneficence, has distinguished California by great and decided natural advantages; and these . . . will make her either a very great or a very sordid and petty State. She can take no middle course. . . . I anticipate for her a proud and happy destiny.

Burnett concluded with pledges of his cooperation and with good wishes to the legislators.[12]

It was a beginning well received, but only a beginning. There were no local precedents to guide the governor and the legislature, and there were serious problems, not the least of which was the condition of limbo owing to Congressional inaction. To meet these problems Burnett brought some experience, but according to State Senator Elisha O. Crosby he also came with a distinct lack of resolve and self-assurance, a timidity, and a fiscal conservatism, all foreshadowing difficult times.

Burnett's experiences as governor accurately mirrored his personality and character. Like most political figures, his contributions lay at some point between the apprehensions of his enemies and the expectations of his friends. He strove hard to handle matters with integrity—to live up to the moral teachings of his forebears; and no one hinted at dishonesty in his administration. But Crosby was right. Burnett would not have a hand in the till, but neither would he have a firm hand at the tiller. He lacked a taste for the tough political decisions; he was a philosophical leader, but the infighting was not his meat. He could take on Congress, assail General Riley, or write a volume on his religious convictions, but these confrontations were on broad points of philosophy. Upon addressing the legislature on the governance of the state, he clung to broad outlines and gave little executive leadership. When the lawmakers did not heed his advice, he accepted the reversal without a fight.[13]

There was no disagreement over the first step, to proceed as if California had been admitted to the Union. The legislature needed no urging whatsoever on this point, but Burnett urged it nevertheless, citing the precedents of Missouri and Michigan, where legislatures convened before admission to statehood.[14]

The first legislature, meeting without benefit of state-supplied paper and pens, was aware of the need for immediate sources of government funds, and here it broke with the governor's recommendations. Burnett's private indebtedness may have been a source of his caution, for he favored a strict "pay-as-you-go" basis of state finance, despite a constitutional clause which authorized the sale of government bonds. The going interest rate was in the neighborhood of 5 percent per month, and the chief executive thought it unfair to saddle future citizens with burdensome costs of a previous government. His proposal for real and personal property taxes preceded that of a later Californian, economist Henry George, in suggesting a tax on unused land designed to break up the big landholdings. Owners of large estates would be obliged to put their idle land to work or sell it rather than pay high taxes on it, and either way California agriculture would be diversified and expanded. This was turned down, as was his plan to cope with tax collecting from a transient population by requiring that collectors accompany assessors. Nonpayment of taxes would be grounds for denying the delinquent person the right to bring civil suit in California courts. Burnett had experience with this device in Oregon, but it was rejected by the California lawmakers, along with his advice against bonded indebtedness.

Lawyer Burnett had some ideas about the state legal structure. He proposed a unique combination of code law for civil cases (somewhat like the Roman and Napoleonic code form as used in Louisiana) and English common law for criminal and commercial cases. The legislature, however, adopted the English common law throughout. With respect to the incorporation of cities, the governor proposed a single system under general law. In one of his rare vetoes, he rejected special legislation for the incorporation of Sacramento, but his veto was overridden, and California since that time has had both charter and general law provisions.

Law and order in a bawdy, gold-rush society was a major problem, and Burnett had some plans for dealing with it. There were not enough jails to lock up the accused or the convicted, and thus punishment was usually too severe or not severe enough to fit the crime. Offenders were either turned loose or physically harmed—by hanging, ear cropping, lashing, or other measures. There was little provision for the intermediate measure, detention. Burnett's solution was more speedy justice and strong punishment (including the death penalty for robbery and grand larceny) until adequate county and state prisons could be constructed, but he firmly opposed vigilante actions. As both frontier lawyer and judge, among Mormons, miners, cattle thieves, and claim jumpers, he distrusted mob "justice." His counsel was often rejected or ignored, and true to his nature he did not press his views. He did call the state militia in August 1850 to suppress squatters who were threatening order and the sanctity of private lands— some of them his own—in Sacramento.

Burnett has been criticized for a statement to the legislature, January 1851, that "a war of extermination will continue to be waged between the races, until the Indian race becomes extinct . . .," but this was a prophecy, not a policy. He added that this "inevitable destiny" was anticipated with "painful regret." Peter further observed concerning the Indians, "We have suddenly spread ourselves over the country . . . and appropriated whatever proportion of it we pleased to ourselves, without their consent and without compensation. . . . [They] have some conception of their right to the country, acquired by long, uninterrupted, and exclusive possession." The whites drove the Indians to starvation, he noted, then levied war on them for the very natural killing of stray livestock of the settlers. Before a legislature hostile toward the Indians, this was an unusually bold statement for a timid governor. Although there were many calls for the militia to "defend" against the Indians, Burnett refused all but two, sending the state forces only to El Dorado County and to the Colorado River.[15] While he was not a great champion of the aborigines, his observations at Fort Laramie and in Oregon and northeastern California show an admiration of, and sympathy for, their race which perhaps placed him ahead of most pioneers of his era. He was a product of his time, and like the other early western governors, he failed to exert the force to counter the preponderant view of the settlers that the Indian should be wiped out or banished to the wastelands.

Toward black residents and potential residents of California, Burnett was less charitable. He was both a vigorous opponent of slavery and a segregationist. The California constitution, he stated, wisely excluded slavery, but it also "excluded this class of persons [Negroes] from the right of suffrage, and from all offices of honor and profit under the State." Confronted with these circumstances, he argued, they would inevitably remain in a subordinate and degraded economic and social position. "Either admit them to the full and free enjoyment of all the privileges guaranteed by the Constitution to others, or exclude them from the State."[16] These could have been noble words for the times had he not pressed for exclusion instead of equality before the law and had he not later (as a supreme court justice) voted to support slave status for a black resident in the famous Archy Lee case. Burnett was not alone in his proposal to ban free blacks from California. Such a measure had been adopted at the convention in Monterey but was dropped for fear that it would cause Congress to refuse statehood. The legislature too rejected the proposal.

California's first year of statehood, *de facto* though it was, ended on a relatively quiet note. Party battles had not advanced to the dueling stage as they would in the near future, and the record told of a ship of state well launched for the turbulent place and time. The loudest political event had been the salute fired in San Francisco on October 18, 1850, upon the arrival of the mail steamer Oregon. This vessel carried the news that the Thirty-first Congress had admitted California as the thirty-first state of the Union on September 9. Burnett had little to do with this directly, but his quiet dealings with the legislature may have indirectly smoothed the way. A Congress which was reluctant to tamper with the North-South balance of power in the Senate might have been only too willing to seize upon political turmoil in California as an excuse to deny admission again. On the debit side, had Burnett's proposal to bar free Negroes been adopted, it could have given Congress the pretext to block admission.

When Peter delivered the annual governor's message to the Second Legislature on January 7, 1851, he got a cool reception, probably in part because of his unpopular statement on the touchy Indian question. Two days later he resigned from the governorship, citing the press of personal business as his reason. True, he had not formally finished paying off his Missouri debts (they were paid, however, within the year); the taxes on his Sacramento property were high; and his land speculation at Alviso—the supposed gateway to the capital at San Jose—was not providing the envisioned returns. Perhaps his $10,000 annual salary was considered inadequate to offset the business sacrifices. But an unstated reason no doubt affected his decision, the same reason that had prompted his resignation as wagonmaster on the Oregon Trail. He had no stomach for the often bitter day-to-day battles. He had played his role, and now it was over. Like the great migration to Oregon, California was organized and well started on the long trail. He was a ship's architect but not its captain in battle. Half his years lay ahead of him, but he had finished his contribution to the American westward movement.

Burnett joined with his sons-in-law C. T. Ryland and W. T. Wallace in law practice at San Jose. Early in 1852 he received a temporary appointment to the Supreme Court of California; later that year he moved to Sacramento, where he watched over his property and served a term on the city council. By 1854 he retired from the practice of law, and in 1857 Governor J. Neely Johnson appointed him again to the Supreme Court (to fill another unexpired term). Peter was elected to that body later the same year, serving until the fall of 1858. Five years later he accepted the presidency of the Pacific Bank of San Francisco, a position which he held for more than sixteen years.[17]

Peter and Harriet Burnett raised a family of six children, Dwight, Letitia (Martha), Romie (Rometa), John, Armstead, and Sally, all of whom came to California. (Armstead and Sally were married on the same day, November 21, 1860, and both died within a year and a half of that date.) Soon after Harriet's death in 1879, Peter gave up the bank presidency. He invested his savings in United States bonds and remained in busy retirement[18] until his death in 1895, at the age of eighty-eight. He was buried at the family cemetery in Santa Clara.

In California, Peter Burnett had found that illusory treasure at the foot of the rainbow, although in unexpected form. He had gone to Oregon in search of land and had left just before Congressional action would have partly fulfilled his wish, and when he went to California seeking his fortune in gold, he found it in land. His goals had been met, even to the one which he had laid up in his heart as a diffident, unpolished lad visiting in Tennessee—out-distancing his well-to-do relatives there. But his political and financial achievements apparently did not really change him much. Burnett would remain the simple, genial type, clinging to his deep

religious feelings and to his tradition-locked standards of personal behavior. If one were to catch him for a portrait in his best hour, in his most
typical character role, it would not be as politician or career man in
business suit and dark cravat, not as stately arbiter in judicial robes, but as
the figure with calloused hands and green-glazed cap, seated by an
inviting campfire on the banks of the Yuba, swapping yarns with his
mining friends old and new.

12 ⊨ *Mirage*

DR. GLEN O. HARDEMAN IN THE GOLD RUSH

"I HAVE AN ALMOST IRRISISTABLE LONGING to go to Santa Fe or the mountains, but I must give that up. What pleases the fancy is not always the most substantial, and 'all is not gold that glitters.'"[1] These musings of nineteen-year-old medical student Glen Owen Hardeman in December 1844 seem almost prophetic of James Marshall's discovery at Coloma some three years later; but of greater significance, they highlight, in documented form, the westward urge which possessed Thomas Hardeman and his wayfaring descendants.

Five years passed, and their passing brought vast changes to the nation—the acquisition of Texas, Oregon, and California and the Mexican cession, capped by global tremors resulting from the gold discovery. Changes there had been for Glen Hardeman also; he had taken two medical degrees and established a practice in Missouri. But one thing was unaltered—that fancy, that irresistible longing for western adventure. If bets had been placed on the candidates least likely to take the trail to Santa

Fe in 1849, Glen would probably have been among those singled out. His father John and his uncle (and namesake) Glen Owen had both died while returning from New Mexico. As recently as 1847 the Pawnees had clashed sharply with travelers on the trail. Meanwhile, young Glen had just taken over a well-established medical practice from a family friend who was retiring. Yet the fall of 1849 found him succumbing to the West's new epidemic of "yellow fever"—California gold—and he was off for the diggings, choosing, of all routes available, the Santa Fe Trail!

Glen was the favorite grandson of patriarch Thomas Hardeman. They lived in the same household for five years, and after John's death in 1829, Thomas was like a father to the young children. Perhaps the seedlings of Glen's wanderlust were planted even then as the old man filled his head with stories of the frontier. But while there were strong forces in his time and state pulling multitudes westward, Glen was subjected to some tugging in the opposite direction. His mother Nancy opposed his westering urges, as did his older brother Locke. Glen spent a large part of his time at the latter's home near Arrow Rock. Locke, who had his father's blue eyes, brown hair, and general facial features, lived in Missouri most of his life. Unlike a host of his kinsmen, he eschewed, or disdained, the "folly" of frontiering. He traveled widely in the East and South as a merchant and slave trader[2] but always returned to his farm and his white colonial two-story house with its square columns and spiral staircase. Locke invented a hemp breaker, a portable livestock fence, and a horse-drawn reaper which, according to one report, was copied and patented by Cyrus McCormick.[3] He sampled, then abandoned politics after serving one term in the Missouri House of Representatives.

"What I feel for you," John Hardeman wrote to his son Locke in a departing message, "it will be impossible for you to know until you become a father."[4] Locke was a life-long bachelor, but he cared for his younger siblings, Glen and Leona Hardeman, with all the attentiveness and guidance of an affectionate father. It was largely through Locke's influence that Glen stayed his desire for frontier wandering and went east to prepare for the profession of his Uncle Blackstone. He studied medicine at Kemper College in St. Louis during the mid-1840s and received an M.D. degree from the University of Missouri in 1848. The following year he tacked on a second M.D., this one from the University of Pennsylvania in Philadelphia. Soon Glen was back in Missouri, where he opened practice at Arrow Rock, Brunswick, and Marshall.[5]

The year 1849 was a bustling one in central Missouri, where a trickle of forty-eighters had become a deluge as word of California gold was confirmed by presidential announcement. The little town of Arrow Rock, located in Saline County where the old Santa Fe Trail crossed the Missouri River, was a focal point through or near which poured thousands of forty-niners. Saline surrendered about 150 of its residents in the spring of '49. Dr. Hardeman, twenty-four years old, unmarried, and fresh from the confines of college, found his profession dull compared to the appeal of the West. He seemed to be a fitting descendant of a venturesome breed. His cool blue eyes would one day look at the end of a gun barrel without yielding up a principle. Glen was five feet ten or eleven inches tall, with medium build, brown hair, lean face, and firm-set mouth and chin. He had a keen sense of humor, and he displayed toward his companions a feeling of loyalty or conscience—the kind of concern that would bring him to wait along the trail for the hindmost rather than to rush ahead with the crowd toward the gold mines.

John A. Bingham, a classmate of Glen's at Kemper, came to California through Santa Fe and El Paso in 1848 and returned to St. Louis after a successful mining season. He wrote a detailed description of the Santa Fe Road to Glen,[6] who prepared to leave over the same route to California in September 1849. Such a starting date for the Platte–South Pass route would have spelled winter disaster in the mountains. But the Santa Fe Trail was passable at any season, and the fall months had certain advantages, not the least being relief from the sweltering heat. Some 10,000 to 15,000 gold seekers selected that route during the rush years. Hardeman's caravan was no small aggregation; he was impressed by the "immense" preparations at the first rendezvous just west of Marshall. There were many wagons and pack trains and "a 2 wheeled 'hand barrow' easily propelled by one man."[7] During the next several years these became quite common.

A quarter century of Santa Fe traders had not dimmed the prospects for taking buffalo along the trail, as Glen was soon to discover. Wolves, too, were seen in numbers, and "wild Indians" were spotted as they stalked the caravan from a distance. Guards were posted nightly, and on one occasion the entire outfit was rudely awakened by the crack of a sentry's rifle. The guard reported that he had seen and fired at a moving form in the prairie grass. No one slept for the remainder of the night, but dawn disclosed only a dog, shot by the sentry in the gloom—a reenactment of the Oregon Trail and Sutton's "four-legged Indian." A few weeks later the episode was repeated—another sleep interrupted by a sentry's gunfire. This time daylight revealed a dead Indian, knife in hand, near the wagons. Glen guessed that he had planned to cut the horses loose and stampede them.

Upon reaching the New Mexico settlements, Hardeman followed the Rio Grande south to El Paso. Whether because of unfavorable reports from returning prospectors, fear of cholera, apprehension over the Apaches, or for some other reason, he decided to abandon the California trip. With several companions, he went south into Chihuahua, traveled by pack mule "across the High table lands of Mexico," and doubled back to the southernmost stretch of the Rio Grande, approximating the route his father John had taken twenty years earlier. The Mexican War having ended only two years before, it was not the safest time for Americans to be caught wandering below the border. Following down the river to its mouth, these wayward argonauts chugged by steamboat through the Gulf of Mexico to New Orleans and Missouri.[8]

Whatever prompted the change in plans and the premature homeward journey, Glen's passage to California was not prevented, but only postponed. His second effort was in keeping with one of his personality traits. When he failed at something, his sense of personal shame impelled him to reach for a new and firmer resolve with which to tackle the assignment again. As a young man he was an inveterate pipe smoker. One evening he decided to quit the habit, and, removing the corncob bowl from the pipe, he tossed it into the bushes. He split the pipe stem in two with his knife and threw one half on each side of the walkway as he entered the house at Arrow Rock. That night after dark he was back with a candle, searching on hands and knees for the pieces. He tied the stem halves together, stuck them into the bowl, and had a smoke. Next morning, in disgust at his lack of will, he flung the pipe into the fireplace and never smoked again. So it was with his search for gold. Before the year 1850 was out, Hardeman had found his rededication and begun his second quest. John L. Hardeman urged his brother to forget California, but he might as well have been King Canute ordering the tide to go back. Armed with the experience of his recent trip, and with some knowledge of the Spanish language, Glen again headed for California, this time via a faster and, in some respects, easier route.

If the Isthmian passage which he chose had some advantages over the Santa Fe Trail, it was also more expensive. To finance the trip, he took several slaves by steamer and sold them in Louisiana for $2,300, a figure which he considered a "sacrifice." He went to New Orleans and booked passage for Havana and the port of Chagres on the 3,000-ton steamer *Ohio*, commanded by Captain J. F. Schenck.[9]

On the morning of November 14, 1850, the *Ohio* left New Orleans. The Gulf of Mexico was calm, and the passage was so smooth that there was none of the customary seasickness between New Orleans and Havana. Hardeman's single-berth room, "though somewhat resembling the cell of a dungeon," was comfortable enough. He watched the passing ships and settled back to read the occult philosophy of Bulwer's *Zanoni.* The weather held clear, and on the afternoon of November 16, the island of Cuba hove into sight "looking like a distant cloud resting on the water." On board the *Ohio* were several Spaniards who were "on tiptoe of expectation to catch a sight of their beloved Havana." The vessel reached harbor just as the sunset gun sounded, and since no ship was permitted to dock after that time, the captain was compelled to steam to and fro before the city, until dawn. Dr. Glen Hardeman's own description of that night conveys the feeling of a wandering descendant of wanderers.

> The most glowing accounts written do not overrate the beauty of the harbour and scenery around. The loveliness of a clear moonlight night— enjoyed from the deck of a vessel in the harbour is absolutely indescribable.[10]
> It was surely the most beautiful . . . sight I ever beheld. The full moon shone as bright as day; the houses could be seen . . . with tall palm trees towering above the roofs. I sat up the balance of the night entranced with the lovely scene.[11]

He described the hustling harbor with its "annoying" customs and health officials; its plethora of ships and soldiers from Spain, on hand as a precaution against recurrence of the Lopez insurrection; its hundreds of small sailboats and rowboats busily carrying passengers or tropical fruits. Glen spent several days in port, but the military air was chilly, and he stayed ashore only long enough to visit a few sites.

On November 18, the Panama-bound passengers were transferred to the United States Mail steamer *Georgia,* commanded by Captain David Dixon Porter, later hero of the battle of Vicksburg and an admiral in the United States Navy. Porter was working in the passenger trade while on extended leave from the Navy following his active service during the Mexican War. Either on this or his return trip Glen was on the same vessel with another well-known figure, Italian General Giuseppe Garibaldi.

Out of Havana, en route to the Isthmus, the *Georgia* coasted along the western end of Cuba and passed Cape San Antonio, the western tip of the island, by November 20. On the following day the seas became heavy, and the vessel, known to sailors as one of the worst "rollers" in service at the time, pitched and tossed until the diarist became seasick. The journal thus came to an untimely close, not to be resumed except for a short account of the return trip. Fortunately, brief memoirs, a packet of letters, a ledger, and some sketches provide a measure of continuity to his travels.

The Caribbean leg of the trip was soon over as the Isthmus of Panama came into view during a heavy tropical downpour. Glen observed, on the bluff above the mouth of the Chagres River, the old Spanish fortress of San Lorenzo, still unreconstructed from bombardment by Henry Morgan in 1671. Debarking at the town of Chagres, Hardeman spent the night in "what they call a hotel." Exasperating delays were frequent in this "mañana" land, but he and several other travelers were more fortunate than many. After "long dickering and palavering with the owners of canoes," or bongos, the little group secured the services of two Negro boatmen, and later in the day they moved up the Chagres River to undertake the "most vexatious" task of negotiating the sixty-mile trans-Isthmian route.[12]

Darkness settled fast on the river in the wake of the setting sun, the travelers noting that there was little twilight in the tropics. They paddled to shore, and after failing in an attempt to light a palm log, sat up the entire rainy night in discomfort as the water rolled down their backs. The boatmen, clad in shirts reaching down to their heels, suffered from the cold, while Hardeman, huddled in his "India rubber coat . . . fared

Among the thousands of prospectors lured to the California gold fields was Dr. Glen O. Hardeman, who took the sea route via Panama. He stopped briefly at Chagres, a deceptively beautiful, disease-infested site. *From* Century Magazine, *1891*.

better than the others." The remainder of the voyage up the Chagres was without noteworthy incident; the two skilled canoeists "walked" the boat up river, their long poles shoving against the stream bed, or paddled to "one side or the other as the current happened to be swift or slow." Provisions on this leg of the journey consisted largely of sardines and the eggs of gulls, pelicans, and other sea birds.[13]

Glen Hardeman, a lifelong student of nature, noted the presence of considerable wildlife in the Isthmian region—pelicans, parakeets, sloths, monkeys, and alligators. The jaguars, he concluded, had been frightened back into the woods away from the trail by the din of passing adventurers.

After several days the party reached the town of Gorgona, from which overland trails led to Panama City on the Pacific. At Gorgona Glen began the twenty-mile plod along the old Spanish Panama-to-Portobello silver trail, which had been for several centuries the path of bullion-burdened pack animals. At one time cobblestoned, the road had deteriorated badly, although it still provided all-weather passage. He rented a mule, a decision which he later regretted because the rain and mud made traveling on foot more expedient; and he walked much, sharing the animal with a fellow adventurer. Crowds of homeward-bound gold seekers, generally having little to say, were encountered along the trail, their weary expressions making words unnecessary. Hardeman's first letter to his brother at Arrow Rock stated that he was distressed at having been separated from his friends. He was no doubt equally distressed over his separation from the trunk which he had shipped from Gorgona to Panama City. He did not see it during the entire overland journey, and after an anxious search, "came across . . . the trunk lashed to the back of an ox" and "did not recover it until the last hour for sailing of the Steamer."[14]

The vessel he referred to was the Pacific Mail Steamship Lines side-wheeler, *Panama,* commanded by Captain J. T. Watkins. The ship was crowded with passengers to the point of discomfort, in order to milk all possible income from the feverish demand for transportation. The process of taking cattle aboard elicited a detailed description.

> I witnessed the shipment of our beef cattle which were floated out to the vessel anchored a mile or two in the harbor. Two steers at a time were lashed by the horns to a pole across a canoe—were hoisted on board at the end of a rope over a pulley in the rigging.

If the process of bringing the twenty or thirty steers on board was interesting, the act of consuming the meat was not. With his youthful appetite, Hardeman was acutely aware of the ship's bells sounding the meal hours. "Provisions," he related, "were hard to get so far from the markets of the U.S. We lived mainly on sardines and very poor beef."[15] This was varied occasionally by large land turtles from the Galapagos Islands and by marine life caught on the voyage to San Francisco.

No prior sailing to California had aroused as much concern and anxiety as did this one. The *Panama,* when it embarked from the Isthmian port of the same name on December 4, 1850, carried the usual cargo and more. Of its 150 passengers, 25 were women, the largest proportion of ladies ever to sail to California on any vessel to that date; and some children, too, were on board. Most of these were families traveling west to join men who had come "but for a day" to the diggings and had elected to remain. The trip from the Isthmus to the Golden Gate was normally made in about eighteen days; by December 22 and 23 expectations were high, but the *Panama* did not appear. Day after uneasy day passed. On December 26 the San Francisco *Alta California* noted much anxiety in the city, but stated that there was no cause for alarm. Two days later hopes were lifted as a vessel with black smoke billowing from its stacks came into view, but optimism gave way to increased alarm as it turned out to be the *Constitution,* which had left the Isthmus some days after the *Panama*. This ship reported heavy weather but had no news of the missing liner. Newspapers predicted that the *Northerner,* which had sailed from Panama City on December 10, would bring word of the tardy steamer, but the *Northerner* arrived on schedule, and the *Alta California* carried the brief, ominous news item, "No tidings of the *Panama* are reported." The gloom thickened. "Fools and cranks" compounded the agony by circulating false reports that the missing vessel had been sighted. Finally, on January 2, 1851, the "long looked for" *Panama* docked safely at San Francisco, its passengers only then learning that they had been presumed drowned.[16] The mystery of the ship's disappearance was at last explained.

Four days out of Panama City, the vessel had lost its steam power when the crosstail broke. Emergency repairs took eight days, during which time the *Panama* traveled under sail. On December 20 it anchored at Acapulco, a regular stop, to take on water, coal, and other provisions. Here Glen went ashore and wrote a letter home as he sat in a "crowded noisy room with an auction going on at the door."[17] As they steamed north off the coast of Mexico, numerous whales were sighted, and a very large white shark and a dolphin were caught. There was a brief stop at Mazatlán, then the ship proceeded to San Diego, near which it suffered a broken cylinder valve. Repairs were made in eight hours, but there was further loss of time when, apparently near San Diego, a fouled anchor chain nearly wrecked the vessel. Monterey, a regular stopover, was bypassed because of dense fog.

At San Francisco, most of the argonauts quickly booked passage to the gold country. That Glen Hardeman may have been seeking either more or less than gold is suggested by his different course of action; he headed immediately for San Jose and a reunion with his cousins, the Burnetts. Without doubt, family ties were a shaping force in his western ambitions.

The Bay landing for San Jose and for much of the Santa Clara Valley was the town of Alviso, established in 1849. Here, nine miles north of San Jose, Glen joined his relatives and established his first California residence. He was impressed by the mild winter climate and observed shortly after his arrival, "As for returning to Missouri—I expect to stay here 15 or 20 years if not for life." But he was by no means certain that his long stay would be at Alviso.

> Everything wears such an artificial aspect here that until I get a better insight into things I am afraid to make a permanent location. Coz. Peter [Burnett] advises me to settle here & wait for the growth of the place thinking it will be a considerable town but I am afraid that his hopes in that respect may get the better of his judgement for he is one of the proprietors of the town. . . . There is a great probability of the seat of government being removed from San Jose which will very much retard its growth.[18]

Regarding the future of Alviso, the newcomer's judgment proved better than that of the former governor. As at Linnton, Oregon, Burnett's speculation failed to pay off; the town did not flourish, and the capital was moved from the Santa Clara Valley.

While waiting to get his bearings for a permanent location, Glen tried to make a start in medicine. The year before his arrival a severe cholera epidemic raged in the South Bay area, but in early 1851 he observed,

"This valley is unaccountably healthy & I doubt but that it will be a long time before there is practice enough . . . to justify a physician devoting his whole time to it."[19] In order to cover his expenses, he went into a business with Peter Burnett's brother.

Hardeman and Thomas Burnett, when they joined together in a gardening partnership, may have been acting on the advice of Peter, who, in his inaugural address of December 1849, paid tribute to California's commercial and agricultural prospects, stating that they were "greater and more commanding than our mineral resources." This was a strong statement for the peak year of the gold rush, but an accurate one. Soils around Alviso were considered as good as any in the valley. The two men purchased four oxen, a wagon, implements, and an assortment of garden seeds. Word had come from Sacramento that great profits had been made from onions in the mining country, and the gardeners devoted much of their acreage to this commodity.

Artesian water from the hills on each side of the valley pressed upward underneath the clay soil, keeping it relatively moist during the dry summer months. But the winter of 1850–1851 had been unusually dry, and Hardeman and Burnett decided to forestall possible crop losses by irrigation. They built a windmill and pump, and proceeded to water their growing investment.[20] A native passer-by who saw the contraption working was reported to have observed, "Los Americanos saben mucho" (The Americans know much). Irrigation had been practiced at a number of missions in California, but this appears to have been the first use of the windmill for that purpose in the Far West. As it did in later years on the Great Plains, the device spread through California following this introduction. With prices at a high level, Glen speculated that he should clear between $1,000 and $1,500 on his share of the agricultural venture.[21]

Hardeman boarded first with his partner and then with a Mr. Ricketts, who was in the warehousing business at Alviso. The doctor tasted of the local social activity, taking the opportunity to "shake a foot" at a "fandango" given at ex-governor Burnett's home when his eldest daughter Martha married J. T. Ryland, a lawyer and a friend of Glen's from Missouri.[22] Meanwhile, the "doctoring" business was not providing Hardeman with much income, and he decided to leave his future farming fortunes in the hands of the elements and Thomas Burnett, at least temporarily, while he had a fling at the diggings.

On April 1, 1851, Glen left Alviso for the mines at Mariposa,[23] the southernmost point of the mother lode southeast of Stockton—nearly the opposite end of the mining range from where "Pete" Burnett had rocked his hastily made cradle. He expected either to pan gold or practice medicine at "one of the mining towns where there is plenty of sickness— though plenty of doctors—for they are plenty as blackberries here."[24] The prevalence of physicians in the gold rush has been often noted. Dr. Fayette Clappe, sometime husband of Dame Shirley, was one of twenty-nine doctors in the Rich Bar community of about 1,000 people. Why this inordinately high percentage of physicians in a rough, frontier environment? They were as susceptible as anyone else to the appeal of glamour and the prospect of quick wealth, and perhaps more so in some instances where appetites had been whetted by the good things in life. Doctors had an extra string to their bow; failing in either mining or medicine, they could try the other. They must have concluded that the population boom, frontier privations, and gold would provide ample patients who could pay the fees. But too many medical men had the same idea. The physician was in a better than average position to gamble, particularly since his capital investment—training, medical bag, and a few books—was not difficult to transport.

Whatever the reasons, doctors came in large numbers to ply their professions, to exchange the scalpel for the shovel, and perhaps because of that "irresistible longing." Fourgeaud and Townsend of San Francisco, Den of Los Angeles, McKinstry of New Helvetia, Bale of Monterey, Leonard of San Francisco and Sacramento were only the most prominent. Dr. J. P. Leonard stated that "the complaints most common in the mining districts are congestive, intermittent and remittent fevers, and disorders of the bowels." Although he did not refer to it by name, poison oak, similar to the poison ivy of the older states, was listed as a prevalent malady. Cholera and diphtheria were among the most dreaded diseases. Leonard concluded that "intemperance, dissipation, disappointments, privations, exposure, etc.," usually had more to do with fatality than the diseases themselves.[25]

Dr. Hardeman was accompanied to the southern mines by Peter Bur-

TOP: Dr. Glen O. Hardeman (1825–1905), yielding to an "irresistible longing" to tackle the frontier, traveled to Santa Fe, Chihuahua, Panama, and California from 1849 to 1852. *Courtesy the Hardeman family.* LOWER: During the Civil War and the days of the Missouri bushwhackers, Hardeman carried this 1851 model, 36-calibre Colt revolver. *Courtesy the Hardeman family.*

nett's brother White (who had returned briefly to Alviso from his recent trip to the gold country), H. M. T. Powell and his son Walter Powell, and seven others. Most of the men took horses or mules, the Powells driving oxen which pulled the only wagon in the company. By mid-afternoon of the first day they arrived at the secularized Mission San Jose and bought supplies. The following day they passed the Livermore Ranch. By sundown the slow oxen and wagon were well to the rear, and the elder Powell, understandably grumbling at the thought of being left alone in the unsettled country, expressed in his diary a note of relief when he saw that Hardeman and Tandy had waited for the wagon at the gap (probably Livermore Pass) leading into the San Joaquin Valley.[26] Powell was haul-ing goods belonging to other members of the party.

On the following day, having been drenched by an all-night rain, the group moved from the flower-studded foothills into the valley. The lowland was dreary, desolate, monotonously flat, with bleached horns of tule elk strewn about. Ahead of them, the men could see a ribbon of timber which stood guard over a sluggish stream—the San Joaquin River. They crossed on Slocum's Ferry at a cost of three dollars apiece per man and a like amount for each animal. The prospectors caught enough fish to vary their diets, then pressed on, reaching Stockton April 4. There they picked up both additional supplies and more sojourners. With the snow-capped Sierra visible in the background, they trudged toward Mariposa, the land of the butterflies.

As they neared their destination, the members of the party were again pelted by rains and sobered by reports of hostile Indians equipped with poisoned, glass-tipped (obsidian) arrows. On one occasion, Powell threat-ened to join another party if his companions did not stay close enough to afford adequate protection. The threat was effective. They reached Mariposa about April 11, having encountered nothing more serious than rumors, rattlesnakes, and a few Indian women weaving baskets. On the following day they were panning the sands and gravels of a bar near the house of Colonel John C. Frémont.

Most of the men from Alviso worked close together in these placer deposits. And hard work it was; scarcely the "something for nothing business" which Thorstein Veblen later called it. "Hands blistered, arms and ankles skinned, and sore all over; back almost broke" was one of

Powell's descriptions of the drudgery. The miners worked with their feet bathed by the chill of the stream and their bodies soaked alternately by perspiration and heavy rainfall. The downpour came almost daily from April 15 to 23, its monotony broken by unwelcome snowfall and hailstorm. Only Powell had a tent, and soon everything in it was soaked. The others huddled beneath "pine arbours" during their non-working hours, having stored their flour and sugar in Powell's tent. Rising waters flooded them out of their mining claims and they trudged several miles with rockers, shovels, and other equipment before finding a suitable area free of claimants. The storms were not without their benefits for Glen and his companions, as a number of miners abandoned their claims.

The resulting improved site selection was to little avail, however. Powell observed on April 25, shortly before he gave up mining and headed for Stockton to devote his energies and wagon to the freighting business, that most of the party was doing poorly, but "S. W. Work, Armstrong and Dr. Hardeman were doing pretty well." This view was something short of unanimous, for on June 1 Hardeman wrote, "Mine has been the experience so far of most newcomers in the mines—I have just about made my board—but I have all the chances before me & expect to make some little out of the claim I now have." It is clear that he did not take enthusiastically to the uncertain toil of the miner from his declaration, "If I cannot live except by manual labour in this country I will put out for some other." In the same letter he stated, "I don't despair by any means of doing something here yet & it shall be done at my legitimate business—I will make enough in the mines this winter to get a start—then for a respectable living in a way that I have a right to expect after having invested as much as I have in schools."[27] He seemed to harbor all the optimism of Dickens's Mr. Micawber, with much of his chronic bad luck as well.

Glen expected to remain at the Mariposa diggings until September 1851, then return to Alviso to settle the gardening partnership with his cousin. He anticipated mining through the winter and trying medical practice again in the spring of 1852, this time at a new location. Already it was apparent that the gardening gamble would not pay off, for "the season turned out favourably & such enormous quantities will be raised that prices will rate with those at home. The day of big prices has past. If I get

[229

back what I invested I will be satisfied."[28] But there would be no such bountiful yield to his pick, pan, rocker, and perspiration in the Mother Lode region. Mariposa was not destined to become his Golconda, nor his Ophir; nor was any other mining center. By July 7, 1851, he had abandoned the scarred lands of the southern mines and returned to Alviso.

Hardeman changed his plans and did not go back to the gold country during the winter. Perhaps, from the expensive stamping mill which he had seen at Mariposa, he sensed what history was soon to enunciate: that at this time, three and one-half years after the discovery, the peak placer-mining days for individual miners with little capital were over. Glen boarded at the home of White Burnett (who had also returned from the diggings) from July 16 into December. Information on the remainder of his stay in California is sketchy. On August 25 he rented oxen from a lime concern, undoubtedly the Rockland Lime Company identified in his sketches. As late as December 1851, he intended to remain in the state for at least another year, having invested money in a business which promised what he termed good prospects. In all likelihood this was the lime company, since he spent some weeks in the area where it was located, the hill region west of the Santa Clara Valley. If he had Micawber's optimism, Glen surely had as many schemes as Mark Twain's Colonel Mulberry Sellers—farming, doctoring, mining, and now the new investment with promise. However, "times soon changed," his debts were mounting, and on February 14, 1852, he extricated himself from the latest venture by selling his interest for $750, two-thirds down, with the balance due in four and six months. With an obvious note of relief he stated that he considered himself "well out of the scrape."[29]

It was becoming obvious that Hardeman's projected fifteen to twenty years' (or lifetime) stay in the Golden State was moving to a much earlier close. The collapse of all his money-making schemes was a major deter-minant, but there were other factors. The irresistible longing had been satiated. He longed now for a return to refinement and comfort. An occasional reference to a certain "Miss P." in his letters to his brother may contain a further clue. Perhaps this was Permelia Townsend, whom he married the year following his return. And he was quite obviously homesick for old acquaintances and family, asking frequently to be remembered to the friends at home and inquiring, to no avail, as to the whereabouts of his comrades Troup Smith and Wetmore, who had also struck out for the golden-hued mirage of the Far West.[30]

Letters from his Missouri kin gave Glen anything but encouragement to continue his frontier fling. In June 1851, his mother Nancy wrote the news of his half-sister Lucretia, who died in childbirth earlier that month, and implored him to read his Bible and go to church often. And she chided, "I hope when your California fever cools, you will come home and settle down to something."[31] Glen's half-brother John Locke Hardeman wrote that those argonauts who had returned to Missouri "all tell a dismal tale of losses and privations," but he neglected to note that those who suffered losses and privations would be likely to return. "To be a Californian is, with us, equivalent to being a bankrupt," he continued, then in a more paternalistic vein, "You had need to taste of adversity. Do not fall by it and you will be the better for having been tried."[32]

The traveler shrugged off these remarks for some time, but they may have added to his discontent. His mind apparently was made up to return some weeks before his departure. During the last six weeks on the Pacific Slope he penciled a number of sketches, as if he had an impulse to capture and hold some visions of his temporary home—visions in a form more tangible than memories and written words. As far back as his days at Kemper College, Glen had a reputation for drawing pictures, and his personal papers contain scores of sketches—portraits, landscapes, and objects of scientific interest.[33] Most of the scenes drawn in California were dated shortly before he left for home.

After he made his decision to return to Missouri, Glen faced the usual delays. He expected "to get off without fail by every steamer, but was disappointed week after week until the 18th of February," 1852. On that date he again boarded the *Panama*. This vessel, which had been long delayed in reaching San Francisco fourteen months earlier, was late again, having suffered a broken lever shaft south of San Diego on January 26.[34] Close calls and delays were not entirely absent on the return trip. The steamer docked at Acapulco on February 26 and reached Panama City March 4. Less than two days later Hardeman had recrossed the Isthmus to Chagres, there to experience a five-day layover. This town was so plagued by malaria and yellow fever (sometimes called Chagres fever or Panama fever) that some life insurance companies wrote cancellation clauses into policies effective if policyholders remained overnight there.

While aboard ship some time after leaving Chagres, Hardeman witnessed the only incident of the return voyage which provoked comment, a burial at sea. An old man put out a fire, "but in suppressing what might have proved a disastrous accident to the vessel" he inhaled sulphuric acid fumes and died. Thus spared a possible catastrophe, the vessel reached Havana on March 14, and six days later Glen disembarked from the *Ohio* at New Orleans.[35] By May 1852 Glen Hardeman had resumed his medical practice at Arrow Rock under circumstances which, if less exciting than his late journey, were more predictable and profitable.

From New Orleans, before commencing the up-river leg of his homeward trip and with disappointment fresh in his thoughts, Glen wrote what must have seemed to him at that time an appropriate epitaph to his California experience:

> I find myself here with $250 in my pocket, and that is all I have to show for California. I have spent three years and you know what part of my fortune in learning a practical definition of folly. I have seen the wreck of my hopes of wealth and must endeavor to content myself with something humbler. I wish now to see if I cannot extract a little happiness out of this world—a thing I have not known for several years past.[36]

Fifty years later, his perspective perhaps sharpened by the same expanse of time that had dimmed his memory, he wrote what may have been a more fitting conclusion by recounting an incident that occurred while he was crossing the Isthmus en route to California in late November of 1850.

> I . . . had an amusing adventure while floundering along in the mud. . . . An old man stepped out in front of me and said, "Young man, I would be doing you a service to knock you in the head right here." I laughed & asked why he would treat me in such a way. "California," said he, "is a cruel, bloody place and you'll be sorry you ever went there." I shook hands with him and passed on.
>
> I never met any cruel bloody adventures in California and can not say that I gained anything more than experience. I did not make a fortune but still do not regret the trip.[37]

Over a span of more than two and one-half years, Dr. Glen Hardeman had breathed deeply of the culture and the natural environment along the western byways. The experiences must have been no small shaping force in his life. He had been interested in the California Indians, some of whom he paid to do his laundry. An obsidian or volcanic glass arrow point, found on the way to Mariposa, was one of his prize mementos of California, and around it he assembled hundreds of Indian relics, many collected by his father, and mostly from the Midwest. In later years he studied the culture of the Eskimos, the inhabitants of the tropics, and various Indian tribes; he was particularly fascinated by the written Cherokee language of Sequoyah. From poetry to politics, from temperature records to wildlife and taxidermy, Glen gave rein to his curiosity. Like his father, he was an agnostic, a writer of philosophical discourses, and a devotee of the sciences. He subscribed to scientific journals, kept clippings and drawings of nature's specimens and events, and had his sons ship skins of animals and birds to him from the Far West. An amateur taxidermist, he mounted scores of North American birds and mammals, including the quetzal of Central America and the ptarmigan of the sub-Arctic. And he took a hand in nature's plan by sending live pairs of opossums from Missouri to be released for propagating in California and importing pheasants from the Northwest to the Midwest.[38]

Among Glen's interests, none appeared to be more keen than his admiration of things Spanish, a direct outgrowth of his travels in Mexico, Central America, and California. He studied Spanish culture, literature, history, and language, and collected various items from areas of Spanish civilization. His favorite dog was named Sancho Panza. If he had drunk amply from the cup of life in the West, Glen had also reached its dregs. He knew the chagrin of Cervantes's peasant squire better than the touch of Midas, as course after course of tempting repast was set before him, only to be removed without his partaking of it. Now he settled into a more sedentary life in the familiar surroundings of Saline County, Missouri. His slaves (he had a total of thirty-six or thirty-seven, although not all at the same time) produced hemp, corn, and other crops.[39] Glen practiced medicine and raised a family which would soon make its own imprints on the Far West. But his settled life would not last. His nerve, steeled by two trips to distant frontiers, would soon face new tests in a western border region torn asunder by agonizing civil war.

13 ⊨ *West Wing of the House Divided*

THE ONSET OF THE CIVIL WAR bent many divergent lines of thought and action into sharp focus over most of the nation. A clear geographical line, or more properly a corridor, from the Atlantic to the Great Plains separated markedly different principles, interests, and feelings north and south. Loyalties were by no means undiluted within each section, but in the border zone between the sections, allegiances were highly unpredictable, often setting neighbor against neighbor. Out on the frontier, the zone of these uncertainties flared out north and south, capping the "T" of the east-west border corridor. New Mexico, with its heavily Spanish-American population, centuries-deep Mexican roots, and a mere dozen years under the United States, was at most lukewarm toward the burning sectional issues. Beyond Arkansas, the Indians, with the exception of some slaveholders, were at first uncommitted to either part in the white man's dispute. And the western half of Missouri, with its mingled unsettledness of intersectional border and western border, was probably the most confused area of the nation. The remainder of the West was too far from the battle theaters to be internally torn apart.

Many of Thomas Hardeman's descendants fought in the Civil War; there were thirteen from Tennessee and a number from Texas and Missouri. Nearly all chose the gray uniforms of the Confederacy,[1] and in view of their heritage and regions of residence their loyalties to the seceded section were not surprising. Nor was it unexpected that several of them were extensively involved in battles for control of the West.

The desert Southwest, although its campaigns have drawn proportionately little comment from historians, was central to Confederate strategy early in the conflict. There has been some speculation that the first southern move was made prior to secession, when pro-South Secretary of War John B. Floyd consigned and assigned to New Mexico much materiel and large numbers of army officers sympathetic to the South. Despite reasonable explanations, this policy, in retrospect, bore some earmarks of conspiracy, and with the advent of secession an array of prominent officers in New Mexico defected to the Confederacy. Among them was Henry H. Sibley, who went to Texas and later to Richmond, where he convinced Confederate President Jefferson Davis to use New Mexico as the gateway for attempted conquest of other western lands.

The plan to take the Far West was vague but grandiose in scope, leaning on the supposed loyalties of ex-Southerners who had gone west. New Mexico should be easy prey; Colorado and California could then be drawn into the southern orbit; Mormon discontent over recent Federal troop actions would bring Utah into the fold; and the customary political chaos south of the border might result in annexation of the north Mexico states to the burgeoning Confederacy. On paper this looked like a fair bid to secure a defensible stronghold, quantities of gold and silver, an outlet to the Pacific for raiding, blockade-breaking, and commerce, and a running start on diplomatic recognition and military aid from England and France. The southwestern scheme could conceivably win the war and perhaps with remarkably little effort. Henry Sibley was given a general's commission and told to get on with it; he returned to Texas to begin recruiting, but meanwhile the first steps had already been taken.

Early in July 1861, Lieutenant Colonel John R. Baylor led the Confederate Second Regiment of Mounted Rifles to El Paso and occupied Fort

Bliss in western Texas before it could be controlled by Union troops from New Mexico. He then readied his 250 Texas cavalrymen to move up the Rio Grande. Colonel Edwin R. S. Canby commanded the Federal forces, whose main purpose had been to control the Indians of New Mexico. Canby's unit had been recently reinforced, but defections to the Confederacy had seriously reduced his complement of officers. He anticipated attacks along the Rio Grande or the Santa Fe Trail and arranged his defenses accordingly. His southern anchor was forty miles north of Fort Bliss at Fort Fillmore, where gray-haired Major Isaac Lynde and about 700 troops awaited Baylor's approach.

Colonel Baylor's men were outnumbered, but they were tough South-westerners conditioned to the severe environment; and Fillmore, with its surrounding heights, had been built to withstand Indians, not artillery. It was scheduled to be abandoned soon. Baylor brought his regiment north through the friendly Mesilla Valley, where most residents were Southern sympathizers. A deserter from his ranks deprived him of the element of surprise, and as he neared the town of Mesilla the sounding of a long-roll and the sight of dust kicked up by Lynde's troops gave warning that the Texans would soon be attacked. Baylor positioned his men at the south end of the town, taking advantage of adobe houses, corrals, and corn fields. Confederate Company A, under thirty-year-old Captain Peter Hardeman, a Freemason and farmer from Gilleland's Creek, Travis County, Texas, formed Baylor's front line. Tennessee-born Peter, confused by some historians with his first cousin William, was a grandson of Thomas Hardeman and son of Dr. Blackstone Hardeman, who had come to Texas in 1835. Judging from an opinion written by a corporal in his company, either Peter Hardeman was something of a tyrant as captain or one or more of his troops disliked military discipline. "He treats us more like slaves than anything else."[2] While his brother Blackstone, Jr., served as a state legislator at Austin, Peter was moving his ninety-man company up the Rio Grande.

Baylor rejected a demand for surrender, and the war in the West began at five o'clock on the evening of July 25, 1861, when Lynde opened with a howitzer barrage and cavalry assault on Hardeman's forces. Loose sand and rank corn growth disordered the advance of the Union men as Hardeman's group countered with a line of rifle bursts from behind an adobe corral.

Three Union soldiers were killed and six wounded, and with darkness gathering Lynde saw no course but to retreat to the fort. One company of Baylor's crew had driven off a 380-man force while suffering no casualties.[3] Anticipating an attack the following day, Baylor held his position.

But Lynde, fearing Confederate howitzer fire from the heights and lacking an adequate water supply for his livestock at the fort, destroyed such property as his men could not take, fired the fort, and fled. Since Texans had cut the road north to Fort Craig, Lynde took his 700 troops through San Augustine Pass toward Fort Stanton, which lay 140 miles northeast.[4] Scanning the dust column through his field glasses on July 27, 1861, Baylor plotted the retreat and gave pursuit, after dispatching Major E. Waller to salvage what he could from the smoldering fort. Waller misunderstood the command and took all the Confederate forces except Hardeman's company, a mistake which turned out to be fortunate for the Texans. The delay prevented them from overtaking Lynde's men until the latter were exhausted from heat and lack of water. Instead of a battle, there was a roundup by Hardeman's company as they charged over the pass, through the strung-out column of thirst-crazed Union soldiers, and prevented them from combining their full forces at San Augustine Springs five miles beyond the pass. The several hundred men who had reached the springs were in battle array, but the flow of water was inadequate to meet their immediate needs, leaving them with little inclination to fight, and they were quickly subdued by Peter's outfit.

Baylor's main body of troops followed, having "no trouble in taking prisoners and disarming them by the squad"[5] on that hot day of retreat. The victory had been surprisingly easy and bloodless, a matter of conditioning and plainsmanship rather than marksmanship. The Federals had violated two cardinal rules of desert travel—take enough water to last until the next supply and divide the party to give the springs recovery time between groups. If, as questionable reports claim, many troopers filled their canteens with whiskey from the fort dispensary, Lynde may not have been entirely to blame.

Baylor said of the skirmishes that "too much praise cannot be given to the officers and soldiers under my command, and especially to Captain Hardeman and company, who were the only part of the command engaged with the enemy."[6] Peter was soon advanced to the rank of colonel. Baylor disarmed and paroled the captives. The victory was important both materially and psychologically, as southern New Mexico was cleared of Union soldiers, the Confederate Territory of Arizona was set up, and the South looked toward step two in its scheme of western conquest.

The engagement often referred to as the "battle of the brothers-in-law," meanwhile, was forming up. The decisive phase of the New Mexico war found Colonel Canby facing Confederate Brigadier General Henry H. Sibley, who is believed to have been married to a sister of Canby. Such unlikely antagonisms are sometimes bred by civil wars. Both men were veterans of service in New Mexico. Canby had about 2,500 men, and he was painfully aware that, owing to critical Union needs in other theaters, reinforcements might not be available. He retrenched to Forts Craig and Union, issued a call for volunteers from New Mexico and Colorado on June 14, 1861, and waited for the impending invasion from Texas. Sibley, for his part, was busy raising an assault force.

One of General Sibley's recruiters was Captain William P. Hardeman, forty-three-year-old planter from Guadalupe County. William, or "Gotch," had already become a party to the sectional conflict. As a delegate to the Texas Secession Convention in 1861 he had voted to separate from the Union, and now he separated from his family, his thirty-one slaves, and the long rows of cotton and sugar cane on his two-square-mile San Marcos River plantation.[7] His reputation, garnered from a dozen years of campaigning against Mexico and the Comanches, enhanced his recruiting abilities.

William raised a force from Guadalupe and Caldwell counties, and they became Company A of Sibley's brigade. The ex-ranger was commissioned senior captain of Colonel John Riley's regiment. Because of his experience and the fact that he had explored New Mexico (in the 1850s), Hardeman was placed in the lead. "Armed to the teeth with shot and squirrel guns," his outfit struck off westward on November 7, 1861, with the other units strung out behind at intervals to let water holes seep full.[8]

Through mesquite and chaparral, across desert plain, arroyo, and barranca, the army made the trek from San Antonio to Fort Bliss and the Rio Grande in late fall and early winter. There Baylor joined the brigade, swelling its size to 3,700 men, and thus both Peter and William Hardeman became officers in the same western army. In January 1862, Sibley marched up the Rio Grande Valley toward the Union stronghold at Fort Craig, expecting that sentiment in New Mexico would swing the territory over to his cause. In this, he and other southern leaders were overly optimistic. Through the southern part their expectations were realized, but farther north New Mexicans had known the Texans as invaders and hated them no matter what flag they carried. This feeling was heightened by the fact that, despite strenuous efforts of the officers, many of Sibley's men were ruffians, looting friend and foe alike in their line of march.

As Peter Hardeman's company had formed the advance guard near Fort Fillmore, so William, with his 800-man company, led the march to Fort Craig. When Sibley ordered the taking of Alamosa (thirty-two miles south of Craig), Gotch Hardeman drew the assignment. He force-marched sixty miles and surrounded the objective, but the Unionists had withdrawn to Craig.[9] Like Fort Fillmore, Craig was not designed to cope with howitzers, and Canby uneasily awaited Sibley's approach, knowing that artillery could smash the fort from the mesa above. On February 7, the Southerners reached an open plain a mile below the bastion, then detoured to Valverde, a small town—or campsite—about seven miles north of the fort. Both commanders appeared willing to fight it out away from the fortification, as Canby came out cautiously, hoping to block his enemy from reaching the water supply of the stream at the limited places where shallow embankments made river access practical.

After two weeks of sparring and positioning, the opponents joined battle on February 25 in a bend of the old, dry river bed at Valverde. Superior numbers and deadly howitzer fire from the batteries of Captain Alexander McRae seemed to be winning the day for the Yankees. The battle might have turned heavily in their favor but for the small arms fire from the companies of William Hardeman and James Crosson and artillery from Trevanion Teel's two cannons.[10]

Meanwhile, because of illness and insobriety Sibley gave his command to Colonel Thomas J. Green and left the battlefield. Green and Major S. A. Lockridge knew that McRae's five howitzers had to be silenced if the Confederates were not to be chopped to pieces by grapeshot and canister. Lockridge called for volunteers to storm the artillery nest, and about 500 Texans, including William Hardeman, obliged. Armed with bowie knives, revolvers, rifles, and shotguns, they burst over a hilltop and

[239

charged 700 yards through a hail of rifle and artillery fire, driving out the defenders and capturing the big guns. McRae defended his battery to the death, and Lockridge fell dead alongside him. Hardeman was twice wounded during the charge and was forthwith promoted to regimental major for distinguished gallantry.[11] It was the first of several Civil War wounds and promotions for this veteran of frontier battles.

The loss of McRae's artillery was a double blow to Canby as it was quickly turned against him by William Hardeman, James Walker, and Henry Ragnet. The battle ended by sunset. Union troops sloshed back to the west bank of the Rio Grande, suffering some losses en route. It was a costly defeat and an almost equally costly victory. The casualties numbered about 300 Union and 200 Southern, with damage to the morale of the numerically superior Federals. But there were heavy losses to Sibley's wagons, provisions, and mules resulting from a Yankee thrust at his poorly positioned supply column.

Lacking supplies for a long siege, Sibley bypassed Canby and Fort Craig. He hurried north to Albuquerque and Santa Fe, captured some supplies, and was either unwilling or unable to stop his men from destroying large quantities of goods which he could ill afford to sacrifice. The pillagers among his men cost him any chance of support from the local population. He left William Hardeman to protect the arms, ammunition, medicines, and other supplies at Albuquerque and "to guard the hospitals there which were full of our sick soldiers."[12] East of Santa Fe, at Glorieta Pass, the Confederates met a force of Colorado volunteers in an indecisive battle. But behind the Southern lines, Major John M. Chivington (of later Sand Creek Massacre fame) and 500 Colorado volunteers chanced upon the poorly protected Confederate supply train of seventy to eighty wagons and destroyed it, along with hundreds of horses and mules. This loss spelled disaster for Sibley and forced his abandonment of New Mexico.

His retreat did not go unchallenged. Colonel Canby had moved up from Fort Craig to attack his brother-in-law's units from the rear. On April 8, 1862, Canby arrived at Albuquerque with 860 regulars and 350 volunteers and attacked William Hardeman's position. Later Canby called it a "demonstration" to permit him to rendezvous with Colonel Paul's troops from Fort Union, but his own Colonel Benjamin Roberts said the dem-

onstration was followed by two days of "sharp skirmishing."[13] Years later
a Confederate officer wrote:

> Fifteen hundred Federal soldiers attacked the position. Hardeman was
> advised of their approach and could have retreated, but his retreat meant the
> surrender of the army, for behind it was a desert, destitute of supplies. For five
> days and nights, his men never leaving their guns, he sustained the attack
> and held the position until reinforcements arrived from Santa Fe. This
> defense saved the army.[14]

This Southern view was probably overdramatized, although there is
little doubt that loss of Albuquerque and its supplies would have meant
the surrender of Sibley's army. Canby may have minimized the battle
because of his failure to win it over an enemy burdened with hospitals full
of sick soldiers. His force outnumbered Gotch Hardeman's 130 to 250
men by at least four to one, perhaps as much as ten to one, but Hardeman
shifted his mountain howitzers (three twelve-pounders and one six-
pounder) rapidly from one emplacement to another, firing quickly from
various points to give the impression that he had many guns. This
probably deterred the cautious Canby, as did the knowledge that a
full-scale assault would destroy the town and cause many casualties among
civilians, who were virtually held hostage by Hardeman's command.[15]

When Sibley arrived from Santa Fe, William advised retreat, since
supplies were low and the Unionists could bring up strong reinforcements. The hunter had become the hunted as Sibley began the long march
back to Texas. At Peralta, thirty-six miles south of Albuquerque, Canby's
contingent caught and skirmished with the Confederates on April 15.
Hardeman, who had gone ahead to attack and preoccupy Kit Carson's
garrison at Fort Craig, wheeled about and reportedly saved Green's
regiment by his return.

The Texans appeared trapped, with Canby nipping at the rear, a
waiting Union force at Craig, harsh desert to the left, and the Rio Grande
on the right. The river was nearly half a mile wide, with flowing chunk
and mush ice up to four inches thick. On the night of April 15 a sandstorm
blew up, and the Confederates took advantage of the screen. Abandoning
some wagons, equipment, and their sick and wounded, they waded to the
west bank of the icy stream, holding guns and ammunition overhead.[16]

They then proceeded down the river, camping on occasion in sight of their pursuers on the opposite bank. Under cover of night they again shook the Federal hounds from their heels, this time by striking west into rugged mountain terrain.

The theory that Canby allowed Sibley to escape in order to avoid feeding the prisoners is not logical. He would have done better to capture, disarm, and parole them, as Baylor had done with Lynde's troops. Nor does the "spare my brother-in-law" accusation carry weight; it is out of keeping with Canby's career. And the opinion popular among historians, that the Union officer masterfully allowed geography to win for him, is less than satisfactory. It was the bold, un-Canby-like stroke of Chivington (while Canby was 150 miles away) that made possible the hands-off, powderless victories. Canby was hypercautious—the George McClellan of the Far West. He had fought a pitched battle at Valverde, and he would not be drawn into another if he could win without it. The Texas column was like a rattlesnake, willing to slither away into seclusion but able to strike if pressed.

There was no further contact between the forces as Sibley's elusive band snaked its way through mountainous, brushy wilds, with only a few days' rations of food and water. There was talk of abandoning all the artillery. William Hardeman was given the assignment of moving the big guns captured at Valverde. According to several accounts, he and his men saved the artillery pieces for later battles by raising and lowering them over precipitous obstacles with ropes.[17] Peter Hardeman and Bethel Coopwood were apparently useful as guides on the ten-day detour arc west of the Rio Grande, as both had been in the area before. After his victory near Fort Fillmore, Peter had led a scouting party of twenty-five men through this country. Finding tracks of Indians driving a herd of sheep, they pursued the "red rascals" west of the Rio Grande, north into the mountains, across the headwaters of the Rio Mimbres, and as far as the tributaries of the Gila River.[18]

Sibley's withdrawal path doubled back to the Rio Grande at some point between Fort Craig and Fort Bliss, where Confederate sympathies in the Mesilla Valley afforded supplies and some protection. A participant in this brilliant retreat silhouetted the scene in sharp literary relief:

Substitute mules for camels and a dreary, barren, desolate, mountainous and trackless waste, for the great Desert of Africa and you have it. A caravan indeed; not of adventurous and money seeking individuals, but a caravan of care worn, disappointed, feet sore soldiers . . . defeated from want of supplies . . . and reinforcements.[19]

At Fort Bliss, Sibley instructed William Hardeman to proceed ahead to Texas and recruit more men for a renewal of the attack on Canby, but William argued that he should assist the exhausted army across the parched plains, with which he was the most familiar. Sibley relented, and the group, having lost half its manpower and nearly all of its more than 300 wagons, moved on rations of bread and water and straggled into San Antonio in midsummer 1862.

The Texans had acquitted themselves well in every battle, with not one defeat in combat; yet Sibley's expedition was a disaster, costing 500 Confederate lives. Even if he had captured Fort Craig and Fort Union, however, he probably could not have withstood Carleton's California column of 1,500 men (which was en route to New Mexico) and the large relief force being organized at Fort Leavenworth. Various reasons have been cited for Sibley's failure—long supply lines, unruly troops, hostility of New Mexicans toward Texas, his own drunkenness, and Canby's geographical strategy. The one most overlooked and perhaps the most important was Sibley's ineptness in logistics; both at Valverde and Glorieta Pass, he committed or permitted nearly fatal mistakes with his supply column —mistakes that probably could have been avoided—thus converting a difficult supply problem into an impossible one.

The Confederacy kept alive its plans for conquering New Mexico and securing a corridor to the Pacific. Lieutenant Colonel Peter Hardeman was given command of the unruly Arizona Brigade, but he became seriously ill. General J. Bankhead Magruder subsequently put William Hardeman in charge of the force for the purpose of organizing and leading another invasion of New Mexico, but the need for leadership in the Gulf theater was pressing. William was ordered back from frontier duty and transferred to the East Texas–Louisiana zone, where he amassed an outstanding record at Fort Butler, Pleasant Hill, and Mansfield, in the forty-three-day rollback of General Nathaniel Banks's numerically superior Union army, at the battle of Yellow Bayou, and at Franklin. He was promoted to Brigadier General.

After Peter Hardeman regained his health, he commanded the Texas-Arizona battalion in the border war zone west of Arkansas from August 1863 to early 1865. Here he served in league with large numbers of Choctaw, Cherokee, Creek, and other Indians who had been lured, threatened, or cajoled into the war on the Confederate side, sometimes by their own slaveholding chiefs, in other instances by known and trusted Southern leaders such as Albert Pike. (Some Indians also sided with the Union.) Most of Hardeman's duty during his eighteen months on this frontier consisted of holding, skirmishing, scouting, and falling back again; there were no major engagements.

A case of mistaken identity nearly caused a bloody shootout and perhaps sheds some light on Peter Hardeman as a frontier officer. He was placed in charge of the brigade during an interregnum between the commands of brigadier generals Smith Bankhead and Richard Gano during October 1863. On the tenth day of the month, while he was encamped in the Choctaw Nation west of Fort Smith, Arkansas, his advance pickets informed him of a sizable force of Union troops settling in for the night about eight miles away. Hardeman led 300 mounted men to the Federal encampment under cover of darkness. Dismounting nearby, he took six men for a close-up scouting operation. It was three o'clock in the morning and all was quiet and very dark, the fires having burned down to smoking ashes. Peter avoided the sentries and ascertained that there were about 400 troops in the camp. Returning stealthily, he ordered his men to mount and took the full complement to within 300 yards of the enemy, where he waited for enough daylight to attack. Just as day was breaking he moved to within 100 yards before being discovered, then charged, surrounding the rudely aroused soldiers and splitting them into two groups before they could form for battle. At this moment Hardeman and his men discovered that their "enemies" were Confederate guerillas under the notorious William "Charles" Quantrill. They had been mistaken for Unionists because of Federal flags and regalia which they sported after their one-sided victory over a northern force at Baxter Springs, Kansas, a few days earlier. Peter Hardeman's firm order that there was to be no shooting until he personally gave the command was of critical importance. He observed later:

If there had been one gun fired there would have been one of the bloodiest fights of the war in proportion to the number of men engaged . . . and my having surprised them so completely gave me decidedly the advantage of them. . . . Col. Quantrill paid me quite a compliment. He said to me, "Sir, you are the only man that has ever so completely surprised me."

This encounter was never officially reported, although Peter Hardeman's recently discovered letter is corroborated briefly in the memoirs of John McCorkle, a member of Quantrill's raiders. McCorkle stated that the guerillas were surrounded in a surprise move, but he incorrectly credited McIntosh (probably a reference to either Chilly or Daniel McIntosh, leaders of Creek Indian battalions) rather than Hardeman as the commanding officer of the sleuthing party of Texans.[20] Both Peter and William Hardeman would play further frontier roles, but in different nations, during the immediate postwar era.

In the meantime, another of Thomas Hardeman's grandsons was serving as an officer in a part of the trans-Mississippi West ravaged by Quantrill and other marauders. Dr. Glen O. Hardeman, unsuccessful as a California gold miner, had returned to his medical practice and farming in Missouri. By the time the Civil War broke out, that state had been in the Union for forty years, but the tranquility was a thin veneer. War bent the frontier line sharply eastward into central Missouri. Caught between the upper and nether millstones in a grinding embrace, that area became a strip of terror characterized by the shallow allegiances typical of the intersectional border corridor and by the light military garrisons of western zones of conflict. One was seldom certain whether his neighbor's color was blue or gray, and if certain today, he could not be sure tomorrow, for switching sides was commonplace. Young men and old boys joined the moment's most romantic figure, whether Union, Confederate or unaligned bushwhacker. That noble inscription emblazoned on the state's Great Seal, "United we stand, Divided we fall," had itself fallen.

Compounding this problem of patriots of a day was the siphoning off of military forces to main theaters of war. In the resultant power vacuum, ruffians roamed and plundered almost at will over the western half of Missouri. As the state had not seceded, and was therefore Union territory by implied preference, all ravaging was by definition Confederate. Bushwhackers, spurred on by such outlaw leaders as Bill Anderson and William Quantrill, terrorized and looted the land, often for personal gain rather than sectional allegiance. Frequently they consisted of local hoodlums, sometimes deceptively dressed in blue uniforms stripped from fallen Federal soldiers, or masked by the United States flag. With interim Governor Hamilton Gamble's provisional Union government at Jefferson City and former Governor Claiborne Jackson's rump Confederate government at Neosho, the uncertain loyalties of the populace were mirrored at the level of state politics. It was a local insurrection within a national civil war.

Glen Hardeman was a different example of the unpredictable nature of Missourians' allegiances. He was a slaveholding descendant of slaveholders in Saline County, an area where Confederate sympathies were little short of unanimous, and he could have kept his own counsel, stayed home at the big, comfortable house near Arrow Rock, and profited from wartime medical practice. But Glen, like his father and grandfather, was known for blunt expression of his feelings, and his adventures on western trails and waters had shown that he did not always shun danger. In Saline County there was danger in dissent.

Not a single vote in that county was cast for Lincoln in the 1860 election. Bell received a majority, and Douglas carried Missouri, his only state victory. As was done in many slaveholding sections, Saline County residents met to consider the crisis arising over a president-designate in whom they had little confidence. They convened at the Marshall courthouse on December 15, 1860, heard from a committee on proposed actions, and set up a special group to consider alternatives. The latter committee, of which Glen Hardeman was a member, presented a guarded resolution supporting the Union and the Constitution, but stating that strong Southern reaction would be justified and supported if the North continued to override the constitutional rights of the South. Northern subversion of the fugitive slave law was condemned, and there was a call for a meeting with the other slave states at Nashville. The resolution passed.

If Glen agreed with this stand, his beliefs soon underwent a rapid and radical change. He was a firm advocate of union, and from the beginning of secession had spoken out publicly for the northern cause, at personal sacrifice and danger to himself and his family. With the advent of the

Emancipation Proclamation, although he was not required to do so in Missouri since it was not in formal rebellion against the Union, he freed his slaves, hiring as paid laborers those freedmen who wished to remain with him. Further, he reported disloyal activities to Federal authorities and volunteered for duty in the army of the Union.

On August 20, 1862, Hardeman was commissioned as Surgeon of the Seventy-First Regiment in the Enrolled Militia of Missouri. He served for two years in that capacity, then resigned to accept an appointment as Union surgeon on the Medical Staff of the Troops of the State of Missouri, having passed the examination of the State Medical Board for this assignment on August 27, 1864.[21] He probably served in the field during Sterling Price's campaign later that year.

Historian George W. Adams has observed that "the absence of thousands of doctors from civil practice left a golden harvest for those who remained at home. Consequently, it took fervent patriotism or sheer inability to build up a practice to draw physicians into government service."[22] Since medical men were exempt from the draft, the statement may be applicable to most parts of the Union. However, there was a more compelling reason for doctors to enter the service from western border regions. The bushwhacker policy of raiding homes and killing adult males who were not Confederate sympathizers rendered life in the armed forces much safer than at home. While neither the patriotism nor the ability of Dr. Hardeman can be assessed, he was a strong Unionist in an overwhelmingly pro-Southern county and had informed Federal authorities on the identities of bushwhackers. He was therefore a marked man and would have been shot on sight by many a border ruffian.

According to unverifiable family lore, early in the war a group of bushwhackers came to the Hardeman house and ordered the occupants to open the door. Glen said that he would report the men to Federal authorities on the very next day. At this, one of the bushwhackers turned his gun on Hardeman, but Permelia, his wife, threw herself in front of him and the assailant did not shoot. Years later, when passions had cooled somewhat, the ex-bushwhacker was reported to have said that the doctor was a brave man but that he would have been killed that night if it had not been for his wife. Shortly after this episode was alleged to have taken place, Glen left for military duty.

Proof of the wisdom of his leaving home was not long in forthcoming. The thud on the door in the dead of night and the hoarse demands of bushwhackers were frequent events at his home during the war years. Life was a frightening ordeal for Permelia and their children, although the ruffians did them no physical harm. It was considered relatively safe for women, even the wives of Union soldiers, to remain at home, since the bushwhacker code, enforced by such leaders as "ladies' man" Quantrill, decreed that no women should be harmed, even though men were at times killed before the eyes of their families.

At two o'clock on the morning of October 16, 1862, a group of twenty-five bushwhackers surrounded the Hardeman house, then ordered that the doctor open the door. His wife told them that he was not home. Led by a young man named O'Donnell, they demanded that she give them a candle, after which they searched the house. They took guns, blankets, socks, and a few yards of cloth. Ransacking bureau drawers, "they even took as small a thing as comb and brush." The raiders were upset at not finding any whiskey, as they had been told that the doctor kept a supply in his house. Outside the building they seized Bob, the horse, and rode him off, leaving an old horse in the yard.[23]

On the night of August 3, 1864, sixteen men, "searched every room in the house and broke open all the trunks," taking a blanket, clothing, a knife, some bullets, and other items. Referring to Dr. Hardeman as "the God Damn rascal that went to Lexington [in Saline County] and brought the Feds down here," they found a Union flag in the house and "went off with it hoisted over them." Two days later, five bushwhackers came to the farm and searched the cabins, but did not enter the house. One of the men, William, had sworn that he would shoot Glen for reporting him. Several months after this raid, Tom Woodson, a local bushwhacker, threatened to burn the Hardemans' house.[24] These maraudings and threats left the families of Union soldiers as well as loyalist refugees in a constant state of uneasiness and great destitution.

October 1864 found more than the usual turbulence in Saline County, as Confederate General Sterling Price led an army through Arrow Rock, plundering what little the previous bushwhacker raids had left, conscripting soldiers, and kidnapping freed Negroes. Some of the freedmen working for Glen Hardeman, including a sixteen-year-old boy named Peter,

While her husband Glen O. Hardeman served in the Union Army, Permelia Townsend Hardeman managed the farm near Arrow Rock, bearing both the insults and plunderings of the bushwhackers. *Courtesy Russella Hardeman Matthews.*

were seized and taken south by Price. Peter was located in Arkansas a year later by Hardeman's efforts, with the help of the Commissioner of Freedmen for the Arkansas Department and Captain John Montgomery of Johnson County, Missouri.

Following the raid by Price and the attendant unrest, several detachments of Union troops were sent to Saline County to quell the bushwhackers and attempt to break up dens of thieves along the Missouri River. These temporary measures were followed by a move to organize a local defense force of several companies to restore civil law and order. Hardeman and Colonel W. A. Wilson, "two of the best and truest Union men in the county," were picked to organize these provisional companies.[25] Winter was a good time to form such defense groups, since bushwhacker activity was reduced by cold weather. The degree of success of these efforts is not established, but episodes such as the raids of the James brothers punctuated the fact that, despite the formal ending of the war, peace was a long time in coming to west-central Missouri. Four years of hatred, neighbor against neighbor, would not soon be assuaged.

After Appomattox, the three cousins and veterans of western campaigns continued to pay dearly for their loyalties. Glen Hardeman was a winner in a loser's section; William and Peter were losers in a winner's nation. Glen, at home in central Missouri, could no longer enjoy the respect which he had commanded before the deep wounds of fratricidal war—wounds that his surgical skills were powerless to heal. Nor was there redemption through the respect long accorded his family in Missouri. The doctor had turned blue-coat in a sea of gray sympathies, and the grays who could not forget turned him away. In 1866 he moved from Arrow Rock to Franklin County in eastern Missouri, settling on a farm near Gray's Summit. A number of Negro laborers went with him. About five years later, hoping that hatreds had died down in the land of his childhood, he went back to Arrow Rock. It was to no avail; Saline County had neither forgotten nor forgiven. After fifteen months he returned to reside permanently at Gray's Summit.

Down on the Texas plains, the verdict of civil strife was even more agonizing as the inveterate frontiersmen William and Peter Hardeman saw it. They preferred to seek new homes in foreign lands rather than surrender and exist under Yankee-dictated rule. The United States, long a haven for emigrants, now witnessed an exodus as thousands of its own citizens, having failed in their all-out effort to form a separate nation, took flight. Millions of others might well have opted for the same course had they possessed the necessary folly, courage, or money to do so.

What were the reasons for the departure of these refugees, numbering perhaps 10,000? They are easier to guess at generally than specifically. War has a momentum of its own, swaying men's minds and warping judgment—spawning pride, shreds of hope, and refusal to believe that the dead have perished and the sufferers have suffered in vain. It was as much a problem of making peace with themselves as of coming to terms with the enemy. Pride and paranoia were no doubt paramount reasons for the hegira. Others were refusal to surrender to the despised foe; fear of punishment on the part of some high officials; inability to face destruction or degradation of their homes; unwillingness to live in a topsy-turvy society controlled by what they viewed as "damnyankees" and "niggers." Too, there was a history of Southerners' fascination with Latin America, as witness the filibustering expeditions of the 1840s and 1850s. The paranoid style, the conviction that the enemy's motives were absolutely despicable, was a characteristic of both sides during Civil War and Reconstruction. It is one of mankind's dilemmas—and strengths—that people commonly can differ very widely in their views yet be so dedicated to their respective beliefs that they are willing to fight and even die for them. Such feelings may have been buttressed by the insecurity and fear emanating from an awareness that politically, economically, and socially, the "bottom rail was on the top." Another dimension of fear—the other side of pride—was the society- and family-conditioned dread of abject humiliation that was greater than the fear of death itself and doubtless accounted for much of the dueling, the postwar suicides in the South, and the exodus. Finally, ignorance of the dire Confederate military situation in the East may have led some of the officers in the Southwest to conclude that if they fled, they could return another day to fight.

General William P. Hardeman, his wealth of pride perhaps overbalancing a trace of hope, and uncommonly willing to accept the challenge of the arid Southwest, joined a Mexico-bound party of fifteen high-ranking Confederate officers at Austin two months after war's end. This company included three generals, Clay King, Alexander W. Terrell, and Hardeman, three colonels, a major, and a captain. Terrell had been a San Antonio judge and had served under Hardeman in the Arizona Brigade. The two were long-time associates; both were regimental commanders at Pleasant Hill and Mansfield, and both had been wounded within a two-day period. Now they were companions in a veritable furnace of Nebuchadnezzar. Terrell was the leader, and the chronicler, of the flight of this small band.[26]

Hardeman and Terrell carried letters from Governor Pendleton Murrah of Texas to European-born Emperor Maximilian of Mexico, requesting aid to the exiles. In Terrell's view, this was back-up insurance, since his first hope was to ally himself with the Emperor's archenemy, Benito Juarez. Maximilian, part benevolent idealist, part opportunist, was an imperial hanger-on from the French debt-collecting invasion of Mexico during the 1860s. He had arrived in 1864 and with French troops was attempting to suppress Juarez and secure Mexico for Napoleon III while the Monroe Doctrine of the United States lay helplessly subordinated to the Civil War. But Juarez was strong in the north, and the Union victory boded ill for the puppet emperor from Austria and his consort Carlotta.

A vague Confederate plan was for leaders such as General Joseph Shelby to move a large army of escapees across the Rio Grande, but Terrell, Hardeman, and their small group became impatient and headed south-westward from Austin through San Antonio in June 1865. Riding horseback and leading several pack mules, they shunned main thoroughfares since some 50,000 Federal troops under General Philip "Shenandoah" Sheridan were patrolling the countryside and the Rio Grande to prevent such escapes, to frustrate the hopes of a resurgent Confederacy, and to dampen French aspirations in Mexico.

The Nueces River, bank-full from recent downpours, presented an obstacle to the refugees. The best swimmers secured lariats fast to each bank, and using these taut ropes they were able to shuttle a hastily built log raft back and forth until all possessions were ferried to the south shore. Aided by Hardeman's field glasses, they slipped through the Union patrols and galloped on toward the north bank of the Rio Grande.

Freedom lay just beyond the swollen current of the great river, or so the officers hoped. Near Roma on the Texas side, they were informed by two Mexicans that there was a ferry at Alamo, eight miles upstream. Yankee soldiers had told the Mexicans that they would capture or kill any Confederate attempting to flee across the border. Captain Roberts (probably Judge Oran M. Roberts) had a Mexican foster brother in Roma who told the party that on the south bank four miles upriver there was a small craft which could carry four horses at a time across the stream, perhaps enabling them to avoid the enemy's patrol at the Alamo crossing.

The men rode hard along the bank until they discerned the old ferry boat across the stream. The waters were cold, and as they swam to fetch the craft Gotch Hardeman must have recalled, with feelings other than nostalgic, the icy night-crossing of the same river far up at Peralta four years earlier. The boat secured, the fugitives transported one cargo after another of horses, mules, and provisions, carrying their last load to the south bank not a moment too soon. Some of Sheridan's soldiers arrived from the Alamo crossing several miles above in time to fire an ineffective volley across the international waterway. Neither Moses at the parting of the Red Sea nor Boone stumbling upon an abandoned canoe on the banks of the Ohio as he fled from the Shawnees could have felt more divinely led than the little party of Confederates.

On Mexican soil, Hardeman was no doubt increasingly useful, as the escape route led through territory which he had scouted years before. Such advantage was largely offset by the mutual hatred between Texan and Mexican. Nearing the town of Mier—of Black Bean Massacre fame—the beleaguered column must have been keenly conscious of both the scourge behind and the plague ahead.

A short ride from the Rio Grande brought them face to face with the greatest danger extant in that region. They suddenly found themselves surrounded by a fierce-looking ring of bandits from the guerilla gang of the notorious "Red Robber of the Rio Grande," General Juan Cortina. The Confederates were well armed, each with two revolvers and a rifle, and Cortina's band was reluctant to risk the cost of a frontal assault. A spurious air of amity prevailed, as the Mexicans provided green corn fodder for the famished animals of the Texans. Terrell and his men drew their horses into a tight circle, facing outward; each man was prepared to mount and ride with guns blazing at an instant's warning. The horses ate.

A potential haul of fine weapons was viewed with covetous eyes by the brigands, who told the Confederates to surrender them. Terrell and his men responded that they would only hand them over to the *commandante* of the town garrison at Mier if that official insisted upon it. Cortina's hombres saw this as a better prospect than facing the notorious guns of the Texans, and they dashed off to Mier with a subterfuge of their own. They would tell the townspeople that the approaching Americans had slaughtered Mexican men and ravished women on their way to Mier. Hardeman, Terrell, and the others rode unsuspectingly into an alerted guard of green-clad soldiers and an angry crowd of civilians who nudged them toward the calabozo. The Texans were, after all, in violation of Mexican territorial rights since they were armed foreigners on Mexican soil. And they were in a town that believed the only good Texans were dead ones. The crisis deepened as the men were told to hand over their arms.

Unknown to the despairing officers, good luck was again riding close on their heels. Not able to communicate satisfactorily, they asked for an interpreter, and a messenger was sent for a bilingual town resident. After some uneasy minutes of waiting, the Confederates saw a man who galloped toward them, dismounted, and shouted "Amigos!" embracing Terrell and Hardeman. He was Narciso Leal, who had known the two officers years before in Texas, and had been an interpreter for Judge Terrell in San Antonio. Leal promptly denounced the bandits' story and urged the alcalde of Mier, Ramón Ramirez, to extend Mexico's hospitality to these "honorable gentlemen," who were, after all, engaged in an expatriation process which was respected and widely used in Latin America.

The crowd dispersed; Leal's reputation was better than that of Cortina's *banditos*. The tired refugees were given a place to rest for the night (in the same rock fort where Texan invaders had surrendered twenty-two years before), but not until their guns and knives had been placed for safe keeping in the locked office of the *alcalde*. The treatment was civil enough, yet the fugitives knew well that, politeness or not, they were prisoners.

The officers had some bargaining power, however, for Colonel Garcia, the *commandante,* was not without his price. He sat menacingly in a position which made escape impossible without his notice, but when approached with an offer he accepted a horse, a revolving rifle, and a supply of liquor in exchange for the freedom of the Confederates. He

General William P. "Gotch" Hardeman, a veteran of more than fifty battles dating from the Texas revolution through the Civil War, exiled himself to Mexico in 1865 rather than surrender to Union forces. *Courtesy Texas State Library.*

secured their weapons from the *alcalde's* office, keeping the rifles to pacify Cortina. They must leave that night to avoid the Red Robber, who was not far away. At the appointed hour of darkness, the men were quietly aroused. They strapped on the saddles which had doubled as pillows during an uneasy evening and followed Garcia. To the last moment, they were uncertain as to whether or not his word was as good as his bribe.

Avoiding the tell-tale clatter of hoofs on the hard, deserted streets of Mier, they rode up an abrupt arroyo embankment and broke out upon a semi-desert tableland which stretched away to the southern horizon. The Texans were given a feast of roasted kid, bread, and wine and sent on their journey, with Garcia's son accompanying them to smooth the way with ranchers en route to Monterrey.

A warm breeze blew in their faces, occasionally stirring sand and dust, as these knights of the dead Confederacy galloped through sparse desert growth toward an uncertain reception deeper into Mexico. Somewhere at about that time, and perhaps on that night's ride over moon-whitened sands, William Hardeman crossed the paths of other frontier-roaming members of the family—Santa Fe trader John, whose trail led almost entirely across Mexico in 1829, and Glen, whose unfruitful gold rush route of 1849 spanned the Chihuahua tablelands between El Paso and the Gulf of Mexico.

The nocturnal flight from Mier was fraught with uncertainties. Sheridan probably would not pursue them directly, but Cortina had been cooperating with the Union officer to head off refugees.[27] And they did not know what to expect when they crossed from Juarez country to the domain of Maximilian. The boundary between these two contenders for control of Mexico lay at the north edge of Monterrey, and when the travelers sighted the town about June 28, Garcia's son, a Juarez man, left them. He had been a valuable asset, thanks to the pack of letters from his father which cleared the way with the ranchers and the free meals he was able to obtain from Garcia's friends. He would accept no pay; Hardeman offered his horse, but it was refused. This chestnut-sorrel stud animal later established a reputation at San Luis Potosí, where 250 Arabian horses were kept for Maximilian's officers. Terrell noted that these "fine Arab" mounts were adapted to the high altitude, but none of them was as fast as Hardeman's horse. The former ranger rode it from Monterrey to the Mexican capital instead of taking the stage with his friends.

Mexico City offered the gathering clan of refugees an interesting social fare of expensive hotel living, fandangos, royal court festivities, and houses of gambling and prostitution—this while they awaited the pleasure of the Emperor to map out a program which would formally integrate the fugitives into Mexico's future.

Maximilian, who had channeled French arms and supplies across the Rio Grande to the South in the late months of the war, was reluctant to enlist thousands of Confederate exiles into his army for fear of direct intervention by the United States. He did, however, take a few generals into his military force, including Hardeman and Terrell, who were appointed as battalion commanders, each at a salary of $3,000 per year.[28] But most of William's activities in Mexico were related to Maximilian's vast colonization and land development schemes. Sent by the government to locate and survey public lands in the wild frontier regions of Durango, he was given no protection against guerillas and robbers, and no pay until after the completion of the survey.[29] Through Matthew Fontaine Maury, a Southern naval officer whom Maximilian had appointed Imperial Commissioner of Immigration, Hardeman and Judge Oran Roberts were designated as settlement agents for a Confederate colony near Guadalajara. And in partnership with California's dueling judge, David S. Terry, Hardeman purchased a 22,140-acre *hacienda* in the West Coast section of Mexico. The two Confederate *hacendados* offered to grubstake colonists by advancing livestock and provisions on a sharecrop basis.[30]

These investments and assignments, and such returns as they may have yielded, were not enough to keep William Hardeman long in Mexico. He backtracked across the Rio Grande in 1866, bringing nothing from the land of the serpent and eagle except memories and impoverished circumstances. Most of the other exiles likewise gave up and filtered back home. The "anarchy, bloodshed, oppression and outrage" south of the border were intolerable.[31] It was now expedient to return to the United States; such retribution as was visited upon the defeated South had been against property, not life, and the passionate hatreds of humiliating defeat may have been dissipated by time and by failures abroad. Like state secession, personal secession for most of the refugees had failed.

Mexico was probably William Hardeman's last frontier challenge. His forays had spanned thirty years of his life. He was subsequently a public servant in his beloved Texas on numerous occasions, and was influential in averting a bloodbath for the state in the Reconstruction-charged Coke-Davis dispute of 1874. William fulfilled a number of largely honorary state functions—Inspector of Railroads, Superintendent of Public Buildings and Grounds, and later, Superintendent of the Confederate Home at Austin. In the 1890s an old acquaintance, fellow Confederate officer, and companion-in-exile, John Henry Brown, made an observation which suggests that, like his grandfather Thomas Hardeman, William was a merger of untamed and civilized ingredients:

> His early life was spent in camp and field with the pioneer hunters and Rangers of the Republic and, yet, it would be difficult to find in any social circle a man more gentle in his bearing and refined in his manners.[32]

In April 1898, the eighty-two-year-old frontiersman died of acute Bright's Disease and was buried in the State Cemetery at Austin.[33]

Uncounted thousands of Southerners exiled themselves to other lands such as Brazil, Venezuela, Cuba, Egypt, and Europe. Colonel Peter Hardeman of the New Mexico and Indian Territory campaigns chose the Southern Hemisphere, embarking from New Orleans en route to the Brazilian frontier in April 1869, probably on the brig *Eliza Stephens*. His wife, the former Nancy Caroline Keese of Tennessee, and their children accompanied him, as did his father-in-law Thomas L. Keese. Brazil's Emperor Dom Pedro II enticed settlers from the Confederacy by various means, such as assisting agent-colonizers, making financial loans, paying part of the transportation costs, extending clemency on import duties, and offering land at minimal cost. Brazilian slavery, an additional attraction, induced some Confederates to take their Negro laborers along, although abolition was gathering momentum; a free birth law had already been enacted.[34] The Census of 1860 for Travis County does not show Peter Hardeman as a slaveholder, although he had slaves in 1863.

Most Confederate colonies in Brazil were established in three areas—in the province of Pará 600 to 700 miles east of the city of Pará; in Espíritu Santo 300 miles above Rio de Janeiro; and in São Paulo. Smaller settlements extended as far south as Rio Grande do Sul. Peter Hardeman and a number of other Texas refugees sank roots at the colony of Americana near São Paulo. Frontier-type experiences were the norm in the Confederate Brazilian colonies. There were hardships en route; after landing there were often destitution, disease, floods, mud, bugs, beasts, and reptiles to contend with. The colonists plunged into farm life, growing corn, sugar cane, cotton, tobacco, vegetables, and fruits. In one attempt at upgrading Brazilian production, Peter Hardeman was involved in the details of shipping "a Saw Mill Complete" from New Orleans to Rio de Janeiro in 1869.[35] In their few spare moments, the 2,700 Southerners in Brazil strove to recreate their culture of the antebellum South; the distinctive dialect, the spirituals, the strains of "Dixie" echoed around the fires and through the highlands of Brazilian Americana. The stars and bars appeared on buildings and Indian pottery, and the drawl and songs have worn through four generations to the present day. Such nostalgic echoes had a hollow ring, and most of these exiles who survived the unaccustomed diseases returned to their former homeland within a few years. But some, including Peter Hardeman and his family, stayed on. He lived until 1882 and was buried near Cillo, a village five miles from Americana. His descendants have remained in Brazil.[36]

Doubtless no more trying hour has ever befallen the United States than the Civil War. It clawed through the surface—through the camouflages overlying human feelings—and left bare much that was base, ugly, and at times noble. Like the jarring of a chessboard or a sounding note in a game of musical chairs, it caused the sudden loosening and jumbling of issues and individuals which had been carefully, although not always justly, positioned over the years. There were issues to be repositioned—issues involving social, political, and legal structures; labor systems; tariff policy; national banking and currency structure; land distribution practice; and improvements at taxpayers' expense. And there were freedmen, soldiers, and homeless civilians who had to deal with the problems of finding new squares or chairs upon which to establish themselves. So much had been jumbled in the South, it became difficult to resume the game. Perhaps it was predictable that some of the descendants of Thomas Hardeman, who were jarred loose from their established positions by the war and its aftermath, slid across the game board to the edge labeled "Frontier."

14 ⊢⊣ *On the "Passed-Over" Frontiers*

THE TEXAS FARM BOY, saddle-weary from too many hours on the long
drive, got off his horse and sat in the shade of a small tree to watch Colonel
James Ellison's cattle.

> The first thing I knew, Tom Baylor was waking me. I thought, "Well, I
> have gone to sleep on guard. I had just as well put my hand in Colonel Ellison's
> pocket and take his money." I never got off my horse any more when on duty,
> though I have seen the time when I would have given five dollars for one-half
> hour's sleep. I would even put tobacco in my eyes to keep awake. Our regular
> work was near eighteen hours a day, and twenty-four if a bad night, then the
> next day, just as though we had slept all night, and most of us getting only
> $30.00 per month and grub, bad weather making from twenty-four to
> forty-eight hours. . . .[1]

These lines are from the pen of Walker Berry Hardeman, one of the
numerous great-grandsons of Thomas Hardeman, on the waning frontier
in the late nineteenth century.

The big-shouldered trans-Mississippi lands had seen many changes before a post-Civil War generation of the Hardeman family pointed its course toward the wilderness. Rails had laced the continent's extremities together, the proud Indian and the lordly buffalo were being ruthlessly ravaged; field, forest, and mine were yielding to hungry hordes of migrants in every corner of the backlands. The frontier of Frederick Jackson Turner's description, if indeed it ever existed, was almost gone. But the wild and thrilling West of yesteryear was still much alive—perhaps larger than life—in the memories of those who had seen it alive and wild. While reckless migrants had burst to the Pacific shores and to intermediate attractions, there was much filling to be done in the "passed-over" frontiers of the Great Plains and intermontane regions, where stalactite of eastern extension would meet stalagmite of western accretion.

It was inconceivable that the descendants of Thomas Hardeman, with their frontier orientation—their bent for being where the action was— would miss what was perhaps the most publicized of all the phases of American westward development, the great cattle drives north from Texas. They were among the drovers and trail bosses of a number of herds bound for Kansas or Nebraska or for Colorado, Wyoming, or New Mexico. As frontier farmers, the Hardemans had always owned cattle; Thomas had taken them to the Cumberland Basin, and both he and his son John had raised cattle in Missouri. But all the herds owned by the Hardemans since the seventeenth century would have totaled up to only a small fraction of the immense numbers which Will and Monroe and Walker Hardeman drove north from Texas.

American settlers struck some of the world's greatest cattle country when they reached Texas. That fertile, grassy expanse stretching from the Hardemans' home counties, Guadalupe, Caldwell, and Gonzales, south and southwest to the Rio Grande was the cradle of the Great Plains cattle empire. Since the eighteenth century tough cattle of Spanish-Mexican stock, conditioned to the semi-arid southwestern environment, had been multiplying in this superb natural habitat. Largely left alone by the Indian (who was content with the buffalo), these animals dotted the landscape in the millions by the mid-nineteenth century. William and Peter and Thomas Monroe Hardeman saw them on a score of military forays and no

doubt thanked their nimble horses for eluding the charge of many a
long-horned bull.

Several trail herds were driven from Texas to markets in New Orleans,
Ohio, Missouri, and the Colorado gold mines between 1846 and the Civil
War, but it was postwar America, with its released manpower, its
growing cities, and its westward thrusting rails which spilled the historic
droves from the great corral of South Texas. These livestock helped to
replenish southern herds destroyed by the war, supplied the Kansas
railheads which connected with population centers in the North and
Northeast, and stocked the Great Plains and other points beyond the
mid-continent line of settlement. Several of the Hardemans were drovers
in at least two of these categories.

The pattern for the drive north quickly became standardized. A herd of
1,500 to 2,000 stock driven by eight to twelve cowboys was optimum.
Leading the way was a chuckwagon, the cook selecting midday stops and
campsites. The horse wrangler drove the "remuda," or herd of remounts
for the cowhands, behind the chuckwagon. Then came the cattle, moving, drifting, grazing slowly in early morning, speeding up till noon,
then grazing during the heat of the day. From mid-afternoon till dark the
pace was rapid. After about a week of "trail-breaking," the animals were
able to maintain a steady gait. The task of the cowboy in keeping the herd
moving at the proper pace was wearying, tedious, and often dangerous.
Upon reaching Sedalia or Abilene or Dodge he was ready for an unwinding
celebration.

The Missouri Pacific railhead at Sedalia, Missouri, left much to be
desired as a terminal owing to the timber, hills, and hostile farmers who
fought to shield their herds from competition and "Texas fever." By the
summer of 1867, Illinois meat marketer Joseph M. McCoy opened
Abilene, Kansas, at the end of the Kansas and Pacific rails, and a year later
large numbers of Texas cattle were taking the Chisholm trail to that
bustling center. Within a few years, Ellsworth, Newton, and Dodge City,
the latter two on the Atchison, Topeka, and Santa Fe line, were funneling
hundreds of thousands of animals onto stock cars bound for centers farther
east. Ultimately, some 4,000,000 Texas cattle and hundreds of whoop-
ing, famished cowboys passed through these bawdy Kansas towns. But
the drives to those towns were among the shortest of the long drives. The

market was soon glutted, and cattle were showing their ribs from the harsh miles of the Chisholm and Western trails. The practice of stocking animals on ranches in Nebraska, Colorado, Wyoming, and Montana was soon adopted, and trails were lengthened by hundreds of miles. In these areas the cattle recuperated and put on weight before being shipped east by rail.

Most of the cowboys of the long drive are little known or unknown. Will Hardeman, trail herder of 1869, is a case in point. In all likelihood, he was William F., eldest son of San Jacinto warrior and Texas Ranger Thomas Monroe Hardeman and older brother of another drover, Monroe Hardeman. For accuracy, he must remain "Will Hardeman." He made the drive to Abilene with J. M. Cowley, a rangy Alabaman who had driven a herd of horses and mules from Texas to Mississippi in 1865. In the spring of 1869, Cowley, Will Hardeman, George Eustace, S. M. Eeds, and Cout Rountree took 1,500 head of cattle up the Chisholm route under trail boss J. H. Smith, going by way of Waco and Fort Worth, where they purchased supplies. The weather was chilly and wet most of the time; swollen streams were a frequent hazard, and one of the drovers was drowned while swimming his horse across Smoky River.[2]

Monroe Hardeman, second son of Thomas Monroe and great-grandson of Thomas Hardeman of Albemarle, was a frequent rider along the cattle corridors. In 1877 he and J. F. Ellison worked on the trail as utility hands for the latter's father, Colonel James Ellison, a big cattleman of Caldwell County. Their foreman was R. G. "Dick" Head of Lockhart. Again in the spring of 1881, this same Hardeman, along with Samuel Dunn Houston, drove cattle north for Head.[3]

Two springs later Monroe Hardeman was trail boss for Dick Head. He collected cattle in Mason and Coleman counties and drove them into Indian Territory. Among Monroe's cowhands were Henry Steele, Joe Lovelady, Pat Garrison, and a Negro named Charlie Hedgepeth. The Texas range had been dry, and the animals were lean at the start. But dryness gave way to severe thunderstorms and high water as Hardeman and his men drove the herd over the Western Trail. The Washita River was rising, and the crossing was difficult. At Dodge City the animals were rested for several days but were too thin to market. This drive continued on to Ogallala, Nebraska, where the herd was sold. The new owner hired on Hardeman and his crew, and they took the same stock west to Cheyenne, Wyoming, arriving there in August 1883, after a drive of 1,500 miles.[4]

Monroe Hardeman was back in the trail boss's saddle again the following year, driving for M. A. Withers out of La Salle County. He crossed the north Red River in the Wichita Mountains and entered Washita Valley where "the whole face of the country was alive with herds." Hardeman and George Block went five miles up the south bank of the Washita, then swam the cattle across the river. By this maneuver they were able to outdistance all the other herds in the area. Several stampedes provided lively entertainment along the way to Dodge City. As in the previous year, after a celebration in that town, they herded the beeves on to Ogallala, thence up the Platte River to the Julesburg Junction[5] in northeastern Colorado.

Meanwhile, another great-grandson of Thomas Hardeman, Walker Berry Hardeman, was taking his turns at the trail. The only son of ranger and Plum Creek veteran Owen Bailey Hardeman, Walker was a long-faced, blue-eyed cowhand, born at Prairie Lea, Caldwell County, March 19, 1857. His years at the district school, the Texas Military Academy, and Coronel institute at San Marcos must have left him with some unsatiated longings.

> I was just a farmer boy, started to church at Prairie Lea one Sunday, met Tom Baylor (he having written me a note several days before, asking if I wanted to go up the trail) and the first thing he said was, "Well, are you going?" I said, "Yes," so he said, "Well, you have no time to go to church." So we went back to my house, got dinner and started to the "chuck wagon and remuda," which was camped some six miles ahead. There I was, with a white shirt, collar and cravat, starting on the trail. You can imagine just how green I was.[6]

That was in the mid-1870s. Seven grueling months on the trail would season the greenness out of Walker Hardeman, and for the next decade he would herd thousands of cattle northward over lonely prairie miles. On his first drive he went with two men whose kinsmen had been close associates of his uncles William and Peter Hardeman: Tom Baylor, a cousin of John R. Baylor, and Ham Bee, relative of General Hamilton Bee. It required a month to "put up" Ellison's herd south of Bryan. Despite hardships and some problems with an old Kansas farmer, it was a favorable season, and

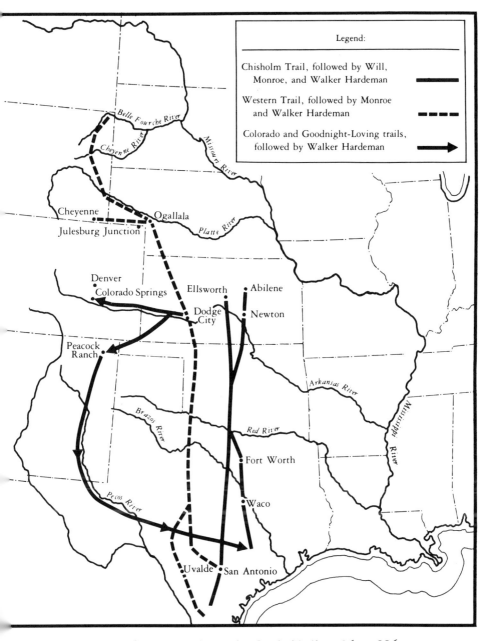

Map 6. The Hardeman Family on the Cattle Trails, 1869–1886.

the cattle were kept in good condition by lush grass as much as ten inches high. The herd hands were well fed with milk, eggs, and pies purchased along the way.

On one occasion a dozen stray cattle got into their herd, and it was too late to cut them out and deliver them to the owner. Two butchers in Kansas offered them $300 for the strays, with no bill of sale to embarrass the drovers later. But Colonel Ellison had not built his reputation on shady deals, and the animals were held for their rightful owner. The Ellison herd was driven through to Ogallala, from which point Hardeman, Baylor, and Bee took another herd northwest to the distant Belle Fourche country of northeastern Wyoming. On this drive they crossed a stretch of sixty miles without water.

Harsh conditions, these, for a self-confessed green cowhand; it could hardly have been the paltry dollar for each day in the saddle that whetted the herdsman's appetite for the trail. Perhaps it was the solitude, the time for reflection, or the smell of grub sizzling as day broke over the camp; the blazing sunsets or the color of the cow towns gaudily blossoming atop the dry stem of the trail. Half a century after his cattle driving days were over, Walker Hardeman reminisced:

> Not one I rode with did I ever hear say, when a trail drive was completed, that he'd go again next year. It was a time-worn saying in every outfit, when the boys turned back after a drive was made, that "they'd rather be a yellow hound dog under a farmhouse than to trail another herd." But nothing was ever as sweet in our ears as the night guard singing the cattle onto the bed ground, and a fiddler playing "Turkey in the Straw" or "Little Brown Jug," while the rest knocked the black out of the pigeon wing, the double shuffle and their boot soles at the same time. Never was there such a generous, free-hearted, wholesome, honest-to-goodness set of men as the open range cowboys of yesterday, and I count it one of the highest honors of my life to have been one of them. [7]

Whatever the allure, like many another drover, Walker came back again and again. In 1883 he went up the trail with William Jackman, later sheriff of San Marcos, Texas. From the Stafford brothers' ranch in Caldwell County, they drove a big herd—3,000 cattle and 400 horses in addition to the 100-horse remuda. The marketing of horses is a neglected but highly significant phase in the history of the long drive. Not only were horses taken specifically for marketing, but a large part of the remuda could be sold, since fewer mounts were needed for the homeward leg of the journey. Lee Wolfington was on this drive, as were Dan, a fifteen-year-old lad, and eight other cowhands. One evening in Indian Territory, Hardeman was "holding" the cattle and Dan was guarding the remuda at a spot within three miles of a group of 400 Indians. Two of the Indians, after eating supper with the drovers, headed toward their own camp then circled back and drove off two saddle horses. Dan discovered them and gave the alarm with shouts and gunfire. Fearing an attack from the encampment of Indians, several cowmen rode to the scene and quickly recovered the mounts. Indians were sometimes a serious threat to the drovers but were more often an inconvenience. They charged a few cents per head to allow passage of cattle across their lands, and at times they stampeded animals and cut out some for their own use, since buffalo were becoming scarce. Probably the drives harmed as much as helped the Indians by despoiling the grazing lands in the Territory.

There were other human obstacles in the paths of the drovers, and it seemed Walker Hardeman's destiny to encounter all types on this drive. The friction between "ranger and granger," or cattleman and farmer, reached serious proportions in the West, sometimes leading to shootings. Hardeman recorded that one night the herd stampeded through a Kansas nester's cane patch. The farmer came out "bellerin' like a range bull," but Walker eventually calmed him with coffee and grub and a promise that trail boss Jackman would reimburse him for the loss. Two years later Congress passed a law prohibiting interference with settlers by cattle drovers.

One branch of the 1883 drive bent off in a direction unusual for the livestock trade when a buyer at Dodge City hired Walker Hardeman as trail boss to drive horses and cattle from Kansas to the Peacock Ranch in northeastern New Mexico. Hardeman and the crew of Mexican drovers had some anxious hours when their herd stampeded at three o'clock one morning and "split a flock of sheep wide open." Luckily no sheep were killed, else there would have been problems between the trail herders and the sheep ranchers. The scattered horses and cattle were rounded up and taken on to New Mexico, where they arrived in good condition. This drive acquainted Hardeman with two routes of historic importance, the old Santa Fe Trail (known to a number of his relatives) and the return to Texas by way of the Goodnight-Loving Cattle Trail along the Pecos River.

Big ranchers such as John R. Blocker often bought cattle in fall and winter months, branded them in early spring, and sent a herd north every ten to twelve days, beginning with the first growth of grass. Blocker, a square-faced, heavy-necked South Carolinian, had a large ranch in Blanco County north of San Antonio. He was reported to have had a financial stake in 86,000 head of cattle on the trails at one time in 1886. After working for three years with rancher Tom Berry in Frio County, Texas, Walker Hardeman drove for Blocker, Driscoll, and Davis that year in company with Sandy Buckalew and trail boss Joe Robertson. They started far south and went up a rough trail along the east fork of the Nueces, past Uvalde, and north to "The Territory," as part of a chain of herds numbering about 40,000 cattle and 1,400 horses: "a speckled ribbon, as far as the eyes could see in either direction." This drive, too, branched off westward, as Hardeman and Robertson took a herd from Kansas to Colorado Springs, then rode to Denver to "take in the town," and saw Joe Jefferson portray Rip Van Winkle at Tabor's Theater.[8]

Soon after the activities of that year, the epic "long drives" came to an end, victims of barbed wire and farmers and sheepherders and falling prices. Walker left the lonely life of the trail and married a widow, Maggie Edwards Bright. The couple had three children, and the cowhand farmed briefly, then became county commissioner in Caldwell County, Texas. The domesticating of his trail ways closed another phase in the backland preferences of Thomas Hardeman's descendants. As if by a signal to keep the western marathon going, in the very year of Walker Hardeman's last drive the Missouri line of the family began to probe again at the remnants of the frontier.

The children of erstwhile gold miner Glen O. Hardeman caught the flavor and the fever of the Old West from many an hour on their father's knee. They begged to hear his stories over and over. All four sons, Letcher, Locke, Glen, and Joseph, kept faith with their forebears who had taken to the West and the wilderness. The second son, Letcher, was born at Arrow Rock, Missouri, April 30, 1864, an uncertain time and place, with repeated bushwhacker raids on the Hardeman home when he was less than a year old. He was named in honor of Jerrold R. Letcher of Saline County, a friend and fellow student of Glen Hardeman at the University of Pennsylvania medical school.

Letcher Hardeman grew up in a rural setting near Gray's Summit, Missouri, where hunting, riding horseback, and working with horses and mules occupied much of his youth. All these experiences were to assume importance in his career. Typical of an increasing number of farm sons of his time, he forsook agriculture for other pursuits. Congressman Richard Bland of Missouri helped to secure an appointment for him as a cadet at West Point Military Academy, where he enrolled July 1, 1882. It is probable that he chose this profession in part because he knew it would take him west. A heavy percentage of the Army's men—about two-thirds—were garrisoned at forts of the Far West at the time he enlisted.

At West Point, Letcher was nicknamed "Jack" by his classmates, one of whom later described him as "tall, wiry, genial, kindly, painstaking."[9] Four years after his induction, the young Missouri farmer emerged from the cadet cocoon to try his wings in the arid atmosphere of the nation's last frontier.

Lieutenant Hardeman was not long in fulfilling his urge to see the West. Coincidentally, his first assignment, with the Fourth regiment of Cavalry, took him into the barren, angular country of the Southwest which had been the sometime habitat of his gold-hunting father and his trade-seeking grandsire. By September 1886 he was at Fort Bowie in the Chiricahua Mountains of Arizona Territory. This post, east of Apache Pass, was built in 1862 to protect the Mesilla-Tucson road and a nearby spring. After several months Letcher was reassigned to Fort Lowell (Tucson) and later to the San Carlos Indian Reservation. His duties at these stations provide a representative cross-sample of the assignments of young field officers in the territory during the late eighties and early nineties.

Although Hardeman arrived at the time when Geronimo's surrender stilled the last major Indian war in the Southwest, there were occasional calls to swab out pockets of resistance, attack roving bands of "hostiles," and round up tribesmen for confinement on reservations. This type of duty occupied a large part of his four years in Arizona. On June 6, 1887, he and James Lockett led a Fourth Cavalry detachment from Fort Bowie to "picket the country, to intercept, and if possible destroy any Indians who may attempt to get into the Chiracachuas by Dunn's Trail, Emigrant or Woods Canon."[10] In mid-September Letcher led Troop G from Bowie to Fief's Ranch to establish a camp, scout the area, and post pickets to cover Moses, Pinery, and Bear Spring canyons. He was warned to avoid stampedes, since one of the sure-fire weapons of the Indians was to drive off the mounts of the cavalrymen.

Through the late months of 1889 Hardeman made many sorties from his base at San Carlos (a center for the Chiricahua Apaches), scouting and rounding up renegades from the reservation. He was operating out of Fort Lowell in search of wild Indians during June 1890.[11] In the course of these and numerous other mopping-up operations, he reputedly exhibited considerable compassion for the "poor devils," the holdouts and runaways who were understandably less than happy with the cruel turn of affairs which found them hunted like the scattered remnants from a covey of game birds. He was credited with coolness under fire and with having won from the Indians their "respect, submission, their confidence as a strict but just . . . leader." These words were from his fellow officers, however.[12] Could the Indians have spoken for themselves, it is possible that their justifiable resentment against all white intruders would have shown in the description.

One of the effective devices that helped the Army overcome the Indians of the Southwest was the heliograph, used with telling effect by General Nelson Miles's forces in the Geronimo era. The heliograph was a mirror and telescope device that reflected the rays of the sun from station to station, much like modern blinker signals. In that land of wide-spaced ranges and ample sunshine it was a rapid method of sending and relaying coded signals or heliograms over many miles. "Whispering mirrors" were vastly more effective than the smoke signals of the tribesmen and much cheaper than the massive layout of telegraph poles and wires. Lieutenant Hardeman developed more than the usual know-how for officers in the installation and use of the heliograph. By weight of evidence in the documents of the Bowie-Lowell-San Carlos area, it is apparent that he was the heliograph expert relied upon most heavily in his years of duty there. In October 1886 and March 1887 he gave instructions on the use of the instrument to groups at Fort Bowie. That fall he was sent to set up a number of the mirror stations above the canyons in the Fief Ranch area.

TOP: The "Buffalo Soldiers" of the Tenth Cavalry were black and their commissioned officers, including Letcher Hardeman, were white. Here a group from this
post-Civil War regiment is sketched at mealtime by Frederic Remington. *From
Century Magazine, 1889.* LOWER: Colonel Letcher Hardeman, commanding
officer of the Sixth Missouri Volunteers in the Spanish-American War, served for
more than a decade on the Indian frontier of the Far West. *Courtesy the Hardeman
family.*

From these his orders were to keep in touch with the signal posts at White's Ranch and Bowie. Around San Carlos he continued his communications specialty with Company G, Fourth Cavalry, in 1889 by setting up stations to maintain contact with adjacent divisions.[13]

Scores of temporary-duty stints filled out Letcher's routine. Behind the monotonously regular courtmartial assignments, a view of soldiers' offenses emerges as starkly as the sandstone pillars and outcroppings of the Southwest. The cases Hardeman heard and tried usually involved drunkenness or desertion, and the verdict was almost invariably "guilty." He served as a witness before the United States courts in Phoenix and Tucson, as range officer at Fort Wingate, as inspector of quartermaster and commissary supplies, and as an escort for the welcomed army paymasters. Through the escort duties he became familiar with Fort Apache, a post he would later command.

A shift from the hot to the cold frontier in the early 1890s found Letcher Hardeman holding a first lieutenant's commission at Fort Assiniboine, Montana. During his entire stay of more than half a decade at this post he was attached to the Tenth Cavalry. An outgrowth of the changing official attitude toward the black Americans, that remarkable organization was set up by Congress in July 1866.[14] As was also true of the Ninth Cavalry established by the same act, the enlisted personnel of the Tenth were entirely blacks, although all commissioned officers of both outfits were white. This regiment served in Kansas, Indian Territory, Texas, Arizona Territory, the Northwest, Cuba, the Philippines, and on the trail of Pancho Villa in Mexico, and won battle honors at Santiago and in the Far East.

In August 1890, the Tenth Cavalry came under the command of thrice-decorated Civil War veteran Colonel John Kemp Mizner. Twelve months later, in a message hinting at racial discrimination, this former commander of the Eighth Cavalry wrote to the Adjutant-General, pointing out that "for twenty consecutive years the Tenth Cavalry had served south of the 36th latitude, in the most undesirable stations as to quarters or barracks";[15] he might have added too, that they were given the worst cast-off mounts in all the cavalry outfits and that there was no opportunity for black soldiers to become officers. He requested a "gradual" change to a more northerly climate, preferably nothing north of Kansas. Whatever his

272]

Paymaster's escort was one of the routine assignments performed by Lt. Letcher Hardeman in the Southwest of the late nineteenth century. The paymaster's valuable cargo and the rough terrain invited ambush. *From* Harper's Weekly, *June 1887*.

motives in seeking orders to a more temperate climate, he got a less gradual change than he had asked for. Although one troop went to Leavenworth, Kansas, the remainder of the regiment was sent to the far Northwest, where it arrived in a blinding winter blizzard! It was deployed at Fort Buford, North Dakota, and Forts Assiniboine, Custer, and Keogh, Montana. On November 20, 1894, Assiniboine became the regimental headquarters for the Tenth, and by 1898 most of the outfit was there.

A Montana newspaperman, writing a decade after the "buffalo soldiers" of the Tenth Cavalry had left the state, chided the people of Vermont for opposing the assignment of the black regiment to Fort Ethan Allen. He closed his tribute with the statement that:

> The Tenth Cavalry trooper is willing and a fighter but he is also much on show. He'll get along all right with those Vermonters, for he will adapt himself to the conditions which prevail, and if he does not make the men who protested against the regiment being sent there back water then I miss my guess. Havre always had a good word for these "blackbirds," and so has every other town near where they have been stationed.[16]

Whether Lieutenant Hardeman would have agreed or disagreed with that appraisal, he did not indicate. In all the known correspondence of this son of an ex-slaveholder, there is not a single word referring to the color of the men in his command; and this, in light of the volume of letters, is unusual. He referred to them as the men, the boys, the soldiers, and the troops. Although he described "the majority of army boys," in a general statement, as "pretty worthless—absolutely devoid of ambition," he does not relate the comment to the Tenth Cavalry.[17] At that time it was not compulsory for officers to serve with Negro units (and commissioned officers were difficult to get for the Ninth and Tenth Cavalry). Hardeman served by choice with the Tenth for many years, and when he left it was not at his own request.

The far western assignment of the Tenth Cavalry was in keeping with the trend of the time—the concentrating of the army at western forts. Assiniboine, like the vast majority of these military establishments, had been built to control the Indian population. On June 25, 1876, Colonel George Custer and his force of some 265 men were cut down and exterminated by the Sioux and Cheyenne at the Little Bighorn. Three months after this battle a column of soldiers under the command of

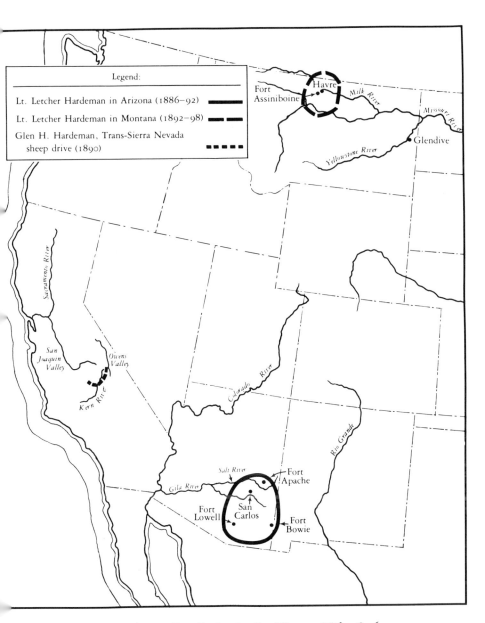

Map 7. The Hardeman Family in the Far West, 1886–1896.

General Alfred H. Terry defeated the Sioux, but Chief Sitting Bull still represented a threat to the North, having escaped into Canada with a small number of unvanquished warriors. Out of fear that Sitting Bull would return, and to control the Blackfeet who had been consigned to a reserve north of the Missouri River, Fort Assiniboine was established on May 8, 1879, by Colonel Thomas Ruger of the Eighteenth Infantry. One of the northernmost military posts in the nation, this large ten-company post was built mainly of brick and named after the Assiniboine Indians of the United States-Canadian border region. It was located on an elevated tongue of the plains, skirted on the south by Beaver Creek about four miles above the confluence of that stream and Milk River. Rocky hills loomed to the south of the fort, while toward the north windswept plains stretched away in a seemingly endless expanse.

The garrison at this post was spared the task of quelling major Indian uprisings, although from time to time it had assignments which broke the routine of duty. It rounded up and returned Indians who had left their designated reserves, and it stood ready to preserve the "pecking order" of that age by protecting railroad management against striking workers, mine owners against workers, miners and stockmen against Indians, and, occasionally, reservation Indians against encroachment by miners. The main characters of the drama, as at most western posts, were the Indians and the soldiers.

Most common of the chores was the rounding up of Cree Indians. These hapless relatives of the Chippewa had been driven across the border into Canada and to the edge of starvation. They frequently ventured south into the United States in search of game, livestock, and handouts. Time and again between 1877 and the early twentieth century they were peacefully rounded up by soldiers and escorted back to Canada. Sometimes they managed to slip back into the United States before their escorts had returned to their posts. Picket fences were utilized in one attempt at containment of the Crees.

Lieutenant John J. Pershing and Hardeman, classmates at West Point and close friends at Assiniboine, were involved on a number of occasions with rounding up Indians.[18] This task was usually accomplished without bloodshed, although not without incident. The soldiers covered hundreds of miles in the saddle, battling heat, cold, thirst, and insects, and killing game to vary their diet. On one of their hunts, Hardeman and Pershing sighted a deer and fired at the same instant. The animal fell, and each man claimed the kill. "It was the only time I ever saw Pershing really get excited," Letcher later observed.[19] During another roundup, Canadian authorities resisted return of the Crees because of a measles epidemic in the area. Supervision of Indians other than Crees, including Blackfeet, Piegans, Gros Ventres, Crows, and Assiniboines also fell to the soldiers at Fort Assiniboine from time to time.

Railroads penetrating the far Northwest inadvertently provided a means of spreading some of the East's labor problems to the backlands, and the Montana of Letcher Hardeman's day was not immune. In April 1894, the Great Northern employees went on strike, interrupting mail deliveries, and the Pullman Palace Car Company strike of May 11, 1894 spread throughout much of the West by late June when Eugene Debs's American Railway Union refused to handle trains with Pullman cars. Federal troops were dispatched to points such as Glendive, Montana, on the Northern Pacific. The disturbance "has not affected us as much as the late strike on the Great Northern did," Hardeman noted. "I don't know how the matter seems there but from this distant point it looks as though there is going to be serious trouble unless that man Debs can be squelched."[20]

Letcher apparently shared the full variety of peacetime assignments while at the Montana fortification. The understaffing of the fort resulted in his falling heir to numerous collateral chores. In October of 1894 he wrote, "I have now the duties of Q.M., commissary and ordnance officer to perform in addition to my troop duties."[21] At the time there were but three troops on the post, and only four officers were available to rotate guard duty. Hardeman was also judge advocate in a general court martial at roughly the same time. He had a novel solution to another problem.

> I invested in a couple of hogs for my troop the other day. Expect to utilize the scraps from the troop mess in feeding hogs. This troop was turned over to me in debt and I have been trying every way to get them out and am just beginning to see daylight now.[22]

Letcher's expertise with the heliograph was followed by another specialty at Assiniboine, an assignment which would shape his next twenty years with the army. The fort records show his increasing involvement with mules and horses, transportation and the remount service—a linkage with his boyhood days in Missouri furrows.[23]

There were occasions for things other than official duty at the fort on Beaver Creek. The day of the illegal traffic in liquor, narcotics, arms, ammunition, and livestock was apparently gone, as was the halfbreed hangout for fakirs, gamblers, and prostitutes which had flourished a mile from Assiniboine during the 1880s. By the time Hardeman had arrived, conditions were more settled. Like a number of other officers, he lived with his family at the outpost. As a Missouri lad he had been interested in hunting, and wild game abounded in Montana. The numerous wolves, coyotes, and large game animals near the fort offered frequent sport and target practice, and he kept hounds to pursue wolves, coyotes, and foxes. He and his family took advantage of other forms of entertainment, including horseback riding, and in winter, sleigh trips to Havre.[24]

Unhappily for the historian, Hardeman's letters are those of a soldier to whom brevity and understatement seemed a virtue. Perhaps the Montana scene appeared bleak and forbidding by comparison with his memories of life in the more humid, temperate, and wooded environment of Missouri. He found the cold of winter and the mosquitoes of summer disagreeable. His pen returns repeatedly to conditions on the farm. Perhaps, too, this mirrors the fact that to the soldier, the situation in the Northwest no longer offered the excitement of the previous several decades. The great mining rushes were past, the Indian menace was minor, the Northern Pacific and Great Northern had stitched the Northwest to the Union, and Montana had been a state since 1889.

That Assiniboine, from its beginning to abandonment in 1911, was relatively tranquil has been interpreted as evidence that its creation was a case of too much, too late. On the contrary, lack of bloodshed was a tribute to its success, since its role was the prevention of violence. The site was well chosen: sufficiently far north to cut off any likely southern sorties of the Sioux, yet holding a position near the center of the Blackfeet Reserve and providing security for nearby stockmen. Its brick construction made it all but immune to attack by Indians. The immediate threat from Sitting Bull was erased by 1881, but for another fifteen years an uneasy feeling pervaded the atmosphere, an apprehension that the smoldering ashes of a once vast Indian stronghold might again be fanned into flames. This concern was heightened by the Apache War and the "Ghost Dance" uprising of 1890. But the demise of the buffalo, the rise of the "iron horse," the employment of rapid-fire weapons by the Army, and the arrival of "civilization" quickly reduced the Indians to demoralized dependents. The soldiers of Letcher Hardeman's time were in a sense anachronisms, with little to do but stand guard and peacefully preside over the dissolution of the redoubt of the native race. They were virtually "mothballed" in the forts of the West until they were called upon to play more active roles.

With the outbreak of the Spanish-American War and the swelling of the armed forces by large numbers of green volunteers, many officers moved from the regulars into positions of temporary advanced rank in command of "Vol" units. On May 23, 1898, Major Letcher Hardeman was placed in charge of the Second Missouri Volunteer Infantry, which he mustered in at Jefferson Barracks near St. Louis. Two months later he became Colonel in command of the Sixth Regiment, Missouri Volunteer Infantry.[25] But what Theodore Roosevelt called the "Splendid Little War" was over and won by the time Letcher's outfit arrived in Cuba, and after a none-too-eventful stay he returned to the United States in April 1899, resuming his duties with the regular army as a first lieutenant.

The shock waves from the war were not soon stilled. Gluttons for empire won the day, and American armed forces were called upon to extinguish the flames of "rebellion" in the Philippines. In February 1901 "Jack" Hardeman, now a captain, began a two-year tour of duty in these islands as regimental quartermaster in the Eleventh Cavalry.[26] This assignment was a reprise of some of his duties at Fort Assiniboine; his experience with mounts, which were the backbone of the army's transportation, was recognized. He commanded the remount station of Fort Reno, Oklahoma, from 1908 until 1912. Hardeman was promoted to major in 1911, and the following year was made commanding officer of Fort Apache. After a two-year term with the Fourth Cavalry at Schofield Barracks in Hawaii, he retired in 1915.

Five months after his retirement, World War I pulled him back to active duty. He served as a recruiting officer for nearly two years until the critical need for mounts in Europe brought him again into the quartermaster corps. For his contributions as Chief of the Remount Service in

Washington, D.C., and in France, 1917–1918, he received the Distinguished Service Medal,[27] having requisitioned hundreds of thousands of horses and mules for wartime use. He also devised the means of sale of 200,000 surplus animals after the war, saving the government large sums of money. In June 1919, after nearly thirty-seven years active service, he retired at the rank of colonel.

The retirement of Colonel Hardeman signaled more than the end of a man's career. It coincided closely with the end of an era for the Army of the United States—the era of the army mule. That legendary beast of burden, comical and cantankerous, indomitable and long indispensable, with "no pride of ancestry and no prospect of progeny," was rapidly replaced by mechanized transportation. But its place in the history and folklore of the army is secure. It is probable that no other soldier in the army's existence had as much to do with as many mules and horses as did cavalry and remount officer Letcher Hardeman in his management of the "mule corps." It was appropriate, perhaps, for a man whose grandfather was one of the first breeders of Missouri mules.

Letcher Hardeman's second retirement was more permanent than the first, and he was able to devote more time with his family. In 1891 he had married Adelaide Parker Russell, daughter of John G. Russell, a Missouri manufacturer. The couple had two daughters, both born in the Far West.

As he had spent his first eighteen years, so the retired officer was to spend his last eighteen, with the plough and the pruning hook rather than the sword and the spear. The nostalgia of boyhood days on the farm kept its hold upon him, and late in his military career he had bought Spring Hill Farm at Rapidan, Virginia, as his place of retirement. His lifelong fondness for mules and horses manifested itself here, where he used them to plow and cultivate. He went to sales out of curiosity, to check on the prices and conditions of animals.[28] Letcher Hardeman spent his remaining years on his farm and died there on February 16, 1937.

Medicine, like westward wayfaring, had begun to establish itself as a family tradition, at least to the extent of several practitioners, including former frontiersmen Blackstone, John M., and Glen O. Hardeman. Glen's eldest son, John Locke, was born in Saline County, Missouri, in 1855, three years before the death of the uncle for whom he was named. Locke's early seasoning for life was waking up at night to the thud of the bushwhacker's boot at his mother's door. After the Civil War, when the family found a less hectic home environment in Franklin County, Locke began to read medicine under his father's guidance. After two years at the University of Missouri, he moved to St. Louis Medical College and was awarded the M.D. degree in 1878. Several years of practice in the Missouri towns of La Due and Brownington, although apparently successful, were not enough to blot out his thoughts of the California image graven there by a thousand tellings of his father's experiences. Like Glen in central Missouri during the gold rush, he grew restive and became the second physician in the family to establish himself in the Golden State. He built his medical and surgical practice at the San Joaquin Valley town of Porterville, in partnership with a Dr. Brumfield. Locke married Vira Jeffries of Missouri and they had two children. He lived at Porterville for the rest of his life. Bear and deer hunting and trout fishing trips into the mountains[29] fed his need for fulfillment of ambitions kindled in his early years by stories of the West.

The third son of Glen O. Hardeman, Glen H. (for Hodgen, in honor of his father's friend Dr. John T. Hodgen, inventor of the Hodgen splint), was born in Franklin County, Missouri, in 1868. Like his father and oldest brother, Glen began the study of medicine, attending Central College, Fayette, Missouri, as preparatory. However, his parents were in advanced years and he interrupted his career (permanently, as it turned out) to go home and care for them and their farm.[30] Several years later, in 1890, he visited his brother Locke in California.

Glen H. Hardeman, a blue-eyed, moustached young man of twenty-two years, was an interested observer of the West. His mode of transportation was somewhat more comfortable than that of his forefathers. Three years before his visit, the Santa Fe line had fractured the Southern Pacific's rail monopoly of California, and Glen chose to journey over the Santa Fe's iron bands. As he settled his wiry six-foot frame into the coach and looked about, he was "very much disappointed in the scenery" of the Southwest.[31] The green hills overlooking his Missouri home had conditioned him against the "dreary wasteland" of the arid parts of the West much as they had influenced his brother at Fort Assiniboine.

The last twenty-five miles of Glen's trip to Porterville were made by buggy "over a road so dusty that at times the horses were almost indistinguishable. . . . I thought Missouri was dusty enough at times," he observed, "but never in my life have I seen it anything like it is here—especially where the heavy hauling has been done. . . . The farmers unite and haul straw on the roads to keep down the dust."[32]

The gargantuan wheat fields of the San Joaquin Valley were an awesome sight to Hardeman's midwestern eyes. Ruinous droughts had crippled the cattle industry in the 1860s, and winter wheat, well suited to much of the Central Valley, became California's leading crop. Soil depletion, foreign competition, depression, and irrigation had combined to render wheat less profitable than some other farm products, and what Glen Hardeman described were among the last throes of the great wheat bonanza in California.

> I passed through a ranch of 22000 acres of wheat between here [Porterville] and Tulare. Several steam harvesters were at work cutting and threshing at the same time, cutting a 20 foot swathe. There were also a dozen or more headers and 3 or 4 horse power harvesters in the same field or rather on the same plain.
>
> They have been cutting the wheat steadily for 2 or 3 months or more and will continue till September. Thousands of acres of wheat, ripened weeks ago, yet remain standing, waiting for the harvester. There is no wind to blow it down and no rain to damage the wheat lying in sacks scattered over the plains.[33]

The Porterville of 1890 was described as a hot, dusty little town of 1,000 people, huddled against the foothills which etched the border between the valley and the southern Sierra Nevada. Electric lights, powered from the Tule River, provided a modern touch. Green, irrigated oases of varied fruit culture speckled the land, but the endless sea of wheat dominated the low country as convincingly as the Sierra overwhelmed the scene east of the town. Glen spent some time reading, as an indoor escape from the dust, but also ventured into the surrounding countryside to hunt wildlife specimens, such as California quail and jackrabbits, for applying his techniques as an amateur taxidermist, shipping the skins to Missouri for later mounting. In July 1890 he went farther afield for a few weeks' experience in the Sierra Nevada, a trip which made a life-long impression on him.[34]

This was the era when Francis Parkman wrote: "The Wild West is tamed and its savage charms have withered." It was the time that the United States Bureau of the Census and historian of the West Frederick

Glen H. Hardeman, the third son of Glen O. Hardeman and
father of the author, sought out the remnants of the frontier by
joining a trans-Sierra sheep drive in 1890. *Courtesy the Hardeman
family.*

Jackson Turner were giving the frontier a decent burial. Tragic, it seemed, that a line, a force, a process which had been so vital to American life was interred at the very time it had first won recognition—had first become appreciated. But the savage charms which Parkman saw withering still possessed savagery and charm to some inveterate outdoorsmen. That indomitable Scots mountaineer John Muir was pushing the idea of a Yosemite Park at the very time Glen Hardeman was assaulting the granite inclines and following the clear streams of the Sierra.

On this trip, just four years after his cousin's last stint on the great cattle trails, Glen assisted in driving a large herd of sheep along part of the trail from summer grazing highlands at the northern end of Owens Valley across the southern Sierra Nevada and into the wintering grounds of the San Joaquin Valley.[35] The drive of 300 miles and more had been made yearly for three decades. This historical transhumance is still an occasional event after more than a hundred years and despite the advent of modern motor trucking. The high meadows between the Sierra and White Mountains are better for sheep feeding, breeding, and wool-growing conditions than is the summer environment of the Central Valley. The drive of 1890 spanned the Sierra Nevada well to the north of the present Tehachapi Pass route authorized by the federal government. Judging from the place names which Glen mentioned, the trail must have led along Cottonwood Creek and over the pass of the same name, into Whitney Meadow, along Golden Trout Creek, south and southwest to Horse Meadows and the Kern River, and thence near Parker and South creeks westward into the San Joaquin Valley.

The young Missourian was accustomed to sheep raising, but the small, enclosed fields on his father's farm had not prepared him for the sight of the large flock being herded across the mountains. There were drovers riding and shouting, dogs yapping at the flanks of stray animals, and several goats to lead the sheep across streams on fallen logs. Glen got his wildest taste of the then not-so-wild West on this drive. Like the other men, he carried a 38-caliber revolver to frighten off predators such as mountain lions. He was awakened one night by a growling sound which seemed to spell danger. Reaching quietly for his six-shooter, he realized that the noise was the snoring of a sleeping companion.

The only use of the revolver on that drive was as a means to catch fish.

Fresh from a small wooded Missouri farm, Glen H. Hardeman was awed by the gigantic wheat fields and huge steam-powered combine harvesters such as the one shown above in the San Joaquin Valley of California. *Courtesy History Division, Natural History Museum of Los Angeles County.*

Glen Hardeman was assigned the pleasurable chore (for he was an avid fisherman) of providing food for the sheepherders. On one occasion he eyed a large trout which lay at the bottom of a pool ignoring his fly, cast after cast. Finally he fired a shot at the fish, which lay unmoving as the water calmed and the bullet sank harmlessly to the bottom. The trout, perhaps awakened, rose to the next cast and was soon tucked away in Glen's hunting coat pocket. He caught many golden trout on this trip, lugging 108 fish back to the hungry herdsmen on his best day, guided by the light of their fire and arriving at camp after dark. Most of the trout were small, and all were taken with the simplest of equipment, a brown hackle fly tied to a willow pole by a six-foot line.

Some years after his return to Missouri, Glen, who was a great-grandson of Thomas Hardeman, married a distant cousin, Marion Evans, a great-great-granddaughter of that same frontiersman. Until his death at his Missouri farm in 1948, Glen Hardeman told his five children about the Sierra experiences on countless occasions. He felt a kinship with those mountains—with much the same intensity, though not the intimacy, of a John Muir. His contagious enthusiasm inspired still another generation to pack into remote parts of that range.

Joseph Townsend Hardeman, the youngest son of Dr. Glen O. Hardeman, was born in 1872. Like his three brothers, he plotted a western course early in life. By 1895, as an employee of the Gauss-Shelton Hat and Glove Company of St. Louis, he was based in Omaha, Nebraska, traveling to far western cities, one of which appealed to him as a place to "hang his hat" literally. He established the J. T. Hardeman Hat Company in Seattle, Washington, where for a number of decades he manufactured men's felt hats. Joe too had a keen feeling for the wilderness areas. He and his wife, the former Julia Russell (who was a first cousin of the painter of western scenes, Charles M. Russell), and their daughter became permanent residents of Seattle. Joseph died in 1943.[36]

The late nineteenth-century West of Letcher Hardeman, and Locke and Glen and Joe, was little more than a dying echo of the frontier of Thomas Hardeman on the Holston or the Tennessee, and of the Missouri River of John's day. Gone were the challenges and privations of the great trails, the Santa Fe, the Oregon, the California, and the Chisholm. But it was the West of their time—the only West remaining to explore and "conquer."

Despite the demise of the "wild" West of his forebears, Missouri-born Joseph T. Hardeman plotted a western course early in life. *Courtesy the Hardeman family.*

In the reports they left, there was in evidence a certain historical nostalgia, a longing to find the wilderness as excitingly dangerous as it once had been. The accounts of hot Arizona duty, of those dreary years at Fort Assiniboine, of life at dusty Porterville, and days on the Sierra sheep trail were those of men who paused momentarily at points in time and place where, almost imperceptibly yet unmistakably, there occurred the fading out of the Old West and the phasing in of the New.

15 ꓧ Westward Impulse in Microcosm
SOME CONCLUDING VIEWS

You will find something more in woods than in books.
Trees and stones will teach you that which you can never
learn from masters.

— BERNARD OF CLAIRVAUX

THE FRONTIER EXPERIENCE of Thomas Hardeman and his descendants was, to an extraordinary degree, a microcosm of the country's westering impulse, a sampling of that great human movement in its various dimensions. Insofar as currently available records show, no other western pioneering family participated in America's frontiering efforts over such a long period of time or such a wide geographic area. The Hardeman influence was felt over the southern half of that part of the nation east of the Mississippi and in nearly the whole of the trans-Mississippi West, with probes into Mexico, Brazil, and the Far East—from the 1750s to the early twentieth century. Sizable numbers of the family held prominent positions of leadership in the West; they represented a broad spectrum of occupations and professions; and finally, they were document writers and savers generation after generation, thus enabling the story to be pieced together.

Among the occupations in which the Hardeman family engaged, the three most frequent were agriculture, politics, and the military; most of the westernized representatives were involved at some time or another in all three. At least two members, Thomas and his son Bailey, were mountain men, half a dozen were gold miners, seven were merchants, five built and operated mills, three had distilleries or wine presses, three were innkeepers, and several were land promoters. There were two ferry boat owners, five physicians, four or five lawyers, two clergymen, several herdsmen, a surveyor, some cotton ginners, and a judge. The fourth estate was represented by editor Peter Burnett. Obviously these are minimum tabulations; could the full story be fathomed, it would show other representatives in perhaps other frontiers and trades. As cases in point, Lent and Nash Hardeman, grandsons of Thomas, moved at least temporarily to the trans-Mississippi West, and some descendants of Thomas's brother John migrated from Georgia to Texas. Unfortunately for the preserving of a balanced and accurate view of history, most first-hand accounts of the West, and of America in general prior to the twentieth century, were written of, by, and for adult white males. So it was with Thomas and Mary Hardeman and their descendants. Very few of the extant letters were written by female members of the family. It is likely that a number of offspring of the Hardeman daughters went frontiering, but most have been lost with the dropping of their mothers' last names upon marriage. In addition to the Burnetts, the brothers Hardeman and Solomon Stone, nephews of Thomas Hardeman, "were wayward and roving. Both went to Mexico at an early day."[1]

But the tally adds up to a significant if indefinite impact on the business, political, and professional activity in the West. Generally missing from the list of occupations were handicrafts. Many of the Hardemans, of course, were slaveholders who relegated the menial tasks to their servants. Thomas and his descendants were not averse to doing manual labor, but they were seldom laborers by occupation, and there is occasional evidence that they took a condescending view of common labor as an occupation.

What the Hardemans did in the West is much clearer than why. Since Frederick Jackson Turner's "The Significance of the Frontier in American History" was presented in 1893,[2] volumes have been written on the motives of westward migration, and hypotheses have been propounded, debunked, and supported in a torrent of literature. No other subject has been more heatedly debated by American historians. The very terms *frontier* and *westward expansion* are at times misleading and inaccurate. The push to the outlands was not always in the design of a tier, nor was it always westward. Yet these terms are so deep-rooted in literature and folklore that they are not likely to yield to more precise expressions. They are employed with a measure of the usual abandon in this volume, as they have come to mean generically what they do not always mean literally. American historians have been less bold in coining a jargon than have scholars in some other disciplines, but perhaps they need such a term as *sertão,* a Portuguese-Brazilian word which, by greater generality, achieves greater accuracy in referring to the backlands than do frontier or West; and an expression such as *settled frontier,* applicable to areas which have advanced beyond the frontier stage except in certain characteristics.

The Hardeman documents can be searched in vain for a frontier concept in the agrarian mode as applied by Turner. Apparently the Hardemans thought of the backlands not as a moving line or process of settlement, nor as the hither edge of free land, but as a fixed area of trails, soils, resources, adventures, opportunities, developments. The literal study of the frontier is analogous to an investigation of an extinct species, while the West is a living, ongoing subject. Properly, a study of the frontier would force attention away from an area as soon as the frontier line had passed it and would rob the West of much valuable history.

Frontier hypotheses have proved at least as vague as the frontier concept. The notion of the West as the "true point of view in the history of this nation" is a narrow observation which historians have long rejected. Yet stress on this idea was as overdue as it was overdone, since scholars had too long ignored the significance of the frontier and the West. The heavy involvement of the Hardemans with that general area lends no weight to the "true point of view" concept. It merely shows an unusual western emphasis on their part.

The Hardeman experience may shed some light on the formative force of free land. Turner, owing some recognition to prior writings such as those of Italian economist Achille Loria, saw two principal and related forces which enabled the frontier to exert its pervading influence—the land in general and free land in particular. The notion that the wilderness mastered the colonist was part of an implied geographical determinism.

Land was viewed as the dynamic shaper, while people, the more passive ingredients, were molded by the whim of the environment. Critics have countered that man was the commanding element which mastered the wilderness and that, in any explanation of American history, capitalism, industrial labor, urban development, the plantation, and other institutions must not be pushed into the background.

Free land was supposed to have had almost magical powers. "The most significant thing about the American frontier is that it lies at the hither edge of free land." And in another passage, Turner expounded: "The existence of an area of free land, its continuous recession, and the advance of American settlement westward, explain American development." It is generally conceded that these observations overstate the case, that prior to the Homestead Act of 1862 land could be owned only for a fee, not free, and that after that date the costs of reaching free land were prohibitive for many people. To be sure, squatters settled as if the land were free, knowing that they must pack up or pay off when the government surveyors reached them.

Land was the occupational common denominator for nearly all the westbound Hardemans. Cheap land in back-country Carolina and Tennessee offered liberation from tenancy for Tom Hardeman. This land was not free, since it was given in exchange for past military duty, as was the case of some grants to Texas migrants. Thomas evinced an uncommonly large land hunger for a non-speculator, the desire to set up his children on plantations. Perhaps this urge for family security was a more basic determinism, and acquisitions of real estate in Tennessee, Louisiana, and Missouri were merely the most accessible means of meeting that need. The traders, salesmen, cattle drovers, soldiers, and miners were seeking something other than acreage, but they had home bases that were measured in land. Peter Hardeman Burnett saw land prospects in Oregon as a way out of his debts, then by chance made his modest fortune in a California land promotion deal.

That land was an important concern in a number of the Hardeman migrations tells little about reasons for the westward movement, since land holding was almost universal in all settled parts of the United States. It was no revelation to state that a people who relied on land for 90 percent of their national livelihood were concerned with the soil. Land was the *sine qua non,* but it was the beginning, the foundation for the economic structure, not the entire structure itself. Because nearly all easterners owned land, one can reverse the hypothesis and argue that land was a prime reason why most people did *not* go west. Despite the common denominator of landed property, the Hardemans' most noted achievements in the West, with the exception of John's experimental and ornamental creations in Tennessee and Missouri, were in things other than agriculture.

The economic "safety valve" theory, that the frontier assisted in maintaining civil tranquility, particularly in hard times, by peacefully drawing off unemployed and dissatisfied elements from the East, was endorsed by a number of scholars. Others have indicated that westward migration was greater during prosperous times than during depressions, that it consisted more of farmers than disgruntled industrial laborers, and that farm mechanization caused cities to become safety valves for the resulting surplus farm population. Furthermore, the frontier era was a period when, relative to Europe, industrial labor was scarce in America, reducing the likelihood that excess steam from laboring classes would blow off toward the West.

Thomas Hardeman and Peter Burnett, seeking relief from tenancy and debts, respectively, during economic lulls, offer limited corroboration to the safety-valve concept. Burnett was not fleeing his creditors but was seeking larger income to pay them off. He secured their permission before leaving Missouri. The overwhelming evidence from the Hardeman experiences is that the relief valve was not a factor. On the contrary, most of the frontiering migrants from this family left large, productive estates and other enterprises to go west. Not depressed conditions, but success seems to be positively related with the frontierward impulse. It is probable that the principle of the safety valve was least applicable to trading and mining in the backlands and not consistently applicable anywhere. Like free land, poverty is simply an inadequate explanation of the westward movement, except perhaps the poverty of soils grown tired from overcropping.

In a psychological sense it can be argued that all who voluntarily became pioneers did so because of a safety-valve motive—to seek improvement of their feelings of physical well-being or personal worth, to gain security for selves or family, or to gratify some basic appetite. There can be no meaningful estimates of the numbers of people who went west because of personal frustrations, disappointments in love affairs and marriages, trouble with the law, embarrassing physical disabilities, and the like. Important as such matters have been to history, they are usually lost to the fund of knowledge, since people rarely keep reliable records of them. Family sorrows undoubtedly helped to populate the frontier, if Thomas, John, Bailey, and Thomas Jones Hardeman can be counted as indicators, since all left for the outlands shortly after deaths in their immediate families. People, like plants, seek to grow and move toward the light, or what they judge to be the light. To Tom Hardeman and his offshoots of the family tree, the Great West was the light, as it was to much of the expansive force of the nation.

The westward migrations of the Thomas Hardeman genus convincingly contradict the "successive waves" view. This theory involved two mutually inclusive patterns. The first was a tier-on-tier progression. "At the Atlantic frontier one can study the germs of processes repeated at each successive frontier." The leap-frogging and trail-following migrations of the Hardeman family conflict radically with this concept. Secondly, westward travel was seen as embodying a rather definite sequence of frontier occupations. In the vanguard, passing through Cumberland Gap in the late eighteenth century, were the trapper and hunter, followed at intervals by cattlemen, miners, and pioneer farmers. At South Pass in the Rockies a century later, the same sequence theoretically prevailed. Perhaps John Gast's painting of 1872, picturing the successive waves of the frontier process, influenced the early advocates of this theory. Certainly the view gave short shrift to the full range of important frontier types. The profile of the Hardeman family experience tends to show that the successive-waves theory ignored or slighted merchants, soldiers, printers, land speculators, millers, distillers, and professional people in the West. Fur trappers and fur traders did arrive early on the frontier scene, largely because they dealt in a commodity well suited to handling over great spans of distance and time, having high value, low bulk, and relative imperishability. Thomas Hardeman's foray in 1768 was typical in this respect. But after the fur gatherers, the sequence was haphazard.

The idea of the frontier as the wellspring of democracy, from which currents flowed so strongly that they democratized older centers to the east, has been widely criticized. A number of the Hardemans without question had a penchant for political involvement and organization. From the Virginia House of Burgesses to Hillsboro, from Knoxville to Missouri, Washington on the Brazos, Oregon, and California, they figured in the formation of nations, territories, states, legislative assemblies, and local governments. But they carried their democratic experiences from older settlements in the East, usually copying from these to meet western needs. And they voiced their frustrations over the fact that, since the frontier was lightly represented in legislative halls, it had little influence on democratic processes except in swinging the balance of power on close votes. Actually, the further an area progressed away from its frontier stage, the more heavily it became represented and the more it influenced democratic processes.

The frontier as a factory for Americanism, nationality, and sectionalism does not relate in a meaningful way to the foregoing study, partly because the concept is vague and also because it seems to deal mainly with the Americanization of the foreign immigrant to America, and the Hardemans had come from Europe so early that the issue cannot be joined. They had a strong sense of "patriotism" and a well-developed Anglophobia, as shown by their roles in the Revolution, the War of 1812, the acquisition of Oregon, and the Mexican War. But their patriotism became confused and diffused when sectional strife split the North and South.

One of the concepts which has become a part of the folklore of the West is the elbowroom motive for migration. Although largely accurate, it was not so much an antisocial tendency as a desire to expand land holdings. The farmer-pioneer, often restricted to small acreage by economic necessity at first, and driven by the American dream to seek an estate of country squire proportions, saw near neighbors as hindrances to enlarged property holdings. In a choice between close neighbors and far boundary lines, the western farmer preferred the latter, and not necessarily because of a need for individualism and aloofness.

The individualism and cooperativeness allegedly fostered by frontier life are neither as paradoxical nor as frontier-oriented as various theorists have maintained. They are less paradoxical because the cooperation was on a small-scale community level—that of the family and neighborhood— leaving room for individual achievement and recognition; and they were less frontier-oriented than rural and pre-technological. Perhaps a better expression would have been "self-reliance," in terms of both individuals and small groups. If subsistence farming did not necessarily equate with self-sufficiency, neither did commercial agriculture deny a high degree of self-sufficiency or self-reliance. Despite their commercial connections, which existed as of the dates of early records, the agrarian and frontiering Hardemans were self-reliant and nature-reliant to a great extent. They grew, caught, shot, processed, and preserved their own food and provided warm-weather refrigeration. (I recall the century-old underground ice house, where ice, cut from the creek in winter, had been packed in straw and kept to meet the refrigeration needs of spring and summer.) They fashioned some of their clothing and could have made it all if necessary, and they built their own houses, fences, and furniture and many of their tools. If necessity was not the mother of invention, it was the parent of production. Such self-reliance bred at least a limited confidence which served the pioneers well in their accustomed environment, the wilderness, and gave them the courage to face its many dimensions. What generated the widespread attitudes of domination and conquest characteristic of mountainman at rendezvous, miner in boomtown, cowboy at railhead, and sodbuster in the settlement on a Saturday night? Perhaps it was a feeling of superiority born of this self-reliance as much as it was the weeks and months of tension, danger, and deprivation and the sense of freedom from restraining social pressures of home.

Among the supposed motives for frontiering, economic ones have been given widest play. Proponents of economic causation have a credibility advantage, since most people who went west did engage in some kind of economic activity after they arrived. However, it does not follow that they went specifically for the jobs they performed after arriving. Many wandered because of urges unrelated to occupation, their economic pursuits having been effects of the moves rather than causes.

One concomitant of the economic activity in the West was a heedless exploitation of the seemingly inexhaustible resources. Its effects were two-phased—immediate defacing of part of the natural environment, and the fostering and perpetuating of long-range *laissez-faire* attitudes toward the land which signaled resource problems for future generations. Peter Burnett's conservation consciousness was an all-too-rare commodity.

A weakness of many frontier theories is that they start with the general, in a deductive, almost intuitive process. When applied to the specific they often bog down nearly to the point of uselessness except to the researcher who employs them as a springboard and will accept either proof or disproof with equanimity. The place of this study and its family subject can best be determined by its readers. Its family-related cause-and-effect observations, of course, will have limited applicability unless corroborated by other western family studies.

What explains the inordinately high percentage of frontiersmen for five generations in a single family line, when most of the migrants in question were relatively well-to-do in their civilized habitats? Heredity is not an answer, nor is the theory that they were dropouts from the Eastern school of hard knocks. In this study, the family as an environmental unit appears to have been a key factor. Families have been researched before, many with a genealogical emphasis, and a few in broader historical, sociological, or other planes of reference. But family accounts of such incurable western wanderers as the members of the Thomas Hardeman line have not been presented heretofore.

The student of today must think away modern, loosely connected family structures in order to understand the tightly knit, highly interdependent, and often paternalistic socioeconomic unit that was the American family of the eighteenth and nineteenth centuries. Children in those eras spent a much higher percentage of their time within the molding limits of the family than under the wing of any other institution or combination of institutions. Offspring were economic assets to their parents, and sons were much more prone to follow in their fathers' paths of livelihood than the sons of recent generations. As the principal social structure, the most important moral and cultural institution, and a primary economic unit, the pre-twentieth-century family has been slighted by historians of the West in their search for causes of behavior— slighted in favor of broader-based determinisms and influences.

The pervasive, patriarchal imprint of Thomas Hardeman was almost certain to show in the living habits and styles of other members of the family, not only through such maxims as "Never embarrass the family" and "Help the honest and industrious kin," but in migratory tendencies as well. Some families stressed printing, others milling or planting, still others politics, coach making, cooperage, or iron-making. Among other things, Thomas Hardeman and his descendants stressed frontiering. When young children accompany their parents, they are presumed to do so involuntarily, but when grown, independent people follow a relative, they usually do so because of cultural ties. Thomas was followed by mature relatives to the Cumberland, and when he staked claims in Louisiana and Missouri in his advancing years, self-reliant sons and daughters and in-laws followed. Thomas, Bailey, and John Hardeman and Glen Owen all became involved in the Santa Fe trade, and Dr. Glen O. Hardeman's choice of that trail many years later seems to have been more than coincidence. The Hardeman migration to Texas was a joint undertaking of three mature brothers, a sister, and two of their grown nephews, all with their families. Peter Burnett was followed by his (adult) brothers to Oregon and thence to California, and when Glen O. Hardeman reached the Golden State, he went first to the homes of his cousins the Burnetts before he gave so much as a passing glance at the diggings. William, Thomas Monroe, Peter, Leonidas, and Owen Bailey Hardeman voluntarily fought together in a number of southwestern campaigns. To deny the family-based motive as a major ingredient in these traveling associations is unrealistic.

Among the prominent names in the annals of the West, there were enough immediate family linkages of independent adults who went to the frontier of their own volition to suggest strongly that the Hardeman case is by no means an isolated one. Consider as examples the following: Donelson, Applegate, Boone, Robertson, Sevier, Chouteau, Becknell, Clark, Sublette, Waldo, McCulloch, Carson, Sappington, Bent, Perkins, Robidoux, Cooper, Pattie, Blount, Wetmore, Marmaduke, Knox, O'Fallon, Workman, Ryland, Kern, Smith (Thomas A.), Powell, Henderson, Calloway. These and a host of others who are known suggest that there were probably a great many whose names are lost.

Lest the interpretation become too sweeping, it must be acknowledged that, like land holdings, family ties deterred many people from going west with the frontier. But this does not deny the fact that family connections were frontiering motives of major importance. Some of these linkages are readily understandable—economic partnerships, physical defense, and psychological support, or a feeling of collective security in the face of a potentially hostile environment. The comfort of having a known, trusted companion, whether family member or friend, was often a factor in the picking of a travel "team."

Despite the rigors and dangers of the West, physical well-being was often related positively to the westward movement in people's thinking. Harriet Burnett's health is one of innumerable examples. The letters of Henry Lee and Willie Blount to John Hardeman, and Antoine Robidoux's report of health conditions in California to residents of Platte County, Missouri, reflect an almost universal concern with the supposedly un-healthful air (particularly at night) of river valleys in the East and Mid-west. Farmers had ambivalent feelings toward these fertile fingers of land: rich soils but poor air; fever and ague. Among the prominent Americans who went west at least in part to improve their health were Richard Henry Dana, Francis Parkman, Theodore Roosevelt, and James Wilson Mar-shall. Hazards to life in the West were more spectacular than in older sections to the east—what with Indians, grizzly bears, thirsty land, and frigid mountain winters—but when all evidence is on the scales, life expectancy was about the same in the West as in the East. Surprisingly, it was better at times in frontier regions, because contagious diseases were less readily transmitted where population was less dense, and because there were relatively fewer women, fewer births, and thus lower inci-dences of infant mortality and deaths of mothers in childbearing. Nor was the higher ratio of physicians in the East a great advantage, since medical men of that era knew nothing about germs and could only treat the symptoms of diseases.

A most perplexing element in the Hardeman frontiering equation is the persistent habit of migrating, generation after generation. Among the explanations for this culturally transmitted trait, one appears to stand out. A number of the Hardemans were notoriously enthusiastic storytellers, and in the American western theme, with which they had no little familiarity, they had one of the most popular story subjects in the history of mankind. Whether the medium has been word of mouth, dime novel, wild west show, pulp magazine, radio, movie, television, historical novel, or factual literature; whether the setting has been snapping embers and flickering tongues of fire casting eerie shadows on log cabin walls, or flashing light of telescreen, Americans have a seemingly incurable habit of sitting down and raptly absorbing the lore of their Great West as it is spun off by almost equally great storytellers. Particularly in rural America before the advent of modern transport and communication, when alternatives for evening entertainment were few, storytelling was immensely popular. Children begged for story after story, hearing the same tales night after night and year after year until they knew by heart the exploits as related by their forebears. The serenity of the mountains, the cool freshness of the streams, the dust of the trail, the waving crest of grassy plains, the rustle of leaves became verily a part of the travelers' fibers. The experiences, the impressions were positioned in their minds as carefully as museum pieces and were taken out, dusted off, and displayed again and again around the glow of evening's blaze. Despite some inaccuracies, thus was a culture transmitted, a heritage preserved through the generations. Thus was a fire kindled in many a youngster, a burning urge to see, hear, and feel the living experiences which had branded him imperceptibly yet indelibly in those impressionable years. Branded him, yes, as the willing property of the open range, and set ringing in his ears the entreaty which was the call of the wilderness.

Scholars must exercise caution when delving into long-past psychological causes and effects. Nevertheless it is probable that children, growing up to the countless tellings and retellings of western stories, came to associate these narratives closely with secure and affectionate personal relationships between themselves and their elders. Sitting on a parent's or grandparent's knee or lap or huddled snugly together around a fire was a condition, a concomitant, of storytelling. The psychological need of the child was for the attention and affection, and the stories came with the package. Children begged for stories largely because of this need, and if the stories were habitually western or frontier, as they were in the Hardeman family even as recently as the late 1930s, the youngsters would be inclined to grow up with an attitude of warmth toward the West. Thus a seeming paradox may have a logical explanation—a secure, comfortable feeling about a dangerous, uncomfortable environment. In all likelihood this was particularly true in West-oriented families like that of Thomas and Mary Hardeman and their descendants. In time, the frontierward direction of interest seemed to generate its own momentum.

Old Tom Hardeman, by the word of several grandsons, was an inveterate teller of stories about his encounters with the wilds. So were Peter Burnett and Glen O. Hardeman, as were Glen's sons and others in the family line. I remember vividly the stories of my father, Glen H. Hardeman—accounts of previous generations of family westerners, tales of the trans-Sierra sheep drive, of goats leading a hesitant flock across logs and stones and streams, and descriptions of the swirling waters of the Kern River, its shimmering course overshadowed by endless forests and massive peaks. I remember, too, the spark of desire which would not be quenched until I had followed and fished the same streams and climbed and camped upon those very mountains. Others, and probably many, have had similar experiences. Samuel Dunn Houston, Chisholm Trail companion of Monroe Hardeman, for example, recounts the story of "Willie" Matthews, a New Mexico girl who was so intrigued by countless tellings of her father's cattle driving experiences that in later years she masqueraded as a young man and rode the trail for four months. Houston rated her as an excellent cowhand.[3]

Not infrequently, friends and neighbors in the rural environment fed their own folklore into nearby families and reinforced the wanderlust. The psychology of keeping abreast or ahead of those who had seen and done big things must have had a driving effect on the people who lived near arteries of travel, who saw the goings and comings of the glamorously tough frontiersmen, and who felt a mingled jealousy and admiration. Mark Twain expressed the sentiment well in his boyhood impressions of the romantic river pilot, the hero returning and departing. The same awe is felt in his classic description of the Pony Express rider. Pioneering souls on every hand, whether disappearing around river's bend or rising and falling with the gallop of a panting steed, were lost in a romantic veil of dust or hazy distance. The tingling spirit of America on the move was in the air—a mysticism drawn deep with every breath by anyone with a drop of restless, venturesome blood. And the Hardemans seemed to settle near arteries where the dip and flash of oars and the clump of feet on the trail were constant reminders that excitement and opportunity lay in the outlands—the Natchez Trace, the Holston, Cumberland, Missouri, and Platte rivers, the Santa Fe and Oregon trails, the Willamette Valley, Applegate's Road, and the cattle trails. Such pressures drove many to go against their better judgment and may account for the fact that several members of the Hardeman family were reluctant frontiersmen at times—John, Glen O. Hardeman and Peter Burnett, for example. Only three, Thomas, Bailey, and William, were clearly cut from the Deerslayer pattern.

What were the impelling commands which sent these and other vanguards of American empire to far corners of the continent? Surely the drive behind the westward movement was a mix of various motives. But which, and how much of which? Such terms as Manifest Destiny, free land, safety valve, and economic or geographic or Freudian determinism are not full explanations. In conceding multiple causation, can we not concede further that we deal with an equation having no ultimate solution, and that somewhere in the genius for reason, logic, pragmatism, organization, appetite gratifying, and profit seeking, humankind indulged in the impractical, the illogical, the fanciful, the romantic, the spiritual, even the mystical, and that never were these characteristics drawn into a more confused yet intriguing conglomerate than in the conquest of the American West?

The members of the Thomas Hardeman line produced a bumper crop, a dynasty of uncorraled spirits. They created some westward-moving currents and swam or drifted with many others, forming accretions here and there as the capricious flow commanded. Hesitant wanderers some of them were. It was as if they feared leaving the accumulations of their material success behind but were powerless to resist an inner urge that pushed them toward the horizon. If their wandering instinct was as compulsive as the tide, it was as unobtrusive. Often they seemed cut or stamped for roles of leadership, but they habitually resigned and shrank away from prominence just as the klieg lights swung toward them; they recoiled as if fearful of forfeiting their backwoods heritage by loitering too long in the snare of organized society. Perhaps this explains in part why they did not approach the status of the hunter-hero myth[4] as did Boone and Crockett and Croghan. They did not aspire to it.

Yet following their trail or sail, one quickly finds history in the making, rubbing shoulders with characters whose names are written large across the paths of the West. The Hardemans were seekers of the wilds, but carriers of civilization in their baggage; hunting out primitive spots, they settled for a while, inoculating patients, fashioning exotic gardens, formulating instruments of government, or accumulating treasure which would build an academy. And having done with these civilizing actions, they moved on to wilder horizons. Given the comfortable domestic circumstances which they left behind, all the frontier theories in literature cannot fully account for their persistent westward impulse, any more than all the dissuading arguments could have stayed them from their appointment with destiny in the backlands. They were a family conspicuous for their motion in what Billington has called "a nation of habitual migrants."[5]

Perhaps their feeling was captured by Lord Byron, a Romantic and a wilderness worshiper in his own right:

> There is a pleasure in the pathless woods,
> There is a rapture on the lonely shore.
> There is society where none intrudes,
> By the deep sea, and music in its roar:
> I love not man the less, but Nature more.

The Old Testament prophet Joel wrote, "The land is the Garden of Eden before them, and behind them a desolate wilderness." But to Thomas Hardeman and a spirited complement of his progeny, the wilderness must have appeared to be a bit of Eden itself.

Genealogy

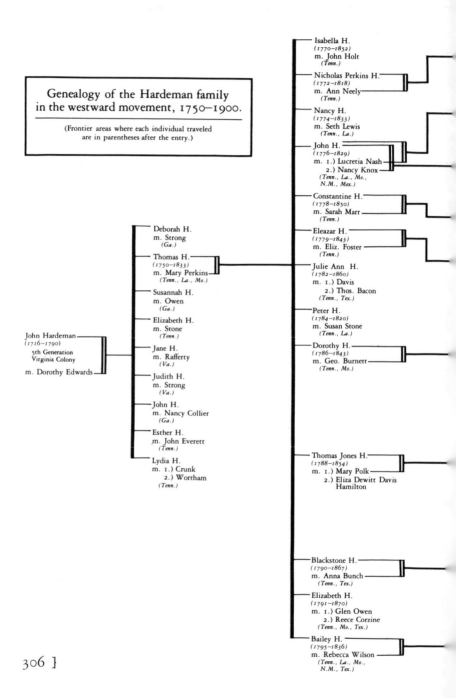

Genealogy of the Hardeman family
in the westward movement, 1750–1900.

(Frontier areas where each individual traveled
are in parentheses after the entry.)

John Hardeman
(1716–1790)
5th Generation
Virginia Colony
m. Dorothy Edwards

Deborah H.
m. Strong
(Ga.)

Thomas H.
(1750–1833)
m. Mary Perkins
(Tenn., La., Mo.)

Susannah H.
m. Owen
(Ga.)

Elizabeth H.
m. Stone
(Tenn.)

Jane H.
m. Rafferty
(Va.)

Judith H.
m. Strong
(Va.)

John H.
m. Nancy Collier
(Ga.)

Esther H.
m. John Everett
(Tenn.)

Lydia H.
m. 1.) Crunk
   2.) Wortham
(Tenn.)

Isabella H.
(1770–1852)
m. John Holt
(Tenn.)

Nicholas Perkins H.
(1772–1818)
m. Ann Neely
(Tenn.)

Nancy H.
(1774–1833)
m. Seth Lewis
(Tenn., La.)

John H.
(1776–1829)
m. 1.) Lucretia Nash
   2.) Nancy Knox
(Tenn., La., Mo.,
N.M., Mex.)

Constantine H.
(1778–1850)
m. Sarah Marr
(Tenn.)

Eleazar H.
(1779–1843)
m. Eliz. Foster
(Tenn.)

Julie Ann H.
(1782–1860)
m. 1.) Davis
   2.) Thos. Bacon
(Tenn., Tex.)

Peter H.
(1784–1820)
m. Susan Stone
(Tenn., La.)

Dorothy H.
(1786–1843)
m. Geo. Burnett
(Tenn., Mo.)

Thomas Jones H.
(1788–1854)
m. 1.) Mary Polk
   2.) Eliza Dewitt Davis
      Hamilton

Blackstone H.
(1790–1867)
m. Anna Bunch
(Tenn., Tex.)

Elizabeth H.
(1791–1870)
m. 1.) Glen Owen
   2.) Reece Corzine
(Tenn., Mo., Tex.)

Bailey H.
(1795–1836)
m. Rebecca Wilson
(Tenn., La., Mo.,
N.M., Tex.)

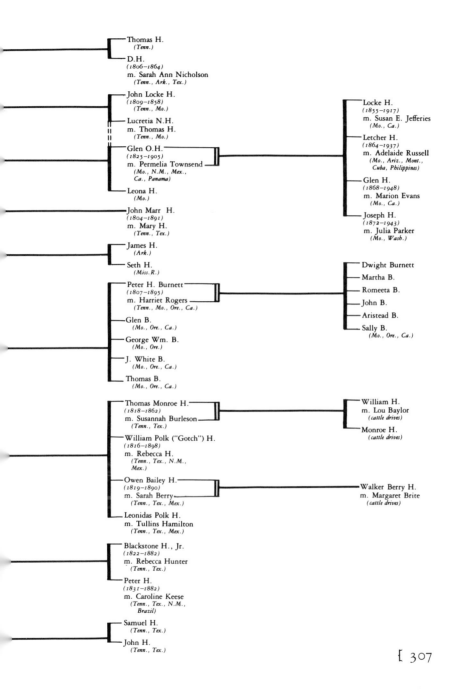

Thomas H.
(Tenn.)

D.H.
(1806–1864)
m. Sarah Ann Nicholson
(Tenn., Ark., Tex.)

John Locke H.
(1809–1858)
(Tenn., Mo.)

Lucretia N.H.
m. Thomas H.
(Tenn., Mo.)

Glen O.H.
(1825–1905)
m. Permelia Townsend
(Mo., N.M., Mex.,
Ca., Panama)

Leona H.
(Mo.)

John Marr H.
(1804–1891)
m. Mary H.
(Tenn., Tex.)

James H.
(Ark.)

Seth H.
(Miss.R.)

Peter H. Burnett
(1807–1895)
m. Harriet Rogers
(Tenn., Mo., Ore., Ca.)

Glen B.
(Mo., Ore., Ca.)

George Wm. B.
(Mo., Ore.)

J. White B.
(Mo., Ore., Ca.)

Thomas B.
(Mo., Ore., Ca.)

Thomas Monroe H.
(1818–1862)
m. Susannah Burleson
(Tenn., Tex.)

William Polk ("Gotch") H.
(1816–1898)
m. Rebecca H.
(Tenn., Tex., N.M.,
Mex.)

Owen Bailey H.
(1819–1890)
m. Sarah Berry
(Tenn., Tex., Mex.)

Leonidas Polk H.
m. Tullins Hamilton
(Tenn., Tex., Mex.)

Blackstone H., Jr.
(1822–1882)
m. Rebecca Hunter
(Tenn., Tex.)

Peter H.
(1831–1882)
m. Caroline Keese
(Tenn., Tex., N.M.,
Brazil)

Samuel H.
(Tenn., Tex.)

John H.
(Tenn., Tex.)

Locke H.
(1855–1917)
m. Susan E. Jefferies
(Mo., Ca.)

Letcher H.
(1864–1937)
m. Adelaide Russell
(Mo., Ariz., Mont.,
Cuba, Philippines)

Glen H.
(1868–1948)
m. Marion Evans
(Mo., Ca.)

Joseph H.
(1872–1943)
m. Julia Parker
(Mo., Wash.)

Dwight Burnett

Martha B.

Romeeta B.

John B.

Aristead B.

Sally B.
(Mo., Ore., Ca.)

William H.
m. Lou Baylor
(cattle drives)

Monroe H.
(cattle drives)

Walker Berry H.
m. Margaret Brite
(cattle drives)

[307

Notes

1. J. Hardeman to T. Hardeman, Fruitage Farm, Mo., May 1828, Glen Hardeman MSS, State Historical Society of Missouri (SHSM), Columbia.

2. Statement of Col. John Reeves, Lyman Draper MSS, 31 S 349, Wisconsin State Historical Society (WSHS), Madison.

3. Memorandum from J. Locke Hardeman to Ferdinand Stith, Franklin, Tenn., June 27, 1834, and T. Hardeman to G. O. Hardeman, Winona, Miss., Feb. 5, 1883, Hardeman MSS, SHSM.

4. Peter H. Burnett, *Recollections and Opinions of an Old Pioneer* (New York, 1880), 2.

5. Background information on the Hardeman family comes from many sources. Much has been assembled in the Hardeman MSS, Tennessee State Library and Archives (TSLA), Nashville, and in the Hardeman MSS, SHSM.

6. Gladys Hardeman, unpublished paper on early history of the Hardeman family, Nacogdoches, Tex., and Samuel C. Williams, "The Hardeman Family," Hardeman MSS, TSLA.

7. Information on the life of Hardeman before his move to the Cumberland Basin in the 1780s comes primarily from Hardeman to Stith.

8. Genealogical data, Hardeman MSS, TSLA. Mary Perkins was born at Henry Cove, Va., Aug. 10, 1754.

9. Statement of land transactions, Hardeman MSS, SHSM, and Washington Co., Tenn. Deed Bk. 3, pp. 249–53.

10. J. G. M. Ramsey, *The Annals of Tennessee to the End of the Eighteenth Century* (Charleston, 1853), 179.

11. "Life of Thomas Hardeman, 1750–1833," Hardeman MSS, TSLA.

12. Katherine K. White, *The King's Mountain Men* (Dayton, Va., 1924), 146, 184.

13. Land indenture and receipt for transfer from Isham Cleaton to Thomas Hardeman, Oct. 8, 1782, Hardeman MSS, SHSM.

14. John Donelson, "John Donelson's Journal," *Three Pioneer Tennessee Documents* (Nashville: Tennessee Historical Commission, 1964), 1–10.

15. Carondelet to McGillivray, New Orleans, Nov. 11, 1792, in John W. Caughey, *McGillivray of the Creeks* (Norman, Okla.: Univ. of Oklahoma Press, 1938), 343.

16. "Life of Thomas Hardeman, 1750–1833."

17. Lanier to Martin, Mar. 16, 1788, Lyman Draper MSS, 2XX.

18. W. W. Clayton, *History of Davidson County, Tennessee* (Philadelphia, 1880), 33.

19. Hardeman to Stith.

20. James Robertson and Anthony Bledsoe to Gov. Samuel Johnston, Hillsboro, N.C., Jan. 4, 1788, N.C. Gov. Letterbooks, Records of the U.S.

21. Hickman's account to Draper, Lyman Draper MSS, 30 S 507–510.

22. Hardeman to Stith.

CHAPTER II

1. Memorandum from J. Locke Hardeman to Ferdinand Stith, Franklin, Tenn., June 27, 1834, Hardeman MSS, SHSM.

2. Davidson Co., Tenn., Deed Bk. G–7, pp. 146, 164, 191; Hawkins Co., Tenn., Deed Bk. 9, p. 344; Williamson Co., Tenn., Deed Bk.A–1, p. 564; Land indentures, Hardeman MSS, SHSM.

3. Margaret Kinard, "Frontier Development of Williamson County," *Tennessee Historical Quarterly*, 8 (Mar. 1949), 27.

4. Williamson Co., Deed Bk. A–1, p. 339; Bk. A–2, p. 382; Bk. B, p. 105; Bk. C, p. 273; Land indenture, Hardeman MSS, SHSM.

5. Bill of sale, Thomas Hardeman to Hugh Gilleland, Jan. 9, 1788, Hardeman MSS, SHSM; Harriet Arnow, *Flowering of the Cumberland* (New York: Macmillan, 1963), 226–27.

6. Samuel C. Williams, "The Hardeman Family," Hardeman MSS, TSLA.

7. Lyman Draper MSS, 31 S 342.

8. Charles A. Beard, *Economic Interpretation of the Constitution* (New York, 1913), *passim,* and William C. Pool, "An Economic Interpretation of the Ratification of the Federal Constitution in North Carolina," *North Carolina Historical Review,* 27 (Apr., July, Oct. 1950), *passim.*

9. North Carolina, *North Carolina House Journal, 1788,* pp. 6, 26.

10. Territory South of the River Ohio, *Journal of the House of Representatives of the . . . Territory of the United States . . . South of the River Ohio, . . . 1795,* p. 4.

11. Samuel C. Williams, "The Admission of Tennessee into the Union," *Tennessee Historical Quarterly,* 4 (Dec. 1945), 296–97; Kinard, "Williamson County," 8.

12. Tennessee, *Journal of the Proceedings of a Convention Begun and Held at Knoxville, Jan. 11, 1796* (rpt. Nashville, 1852), 3.

13. *Ibid.,* 22–24, 27–29.

14. Roy W. Black, Sr., "The Genesis of County Organization, in the Western District of North Carolina and in the State of Tennessee," *West Tennessee Historical Society Papers,* 2 (1948), 112–13.

15. Tennessee, *Tennessee Journals of the Senate and House . . . 1797–1798,* 8–14.

16. *Ibid.,* 269, and W. Blount to J. Robertson, Knoxville, Tenn., James Robertson MSS, TSLA.

17. Lyman Draper MSS, 31 S 349.

18. Letters of Thomas Hardeman and his sons, Bailey Hardeman MSS, TSLA.

19. North Carolina, *House Journal, 1788,* 189, and Territory South of the River Ohio, *Journal,* 20.

20. Williamson Co., Deed Bk. A–1, p. 564.

21. T. Hardeman to P. Hardeman, Franklin, Tenn., Nov. 2, 1810, Dec. 6, 1810, and Mar. 12, 1811, Bailey Hardeman MSS, TSLA.

22. *Ibid.,* Oct. 13, 1809, Nov. 2, 1810, and Feb. 27, 1811; and Certificate of Sale, Hardeman MSS, SHSM.

23. Williamson Co. Court of Pleas and Quarter Sessions, Minute Bk. I, pp. 88, 100, 106–107, 124, 175.

24. *Ibid., passim,* and Nicholas P. Hardeman and John Hardeman Store, Ledger Bk. B, p. 359. Hardeman MSS, SHSM.

25. Hardeman Store, Ledger, Oct. 1806, p. 119.

CHAPTER III

1. Peter H. Burnett, *Recollections and Opinions of an Old Pioneer* (New York, 1880), 5.

2. As quoted in John F. McDermott, "Culture on the Missouri Frontier," *Missouri Historical Review,* 50 (July 1956), 369.

3. John Hardeman Passport, Hardeman MSS, SHSM.

4. Masonic History Agency, *History of Freemasonry in Early Tennessee, 1789–1943* (Chattanooga, 1943), *passim*.

5. For an excellent general treatment of the subject, see Lewis Atherton, *The Southern Country Store, 1800–1860* (Baton Rouge: Louisiana State Univ. Press, 1949), *passim*.

6. John and Nicholas P. Hardeman Store, records, *passim*; debt certificates, Hardeman MSS, SHSM; William N. Chambers, *Old Bullion Benton, Senator from the New West: Thomas Hart Benton, 1782–1858* (Boston: Little, Brown, 1956), 24.

7. Hardeman Store, records, *passim*.

8. *Ibid.*

9. *Ibid.*

10. *Ibid.,* Journal B, Dec. 1803, p. 71; Feb. 1804, p. 101; and Ledger, Dec. 1805, p. 77; Feb. 1806, pp. 85, 92.

11. *Ibid.,* Ledger, Feb. 1806, pp. 89–92, 95.

12. *Ibid.,* July 1806, p. 108, and *passim*.

13. *Ibid., passim,* example, Journal B, Dec. 1803, p. 71.

14. *Ibid.,* Journal B, Dec. 1803, p. 70; Oct. 1804, pp. 192–95; and Ledger, Oct. 1805, p. 81; Feb. 1806, p. 92; Oct. 1806, pp. 120–22.

15. Bill of sale, Andrew Jackson to John Hardeman et al, Feb. 18–23, 1804, Andrew Jackson MSS. Ser. 1, July 23, 1803–Mar. 4, 1806, Microfilm roll 3.

16. Hardeman Store, records, Journal B, Nov. 1803, p. 43, and Ledger, Feb. 1806, p. 85; Oct. 1806, p. 109.

17. *Ibid., passim,* and credit slips, Hardeman MSS, SHSM.

18. Hardeman Store, records, *passim,* and Ledger, Feb. 1806, p. 84.

CHAPTER IV

1. Davidson Co., Deed Bk. D, p. 151, and a Hardeman Family Bible, copy of births recorded, courtesy F. W. Brigance, Murfreesboro, Tenn.

2. Davidson Co., Marriage Bk. 1, p. 2; Genealogical data, Hardeman MSS, TSLA; and P. Nugent to G. O. Hardeman, Greenville, Miss., May 14, 1895, Hardeman MSS, SHSM.

3. Memorandum from J. Locke Hardeman to Ferdinand Stith, Franklin, Tenn., June 27, 1834, Hardeman MSS, SHSM.

4. John Hardeman, workbooks, and License to Practice Law, Hardeman MSS, SHSM; Walter W. Faw, "Bailey Hardeman," Hardeman MSS, TSLA. Williamson County had a number of practicing attorneys who were contemporaries of the Hardemans and who later achieved prominence: Thomas H. Benton, Aaron Brown, Felix Grundy, John Eaton, and John Bell.

5. Letters of Thomas, John, and Peter Hardeman, Bailey Hardeman MSS, TSLA.

6. *Ibid.,* and John Hardeman, Inventory of Property, and Intention of Sale, Jurisdiction of Baton Rouge, Sept. 20, 1805, Hardeman MSS, SHSM.

7. S. Lewis to P. Hardeman, Opelousas, La., Feb. 13, 1815, Bailey Hardeman MSS, TSLA.

8. T. Hardeman to P. and T. J. Hardeman, Franklin, Tenn., Feb. 27, 1811; T. Hardeman to P. Hardeman, Franklin, Dec. 26, 1810, Bailey Hardeman MSS, TSLA; John Hardeman and John Chisholm, Bill of Sale, Williamson Co., July 5, 1806, Hardeman MSS, SHSM; Martha L. Houston, comp., "Tennessee Census Reports, Williamson County—1820," No. 26 (Washington, D.C., 1936), 4, 22.

9. P. Perkins to P. Hardeman, Baltimore, July 13, 1809, Bailey Hardeman MSS, TSLA.

10. *Ibid.*

11. T. Hardeman to P. Hardeman, Franklin, Feb. 27, 1811, Bailey Hardeman MSS, TSLA.

12. S. Lewis and J. Dunlop to The Humane Society for the Abolition of Slavery, Richmond, Va., Natchez, Miss. Terr., Aug. 18, 1806, Bailey Hardeman MSS, TSLA.

13. E. Hardeman to Judge John Overton, Oct. 27, 1830, Overton MSS, TSLA.

14. Williamson Co., Deed Bk. D, p. 166; Court Minute Bk. 1, p. 509; Court Minute Bk. 5, p. 230.

15. Thomas H. Benton to J. and N. P. Hardeman, Duck River, Tenn., Dec. 10, 1804, Hardeman MSS, SHSM.

16. Hardeman Store records, Ledger, Oct. 20, 1804–Jan. 1806, p. 1, Hardeman MSS, SHSM.

17. T. H. Benton to J. and N. P. Hardeman, Duck River, Dec. 10, 1804.

18. T. H. Benton to T. Hardeman, St. Louis, Nov. 22, 1829, Hardeman MSS, SHSM.

19. As quoted in John M. Blum et al.: *The National Experience* (New York: Harcourt, Brace, 1963), 174.

20. Monthly Report of U.S. Infantry Commanded by Lieut. Col. Thomas H. Benton, 39th Infantry, Sept. 30, 1814, Andrew Jackson MSS, Ser. 5, Sept. 26, 1814–Mar. 2, 1815, Microfilm, roll 67.

21. Willie Blount, Statement of Commission of Peter Hardeman, Bailey Hardeman MSS, TSLA.

22. Report of killed and wounded in Gen. John Coffee's Brigade in Battle of Dec. 23, 1814; Soldiers Taken by the British Near New Orleans, Jackson MSS, roll 67; J. Hardeman to P. Hardeman, Franklin, Tenn., Jan. 27, 1815; T. Hardeman to P. Hardeman, Jan. 30, 1815, Bailey Hardeman MSS, TSLA.

23. J. Hardeman to P. Hardeman, Jan. 27, 1815, Bailey Hardeman MSS, TSLA.

24. Roy W. Black, Sr., "The Genesis of County Organization in the Western

District of North Carolina and in the State of Tennessee," *West Tennessee Historical Society Papers,* 2 (1948), 113, 117, and Tennessee General (land) Grant Records, *passim,* TSLA.

25. T. Hardeman to P. Hardeman, Feb. 27, 1811, Bailey Hardeman MSS, TSLA; Maury Co., Deed Bk. E, p. 170; and Peter H. Burnett, *Recollections and Opinions of an Old Pioneer* (New York, 1880), 24–25.

26. Gravestones in and near Franklin, Tenn.

CHAPTER V

1. Statement of Glen H. Hardeman.

2. Memorandum from J. Locke Hardeman to Ferdinand Stith, Franklin, Tenn., June 27, 1834, Hardeman MSS, SHSM.

3. *Ibid.,* and Statement appointing John Hardeman as Attorney in Fact for Thomas Hardeman, Sept. 30, 1816, Hardeman MSS, SHSM.

4. Howard Co., Mo., Deed Bk. E, p. 54, and Bk. D, p. 42; and *Missouri Intelligencer* (Franklin), Nov. 20, 1821. An arpen or arpent was a French unit of measure, equaling about 0.85 acre.

5. *Missouri Intelligencer,* Sept. 23, 1820, and Feb. 19, 1821.

6. *Ibid.,* Jan. 29, 1821, and Howard Co. Deed Bk. D, pp. 42–46.

7. Thomas Hardeman land certificates, Hardeman MSS, SHSM, and Howard Co. Circuit Court Bk. 2, p. 79. Hardeman's neighbor, trapper Ezekiel Williams, helped to lay out the five-mile road.

8. Thomas Hardeman, taxable property list, 1820, Hardeman MSS, SHSM.

9. *Missouri Intelligencer,* Apr. 22, 1820.

10. T. Hardeman to John Overton, Franklin, Mo., June 24, 1825, Overton MSS, TSLA.

11. Peter H. Burnett, *Recollections and Opinions of an Old Pioneer* (New York, 1880), 7. Peter added the extra "t" to his last name.

12. Genealogical data, Hardeman MSS, TSLA.

13. John Hardeman, land certificates and receipts, Hardeman MSS, SHSM, and Howard Co., Deed Bk. H, p. 322.

14. *Missouri Intelligencer,* June 10, 1820, and Nov. 20, 1821.

15. Thomas Hardeman, land certificates and taxable property list; map of Franklin, Mo., Hardeman MSS, SHSM.

16. Hardeman Store, records, Franklin, Mo., 1817–1818, *passim,* Hardeman MSS, SHSM, and Elijah Iles, *Early Life and Times in Kentucky, Missouri, and Illinois* (Springfield, Ill., 1883), 22.

17. John Hardeman, Appraised Value of Property, 1829, Hardeman MSS, SHSM.

18. J. Hardeman to L. Parker, Jefferson City, Apr. 7, 1827, and John Hardeman account with Ward and Parker, St. Louis, Dec. 7, 1825–Nov. 1826,

Parker-Russell MSS, Missouri Historical Society (MHS), St. Louis; *Missouri Intelligencer,* Mar. 25, 1823.

19. Henry Clay to J. Hardeman, Washington, D.C., Jan. 22, 1825, copy in Hardeman MSS, SHSM.

20. L. Parker to J. Hardeman, St. Louis, Aug. 2, 1826; Hardeman to Parker, Jefferson City, Aug. 7, 1827, Parker-Russell MSS; John Hardeman, receipts in account with Smith and Knox, *passim,* Hardeman MSS, SHSM.

21. *Missouri Intelligencer,* June 10, 1823.

22. *Ibid.*

23. H. Lee to J. Hardeman, Westmoreland Co., Va., Apr. 1, 1823, Hardeman MSS, SHSM.

24. *Missouri Intelligencer,* Mar. 25, 1823; John O'Fallon to J. Hardeman, St. Louis, Nov. 3, 1821, and Apr. 14, 1826, Hardeman MSS, SHSM.

25. Alphonso Wetmore, *Gazetteer of the State of Missouri* (St. Louis, 1837), 88–89.

26. *Missouri Intelligencer,* Oct. 29, 1822.

27. W. F. Switzler, *Illustrated History of Missouri from 1541 to 1877* (St. Louis, 1879), 194–95. Switzler was a friend of John Hardeman's sons.

28. George C. Sibley to J. Hardeman, San Fernando, N.M., Feb. 15, 1826, Hardeman MSS, SHSM.

29. Captain Pentland to J. Hardeman, Council Bluffs, May 1824, Hardeman MSS, SHSM.

30. J. O'Fallon to General Thomas A. Smith, St. Louis, Dec. 27, 1827, Jan. 25, 1828, and Sept. 3, 1828, Thomas A. Smith MSS, SHSM; J. O'Fallon to J. Hardeman, St. Louis, Nov. 3, 1821, Hardeman MSS, SHSM.

31. Walter B. Stevens, *Centennial History of Missouri* (St. Louis, 1921), II, 332.

32. As quoted in John F. McDermott, "Culture on the Missouri Frontier," *Missouri Historical Review,* 50 (July 1956), 369.

33. Wetmore, *Gazetteer,* 89.

34. Edwin James, comp., *Account of an Expedition from Pittsburgh to the Rocky Mountains Performed in the Years 1819–1820* (Philadelphia, 1822), I, 89.

35. J. Hardeman to J. L. Hardeman, Franklin, Mo., Mar. 10, 1828, and List of fruits and berries transplanted from Fruitage Farm to Penultima, Hardeman MSS, SHSM.

36. Bill of sale, S. Bascom to J. Hardeman, Philadelphia, July 10, 1818, Hardeman MSS, SHSM.

37. Willie Blount to E. Earle, Bakerdon, Tenn., Sept. 20, 1822, Hardeman MSS, SHSM.

38. John McNairy to J. Hardeman, Sept. 1822, Hardeman MSS, SHSM.

39. Hardeman to McNairy, Franklin, Mo., Nov. 6, 1822, and Hardeman to Blount, Franklin, Jan. 18, 1824, Hardeman MSS, SHSM.

40. John Hardeman, poetry, Hardeman MSS, SHSM.
41. J. Hardeman to J. L. Hardeman, Franklin, Mo., Oct. 5, 1825, Hardeman MSS, SHSM, and Genealogical data, Hardeman MSS, TSLA.
42. *Missouri Intelligencer,* Sept. 18, 1824.
43. T. Hardeman to M. M. Marmaduke, Franklin, Tenn., 1833, Sappington MSS, MHS.

CHAPTER VI

1. J. Hardeman to T. Hardeman, Franklin, Mo., May 3, 1828, and J. Hardeman to J. L. Hardeman, Franklin, May 20, 1828, Hardeman MSS, SHSM.
2. *Missouri Intelligencer* (Franklin), Nov. 20, 1821, Dec. 16, 1823, and Sept. 26, 1827; and Edwin James, *Account of an Expedition from Pittsburgh to the Rocky Mountains Performed in the Years 1819–20* (Philadelphia: 1822), I, 100.
3. B. Hardeman to T. Hardeman, Quintana, Tex., Jan. 25, 1836, Bailey Hardeman MSS, TSLA.
4. "Annals of Bailey Hardeman," Bailey Hardeman MSS, TSLA; and Receipt of Bailey Hardeman's payment, Franklin, Mo., Jan. 16, 1821, Hardeman MSS, SHSM.
5. Tennessee General (land) Grant Records, Bk. T, pp. 540, 917; Bk. U., pp. 788–89; and Bk. Y, p. 722, TSLA.
6. J. Hardeman to T. H. Benton, Franklin, Aug. 11, 1825, Sappington MSS, MHS, and M. M. Marmaduke to J. Hardeman, Santa Fe, Aug. 5, 1824, Hardeman MSS, SHSM.
7. M. M. Marmaduke to J. Hardeman, Taos, N.M., Oct. 13, 1824, Hardeman MSS, SHSM. Except as otherwise noted, the account of Marmaduke's trip is taken from his diary in Archer B. Hulbert, *Southwest on the Turquoise Trail: The First Diaries on the Road to Santa Fe* (Denver, 1933), 69–77.
8. M. M. Marmaduke to J. Hardeman, Santa Fe, Aug. 5, 1824, Hardeman MSS, SHSM.
9. A. Storrs to T. H. Benton, in Hulbert, *Southwest,* 80.
10. Marmaduke to Hardeman, Aug. 5, 1824.
11. *Ibid.*
12. A. Storrs to T. H. Benton, in Hulbert, *Southwest,* 84.
13. *Ibid.,* 89.
14. Marmaduke to Hardeman, Oct. 13, 1824.
15. Except as otherwise noted, the account of Becknell's expedition is taken from his report in *Missouri Intelligencer,* June 25, 1825.
16. Hiram M. Chittenden, *The American Fur Trade of the Far West* (Stanford, Calif.: Academic Reprints, 1954), II, 506.

17. *Missouri Intelligencer,* June 25, 1825, and J. Hardeman to T. H. Benton, Franklin, Aug. 11, 1825, Sappington MSS.

18. U.S. Congress, Senate, *Public Documents,* 22nd Cong., 1st Sess., 1832, II, no. 90, p. 83.

19. Bailey Hardeman and William Scott, Contract, Aug. 27, 1825, Abiel Leonard MSS, SHSM, and List of Traders at Santa Fe in 1825, Ritch MSS, Henry E. Huntington Library, San Marino, Calif.

20. Iris H. Wilson, *William Wolfskill, 1797–1866: Frontier Trapper to California Ranchero* (Glendale: Arthur H. Clark, 1965), 46–48.

21. Josiah Gregg, *Commerce of the Prairies* (Philadelphia: Lippincott, 1962), II, 206.

22. *Missouri Intelligencer,* June 25, 1825.

23. Max L. Moorhead, *New Mexico's Royal Road: Trade and Travel on the Chihuahua Trail* (Norman: Univ. of Oklahoma Press, 1958), 67–69, and Kate L. Gregg, ed., *The Road to Santa Fe: The Journal and Diaries of George Champlin Sibley* (Albuquerque: Univ. of New Mexico Press, 1952), *passim.*

24. J. Hardeman to T. H. Benton, Aug. 11, 1825.

25. Otis Young, *Military Escorts on the Santa Fe Trail* (Glendale: Arthur H. Clark, 1952), *passim.*

26. J. Hardeman to T. Hardeman, May 3, 1828.

27. Trade lists of George and Washington Knox, Nov. 11, 1831, MANM 2982, and Sept. 1, 1832, MANM 3352, MSS, New Mexico State Records Center and Archives, Santa Fe; and S. McClure to M. M. Marmaduke, May 1824, Sappington MSS. Both George Knox, Sr. and George, Jr. were engaged in the Santa Fe trade.

28. T. A. Smith to J. Nicholson, Franklin, Sept. 26, 1829; Smith to G. Knox, Sept. 26, 1829; and Knox to Smith, New York, Feb. 6, 1828; Geo. M. Parker MSS, MHS.

29. T. H. Benton to M. M. Marmaduke, Washington, D.C., Jan. 28, 1828, Sappington MSS, and John Hardeman Passport, 1828–1829, Hardeman MSS, SHSM.

30. J. Hardeman to T. Hardeman, May 3, 1828. Lead had been discovered near the present site of Potosi, Mo., in the 1780s.

31. G. Knox to P. Knox, Cotton Grove, Mo., Sept. 14, 1828, Geo. M. Parker MSS, and Alphonso Wetmore to Lewis Cass, in Hulbert, *Southwest,* 182. Except as otherwise noted, the account of the trip is from Wetmore's Diary.

32. G. Knox to P. Knox, Sept. 14, 1828.

33. J. Hardeman to J. L. Hardeman, Santa Fe, Aug. 20, 1828, Hardeman MSS, SHSM.

34. John Hardeman, Customs House receipts, Fronteras, Sonora Province, Mex., Oct. 2, 1828, and Arizpe, Sonora, Jan. 13, 1829, Thomas A. Smith MSS.

35. G. Knox to P. Knox, Sept. 14, 1828.

36. *Western Monitor* (Fayette, Mo.), Oct. 3, 1829, and Statement of John Hardeman's death, Hardeman MSS, SHSM. John was buried in Girod North Street Cemetery, New Orleans.

37. Thomas Hardeman statement, Hardeman MSS, SHSM.

38. William H. Ashley to T. A. Smith, Sept. 23, 1829, Smith MSS.

39. T. A. Smith to G. Knox, Franklin, Sept. 26, 1829, Parker MSS.

40. J. Hardeman to J. L. Hardeman, May 20, 1828.

41. S. Porter to M. M. Marmaduke, Westmoreland Co., Va., Mar. 28, 1830, Sappington MSS.

42. A. Wetmore to L. Cass, in Hulbert, *Southwest,* 180–81.

CHAPTER VII

1. T. Hardeman to N. Hardeman, Rutherford Co., Tenn., Sept. 27, 1831, and Memorandum from J. Locke Hardeman to Ferdinand Stith, Franklin, Tenn., June 27, 1834, Hardeman MSS, SHSM.

2. T. Hardeman to N. Hardeman, Sept. 27, 1831, and T. Hardeman to N. Hardeman, Bolivar, Tenn., Dec. 24, 1831, Hardeman MSS, SHSM.

3. Williamson Co., Tenn., Deed Bk. L, p. 48.

4. Bailey Hardeman Store records, *passim,* Bailey Hardeman MSS, TSLA.

5. "Annals of Bailey Hardeman," Bailey Hardeman MSS, TSLA.

6. *Ibid.;* Williamson Co., Deed Bk. L, p. 48; and Williamson Co., Private Acts, 1829–1830, Ch. 17, p. 18.

7. Gladys Hardeman, "Bailey Hardeman," MS, Nacogdoches, Tex.

8. *Ibid.*; "Thomas Jones Hardeman," and "Blackstone Hardeman," Hardeman MSS, TSLA.

9. Oct. 14, 1836, Sappington MSS, MHS.

10. Memorandum of captains John H. Moore, Albert Martin, and R. M. Coleman, Gonzales, Tex., Sept. 30, 1835, Austin MSS, Univ. of Texas Archives, Austin.

11. John H. Brown, *Indian Wars and Pioneers of Texas* (St. Louis, 1895), 396–97.

12. H. P. F. Gammel, ed., *The Laws of Texas, 1822–1897* (Austin, 1898), I, 599.

13. Louis W. Kemp, *Signers of the Texas Declaration of Independence* (Houston, 1944), 163.

14. J. K. Greer, "The Committee on the Texas Declaration of Independence," *Southwestern Historical Quarterly,* 31 (July 1927), 244.

15. As quoted in S. H. Dixon, *Men Who Made Texas Free* (Houston, 1924), 299.

16. See William F. Gray, *From Virginia to Texas, 1835* (Houston, 1909), 123.

17. Dixon, *Men Who Made Texas Free,* 300.

18. Eugene C. Barker, *Texas History* (Dallas, 1929), 238–41.

19. *Ibid.*

20. Frank M. Brown, "Annals of Travis County," MS, Univ. of Texas Archives, 39, and statement of Gen. Alexander Watkins Terrell quoted in *The Seguin Enterprise* (Texas), Aug. 20, 1937. Terrell and William Hardeman were closely associated in many battles.

21. Brown, *Indian Wars,* 397. Brown and Hardeman also had a close military association and were fellow-exiles to Mexico after the Civil War.

22. Alex Dienst, "The Navy of the Republic of Texas," *The Quarterly of the Texas State Historical Association,* 12 (Jan. 1909), 193–94, and Ernest W. Winkler, "The Seat of the Government of Texas," in *ibid.,* 10 (July 1906), 154.

23. Brown, *Indian Wars,* 397, and "Thomas Monroe Hardeman," Hardeman MSS, TSLA.

24. William C. Binkley, ed., *Official Correspondence of the Texan Revolution, 1835–1836* (New York, 1936), II, 671–72.

25. *Telegraph and Texas Register* (Columbia, Tex.), Oct. 13, 1836.

CHAPTER VIII

1. Samuel Houston, *The Writings of Sam Houston, 1813–1863*, ed. by Amelia W. Williams and Eugene C. Barker (Austin: Univ. of Texas Press, 1938–1943), IV, 257.

2. T. J. Hardeman, statement to Reuben Hornsby, Hornsby MSS, Univ. of Texas Archives, Austin.

3. Graduates of the University of Nashville, Microfilm, AC no. 153, pp. 13, 18, TSLA.

4. Alexander W. Terrell, *From Texas to Mexico and the Court of Maximilian in 1865* (Dallas, 1933), 61.

5. John H. Brown, *Indian Wars and Pioneers of Texas* (St. Louis, 1895), 397–98.

6. *Ibid.,* 398.

7. *Ibid.,* and *Telegraph and Texas Register* (Columbia, Tex.), Apr. 17, 1839.

8. Mildred Mayhall, *Indian Wars of Texas* (Waco: Texian Press, 1965), 35, and Olive T. Walker, "Major Whitfield Chalk, Hero of the Republic of Texas," *Southwestern Historical Quarterly,* 60 (Jan. 1957), 361.

9. John H. Jenkins, *Recollections of Early Texas: the Memoirs of John Holland Jenkins,* ed. John Holmes Jenkins III (Austin: Univ. of Texas Press, 1958), 67.

10. Joseph M. Nance, *After San Jacinto: The Texas-Mexican Frontier, 1836–1841* (Austin: Univ. of Texas Press, 1963), 35.

11. Militia Rolls (Texas), MS, Texas State Archives, Austin.

12. W. M. Matthews, "Thomas Jones Hardeman," Hardeman MSS, TSLA, and *Bolivar Bulletin* (Bolivar, Tenn.), Apr. 23, 1943.

13. Walter Prescott Webb, *The Texas Rangers: a Century of Frontier Defense* (Boston, 1935), 91.

14. Terrell, *From Texas to Mexico,* 20, 32–33.

15. Mrs. J. B. Steele to H. Smithers, Dallas, Feb. 11, 1941, Texas State Archives, and notes of Judge W. W. Faw, *passim,* Faw MSS, TSLA. Leonidas Hardeman was born at Bolivar, Tenn., Mar. 25, 1825, and died in Texas, Feb. 26, 1892.

16. Samuel C. Reid, *The Scouting Expeditions of McCulloch's Texas Rangers* (Philadelphia, 1860), 38–52. Reid was with Hardeman in McCulloch's unit.

17. Luther Giddings, *Sketches of Campaigns in Northern Mexico by an Officer of the First Ohio Volunteers* (New York: Putnam's, 1953), 143–44.

18. Terrell, *From Texas to Mexico,* 32–33.

19. *Ibid.,* 20.

20. Gladys Hardeman, "Blackstone Hardeman, Sr.," MS, Nacogdoches, Tex.

21. Gladys Hardeman, "Blackstone Hardeman, Jr.," MS, Nacogdoches, Tex.

22. *Ibid.,* and Blackstone Hardeman, Jr., Store, records, Nacogdoches, Tex., 1852–1854, 1861–1862, Hardeman MSS, Univ. of Texas Archives.

CHAPTER IX

1. Edward Henry Lenox, *Overland to Oregon in the Tracks of Lewis and Clark: History of the First Emigration to Oregon in 1843,* ed. Robert Whitaker (Oakland, 1904), 13–14. Lenox was a member of the 1843 wagon train to Oregon.

2. Joseph Schafer, "Notes on the Colonization of Oregon," *Oregon Historical Quarterly,* 6 (March-Dec. 1905), 386.

3. Peter H. Burnett, *Recollections and Opinions of an Old Pioneer* (New York, 1880), 6. Burnett's mother, Dorothy, was born at the Hardeman Stockade near Nashville, May 15, 1786. George Burnet was born in Pittsylvania Co., Va., Sept. 26, 1770. They were married in Davidson Co., Tenn., in 1802.

4. *Ibid.,* 7.

5. *Ibid.,* 20.

6. *Ibid.,* 24.

7. *Ibid.,* 48.

8. *Ibid.,* 52–53.

9. John Minto, "Antecedents of the Oregon Pioneers and the Light These Throw on Their Motives," *Oregon Historical Quarterly,* 5 (March-Dec. 1904), 40.

10. Burnett, *Recollections,* 97–98.

11. *Ibid.,* 98–99, and W. M. Paxton, *Annals of Platt County, Missouri* (Kansas City, 1897), 52.

12. *Ohio Statesman,* Mar. 14, 1843, as quoted in *Oregon Historical Quarterly,* 4 (1903), 174–75.

13. Minto, "Antecedents," 40.

14. P. H. Burnett to J. G. Bennett, *New York Evening Herald,* Dec. 28, 1844, and Jan. 6 and 18, 1845 (a total of five letters); and George Wilkes, "Travels Across the Great Western Prairies and Through Oregon," *Oregon,* Part II (Washington, D.C., 1845), 63–114.

15. Burnett to Bennett, *Herald,* Jan. 6, 1845.

16. James W. Nesmith, "Address," *Transactions of the Third Annual Reunion of the Oregon Pioneer Association* (Salem, 1876), 46.

17. *Niles National Register,* May 23, 1829, and Leroy R. Hafen, ed., *The Mountainmen and the Fur Trade of the Far West* (Glendale: Arthur H. Clark, 1966), IV, 111.

18. Burnett, *Recollections,* 102.

19. James W. Nesmith, "Diary of the Emigration of 1843," *Oregon Historical Quarterly,* 7 (1906), 330–31, and William T. Newby, "William T. Newby's Diary of the Great Migration of 1843," ed. N. M. Winton, *Oregon Historical Quarterly,* 40 (Sept. 1939), 222.

20. *Daily Picayune* (New Orleans), Nov. 21, 1843.

21. Burnett to Bennett, *Herald,* Jan. 18, 1845.

22. *Daily Picayune,* Nov. 21, 1843, and Lenox, *Overland,* 18.

23. Minto, "Antecedents," 44–45.

24. Burnett, *Recollections,* 116.

25. Burnett to Bennett, *Herald,* Jan. 6 and 18, 1845, and Burnett to Penn, Fort Walla Walla, Oct. 25, 1843, in *Jefferson Enquirer* (Jefferson City), Aug. 15, 1844.

26. Nesmith, "Diary," 337.

27. Wilkes, "Travels," 86, and Burnett, *Recollections,* 124–25.

28. *Delineations of American Scenery and Character,* ed. Francis H. Herrick (New York, 1926), 4.

29. Burnett, *Recollections,* 113.

30. Jesse Applegate, *A Day With the Cow Column in 1843,* ed. Dorothy Johansen (Portland: Champoeg Press, 1952), 16–17.

31. Burnett, *Recollections,* 114.

32. *Ibid.,* 117.

33. *Ibid.,* 126, and Wilkes, "Travels", 87.

34. Burnett, *Recollections,* 129.

35. *Ibid.,* 130.

36. *Ibid.,* 232.

37. John C. Frémont, *Narrative of Exploration and Adventure,* ed. Allan Nevins (New York: Longmans, Green, 1956), 304.

38. Burnett, *Recollections,* 135.

39. Frémont, *Narrative,* 304.
40. Burnett, *Recollections,* 135–36.

CHAPTER X

1. This is obvious from the similarity between the letters of 1844 and Burnett's autobiography, published in 1880. By his own statement, the latter was written with his journal before him.
2. P. H. Burnett to J. G. Bennett, *New York Evening Herald,* Jan. 6, 1845. The succeeding quotations from Burnett regarding conditions on the trail are all from this letter.
3. *Niles National Register,* Nov. 2, 1844, reprinted from the *Republican* (St. Louis).
4. Burnett to Bennett, *Herald,* Dec. 28, 1844.
5. Peter H. Burnett, *Recollections and Opinions of an Old Pioneer* (New York, 1880), 178, 180.
6. John Minto, "Reminiscences of Honorable John Minto, Pioneer of 1844," *Oregon Historical Quarterly,* 2 (June 1901), 135–36.
7. Charles L. Camp, ed., "James Clyman, His Diaries and Reminiscences," *California Historical Society Quarterly,* 4 (June 1925), 352, and Theresa Gay, *James Marshall, the Discoverer of California Gold: a Biography* (Georgetown, Calif.: Talisman Press, 1967), 49.
8. Camp, *James Clyman,* 351–52, and Fred Lockley, "Some Documentary Records of Slavery in Oregon," *Oregon Historical Quarterly,* 17 (Mar.–Dec. 1906), 111–12.
9. Burnett to Bennett, *Herald,* Dec. 28, 1844.
10. Lockley, "Slavery in Oregon," 107–12.
11. *Niles National Register,* Nov. 2, 1844.
12. Burnett, *Recollections,* 169.
13. *Republican* (St. Louis), Aug. 9, 1845.
14. "Petition of Citizens of Oregon," *Pacific Northwest Quarterly,* 40 (Jan. 1949), 6–7.
15. John Minto, "What I Know of Dr. McLoughlin and How I Know it," *Oregon Historical Quarterly,* 11 (Mar.–Dec. 1910), 186–87.
16. John Minto, "Antecedents of the Oregon Pioneers and the Light These Throw on Their Motives," *Oregon Historical Quarterly,* 5 (Mar.–Dec. 1904), 43.
17. Burnett, *Recollections,* 253.
18. *Ibid.,* 254, and *California Star and Californian* (San Francisco), Dec. 2, 1848. This issue contains an account by Burnett of his trip.
19. Burnett, *Recollections,* 253.
20. *Ibid.,* 255; *California Star,* Dec. 2, 1848; and Anson S. Cone, "Reminiscences," *Oregon Historical Quarterly,* 4 (Mar.–Dec. 1903), 251–56.

21. *California Star,* Dec. 2, 1848, and Cone, "Reminiscences," 256.

22. Mildred B. Burcham, "Scott's and Applegate's Old South Road," *Oregon Historical Quarterly,* 41 (March–Dec. 1940), 406, 408, and Walter Meacham, *Applegate Trail* (American Pioneer Trails Assoc., 1941), 13.

23. Cone, "Reminiscences," 257.

24. Burnett, *Recollections,* 262, and *California Star,* Dec. 2, 1848.

25. Burnett, *Recollections,* 258.

26. J. Goldsborough Bruff, *Gold Rush: The Journals, Drawings, and Other Papers of J. Goldsborough Bruff,* ed. Georgia W. Read and Ruth Gaines (New York: Columbia Univ. Press, 1949), 175–81.

27. Burnett and others of his time, as well as some modern-day writers, apply the name "Sierra Nevada" to some areas which geomorphologically belong to the Cascade Range and the Modoc Plateau.

28. Burnett, *Recollections,* 265.

29. *Ibid.,* 266–67.

CHAPTER XI

1. Peter H. Burnett, *Recollections and Opinions of an Old Pioneer* (New York, 1880), 270–71.

2. *Ibid.,* 268.

3. *Mercury* (San Jose), Mar. 10, 1864.

4. Burnett, *Recollections,* 274.

5. *Mercury,* Mar. 10, 1864, and *Daily Alta California* (San Francisco), Oct. 23, 1866.

6. The account of Burnett as legal counsel and business agent for Sutter's estate is from William E. Franklin, "A Forgotten Chapter in California History: Peter H. Burnett and John A. Sutter's Fortune," *California Historical Society Quarterly,* 41 (Dec. 1962), 319–24, and Burnett, *Recollections,* 287–88.

7. Franklin, "A Forgotten Chapter," 322–23.

8. The account of Burnett's role in the provisional government move is taken from William E. Franklin, "Peter H. Burnett and the Provisional Government Movement," *California Historical Society Quarterly,* 40 (June 1961), 123–36, and Burnett, *Recollections,* 294, 299, 306–34.

9. The other justices (who elected Burnett chief justice) were José M. Covarubias, Pacificus Ord, and Lewis Dent.

10. Burnett, *Recollections,* 348.

11. *Daily Alta California,* Dec. 28, 1849.

12. The Inaugural Address is quoted in its entirety in Burnett, *Recollections,* 349–51.

13. The best treatment of Burnett's governorship is William E. Franklin,

"The Political Career of Peter Hardeman Burnett" (unpublished Ph.D. diss., Dept. of History, Stanford Univ., 1954).

14. California, *Journal of the California Senate* (1850), 32–33.

15. *Ibid.* (1851), 14–18, and Brett H. Melendy and Benjamin F. Gilbert, *The Governors of California: Peter H. Burnett to Edmund G. Brown* (Georgetown: Talisman Press, 1965), 32.

16. California, *Journal of the Senate* (1850), 38, and (1851), 19–20.

17. P. H. Burnett to G. O. Hardeman, San Francisco, Feb. 18, 1873, and Sept. 12, 1881, Hardeman MSS, SHSM.

18. P. H. Burnett to G. O. Hardeman, San Francisco, Mar. 19, 1873, and Sept. 12, 1881, Hardeman MSS, SHSM, and Burnett to D. W. May, San Francisco, Oct. 6, 1890, Western Historical MSS, SHSM.

CHAPTER XII

1. G. O. Hardeman to J. L. Hardeman, St. Louis, Dec. 1, 1844, Hardeman MSS, SHSM.

2. Correspondence between J. L. Hardeman and M. M. Marmaduke, *passim,* Sappington MSS, MHS. For an account of the life of John Locke Hardeman, see Nicholas P. Hardeman, "Portrait of a Western Farmer: John Locke Hardeman of Missouri, 1809–1858," *Missouri Historical Review,* 66 (Apr. 1972), 319–35.

3. Thomas C. Rainey, *Along the Old Trail* (Marshall, Mo., 1914), 93. Rainey states that McCormick spent a week with Hardeman and used his ideas for the reaper, which was instrumental in revolutionizing American agriculture. Diagram of portable fence, and other papers of J. L. Hardeman, MSS, SHSM.

4. J. Hardeman to J. L. Hardeman, Franklin, Mo., May 20, 1828, Hardeman MSS, SHSM.

5. G. O. Hardeman, medical school diplomas, Univ. of Missouri and Univ. of Pennsylvania, in possession of the writer, and Nicholas P. Hardeman, "Bushwhacker Activity on the Missouri Border: Letters to Dr. Glen O. Hardeman, 1862–1865," *Missouri Historical Review,* 58 (Apr. 1964), 206.

6. Nicholas P. Hardeman, ed., "Campsites on the Santa Fe Trail in 1848: as reported by John A. Bingham," *Arizona and the West,* 6 (Winter 1964), 313, 315–16.

7. Glen O. Hardeman, Memoirs written for grandsons, Dec. 1902, Hardeman MSS, SHSM.

8. *Ibid.*

9. G. O. Hardeman to J. L. Hardeman, Acapulco, Dec. 20, 1850; J. L. Hardeman to G. O. Hardeman, Vicksburg, Miss., Jan. 10, 1851; and Glen O. Hardeman, Journal of a Trip to California, 1850–1852, Hardeman MSS, SHSM.

10. Glen O. Hardeman, Journal. The account of the trip from New Orleans to the Isthmus of Panama is taken mainly from this source.

11. G. O. Hardeman, Memoirs.

12. G. O. Hardeman to J. Locke Hardeman, Dec. 20, 1850.

13. G. O. Hardeman, Memoirs.

14. G. O. Hardeman to J. L. Hardeman, Dec. 20, 1850.

15. G. O. Hardeman, Memoirs.

16. *Daily Pacific News* (San Francisco), Jan. 3, 1851, and *Daily Alta California* (San Francisco), Jan. 3, 1851. Except as otherwise indicated, the details of the difficulties en route from Panama City to San Francisco are taken from these newspaper accounts.

17. G. O. Hardeman to J. L. Hardeman, Dec. 20, 1850.

18. G. O. Hardeman to J. L. Hardeman, Alviso, Calif., Jan. 26, 1851, Hardeman MSS, SHSM.

19. *Ibid.*

20. Glen O. Hardeman, Ledger of accounts in California, 1851–1852, Hardeman MSS, SHSM, and *Pacific Transcript* (Pacific, Mo.), Jan. 20, 1905.

21. G. O. Hardeman to J. L. Hardeman, Alviso, Mar. 23, 1851, Hardeman MSS, SHSM.

22. G. O. Hardeman to J. L. Hardeman, Jan. 26, 1851.

23. Hardeman, Ledger, and G. O. Hardeman to J. L. Hardeman, Mariposa, Calif., June 1, 1851, Hardeman MSS, SHSM.

24. G. O. Hardeman to J. L. Hardeman, Jan. 26, 1851.

25. Robert T. Legge, ed., "Medical Observations of J. P. Leonard, M.D., San Francisco and Sacramento, 1849," *California Historical Society Quarterly,* 29 (Sept. 1950), 211–16.

26. Douglas S. Watson, ed., *The Santa Fe Trail to California, 1849–1852: the Journal and Drawings of H. M. T. Powell* (San Francisco, 1931), 249. Except as otherwise noted, the account of the Mariposa experiences is taken from this source, 249–58.

27. G. O. Hardeman to J. L. Hardeman, June 1, 1851.

28. *Ibid.*

29. G. O. Hardeman to J. L. Hardeman, New Orleans, Mar. 25, 1852, Hardeman MSS, SHSM.

30. Troup Smith, son of Gen. Thomas A. Smith, had died at sea. Wetmore was probably related to Santa Fe trader Alphonso Wetmore.

31. N. Dunnica to G. O. Hardeman, Arrow Rock, Mo., June 29, 1851, Hardeman MSS, SHSM.

32. J. L. Hardeman to G. O. Hardeman, Arrow Rock, May 25 and Aug. 26, 1851, Hardeman MSS, SHSM.

33. H. W. Hough to Mrs. J. W. Evans, n.d., Hardeman MSS, SHSM.

34. G. O. Hardeman to J. L. Hardeman, New Orleans, Mar. 25, 1852; *San Francisco Herald,* Steamer Edition, Mar. 2, 1852; and *Daily Alta California,* Feb. 18, 1852.

35. G. O. Hardeman, Memoirs.

36. G. O. Hardeman to J. L. Hardeman, Mar. 25, 1852.

37. G. O. Hardeman, Memoirs.

38. Hardeman MSS, SHSM, *passim*. The wildlife specimens mounted by Glen O. Hardeman and his son Glen and grandsons were presented to Central College, Fayette, Mo.

39. Glen O. Hardeman, Notebooks, MSS, SHSM, include such information as crops, weather statistics, and names of slaves.

CHAPTER XIII

1. Civil War Centennial Commission of Tennessee, *Tennesseans in the Civil War* (Nashville: Civil War Centennial Commission, 1965), II, 189. Former Texas ranger Thomas Monroe Hardeman lost his life while serving with Gen. Hood's Brigade in Tennessee during 1862.

2. C. A. Shanks to C. S. Taylor, Fort Bliss, Tex., July 23, 1861, copy supplied, courtesy of Dr. Martin H. Hall, Arlington, Tex.; and Gladys Hardeman, "Colonel Peter Hardeman," MS, Nacogdoches, Tex.

3. James C. McKee, *Narrative of the Surrender of a Command of U.S. Forces at Fort Fillmore, New Mexico, in July, A.D. 1861* (Prescott, Ariz. Terr., 1878), 1–2, and J. R. Baylor to T. A. Washington, Sept. 21, 1861, in U.S. War Department, *The War of the Rebellion: A Compilation of the Official Records of the Union and Confederate Armies* (Washington, D.C., 1880- 1902), Ser. I, vol. 4, pp. 17–18.

4. I. Lynde to Southern Dist. of New Mex., July 26, 1861, and Lynde to Dept. of New Mex., Aug. 7, 1861, in *War of the Rebellion*, Ser. I, vol. 4, pp. 4–5.

5. McKee, *Narrative*, 8, 11–12, and J. R. Baylor to T. A. Washington, Sept. 21, 1861, in *War of the Rebellion*, Ser. I, vol. 4, p. 18.

6. J. R. Baylor to Headquarters, Aug. 3, 1861, in *War of the Rebellion*, Ser. I, vol. 4, p. 17.

7. Ralph Wooster, "An Analysis of the Membership of the Texas Secession Convention," *Southwestern Historical Quarterly*, 62 (Jan. 1959), 331, and Hortense W. Ward, "The First State Fair of Texas," *Southwestern Historical Quarterly*, 57 (Oct. 1953), 171.

8. John H. Brown, *Indian Wars and Pioneers of Texas* (St. Louis, 1895), 398, and Theophilus Noel, *A Campaign from Santa Fe to the Mississippi* (High Point, N.C.: C. R. Sanders, Jr., 1961), 10, 118. Noel served in William Hardeman's company during the New Mexico campaign.

9. Noel, *A Campaign from Santa Fe*, 10.

10. Martin H. Hall, *Sibley's New Mexico Campaign* (Austin: Univ. of Texas Press, 1960), 90.

11. Brown, *Indian Wars*, 398, and Muster Rolls, National Archives, Washington, D.C.

12. Harvey Holcomb, "Confederate Reminiscences of 1862," *New Mexico Historical Review*, 5 (July 1930), 316. Holcomb was also a Confederate soldier in the New Mexico campaign.

13. E. R. S. Canby to Adjutant Gen. of the Army, Apr. 11, 1862, in *War of the Rebellion*, Ser. I, vol. 9, pp. 549–50, and B. S. Roberts to L. Thomas, Apr. 23, 1862, Ser. I, vol. 9, p. 553.

14. Brown, *Indian Wars*, 398.

15. *Ibid.;* Roy S. Dunn, "Life and Times in Albuquerque, Texas," *Southwestern Historical Quarterly*, 55 (July 1951), 65; and Hall, *Sibley's New Mexico Campaign*, 172.

16. Noel, *A Campaign from Santa Fe*, 27.

17. *Ibid.*, 28, and Brown, *Indian Wars*, 398.

18. P. Hardeman to J. R. Baylor, Oct. 8, 1861, in *War of the Rebellion*, Ser. I, vol. 4, p. 33.

19. Noel, *A Campaign from Santa Fe*, 28.

20. P. Hardeman to Caroline Hardeman, Rocky Creek, Choctaw Nation, Oct. 12, 1863, courtesy Mrs. Viola Hardeman Kraemer, Tyler, Tex.; and O. S. Barton, *Three Years With Quantrell: A True Story Told by His Scout John McCorkle* (New York: Buffalo Head Press, 1966), 95–96.

21. Certificate of Commission from Gov. Hamilton R. Gamble of Missouri, Aug. 20, 1862, Hardeman MSS, SHSM.

22. George W. Adams, *Doctors in Blue: The Medical History of the Union Army in the Civil War* (New York: Collier Books, 1961), 151–52.

23. P. A. Hardeman to G. O. Hardeman, Arrow Rock, Mo., Oct. 17, 1862, and Aug. 7, 1864, and N. H. H. (name unknown) to G. O. Hardeman, Arrow Rock, Oct. 17, 1862, Hardeman MSS, SHSM.

24. P. A. Hardeman to G. O. Hardeman, Arrow Rock, Aug. 7 and Oct. 9, 1864, Hardeman MSS, SHSM.

25. J. F. Philips to J. B. Barnes, Jan. 10, 1865, in *War of the Rebellion*, Ser. I, vol. 48, Pt. 1, pp. 475–77, and J. R. Montgomery to G. O. Hardeman, Dec. 20, 1865, Hardeman MSS, SHSM.

26. Except as otherwise noted, the account of the flight to Mexico is based on Alexander W. Terrell, *From Texas to Mexico and the Court of Maximilian in 1865* (Dallas, 1933), *passim.*

27. Albert R. Buchanan, *David S. Terry of California, Dueling Judge* (San Marino, Calif.: Huntington Library, 1956), 140.

28. Carl C. Rister, "Carlota, a Confederate Colony in Mexico," *Journal of Southern History*, 11 (Feb. 1945), 40.

29. William C. Nunn, *Escape from Reconstruction* (Fort Worth: Leo Potishman Foundation, 1956), 80.

30. *Ibid.*, 71–72; Buchanan, *David S. Terry*, 146–47; and Andrew F. Rolle, *The Lost Cause: The Confederate Exodus to Mexico* (Norman: Univ. of Oklahoma

Press, 1965), 136. The sheep were shipped by water from California to Mazatlán and driven to Guadalajara.

31. Statement of David S. Terry, as quoted in Rolle, *The Lost Cause,* 109.

32. Brown, *Indian Wars,* 399.

33. *Galveston Daily News,* Apr. 9, 1898.

34. G. Hardeman to N. D. Cone, São Paulo, Brazil, June 6, 1932; M. Hardeman to Gladys Hardeman, São Paulo, Apr. 5, 1949, courtesy of Gladys Hardeman, Nacogdoches, Tex.; and Lawrence F. Hill, "Confederate Exiles in Brazil," *Hispanic American Historical Review,* 7 (May 1927), 194–95.

35. Receipt for sawmill purchased from Charles Nathan, New Orleans, Apr. 12, 1869, Peter Hardeman MSS, courtesy Mrs. Viola Hardeman Kraemer, Tyler, Tex.

36. Hill, "Confederate Exiles," *passim;* Madeline D. Ross and Fred Kerner, "Stars and Bars Along the Amazon," *The Reporter,* 19 (Sept. 18, 1958), *passim;* information provided by Ward Nash Hardeman of Austin, Tex., and Gladys Hardeman of Nacogdoches, Tex.

CHAPTER XIV

1. Walker B. Hardeman, "Punching Cattle on the Trail to Kansas," in Marvin J. Hunter, comp. and ed., *The Trail Drivers of Texas* (Nashville, 1925), 147.

2. J. M. Cowley, "Was a Freighter and Trail Driver," in *ibid.,* 564–66.

3. J. F. Ellison, "Traveling the Trail with Good Men Was a Pleasure," in *ibid.,* 539, and Samuel D. Houston, "When a Girl Masqueraded as a Cowboy and Spent Four Months on the Trail," in *ibid.,* 61.

4. Henry D. Steele, "Played Pranks on the Tenderfoot," in *ibid.,* 137–39.

5. George W. Brock, "When Lightning Set the Grass on Fire," in *ibid.,* 222–23.

6. Walker B. Hardeman, "Punching Cattle," 146–47.

7. Cora M. Cross, "Stories of Trail Drivers of Long Ago: W. B. Hardeman Tells of Trailing Big Herds to Market in Texas Pioneer Days," MS, Fort Worth, Tex., copy supplied, courtesy of Mrs. Viola Hardeman Kraemer, Tyler, Tex.

8. *Ibid.,* and *The Semi-Weekly Farm News* (Dallas), Nov. 15, 1935.

9. *Sixty-ninth Annual Report of the Association of Graduates of the United States Military Academy at West Point, New York, June 13, 1938* (Newburgh, N.Y., 1938), 138.

10. R. A. Brown to J. Lockett, Fort Bowie, Ariz. Terr., June 6, 1887, in U.S. War Dept., Army Commands, Fort Bowie, Microfilm roll A–12.

11. Commissioned Officers Report, San Carlos, Ariz. Terr., Sept.–Nov. 1889, Microcopy 617, and Post Records, Fort Lowell, Ariz. Terr., Letters, 1881–1891, vol. 20, p. 183.

12. *Sixty-ninth Annual Report, West Point,* 138, and *Republican* (St. Louis), June 23, 1898.

13. E. Beaumont to L. Hardeman, Sept. 12, 1887; Order No. 142, Oct. 23, 1886; and Order No. 29, Mar. 21, 1887, in U.S. Army Commands, Fort Bowie, Microfilm roll 2; Commissioned Officers Report, San Carlos, Dec. 1889, Microcopy 617.

14. William H. Leckie, *The Buffalo Soldiers: a Narrative of the Negro Cavalry in the West* (Norman: Univ. of Oklahoma Press, 1967), *passim.*

15. As quoted in *ibid.,* 28.

16. *Great Falls Daily Tribune* (Montana), Aug. 6, 1909, Montana Historical Society, Helena.

17. L. Hardeman to G. O. Hardeman, Fort Assinniboine, Mont., Dec. 12, 1894, Hardeman MSS, SHSM. (The spelling of the name was later changed to Assiniboine.)

18. L. Hardeman to G. O. Hardeman, Fort Assinniboine, March 5, 1896, Hardeman MSS, SHSM, and Muster Roll, National Archives, Washington.

19. Donald Smythe, S.J., "John J. Pershing at Fort Assiniboine," *The Montana Magazine of Western History,* 18 (Jan. 1968), 20.

20. L. Hardeman to G. O. Hardeman, Fort Assinniboine, Apr. 15 and July 8, 1894, Hardeman MSS, SHSM.

21. *Ibid.,* Oct. 14, 1894.

22. *Ibid.,* Dec. 12, 1894.

23. J. K. Mizner to Adjutant Gen., Dakota Dept., Fort Assinniboine, Nov. 8, 1896, and T. A. Baldwin statement, Fort Assinniboine, Apr. 3, 1897, in Fort Assinniboine Correspondence Register, Microfilm roll 54.

24. Herman Werner, *On the Western Frontier with the U.S. Cavalry 50 Years Ago* (n.p., 1934), 81–82; Letcher Hardeman to G. O. Hardeman, Fort Assinniboine, Dec. 12, 1894; and Leona Hardeman to G. O. Hardeman, Fort Assinniboine, March 5, 1896, Hardeman MSS, SHSM. Letcher's sister, Leona, was visiting Fort Assinniboine.

25. *History of the Sixth Regiment of Missouri Volunteer Infantry* (St. Louis, 1899), no pagination.

26. Francis B. Heitman, *Historical Register and Dictionary of the United States Army* (Urbana: Univ. of Illinois Press, 1965), I, 499.

27. *Sixty-ninth Annual Report, West Point,* 138.

28. L. Hardeman to G. H. Hardeman, Rapidan, Va., July 12, 1922, Hardeman MSS, SHSM.

29. G. O. Hardeman to G. H. Hardeman, Gray Summit, Mo., July 22, 1890; G. H. Hardeman to G. O. Hardeman, Porterville, Calif., Aug. 18, 1890; and J. L. Hardeman to G. O. Hardeman, Porterville, Oct. 23, 1894, Hardeman MSS, SHSM.

30. L. Hardeman to G. H. Hardeman, Rapidan, July 12, 1922.

31. G. H. Hardeman to G. O. Hardeman, Porterville, July 16, 1890, Hardeman MSS, SHSM.
32. *Ibid.*
33. *Ibid.*
34. *Ibid.*, Aug. 18, 1890.
35. From stories told by Glen H. Hardeman to his children.
36. Correspondence between J. T. Hardeman and G. O. Hardeman, 1890s, Hardeman MSS, SHSM, and information provided by Mrs. Russella Hardeman Matthews, daughter of Joseph T. Hardeman, Seattle, Wash.

CHAPTER XV

1. T. Hardeman to G. O. Hardeman, Brentwood, Tenn., Dec. 19, 1882, Hardeman MSS, SHSM.
2. Frederick Jackson Turner, *The Frontier in American History,* (rept. New York: Holt, Rinehart, 1962). See especially pp. 1–38 for Turner's hypothesis on the American frontier.
3. Samuel D. Houston, "When a Girl Masqueraded as a Cowboy and Spent Four Months on the Trail," in Marvin J. Hunter, comp. and ed., *The Trail Drivers of Texas* (Nashville, 1925), 60–66.
4. For a discussion of the hunter-hero myth, see Richard Slotkin, *Regeneration Through Violence: The Mythology of the American Frontier, 1600–1860* (Middletown, Conn.: Wesleyan Univ. Press, 1973), *passim.*
5. Ray Allen Billington, *America's Frontier Heritage* (New York: Holt, Rinehart, 1966), 197.

Bibliography

THE FOLLOWING BIBLIOGRAPHY is limited primarily to items which contain information bearing directly on the people who are central to this study and on their activities. Where quotations or unique and necessary background material are involved, other entries have been included. In view of the abundance of published bibliographical reference works on the West and the westward movement, a more comprehensive bibliography in this volume is deemed unnecessary.

I. UNPUBLISHED MATERIALS

Austin MSS, Univ. of Texas Archives, Austin.
Brown, Frank M. "Annals of Travis County." Univ. of Texas Archives, Austin.
Draper, Lyman, MSS, Wisconsin State Historical Society, Madison.
County Court House Records. Deed Books, Court Minute Books, Tax Books, and Marriage Books in Cooper County (Boonville, Mo.); Davidson County (Nashville, Tenn.); Guilford County (Greensboro, N.C.); Hawkins County (Rogersville, Tenn.); Howard County (Fayette, Mo.); Maury County (Columbia, Tenn.); Saline County (Marshall, Mo.); Washington County (Jonesboro, Tenn.); Williamson County (Franklin, Tenn.).

Cross, Cora M. "Stories of Trail Drivers of Long Ago: W. B. Hardeman Tells of Trailing Big Herds to Market in Texas Pioneer Days." MS., Fort Worth, Tex., copy supplied courtesy of Mrs. Viola Hardeman Kraemer, Tyler, Tex.

Faw MSS, Tennessee State Library and Archives, Nashville.

Franklin, William E. "The Political Career of Peter Hardeman Burnett." Unpublished Ph.D. diss., Dept. of History, Stanford Univ., 1954.

Hardeman MSS, Tennessee State Library and Archives, Nashville.

Hardeman MSS, Univ. of Texas Archives, Austin.

Hardeman, Bailey, MSS, Tennessee State Library and Archives, Nashville.

Hardeman, Gladys. Unpublished biographical vignettes of Bailey Hardeman, Blackstone Hardeman, Jr., Blackstone Hardeman, Sr., Colonel Peter Hardeman, and Thomas Jones Hardeman, Nacogdoches, Tex.

————. "Early History of the Hardeman Family." Nacogdoches, Tex.

Hardeman, Glen, MSS, Western Manuscripts Collection, State Historical Society of Missouri, Columbia.

Hardeman, Glen O., medical school diplomas, Univ. of Missouri, 1848, and Univ. of Pennsylvania, 1849. In possession of Nicholas P. Hardeman, Garden Grove, Calif.

Hardeman, Peter, letters and MSS from São Paulo, Brazil. Copies in possession of Nicholas P. Hardeman, Garden Grove, Calif.; some originals loaned by Mrs. Viola Hardeman Kraemer, Tyler, Tex.

Hornsby, Reuben, MSS, Univ. of Texas Archives, Austin.

Houston, Martha L., comp. "Tennessee Census Reports, Williamson County—1820." No. 26, Washington, D.C., 1936.

Jackson, Andrew, MSS, Series 5, microfilm roll 67; and Series 1, microfilm roll 3, Library of Congress, Washington, D.C.

Knox, George and Washington, trade lists, Nov. 11, 1831, MANM 2982, and Sept. 1, 1832, MANM 3352, New Mexico State Records Center and Archives, Santa Fe.

Leonard, Abiel, MSS, Western Manuscripts Collection, State Historical Society of Missouri, Columbia.

University of Nashville, records, microfilm AC—153, Tennessee State Library and Archives, Nashville.

North Carolina. Governors' Letter Books, 1784–1791, microfilm reel 4, National Archives, Washington, D.C.

Parker, George M., MSS, Missouri Historical Society, St. Louis.

Parker–Russell, MSS, Missouri Historical Society, St. Louis.

Ritch MSS, Henry E. Huntington Library, San Marino, Calif.

Robertson, James, MSS, Tennessee State Library and Archives, Nashville.

Sappington MSS, Missouri Historical Society, St. Louis.

Smith, Thomas A., MSS, Western Manuscripts Collection, State Historical Society of Missouri, Columbia.

Steele, Mrs. J. B., letter to H. Smithers, Feb. 11, 1941, Texas State Archives, Austin.

Tennessee. General (land) Grant Records, Tennessee State Library and Archives, Nashville.

Texas. Muster Rolls, Texas State Archives, Austin.

U.S. Army Records, Fort Assiniboine, Mont., Montana State Historical Society, Helena.

U.S. Army Records, Fort Bowie, Ariz., microfilm roll 2.

U.S. Army Records, San Carlos, Ariz., microcopy 617.

U.S. Army Muster Rolls, National Archives, Washington, D.C.

Williams, Samuel C. "The Hardeman Family." Tennessee State Library and Archives, Nashville.

II. GOVERNMENT PUBLICATIONS

California. *Journal of the California Senate* (1850).

Gammel, H. P. N., comp. *The Laws of Texas, 1822–1897.* 10 vols., Austin, 1898.

North Carolina. *North Carolina House Journal* (1788).

Tennessee. *Journal of the Proceedings of a Convention Begun and Held at Knoxville, Jan. 11, 1796.* Rpt. Nashville, 1852.

Tennessee. *Journals of the Senate and House of the Second General Assembly of the State of Tennessee Held at Knoxville, 1797–1798.*

Territory South of the Ohio. *Journal of the House of Representatives of the Legislative Council of the Territory of the United States of America, South of the River Ohio: Begun and Held at Knoxville, the 29th Day of June, 1795.* Rpt. Nashville, 1852.

U.S. Congress, Senate. *Public Documents.* 22nd Congress, 1st Sess., 1832, Vol. II.

U.S. War Department. *The War of the Rebellion: A Compilation of the Official Records of the Union and Confederate Armies.* 128 vols. Washington, D.C., 1880–1901.

III. BOOKS AND PAMPHLETS

Abernethy, Thomas P. *From Frontier to Plantation in Tennessee: A Study in Frontier Democracy.* Chapel Hill: Univ. of North Carolina Press, 1932.

Adams, George W. *Doctors in Blue: The Medical History of the Union Army in the Civil War.* New York: Collier Books, 1961.

Applegate, Jesse W. *A Day With the Cow Column in 1843.* Ed. Dorothy Johansen. Portland: Champoeg Press, 1952.

Arnow, Harriet. *Flowering of the Cumberland.* New York: Macmillan, 1963.

Atherton, Lewis. *The Southern Country Store, 1800–1860.* Baton Rouge: Louisiana State Univ. Press, 1949.

Audubon, John James. *Delineations of American Scenery and Character.* Ed. Francis H. Herrick. New York, 1926.

Barker, Eugene C. *Texas History.* Dallas, 1929.

Barton, O. S. *Three Years with Quantrell: A True Story Told by His Scout John McCorkle.* New York: Buffalo Head Press, 1966.

Beard, Charles A. *Economic Interpretation of the Constitution.* New York, 1913.

Billington, Ray Allen. *America's Frontier Heritage.* New York: Holt, Rinehart, 1966.

Binkley, William C. *Official Correspondence of the Texan Revolution, 1835–1836.* 2 vols. New York: D. Appleton-Century, 1936.

Blum, John M., et al. *The National Experience.* New York: Harcourt, Brace, 1963.

Brown, John H. *Indian Wars and Pioneers of Texas.* St. Louis, 1895.

Bruff, J. Goldsborough. *Gold Rush: The Journals, Drawings, and Other Papers of J. Goldsborough Bruff.* Ed. Georgia W. Read and Ruth Gaines. New York: Columbia Univ. Press, 1949.

Buchanan, Albert Russell. *David S. Terry of California, Dueling Judge.* San Marino, Calif.: Huntington Library, 1956.

Burnett, Peter Hardeman. *Recollections and Opinions of an Old Pioneer.* New York, 1880.

Caughey, John W. *McGillivray of the Creeks.* Norman: Univ. of Oklahoma Press, 1938.

Chambers, William N. *Old Bullion Benton, Senator from the New West: Thomas Hart Benton, 1782–1858.* Boston: Little, Brown, 1956.

Chittenden, Hiram M. *The American Fur Trade of the Far West.* 2 vols. Stanford, Calif.: Academic Reprints, 1954.

Civil War Centennial Commission of Tennessee. *Tennesseans in the Civil War.* 2 vols. Nashville: Civil War Centennial Commission, 1965.

Clayton, W. W. *History of Davidson County, Tennessee.* Philadelphia, 1880.

Dixon, S. H. *Men Who Made Texas Free.* Houston, 1924.

Donelson, John. "John Donelson's Journal," in *Three Pioneer Tennessee Documents.* Nashville: Tennessee Historical Commission, 1964.

Field, Matthew C. *Prairie and Mountain Sketches.* Ed. Kate L. Gregg and John F. McDermott. Norman: Univ. of Oklahoma Press, 1957.

Frémont, John C. *Narrative of Exploration and Adventure.* Ed. Allan Nevins. New York: Longmans, Green, 1956.

Gay, Theresa. *James Marshall, the Discoverer of California Gold: A Biography.* Georgetown, Calif.: Talisman Press, 1967.

Giddings, Luther. *Sketches of Campaigns in Northern Mexico by an Officer of the First Ohio Volunteers.* New York: Putnam's, 1953.

Gray, William F. *From Virginia to Texas, 1835.* Houston, 1909.

Gregg, Josiah. *Commerce of the Prairies.* 2 vols. Philadelphia: Lippincott, 1962.

Gregg, Kate L., ed. *The Road to Santa Fe: The Journal and Diaries of George Champlin Sibley.* Albuquerque: Univ. of New Mexico Press, 1952.

Hafen, Leroy R., ed. *The Mountainmen and the Fur Trade of the Far West.* 9 vols. Glendale: Arthur H. Clark, 1965–1972.

Hall, Martin H. *Sibley's New Mexico Campaign.* Austin: Univ. of Texas Press, 1960.

Heitman, Francis B. *Historical Register and Dictionary of the United States Army from its Organization, September 29, 1789, to March 2, 1903.* 2 vols. Rpt. Urbana: Univ. of Illinois Press, 1965.

History of the Sixth Regiment of Missouri Volunteer Infantry. St. Louis, 1899.

Houston, Samuel. *The Writings of Sam Houston, 1813–1863.* Ed. Amelia W. Williams and Eugene C. Barker. 8 vols. Austin: Univ. of Texas Press, 1938–1943.

Hulbert, Archer B., ed. *Southwest on the Turquoise Trail: The First Diaries on the Road to Santa Fe.* Denver, 1933.

Hunter, Marvin J., ed. *The Trail Drivers of Texas.* Nashville, 1925.

Iles, Elijah. *Early Life and Times in Kentucky, Missouri, and Illinois.* Springfield, Ill., 1883.

James, Edwin, comp. *Account of an Expedition from Pittsburgh to the Rocky Mountains Performed in the Years 1819–1820.* 2 vols. Philadelphia, 1822–1823.

Jenkins, John H. *Recollections of Early Texas: The Memoirs of John Holland Jenkins.* Ed. John Holmes Jenkins, III. Austin: Univ. of Texas Press, 1958.

Johnson, O., and W. H. Winter. *Route Across the Rocky Mountains.* Ann Arbor: University Microfilms, Inc., 1966.

Kemp, Louis W. *Signers of the Texas Declaration of Independence.* Houston: Anson Jones Press, 1944.

Leckie, William H. *The Buffalo Soldiers: A Narrative of the Negro Cavalry in the West.* Norman: Univ. of Oklahoma Press, 1967.

Lenox, Edward Henry. *Overland to Oregon in the Tracks of Lewis and Clark: History of the First Emigration to Oregon in 1843.* Ed. Robert Whitaker. Oakland, 1904.

McKee, James Cooper. *Narrative of the surrender of a Command of U.S. Forces at Fort Fillmore, N.M., in July, A.D. 1861.* Prescott, 1878.

Masonic History Agency. *History of Freemasonry in Early Tennessee, 1789 -1843.* Chattanooga, 1943.

Mayhall, Mildred P. *Indian Wars of Texas.* Waco: Texian Press, 1965.

Meacham, Walter. *Applegate Trail.* American Pioneer Trails Assoc., 1941.

Melendy, Brett H., and Benjamin F. Gilbert. *The Governors of California: Peter H. Burnett to Edmund G. Brown.* Georgetown, Calif.: Talisman Press, 1965.

Moorhead, Max L. *New Mexico's Royal Road: Trade and Travel on the Chihuahua Trail.* Norman: Univ. of Oklahoma Press, 1958.

Nance, Joseph M. *After San Jacinto: The Texas-Mexican Frontier, 1836–1841.* Austin: Univ. of Texas Press, 1963.

Noel, Theophilus. *A Campaign From Santa Fe to the Mississippi: Being a History of the Old Sibley Brigade.* High Point, N.C.: C. R. Sanders, Jr., 1961.

Nunn, William C. *Escape From Reconstruction.* Fort Worth: Leo Potishman Foundation, 1956.

Paxton, W. M. *Annals of Platt County, Missouri.* Kansas City, 1897.

Rainey, Thomas C. *Along the Old Trail.* Marshall, Mo., 1914.

Ramsey, J. G. M. *The Annals of Tennessee to the End of the Eighteenth Century.* Philadelphia, 1853.

Reid, Samuel C. *The Scouting Expeditions of McCulloch's Texas Rangers.* Philadelphia, 1860.

Rolle, Andrew F. *The Lost Cause: The Confederate Exodus to Mexico.* Norman: Univ. of Oklahoma Press, 1965.

Sixty-ninth Annual Report of the Association of Graduates of the United States Military Academy at West Point, New York, June 13, 1938. Newburgh, N.Y., 1938.

Slotkin, Richard. *Regeneration Through Violence: The Mythology of the American Frontier, 1600–1860.* Middletown, Conn.: Wesleyan Univ. Press, 1973.

Stevens, Walter Barlow. *Centennial History of Missouri (the Center State): One Hundred Years in the Union, 1820–1921.* 5 vols. St. Louis, 1921.

Switzler, W. F. *Illustrated History of Missouri from 1541 to 1877.* St. Louis, 1879.

Terrell, Alexander Watkins. *From Texas to Mexico and the Court of Maxmilian in 1865.* Dallas, 1933.

Turner, Frederick Jackson. *The Frontier in American History.* Rpt. New York: Holt, Rinehart, 1962.

Watson, Douglas S., Ed. *The Santa Fe Trail to California, 1849–1852: The Journal and Drawings of H. M. T. Powell.* San Francisco, 1931.

Webb, Walter Prescott. *The Texas Rangers: A Century of Frontier Defense.* Boston, 1935.

Werner, Herman. *On the Western Frontier With the U.S. Cavalry 50 Years Ago.* N.p., 1934.

Wetmore, Alphonso. *Gazetteer of the State of Missouri.* St. Louis, 1837.

White, Katherine K. *The King's Mountain Men: The Story of the Battle, With Sketches of the American Soldiers Who Took Part.* Dayton, Va., 1924.

Wilkes, George. *Oregon.* Washington, 1845.

Wilson, Iris H. *William Wolfskill, 1797–1866: Frontier Trapper to California Ranchero.* Glendale: Arthur H. Clark, 1965.

Young, Otis. *Military Escorts on the Santa Fe Trail.* Glendale: Arthur H. Clark, 1952.

IV. NEWSPAPERS

Bolivar Bulletin (Bolivar, Tenn.), 1943.

California Star and Californian (San Francisco), 1848.

Daily Alta California (San Francisco), 1849–1852, 1866.
Daily Pacific News (San Francisco), 1851.
Daily Picayune (New Orleans), 1843.
Expositor (Independence), 1844–1846.
Galveston Daily News, 1898.
Great Falls Daily Tribune (Montana), 1909.
Independence Journal, 1844–1846.
Jefferson Enquirer and Missouri Democrat (Jefferson City, Mo.), 1843–1845.
Mercury (San Jose), 1864.
Missouri Intelligencer (Franklin), 1820–1825.
National Intelligencer (Washington, D.C.), 1829.
New York Evening Herald, 1844–1845.
Niles National Register (Baltimore), 1829, 1843–1845.
Ohio Statesman (Columbus), 1843.
Pacific Transcript (Missouri), 1905.
Platte Argus (Missouri), 1844–1846.
Republican (St. Louis), 1844.
San Francisco Herald, 1852.
The Seguin Enterprise (Texas), 1937.
The Semi-Weekly Farmer News (Dallas), 1935.
Telegraph and Texas Register (Columbia), 1836, 1839.
Washington Globe, 1844–1845.
Weekly Tribune (Liberty, Mo.), 1846–1847, 1849.
Western Monitor (Fayette, Mo.), 1829.

V. ARTICLES IN PERIODICALS

Black, Roy W., Sr., "The Genesis of County Organization in the Western District of North Carolina and in the State of Tennessee," *West Tennessee Historical Society Papers*, 2 (1948), 95–118.
Burcham, Mildred, "Scott's and Applegate's Old South Road," *Oregon Historical Quarterly*, 41 (March–Dec. 1940), 405–23.
Camp, Charles, ed., "James Clyman, His Diaries and Reminiscences," *California Historical Society Quarterly*, 4 (June 1925), 307–60.
Comer, Clay, "The Colorado River Raft," *Southwestern Historical Quarterly*, 52 (Apr. 1949), 410–26.
Cone, Anson S., "Reminiscences," *Oregon Historical Quarterly*, 4 (March–Dec. 1903), 251–59.
Dienst, Alex, "The Navy of the Texas Republic," *The Quarterly of the Texas State Historical Association*, 12 (Jan. 1909), 166–203.
Dunn, Roy S., "Life and Times in Albuquerque, Texas," *Southwestern Historical Quarterly*, 55 (July 1951), 62–76.
Franklin, William E., "A Forgotten Chapter in California History: Peter H.

Burnett and John A. Sutter's Fortune," *California Historical Society Quarterly,* 41 (Dec. 1962), 319–24.

————, "Peter H. Burnett and the Provisional Government Movement," *California Historical Society Quarterly,* 40 (June 1961), 123–36.

Greer, J. K., "The Committee on the Texas Declaration of Independence," *Southwestern Historical Quarterly,* 31 (July 1927), 33–49.

Hardeman, Nicholas P., "Bushwhacker Activity on the Missouri Border: Letters to Dr. Glen O. Hardeman, 1862–1865," *Missouri Historical Review,* 58 (April 1964), 265–77. Parts of this article have been reproduced in Ch. XIII by permission of *Missouri Historical Review.*

————, ed., "Campsites on the Santa Fe Trail in 1848, as Reported by John A. Bingham," *Arizona and the West,* 6 (Winter 1964), 313–19.

————, "Portrait of a Western Farmer: John Locke Hardeman of Missouri, 1809–1858," *Missouri Historical Review,* 66 (April 1972), 319–35.

————, "Sketches of Dr. Glen Owen Hardeman: California Gold Rush Physician," *California Historical Society Quarterly,* 47 (Mar. 1968), 41–71. Parts of this article have been reproduced in Ch. XII by permission of California Historical Society, San Francisco.

Hill, Lawrence F., "Confederate Exiles in Brazil," *Hispanic American Historical Review,* 7 (May 1927), 192–210.

————, "The Confederate Exodus to South America," *Southwestern Historical Quarterly,* 39 (Oct. 1935 and Jan. 1936).

Holcomb, Harvey, "Confederate Reminiscences of 1862," *New Mexico Historical Review,* 5 (July 1930), 315–20.

Kinard, Margaret, "Frontier Development of Williamson County," *Tennessee Historical Quarterly,* 8 (Mar. 1949), 3–33; (June 1949), 127–53.

Legge, Robert T., ed., "Medical Observations of J. P. Leonard, M.D., San Francisco and Sacramento, 1849," *California Historical Society Quarterly,* 29 (Sept. 1950), 211–16.

Lockley, Fred., "Some Documentary Records of Slavery in Oregon," *Oregon Historical Quarterly,* 17 (Mar.–Dec. 1916), 107–15.

McDermott, John F., "Culture on the Missouri Frontier," *Missouri Historical Review,* 50 (July 1956), 355–70.

Maloney, Alice B., "John Gantt, Borderer," *California Historical Society Quarterly,* 16 (Mar. 1937), 48–60.

Minto, John, "Antecedents of the Oregon Pioneers and the Light These Throw on Their Motives," *Oregon Historical Quarterly,* 5 (Mar.–Dec., 1904), 38–63.

————, "Reminiscences of Honorable John Minto, Pioneer of 1844," *Oregon Historical Quarterly,* 2 (1901), 119–67, 209–54.

————, "What I Know of Dr. McLoughlin and How I Know It," *Oregon Historical Quarterly,* 11 (Mar.–Dec. 1910), 177–200.

Nesmith, James W., "Address," *Transactions of the Third Annual Reunion of the Oregon Pioneer Association* (1876).

————, "Diary of the Emigration of 1843," *Oregon Historical Quarterly*, 7 (1906), 329–59.

Newby, William T., "William T. Newby's Diary of the Great Migration of 1843," ed. N. M. Winton, *Oregon Historical Quarterly*, 40 (Sept. 1939), 319–24.

Penrose, S. B. L., "The Wagon Train of 1843: Its Dual Significance," *Oregon Historical Quarterly*, 34 (1943), 361–69.

"Petition of Citizens of Oregon," *Pacific Northwest Quarterly*, 40 (Jan. 1949), 5–8.

Pool, William C., "An Economic Interpretation of the Ratification of the Federal Constitution in North Carolina," *The North Carolina Historical Review*, 27 (Apr., July, Oct. 1950).

Rister, Carl C., "Carlota, a Confederate Colony in Mexico," *Journal of Southern History*, 11 (Feb. 1945), 33–50.

Ross, Madeline D., and Fred Kerner, "Stars and Bars along the Amazon," *The Reporter*, 19 (Sept. 18, 1958), 34–36.

Schafer, Joseph, "Notes on the Colonization of Oregon," *Oregon Historical Quarterly*, 6 (Mar.–Dec. 1905), 379–90.

Smythe, Donald, S.J., "John J. Pershing at Fort Assiniboine," *The Montana Magazine of Western History*, 18 (Jan. 1968), 19–23.

Swartzlow, Ruby J., "Peter Lassen, Northern California Trail Blazer," *California Historical Society Quarterly*, 18 (Dec. 1939), 291–314.

Walker, Olive T., "Major Whitfield Chalk, Hero of the Republic of Texas," *Southwestern Historical Quarterly*, 60 (Jan. 1957), 358–68.

Ward, Hortense W., "The First State Fair of Texas," *Southwestern Historical Quarterly*, 57 (Oct. 1953), 163–64.

Williams, Samuel C., "The Admission of Tennessee into the Union," *Tennessee Historical Quarterly*, 4 (Dec. 1945), 291–319.

Winkler, Ernest W., "The Seat of the Government of Texas," *The Quarterly of the Texas State Historical Association*, 10 (July 1906), 140–71.

Wooster, Ralph, "An Analysis of the Membership of the Texas Secession Convention," *Southwestern Historical Quarterly*, 62 (Jan. 1959), 322–35.

————, "Wealthy Texans, 1860," *Southwestern Historical Quarterly*, 71 (Oct. 1967), 163–80.

Index

Chickasaw Indians, 14, 17
Chihuahua, Mex., 113, 218
Chihuahua Trail. *See* El Camino Real
Childress, George C., 126–27
Chiles, Joseph, 171
China, Mex., 144
Chireno, Tex., See Hardemans, Tex.
Chiricahua Apache Indians, 270
Chiricahua Mts., Ariz., 269
Chisholm, John, 60–61
Chisholm Trail, 262–63
Chivington, John M., 240, 242
Choctaw Nation, 244
Chouteau family, 298
Cillo, Brazil, 259
Cimarron River, Santa Fe Trail, 100
Civil War in the West, 234–59
Clappe, "Dame Shirley." *See* "Dame Shirley"
Clappe, Dr. Fayette, 226
Clark family, 298
Clay, Henry, 76–77, 81–82
Clay County, Mo., 155
Cleaton, Isham, 12
Cleveland, Benjamin, 12
Clyman, James, 180–81
Coast Range, 192
Coffee, John, 65–68
Coldwater campaign, 19–20
Cole County, Mo., 78
Coleman, Cuthbert, 61
Coleman County, Tex., 263
Colorado, 240, 264, 268
Colorado Navigation Co., 134
Colorado River, 105–106, 211
Colorado Springs, Colo., 268
Colt revolver, 137
Columbia River, 172, 174
Comanche Indians, 108, 136–41
Comtian philosophy, 90
Cone, Anson, 191, 193
Confederate States of America, 234–59
Conrad, Edward, 126–27
Conservation, 168, 170
Constitution, Republic of Texas, 127–28
Constitution, Tennessee, 30, 32

Constitution, U.S., 28
Cook, Hamilton, 125
Cooper family, 73, 298
Cooperage, 5, 37
Coopwood, Bethel, 242
Córdova, Vicente, 138
Corn, 26, 50
Corpus Christi, Tex., 141
Cortina, Juan, 253–56
Corzine, Dr. Reece, 119
Cós, Martín Perfecto de, 124–25
Cotton factor, 43
Council House Battle, San Antonio, 138, 140
Country store, as institution, 43, *See also* Hardeman stores; Merchandising
Cowley, J. M., 263
Crab Orchard, Ky., 13
"Crabstick," Tenn., 82
Cree Indians, 276–77
Creek Indians, 19, 22, 245
Crosby, Elisha O., 209
Crosson, James, 239
Crowley, Ben, 7, 13
Crowley, Sam, 7, 13
Crunk, Lydia Hardeman (sister of Thomas Hardeman, 1750–1833), 13
Cuba, 220, 279
Cumberland Basin, 7, 13, 19, 29–30, 43–53, 155
Cumberland Gap, 6, 13, 294
Cumberland River, 13, 17, 44
Curry, George L., 185

Dalles, The. *See* The Dalles
"Dame Shirley," 226
Dan River, Va., 6–8, 40
Dana, Richard Henry, 299
Davidson County, Tenn., 25, 28–32, 40
Davis, Jefferson, 235
Debs, Eugene V., 277
Declaration of Independence, Republic of Texas, 126–27
Deer Creek, Calif., 196, 198
Deism, 93–94
Denver, Colo., 268

Wilderness Calling was composed on the Variable Input Phototypsetter in eleven-point Garamond No. 3 with two-point line spacing. Garamond was selected for display. The book was designed by Jim Billingsley, composed by Moran Industries Book Division, Baton Rouge, Louisiana, printed by Thomson-Shore, Inc., Dexter, Michigan, and bound by John H. Dekker & Sons Bookbindery, Grand Rapids, Michigan.

THE UNIVERSITY OF TENNESSEE PRESS : KNOXVILLE